The Baron of
Beacon Hill

Also by William M. Fowler, Jr.

William Ellery: A Rhode Island
Politico and Lord of Admiralty

Rebels Under Sail: The American
Navy During the Revolution

The American Revolution:
Changing Perspectives (edited,
with Wallace Coyle)

The Baron of Beacon Hill

A Biography of John Hancock

WILLIAM M. FOWLER, JR.

HOUGHTON MIFFLIN COMPANY

BOSTON 1980

B
Hancock

Library of Congress Cataloging in Publication Data
Fowler, William M
The Baron of Beacon Hill.

Bibliography: p.
Includes index.
1. Hancock, John, 1737-1793.   2. Statesmen — United
States — Biography.   3. United States. Declaration of
independence — Signero — Biography.   I. Title.
E302.6.H23F65   1980   973.3'092'4 [B]   79-22268
ISBN 0-395-27619-5

Printed in the United States of America

W 10 9 8 7 6 5 4 3 2 1

Maps drawn by Samuel H. Bryant.

To my mother and father

Foreword

COMING TO GRIPS with John Hancock is no easy task. His name enjoys immense popularity in America. Next to Washington and Lincoln he probably has more streets and towns named after him than any other person in American history.

Most of his fame rests on that one afternoon in Philadelphia, when he took a quill and sprawled a signature on the Declaration of Independence that has become nearly as famous as the document itself. Indeed, far more Americans know who signed the Declaration than who wrote it. It is a pity that this single act has taken on such awesome dimensions that if Hancock had come down from heaven for this one performance, and then quickly returned, his life would have been justified.

He deserves to be remembered for being something more than his signature. For nearly thirty years he dominated Massachusetts' politics and left his mark on national affairs, as well. From his home atop the hill he looked down on a community that nearly always looked up to him. To be sure, some hated him, but, judging from his charmed political life, many more loved him.

He was an odd combination for a politician: an aristocrat whose rapport was with those beneath him, a sybarite who survived and thrived in an age that prided itself on self-denial, and a revolutionary whose greatest hallmark was moderation.

Over the past few years, numerous individuals and institutions have assisted me. In naming some, I am sure to omit others, and for that I beg their indulgence.

High on the list must be the New England Historic and Genealogical Society. James Bell, director of the society, was a gracious host who always made me feel at home while I was using the society's premier collection on New England history. Two other people at the society also deserve mention. Ralph Crandall, editor of the *Register*, provided good counsel; and David Dearborn, in the society's library, did some useful genealogical research. The society also allowed me to reprint portions of "John Hancock! The Paradoxical President" NEHGR, 130: 162–178, in Chapters 11 and 12. In like manner the Essex Institute permitted me to use portions of "The Massachusetts Election of 1785: A Triumph of Virtue," Essex Institute *Historical Collections*, 111: 290–304 in Chapter 14.

As is always the case, the personnel at the Massachusetts Historical Society were knowledgeable and helpful, especially Winifred Collins and Robert Sparks. The same spirit of cheerful assistance was also present at the Boston Public Library, the Boston Museum of Fine Arts, the Northeastern University Library, and the Archives of the John Hancock Mutual Life Insurance Company.

Court records would have been far less intelligible and useful without the aid of Robert Brink, in the Social Law Library, and the staff in the Probate Court and the clerk's office of the Supreme Judicial Court. A special note of thanks is due to Thomas Parker and the Bostonian Society for allowing me access to Hancock's suit of clothes.

The list of institutions outside Boston is even longer. Special thanks are paid to the Houghton Library, at Harvard University; the Harvard University Archives; the American Antiquarian Society; the Historial Society of Pennsylvania; the Yale University Library; the Huntington Library; the New-York Historical Society; the Clements Library, at the University of Michigan; and the Essex Institute, in Salem.

Support for this biography was provided by a grant from the American Philosophical Society and a sabbatical leave from Northeastern University.

Many years ago, as an undergraduate, I had the pleasure of sitting in on a class, Colonial America, taught by Professor Robert Feer. That began my interest in early American history and launched a friendship with Bob Feer that I shall always remember. Some years later, when I was completing graduate school, Bob began work on a biography of John Hancock. He never lived to complete that project. I am grateful to Raymond Robinson, executor of the Feer estate, for allowing me access to Bob's preliminary notes on Hancock. Those notes, and especially Bob's dissertation, "Shays's Rebellion" (Harvard, 1958), were invaluable.

G. B. Warden of Cambridge took time from a busy schedule to read the manuscript and helped me correct some errors. My editor at Houghton Mifflin, David Harris, provided good counsel and was patient with a tardy author.

No author is a hero to his typist. It was my very happy fate to find a person, Judith Waterman, who could both interpret my writing and type good copy from it.

Finally, as always, I find myself groping for words to thank my wife, Marilyn. Again, she has managed to contribute more than I could ever begin to acknowledge.

WILLIAM M. FOWLER, JR.

Contents

FOREWORD · vii

1 · THE THREE JOHN HANCOCKS · 1

2 · THE EDUCATION OF A BOSTON GENTLEMAN · 16

3 · BOSTON TO LONDON AND HOME AGAIN · 32

4 · ON HIS OWN · 48

5 · JOHN HANCOCK — HERO AND MARTYR · 68

6 · FRANCIS BERNARD VERSUS JOHN HANCOCK · 88

7 · PROTEST TURNS TO VIOLENCE — THE MASSACRE · 106

8 · THE UNFORTUNATE THOMAS HUTCHINSON · 125

9 · TEA PARTY · 143

10 · HANCOCK LEADS THE REBELLION · 162

11 · MR. PRESIDENT · 186

12 · BACK TO BOSTON · 203

13 · GOVERNOR HANCOCK · 222

14 · RESIGNATION AND DEFEAT · 245

15 · A LITTLE REBELLION AND A GRAND CONVENTION · 262

NOTES · 285

BIBLIOGRAPHY · 345

INDEX · 353

Illustrations

following page 176

Thomas Hutchinson by John Singleton Copley
Reverend Samuel Cooper by John Singleton Copley
James Sullivan by Gilbert Stuart
Paul Revere by John Singleton Copley
Ebenezer Hancock. Artist unknown.
Four portraits of John Hancock
Dorothy Quincy Hancock by John Singleton Copley
James Warren by John Singleton Copley
Thomas Hancock by John Smibert
Samuel Adams by John Singleton Copley
The "Bishop," the first Reverend Mr. John Hancock
Hancock-Clarke House Lexington Massachusetts,
home of the "Bishop."
Paul Revere's engraving of the British troops landing 1768
Hancock's mansion on Beacon Hill
"A Prospect of the Colleges in Cambridge in New England." A
view of Harvard as Hancock knew it
Paul Revere's engraving of the Boston Massacre
British cartoon showing a meeting between Lord North
and Hancock

"The Flight of the Congress." A British cartoon depicting
Congress's evacuation of Philadelphia. Hancock is
in the center

John Trumbull's painting of the Committee of Congress
presenting the Declaration of Independence to the President of
the Congress. John Hancock seated at right

Four of the five U.S. Navy vessels named after John Hancock

Frigate *Hancock* 1776

U.S.S. *Hancock* AP-3 off Mare Island Navy Yard during
the early 1900s

U.S.S. *Hancock* CVA 19

U.S.S. *John Hancock* DD 981 The newest of the *Hancocks*

Declaration of Independence

MAPS

The Thirteen Colonies, *page xiv*
The Town of Boston in 1775, *page xv*

GENEALOGICAL TABLE

The Ancestry of John Hancock, *page 4*

The Thirteen Colonies

Kilometers
0 50 100   200   400

0   50   100   200   400

Sam¹ H. Bryant

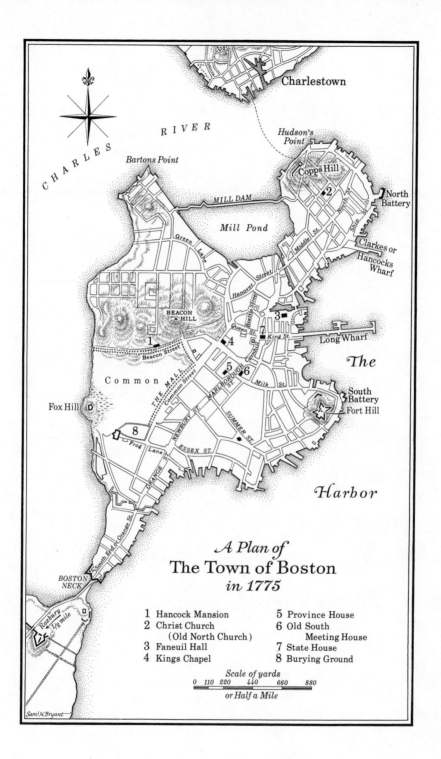

A Plan of
The Town of Boston
in 1775

1 Hancock Mansion
2 Christ Church
  (Old North Church)
3 Faneuil Hall
4 Kings Chapel

5 Province House
6 Old South
  Meeting House
7 State House
8 Burying Ground

Scale of yards
0 110 220   440   660   880
or Half a Mile

Sam! H. Bryant

Chapter 1

The Three John Hancocks

*T*HE TOWNSPEOPLE called him "Bishop," which seems a very strange title for a Congregational minister, but it reflected the softening of eighteenth-century New England theology, as well as the esteem in which they held the man. He was the Reverend Mr. John Hancock, minister of the church in Lexington.

He had begun life in 1671 as the son of a Cambridge shoemaker. Somehow, he mustered enough learning and influence to enter Harvard College with the class of 1689. On admission, students at the college were automatically ranked according to family background and status, so Hancock came in near the bottom, as number thirteen out of fourteen. For the next four years he struggled with Latin, Greek, and other classical studies, mastering them with memory and recitation. By the time he finished his degree, he knew Cicero and Virgil, was able to quote Scripture (in Greek), argue with precise logic, and demonstrate a nodding acquaintance with arithmetic and geometry. All of this, of course, having been learned in an atmosphere of disciplined Puritanism, wherein scholarship and prayer ruled all.[1]

While young Hancock plodded dutifully through his lessons, the world outside was in turmoil. The old Massachusetts charter had been annulled, and in its wake came Sir Edmund Andros and the Dominion of New England. The days of the Puritan oligarchy and rule by the Saints were over. At Harvard, it was feared that Sir Edmund had designs on changing the school; so the rector, Increase Mather, protested to the king and prayed privately for the governor's speedy departure. Perhaps the prayers worked. At any rate, with the Glorious Revolution, Andros got his comeuppance, was removed, and the college was saved. As momentous as all these whirling events were, Hancock seems to have been little concerned about anything beyond his books. In fact, his record at school is singularly uninteresting. Like so many first-generation college students, John Hancock was serious in his studies, conventional in his behavior, and wary of doing anything that might be thought the least indecorous.[2]

After graduation he lived at home and took a turn teaching at the Cambridge Grammar School, helping to prepare other young men for Harvard, as he himself had been prepared only a few years before. Teaching, though, was not his goal. He wanted to be a minister, and his duties at the school provided him with sufficient time to prepare for the calling. He probably delivered an occasional sermon in Cambridge, and from this his reputation grew; in December 1691, he got his first invitation to preach beyond the town.[3]

The invitation came from the town of Groton. The parishioners needed a minister, and Hancock was eager to gain experience even if it meant traveling to such a remote place. Groton was on the northern fringe of Middlesex County, almost on the New Hampshire border and nearly forty miles from Cambridge.

To a young man whose entire life had been spent practically within sight of Cambridge Common, Groton was the end of the earth. Eight times, between January and April 1692, he trudged out to preach and then came home. It took at least a day to get there and in the winter perhaps even longer, but the journey did not diminish his ardor. The congregation liked him and tried to persuade him to remain permanently, but he refused. Instead, he preferred to stay in Cambridge and await a more convenient opportunity.

He got his chance in 1697 when the church in the North Precinct of Cambridge asked him to preach as a candidate for settlement. The agreement called for him to preach from No-

vember until May, but it did not take that long for the members of
the congregation to make their decision, for after listening to
Mr. Hancock they knew by March that this was the man they
wanted to be their minister.[4]

Hancock was ordained in his new post on November 2, 1698.
For the next fifty-four years this church and this community
was to be his home. In keeping with his new station, it was
important that he take a proper wife, and in December 1700 he
married Mary Clarke, whose father, Thomas, was a graduate of
Harvard College and minister to the church at Chelmsford, only
a short distance from home. This was an important move forward for Hancock. Not only was Mary's father of some prominence, but her mother was a member of the Bulkeley clan,
whose roots and influence went deep in the Bay Colony.[5]
Through kinship and friendship, Hancock's world was growing
larger. At the same time, his church grew stronger. In 1698,
when he delivered his first sermon, there were barely 300 people
living in the North Precinct. In less than fifteen years, that
figure had doubled, so by 1713 the community was ready to
break completely from Cambridge and establish their own
town. This they did in 1713, when they incorporated under the
name of Lexington.[6]

Part of the town's population growth was the doing of the
Hancocks themselves. In 1702 they had their first child, a son,
whom they promptly christened John, in honor of his father.
Within quick succession they had a second son, Thomas, the
next year, followed by a daughter, Elizabeth, two years after.
The last two children came a bit later; Ebenezer in 1710 and
Lucy in 1713. Along with the parents and children there was
another member of the household who came to live at the manse
some time after 1700 — old Nathaniel, Hancock's widower
father, who stayed with them until his death, in 1719.[7]

It was a crowded and busy house. Since it was the minister's
home and stood so close to the center of the town, there were
people constantly passing in and out, seeking Hancock's advice.
What they usually left with was a dose of good sense laced with
wit. However, if they came to give advice, the reception was
likely to be restrained. On one occasion, when a committee of

The Ancestry of John Hancock

NATHANIEL HANCOCK
d. circa 1648, Cambridge, Mass.

JOAN or JOANNA ———
fl. 1663

HENRY PRENTICE
d. 1654, Cambridge, Mass.

JOANNA

JONAS CLARK(E)
b. circa 1620
d. 1700, Cambridge, Mass.
ELIZABETH CLARK
d. 1672/3, Cambridge, Mass.

(REV.) EDWARD BULKELEY
bp. 1614, Odell, Beds., Eng.
d. 1695/6, Chelmsford, Mass.
LUCIAN ———

MATTHEW HAWKE
b. circa 1610, Cambridge, Eng.
d. 1684, Hingham, Mass.
MARGARET ———
d. 1683/4, Hingham

JOHN JACOB
b. circa 1630
d. 1693, Hingham, Mass.
MARGERY EAMES
d. 1659, Hingham, Mass.

THOMAS GILL
b. circa 1616, Eng.
d. 1704/5, Hingham, Mass.
HANNAH OTIS
d. 1675/6, Hingham, Mass.
THOMAS LINCOLN
"HUSBANDMAN"
d. 1692, Hingham, Mass.
MARGARET LANGER
d. 1693/4, Hingham, Mass.

NATHANIEL HANCOCK
b. 18 Dec. 1639; w. Cambridge, Mass.
m. 8 Mar. 1663; w. Cambridge, Mass.
d. 2 Apr. 1719; w. Lexington, Mass.
MARY PRENTICE
b. 25 Nov. 1644; w.
m. 8 Mar. 1663; w. Cambridge, Mass.
d. 20 Sept. 1699; w.

(REV.) THOMAS CLARKE
b. 2 Mar. 1652/3; w. Cambridge, Mass.
m.   ; w.
d. 7 Dec. 1704; w. Chelmsford, Mass.
MARY BULKELEY
b. circa 1653; w.
m.   ; w.
d. 2 Dec. 1700; w. Chelmsford, Mass.

JAMES HAWKE
bp. 27 May 1649; w. Hingham, Mass.
m. 9 July 1678; w. Hingham, Mass.
d. 27 Nov. 1715; w. Hingham, Mass.
SARAH JACOB
bp. 28 Feb. 1657/8; w. Hingham, Mass.
m. 9 July 1678; w. Hingham, Mass.
d. 15 Mar. 1693/4; w. Hingham, Mass.

SAMUEL GILL
b. 16 Dec. 1655; w. Hingham, Mass.
m. 13 Jan. 1684/5; w. Hingham, Mass.
d. 29 Mar. 1730; w. Hingham, Mass.
RUTH LINCOLN
b. 19 Nov. 1662; w. Hingham, Mass.
m. 13 Jan. 1684/5; w. Hingham, Mass.
d. 10 Apr. 1751; w. Hingham, Mass.

(REV.) JOHN HANCOCK
b. 1 Mar. 1670/1
w. Cambridge, Mass.
m. 11 Dec. 1700
w. Chelmsford, Mass.
d. 6 Dec. 1752
w. Lexington, Mass.
[H.C. 1689]
ELIZABETH CLARKE
b. circa 1681

JAMES HAWKE
b. 29 Sept. 1683
w. Hingham, Mass.
m. 13 May 1708
w. Hingham, Mass.
d. 10 July 1716
w. Hingham, Mass.
MARY GILL
b. 6 Sept. 1686
w. Hingham, Mass.
m. 13 May 1708
w. Hingham, Mass.
d.
w.

(REV.) JOHN HANCOCK
b. 1 June 1702
w. Lexington, Mass
m. 12 Dec. 1733
d. 7 May 1744
w.
[H.C. 1719]

MARY HAWKE
b. 13 Oct. 1711
w. Hingham, Mass.
m. 12 Dec. 1733
w.
d.
w.

(Gov.) JOHN HANCOCK
Born 12 Jan. 1736/7
where Braintree, Mass.
married 28 Aug. 1775
where Fairfield, Conn.
died 8 Oct. 1793
where
[H.C. 1754]
wife Dorothy Quincy

SOURCES: Charles Hudson, *History of the Town of Lexington* ... (1913), 2:266–268. Donald L. Jacobus, *The Bulkeley Genealogy* (1933), 111–113, 131–132, 152, 213, 446. George Lincoln, *History of the Town of Hingham* (1893), Vols. 2 and 3, passim. Lucius R. Paige, *History of Cambridge, Mass. 1630–1877* ... (1877), 510, 571–572, 629. Clifford K. Shipton, *Sibley's Harvard Graduates* ... (Cambridge, Mass. 1933–1972).

Courtesy New England Historical Genealogical Register.

the church came to advise him that he ought to counsel with the ruling elders, Hancock responded that he was willing to consult with them as long as he could define their duties, which, according to him, consisted of "saddling his horse and holding his bridle."[8] Both at home and in the church there was a grain of despotism in the man, but if he had that trait, he must have had others to compensate, for there is no evidence to suggest that he was not loved at home and respected in the pulpit.

For more than half a century the Bishop sat in his Lexington see, watching his family's economic and social fortunes build on the solid foundation he had laid. Daughter Lucy married Nicholas Bowes, the minister in neighboring Bedford, and her older sister, Elizabeth, moved to Dorchester to become the wife of Reverend Jonathan Bowman. The sons, too, offered a pleasing prospect for advancement. Both John, the oldest, and Ebenezer, the youngest, followed their father to Harvard. Thomas, the middle son, an independent-minded soul, fell out of the pattern and went off to Boston to try his hand in business. All in all, John Hancock took great pride in the very promising future of his family.

Because John was the eldest, he was the first to cast off from Lexington. He entered Harvard with the class of 1719, a relatively undistinguished lot. After four years of study, about all that John Hancock himself was remembered for was being "a conspicuously orderly boy in a bad class." He did, though, manage to get a ranking of eight out of twenty-seven, a neat improvement over his father and a reflection of his family's rising status.[9]

Despite the good offing, John never seemed to match his father. Somehow he lacked the force and dynamism that was so much a part of the old Bishop's character. Perhaps living all those years in the shadow of the great man had stifled him to such an extent that, when he finally went out on his own, he remained unassertive and somewhat fearful of offending anyone. He seems to have been a good but bland man.

Like his father, after graduation he tried teaching for a while, first for a year in Lexington and then for two in neighboring Woburn. Tiring of that, in 1722 he applied for the post of minister in the new town of Westborough, toward the central part of the colony. Westborough rejected him, and in the fall of 1723 he returned to Harvard as college librarian.[10] That winter he was invited to preach at Portsmouth, New Hampshire, as a candidate for a vacant post there. He did not get that job, either, and it may well have been because of a letter written by a schoolmate, the Reverend William Waldron, pastor of the New Brick Church in Boston:

> As for Mr. Hancock whom you have with you I Know Little of Him. He has no great Character for his Abilities Either Naturale or Acquired; The professor told me He did not Know but Hancock might Suit you, for He could make a very handsome bow, and if the first did not Suit He'd Bow Lower a Second time.[11]

John returned to his library but never surrendered his yearning for a pulpit. He stayed at his job for three years. It was neither demanding nor lucrative, but it did provide him time and opportunity to improve his image. His station at the library put him at the intellectual crossroads of the colony. Both those who would be ministers and those who already were had need of his services and often came to see him. By this method, as well as through his father's connections, Hancock came to be known and to know a good many in the ministerial community.

In late winter of 1726, Joseph Marsh, minister of the North Parish in Braintree, died suddenly. His death provided an opportunity that Hancock was not slow to take advantage of, and he immediately began to vie for the post.

Braintree was an old and well-established community. In fact, the local townspeople rightfully boasted that their settlement predated that of Boston, their near neighbor to the north. Physically, it is hard to imagine a more attractive place in the whole Bay Colony. It was large, about fifty square miles (encompassing the present towns of Braintree, Quincy, Holbrook, and Randolph), and laced with streams and tidal marshes. There were numerous hills undulating gently toward the nearby sea, where several beaches and inlets provided spots for small shipbuilding enterprises. Since Braintree was only a few miles

south of Boston, travel to that town and the wider world it
represented was relatively easy.

Marsh's church was in the northern end of the town. It was
not a large congregation — only about forty families — but it
was prosperous and included some families, such as the
Adamses and Quincys, whose future sons would bring fame to
the community. In his eighteen years as their pastor, Marsh had
managed to keep his people on a steady course through calm
seas. Braintree was a peaceable community.[12]

Almost as soon as the old minister was put in the ground, the
parish began the search for a replacement. It did not take long,
and on June 29, 1726, they issued a unanimous call to the Harvard College librarian "to settle in the work of the ministry."
Fortunately for Hancock, it was at the end of the school year,
so it did not take long for him to complete his affairs in Cambridge and move to Braintree, where he took up his residence
in early fall. Although he began to preach immediately, his
official ordination had to wait a month or two. This was a gala
celebration, attended by ministers and neighbors from all the
surrounding towns. Food and drink were provided, and for those
who came a distance, quarters were found. All this, of course,
took time to arrange, but finally on November 2, 1726, John
Hancock was ordained the tenth and youngest minister of the
North Parish of Braintree. The Bishop came down for the festivities and delivered the sermon, which was filled with his
usual vigor and despotism.[13]

From all accounts, young Hancock served his parish well, and
they likewise were generous to him. His salary of £110 per year
was not large, but it was £40 more than Marsh had received,
and the settlement fee of £200 was double what the old minister
had gotten. The salary was probably a reflection of the growth
and prosperity of the church, and, with some careful cajoling,
the new minister convinced his congregation that they ought to
have a new and larger church building. The plans were drawn,
and in 1732 the North Parish moved into their new quarters.[14]

With his new-found prosperity, Hancock began to invest in
land in Braintree and Hingham. It may well have been on a
buying or inspection trip to the latter town that the very eligible

Mr. Hancock met Mary Hawke Thaxter. She was nine years his junior, and the daughter of the late James Hawke, a reasonably well-to-do farmer of the town. She had been married once before, to James Thaxter, but he had died on December 4, 1732. A little more than a year later, on December 13, 1733, she married Mr. Hancock.[15]

Life for the new couple soon settled into the predictable pattern of a small rural town, where everything seems to be dominated by talk of birth, death, crops, and weather. As minister, he baptized, married, and buried his people, including one John Adams, whom he baptized on October 26, 1734.[16] In the spring of 1735 the Hancocks had their first child, a daughter named Mary, after her mother. Less than a year later, on January 12, 1737, a second child arrived, a son named John, like his father and grandfather. The last member of the family came along in November 1741 and was named Ebenezer, after his uncle.

Life was pleasant for the Hancocks. The parish liked their minister, paid him well, and provided him with a comfortable home. His income even allowed him to purchase a slave, Jeffrey, who assisted with household chores and the farming. In return, Hancock served the parishioners as a "faithful shepherd," keeping a vigilant watch over their morals while seeing to their religious well-being. Philosophically and theologically, he was typical of a good many Harvard clergymen, neither particularly brilliant nor dynamic. For him the old Calvinism had softened. His God was no longer a wrathful Jehovah predestining some for heaven and others for hell; rather, He was a kind master and gentle judge. Hancock agreed with the liberal views of the great Boston minister Charles Chauncy and subscribed to his very popular *Seasonable Thoughts*. The Braintree parson even went so far as to tolerate openly the establishment of a neighboring Anglican parish.[17]

Not everyone was pleased with this drift away from the old principles, and beginning in the 1730s and continuing into the forties there was an evangelical movement toward a regeneration of religious spirit that came to be called "The Great Awakening." It was an outpouring of religious enthusiasm that was carried through the colonies by a platoon of itinerant preachers who, wherever they went, praised the Lord and damned the local minister.[18]

One of the more vocal itinerants was Gilbert Tennent, who came to New England in 1740 and for three years preached through the countryside. In one of his sermons, "On the Danger of an Unconverted Ministry," Tennent lashed out at ministers who in his eyes were more concerned with the intellect than the spirit.[19] Rising to defend himself and his fellow ministers, John Hancock of Braintree responded to the challenge. He delivered the reply in Ashford, Connecticut, where he had been invited to preach on the occasion of an ordination. He titled his sermon "The Danger of an Unqualified Ministry." It was a learned and clever, albeit dull, reassertion of the need for an educated and well-trained clergy. He praised Chauncy and condemned the itinerants for sowing "the Seeds of all that Discord, Intrusion, Confusion, Separation, Hatred, Variance, Emulations, Wrath, Strife, Seditions, Heresies, etc. that have been springing up in so many of the Towns and Churches thro' the Province . . ."[20]

When his father journeyed to Ashford, young Johnny was left at home. He was only seven years old, hardly of an age to be concerned about or interested in such weighty matters. Yet, though he and his brother and sister may have been only dimly aware of the currents swirling around them, they were nevertheless very much affected by them. Their father's liberalism guaranteed them a less repressed childhood than he himself had had. They were not being reminded incessantly of Adam's sin and their worthlessness; instead, they learned to love a God who loved them and to have faith in themselves. In some ways this can be seen as a surrender to the secular world, and, indeed, for the rest of his life John Hancock never showed the slightest interest in speculative religion and remained only a perfunctory churchgoer.

From Johnny's birth, it was assumed that he was bound for Harvard. At about the age of five or six he was sent off to a local dame school, run by Mrs. Belcher, and later to one conducted by Joseph Cleverly. It was probably in one of these that he first met John Adams, with whom he struck up a casual acquaintance.[21] Here, with the other children of the town, Johnny learned the rudiments of reading, writing, and figuring.

He could hardly have had a better childhood. He had the best that his parents and Braintree could offer, with a bright, serene, and secure future ahead of him. An easy prediction would have been that he was on his way to becoming the third Reverend Mr. John Hancock.

In the spring of 1744, Johnny's world came suddenly to an end. After a short illness, his father died. The sadness of the event was made even more poignant by the knowledge that the family would have to move, for a new minister would soon be arriving and it would be his right to live in the manse. Where to go? With three children to care for, the oldest only nine, Mary Hancock had a difficult decision to make. Her own parents were both dead, so returning to Hingham was not a likely possibility. Her uncertainty was short-lived, for very quickly there came an invitation from the Bishop and his wife to come and live with them.

Unlike the old days, the parsonage in Lexington was empty and lonely. After John had gone to Braintree and the daughters were married, the only one left at home was Ebenezer. On graduating from Harvard, he had come back to help his father in the church and was expected to take over whenever the old man stepped aside. Unhappily, he died in the diphtheria epidemic of 1741. Grandfather had room to spare and, perhaps, a hankering to help shape the destiny of his namesake, so the invitation went out to Mary and the children to come to Lexington.

It must have been difficult for Mary Hancock to make the transition from mistress of her own house to that of a guest in another, but, in many ways, the two worlds were similar. Life in the Lexington parsonage could not have been wholly unlike that in Braintree, and with the Bishop to guide them, the boys would at least grow up in a proper way.

The only remaining son in the Bishop's family, Thomas, viewed the Lexington household with interest. Although he had left home many years before to strike out on his own, he always felt a responsibility to his family. Indeed, it was Thomas who provided the money to build a good portion of the house in which his father now lived. He was one of Boston's wealthiest merchants, and he and his wife, Lydia, had nearly everything they wanted, except for one thing — children. If Grandfather could wonder whether there would be another Reverend Mr. Hancock, then Thomas, too, must have pondered the fact that there was no one to succeed him in his business.

Weighing all of these issues, some time in 1745 the family came to a decision. Johnny would go to Boston to live with Uncle Thomas and Aunt Lydia and attend Boston Latin School. It is not clear whether the decision was made so that Johnny could enroll in the Latin School or whether that was secondary to his living with Uncle Thomas. What is beyond dispute, though, is that this move altered radically John Hancock's life — and altered the history of America, as well.

Thomas Hancock was quite unlike his father; he was neither a college graduate nor a minister. Yet in other ways he was more like him than either John or Ebenezer was, for he possessed the same drive and autocracy that had made the Bishop a power to be reckoned with. These same qualities, which in some measure seemed to have eluded John and Ebenezer, found a home in him, and he used them not to lay up wealth for another world, but to amass it in this one.

It was out of necessity and a bit of compulsion that Thomas had ventured out from Lexington on a less traveled path. The Bishop's means were modest, and there was already one son at college. There simply was no way he could support two sons in school together. The opportunities in Lexington were obviously limited, so a few days before his fourteenth birthday Thomas packed his belongings and headed off to Boston, where his father had arranged for him to be apprenticed to Samuel Gerrish, a well-known bookseller up on Cornhill. There, he was to "learn the Art or Trade of a Book binder."[22]

For seven years Thomas stayed with Gerrish, mastering all the mysteries of printing, binding, and retailing. At the same time he learned a good deal about the wider world of trade and politics, listening to Gerrish's customers complain about a lack of currency, honoring bills of exchange, the latest act of the governor, or marauding French and Indians along the frontier.

Gerrish's prominence guaranteed that if Thomas stayed long enough in his shop, he was bound to see and meet many of the colony's leading merchants. So while brother John was meeting the intellectual set at Harvard, Thomas was moving in mercantile circles. As he listened to the merchants' conversation, he carefully locked away in his memory the names of men in New York, Philadelphia, London, and elsewhere who could be dealt with and relied on. Most of all, though, what Thomas learned was the business of risk-taking.

Toward the end of his apprenticeship, in 1724, Thomas visited England. At least one reason for the visit was to enable him to establish personal contact with British merchants with whom he planned to trade on his own. He must have made a good impression, for soon after his return home the *Boston News Letter* announced that "Thomas Hancock, at the sign of the Bible and Three Crowns, has for sale *The Danger of People's Losing the Good Impression made by the late awful Earthquake*, a Sermon Preached a Month After it Happened, by the Rev. Mr. Cooper, and all manner of other improving tracts."[23]

The shop prospered, and Thomas decided to venture out a bit and dabble in local politics. His efforts got him elected hogreeve, a lowly office, to be sure, charged with controlling the swine in Boston's streets, but at least a start. In the summer of 1727, only two years after launching his business, Thomas was doing so well that he decided to take some of his profit and try a new endeavor. He joined with John Wendell and shipped off a load of general merchandise for sale in Albany. It worked, and within a year his business and credit were good enough so that he could easily manage a debt of more than £3000.[24]

As a natural extension of his book business, Thomas expanded vertically; in 1728, along with Daniel Henchman, Benjamin Faneuil, and Henry Philips, he built a paper mill at Milton Lower Falls, just outside Boston. It was the first such mill in New England, and the fact that he was in partnership with Faneuil, Henchman, and Philips, all eminent merchants of the town, testifies to Hancock's growing reputation.[25]

With good family connections and the promise of even more success before him, Thomas Hancock had become one of Boston's most eligible young men. The Hancocks seemed to have had a penchant for marrying relatively late, and Thomas was no exception. Finally, on Guy Fawkes Day, 1731 (November 5), he married Lydia Henchman, partner Daniel's only child. Whether the match was made in heaven or in a local counting-house is uncertain, but however and wherever it was made, it further allied Thomas with a powerful Massachusetts tribe. Lydia's great-grandfather had been a hero of King Philip's War and one of the founders of the town of Worcester, in the central part of the colony, where a good portion of the family still lived. Her father, of course, was one of Boston's best-known book dealers, and her mother was Samuel Gerrish's sister. All in all, Thomas did well.[26]

The newlyweds settled down to life in Boston. At the town meeting in March 1732, the members elected Thomas a constable. It was a step up from hog-reeve, and under different circumstances he would have considered it an honor, but in this case his neighbors were playing a joke on him. Being a constable often required working at night, so as a lark the meeting often elected newly married men. Neither Thomas' nor Lydia's reaction is recorded, but he held the job and served his full term.

Having done well on his previous ventures, Hancock continued reaching into other businesses. He bought and speculated in land and continued to import an ever-widening variety of goods, including cloth, tea, manufactures, and books, with the latter becoming less important as he moved from bookseller to general merchant. His shop down near the town dock became a clearinghouse for goods and bills from all over the North Atlantic Basin.

In less than a decade Thomas Hancock had gone from apprentice to prosperous merchant. Indeed, his rise had been so rapid that rumors went about the town that somewhere he had a secret cache of wealth. Thomas had no such cache, just intelligence, drive, and a healthy dose of luck.

To suit their growing stature, the Hancocks decided to leave the crowded inner town and build an elegant home on the spacious slopes of neighboring Beacon Hill. Beacon was the tallest of the three hills that dominated the Shawmut Peninsula, on which the town was built. (The others were Cotton and Mount Whoredom.) It was on its summit that the Puritans had built a beacon fire to warn of approaching enemies, and from this function the hill had taken its name. In 1735 Hancock bought a portion of the south slope abutting the Common, and within a year construction was begun on what would soon become Boston's most famous home.

It was basically Georgian in style. The large center entrance faced the south, with the house perfectly balanced on either side. It stood about two and a half stories and had three dormers jutting out from a gambrel roof. There were at least a dozen main rooms and many smaller ones, including a room for china and several for white servants and black slaves. Outside the house was a series of very elegant gardens, dominated by a wide variety of fruit-bearing and decorative trees. Hancock was building at a time when the orchard craze was sweeping the town. According to one visitor, Bostonians had "run mightily into orcharding," and Thomas was no exception.[27] Directly in front of the house was the road that led up from the town, called appropriately Beacon Street, and on the far side of it was a rail fence put up by Thomas to prevent cows on the Common from wandering into his gardens.[28]

Hancock had become a great merchant, and his home was a testament to that fact. Those in Boston knew of his monument firsthand, and to those in England with whom he did business Hancock himself provided testimony.

> My Gardens all Lye on the South Side of a hill with the most beautiful Assent to the Top and its allowed on all hands the Kingdom of England dont afford so fine a Prospect as I have both of Land and Water Neither do I intend to Spare any cost or pains in making my Gardens beautifull or Profitable.[29]

From this lofty perch Thomas Hancock could view the town, harbor, and far into the countryside; and nearly everywhere he looked he had interests — shops, ships, and land. He was one of Boston's best-known citizens. In 1739 as a mark of respect the town elected him to its highest office — selectman — and then continued to re-elect him for the next thirteen years.[30]

Despite all his success, Thomas never forgot his family. He lent them money, made investments for them, and generally stood by to help whenever he could.[31] It was not that he was an especially kind or generous man. What mattered was that he had grown up in a family ruled by a patriarch, and now, with his wealth, he had gained a status in that family which his birth could have never given him: he was the eldest son. Indeed, with the death of Ebenezer, in 1741, and John, in 1744, he was the only son. By success and default Thomas had become the secular Bishop.

Under the circumstances, it was his responsibility to see to the care of his brother's children, even more so since he had none of his own.

Chapter 2

The Education of a Boston Gentleman

OUNG HANCOCK'S BOSTON was bigger, busier, dirtier, and noisier than any other town in America. Crowded onto a narrow peninsula, laced with meandering streets that looked to all the world as if they had been laid out by a wandering cow or a tipsy sailor, it was often toasted as the "crooked little town of Boston."[1]

But if the streets were random, the people were purposeful. They had managed to balance off a niggardly soil with a bountiful sea and from it to fashion a thriving economy. It had begun with the prolific cod, certainly one of nature's uglier creatures, but also one of her more valuable. From such beginnings, energetic Yankee merchants branched out into other ventures, until these codfish aristocrats had built Boston into one of the leading seaports of the British Empire. Her ships visited ports from London to Cádiz to Jamaica. Toward distant places they carried rum, whale oil, fish, foodstuffs, and any one of a dozen other commodities that could be exchanged for homeward-bound cargoes of manufactures, wines, molasses, and sugar.

To support this far-flung trade, the town boasted numerous shipyards, warehouses, docks, shops, and anything else required in a maritime community. There can be no doubt that for Boston the empire worked, and marvelously so. Although there might be inconveniences in the law, such as prohibitive duties, these could usually be overcome through mutual understandings with royal officials, coupled with lax enforcement. Smuggling, of course, was endemic to the system, and Thomas Hancock, like most of his colleagues, was much involved in the business. It was not unusual for him to tell his captains that, on returning from an illicit voyage, they were to land their cargo in a remote cove or bay in the outer harbor, out of sight of nosy officials.[2] Dealing with these hazards of the law, along with the problems of weather, changing markets, and finance, was difficult enough for Hancock, but in the early 1740s another element was added to vex him — war.

The eighteenth century was a time of almost constant imperial conflict, involving at various stages England, France, and Spain, as well as other, lesser powers. In North America the main antagonists were the French, based in Canada, and the British, in the mainland colonies. Sometimes the border clashes between the two were made official with a declaration of war, but at other times they were simply carried on in the informal but bloody style of frontier savagery.

One of the official wars began in 1739, when a British merchant and smuggler named Robert Jenkins lost his ear in a fray with the Spanish authorities off the coast of Florida. Jenkins took his lopped-off ear home with him as proof of Spanish barbarity. The uproar was so great that, despite the misgivings of some that conflict with Spain would inevitably involve France, war was declared. As had been feared, the War of Jenkins' Ear did merge into a larger struggle, and in 1744 France joined Spain against England.[3]

With the entry of the French, the war came home to New England, and Boston was alive with excitement and expectation. The royal governor, William Shirley, a devoted imperialist, moved quickly and successfully to convince the General Court that, for the safety of the colony and the greater good of the empire, the French fortress of Louisbourg, on Cape Breton Island, ought to be taken.[4]

That news brought joy to the mansion up on Beacon Hill. For some time Thomas had been cozying up to the governor, and that relationship, together with his well-established London connections, had already brought him thousands of pounds in government contracts.[5] Now, with an expedition the size of the one being proposed, Hancock could only have had sugar plums dancing in his head.

After months of intensive and expensive preparation, the expedition set sail in March 1745. Almost 100 vessels, carrying thousands of men, bore off to the north. With the exception of a small covering force from the Royal Navy, the whole business was strictly the work of New England. For weeks, the people of Boston waited anxiously for news. Dispatches told of the fleet's arrival, of the beginnings of the siege, and the French attempts to break it. Then in July came the most glorious news of all — Louisbourg had surrendered.[6]

Boston went wild with joy. People crowded onto the Common, shouting and singing; bonfires were lit; church bells rang; and the rum flowed.[7] Thomas himself could hardly contain his enthusiasm. For him, Louisbourg marked not only a great victory, but the promise of more campaigns and more contracts. It was, of course, during this grand summer of 1745 that young Johnny moved in with Thomas and Lydia.

While Thomas spent his time politicking for contracts, Master Hancock settled into his new home. Aunt Lydia gave him one of the large front bedrooms, from which he could look out across the Common toward the Neck and even to the distant Blue Hills. She instructed the servants to care for his needs and then saw to many of them herself. By all accounts, Aunt Lydia's personality loomed as large as her bulk, and in the years to come she stands out, with the possible exception of her husband, as the strongest single influence on Hancock's life.

Although he was only eight, Johnny could not help being aware of the spaciousness of his new world. From his window he watched an almost constant parade of people coming to visit his uncle. Some were dressed in the scarlet of the army, others in the blue and gold of the navy, and many in plain civilian dress. At dinner he was bored by the talk of London gossip, land speculation, war, and politics. When the meal was finished and the men retired to their port and tobacco, Johnny was sent to bed, where he could still hear muted voices below speaking of places far away and of men whose names were not familiar to him. Uncle Thomas and his friends seemed always to talk of trade and empire, war and politics, all of which was remote from the everyday considerations of an eight-year-old child, but it did at least leave him with a vague notion that his uncle was an important man whose orbit swung far beyond the confines of the narrow town of Boston.

Someday Master Hancock would know a good deal more of empire, politics, king's ministers, battles and generals, but for the time being his main concern was school. In August, shortly after Johnny arrived in town, Uncle Thomas took him to the Boston Latin School to meet its master, John Lovell, and apply for admission.[8]

Johnny had undoubtedly heard a good deal about Lovell, most of it bad, and in the few minutes that it took to walk down the hill to school his mind must have been filled with something akin to terror. As a teacher, Lovell had the reputation for being a hard drillmaster who wielded a quick ferule and showed very little kindness or compassion toward his students. He had first come to Latin in 1729, the year after his graduation from Harvard, and spent five years as an usher in the school. Then, in 1734, when Master Nathaniel Williams retired, the town meeting voted unanimously that Lovell should have his job.[9] For forty-one years Lovell ruled on School Street, retiring only in 1775, when his Tory leanings made life uncomfortable. On the day of Lexington and Concord he is reputed to have dismissed his students by telling them, "War's begun and school's done: *Deponite libros.*"[10] In his four decades of service Lovell trained more than 2000 of Boston's best and brightest boys. His influence was considerable, for if they did well in his school and could persuade him to speak for them, admission to Harvard and the success that that promised was practically automatic.

Like the other two dozen or so students who presented themselves for admission, Johnny was asked by Lovell to read a few verses from the King James's Bible. He did that with ease, and, having established his literacy — the family background spoke for itself — he was admitted to Latin. His age posed something of a problem because he was a bit older than the other first-year students; they were closer to seven, and he was on his way to nine. His excellent training in Braintree and Lexington allowed Lovell to solve this easily enough; the master decreed that Hancock be skipped up to the third year so that he could be with boys of his own age and ability.[11]

In the good weather when there was early light the schoolday began at seven, so Johnny was up early and trudging off down the hill. The school itself was an old wooden structure built back near the turn of the century and crammed onto a small lot just behind King's Chapel, the Anglican church. It was two stories high, about forty feet wide where it faced the street, and twenty-five feet deep. The shingled gambrel-style roof had an incongruous-looking belfry perched atop. As Johnny walked up the steps the bell was pealing and would continue to ring until all the students were seated and the master appeared.[12]

The boys were grouped at benches according to their age. The curriculum, which was fixed, had not changed in years. Under Lovell's piercing gaze, ushers went about their business, drilling students in their lessons. For the lazy, recalcitrant, or slow, "Old Gaffer," as he was not so affectionately called by his students, wandered about, with his ferule at the ready. "It was," according to one alumnus, "a short, stubbed, greasy-looking article . . . The lightest punishment was one clap, the severest form — the most usual, two, one on each hand."[13]

At his bench, hunched over his Greek and Latin texts, including Aesop's *Fables*, Eutropius' Roman history, and Ward's *Lily's Grammar*, Hancock began his career at Latin. By no means was he Lovell's best student, but, then, he was not the worst, either. He undoubtedly got his share of the ferule, and on more than one occasion he had to explain to Aunt Lydia or Uncle Thomas why it was that he had curious red marks on his hands. But if he could be bad, he could also be good and share in the rewards, the highest of which was being allowed to work in Master Lovell's garden.[14] By his fifth year he was ready to begin "making Latin," so he was moved from his bench to a table, where he could begin to write. He translated from Caesar's *Commentaries*, Cicero's *Orations*, and the *Aeneid*. In his last year at the school the capstone was added — Xenophon and Homer.[15]

The narrow curriculum provided for no frills. The purpose of the Latin Grammar School was to prepare a student in the tradition of the liberal arts so that he could follow the same path at college. Classical languages were the foundation, but with his mastery of the ancients he also acquired knowledge of history, philosophy, and theology. Arithmetic, writing, and spelling were not taught on School Street. These less lofty items were left for the writing schools.[16] For one hour each day Hancock and the others would walk over to one of several such schools in the town. In young John's case, he went down to the edge of the Common, where Abiah Holbrook taught the fine art of writing in a building next to the one in which the town cannon were kept.[17] To Holbrook, handwriting was an art. If he had been born only a few centuries earlier he undoubtedly would have spent his lifetime in some remote monastery, illuminating manuscripts. He spent seven years "writing" a twenty-six-page pamphlet, *Demonstration of Penmanship*, an elegant piece of calligraphy.[18]

With Holbrook to guide him, Hancock developed a style of writing that, even in an age known for its fine hands, was outstanding. He may have been an indifferent student at Latin, but to Holbrook he was the best the teacher had ever had, and his famous signature stands as graceful testimony to Holbrook's skill.

Of course Aesop, Caesar, and Abiah Holbrook did not monopolize all of Hancock's time. Like the rest of his chums, he had every Thursday and Saturday afternoon off, as well as Sundays and any special fast days. In his leisure he could ride to Lexington and visit the family or stay in Boston, perhaps gamboling on the Common, getting into the devilish things that young boys are apt to find. The Frog Pond was just in front of his home, and that must have had some attraction. But he would also wander down to the docks, where he could fish and listen to the sailors swapping tales. In the winter, sledding was great fun — starting on the top of Beacon Hill and, with a loud hullo, racing down School Street, past Latin, across Marlborough, and practically to the harbor's edge.[19]

Naturally, he was not alone. Johnny was always gregarious,

and undoubtedly a number of his chums were with him on these adventures. Sam Quincy was probably there. He was one of the few out-of-town students at Latin. He lived in Braintree and knew most of Johnny's old friends from the town. There was also a young English boy with whom he became well acquainted, John Henry Bastide, Jr. His father was a British army engineer in Nova Scotia who had left both his son and wife in Boston. Uncle Thomas was a business associate of the older Bastide and a close friend of the family; he kept a careful eye on both young John Henry and his mother.[20] Another boy in the class whom Johnny knew and may have spent some of his frivolous moments with was James Lovell, son of the master and a future member, along with Hancock, of the Continental Congress. And then there was Benjamin Church, the man who became a "High Son of Liberty," only to sell out his friends for British gold.[21]

Aside from the ordinary boyhood diversions to be found in Boston, there were some special activities that caught young Hancock's attention — scenes of war. On several occasions during the War of Jenkins' Ear he could look out from his window across the Common to a scene of white tents and soldiers, some in the crisp scarlet of the king, others in an assortment of militia uniforms. It was exciting entertainment for the boys of the town, Hancock included, to hang on the fence rail and watch the men marching and wheeling about as officers barked out orders. The harbor, too, was often full of the sights of war, as majestic ships of the Royal Navy, along with scruffy privateers, came and went. The victories of the war were marked with great celebration — candles in every window, bonfires, ringing bells, grand processions, and general jubilation.

Not all was adventure, romance, and glory, though, for with the ebb and flow of soldiers and sailors came the inevitable flotsam and jetsam of the seamier side of life — packed taverns, busy whorehouses, brawls, public whippings, executions, and even a full-scale riot.[22] Exuberance, in all of its forms, is one side of war, but so too is sorrow. At home and on the streets of the town Hancock heard stories of children who had become orphaned, women who had become widowed, men who had lost limbs. They all gave unwilling testimony to the human cost of these imperial adventures. From his lofty hill, though, and with wealth and position to screen out the nastiness of war, he continued to believe that the business of arms was a glorious undertaking, a romantic image that for the rest of his life would contribute to his persistent craving for fame in combat.

Although Boston may have been only occasionally a place for soldiers, it was always a home for politicians. At the age of twelve Hancock got a personal introduction into local politics when Master Lovell and the Latin School fell headlong into a squabble with the town and the vestry of King's Chapel.

It all began in the spring of 1748, when the minister, wardens, and vestry of the church petitioned the town for permission to expand their church building.[23] With a graveyard on the right, a street in front, and a street on the left, there was only one direction in which the church could grow — to the rear. Unfortunately, that was exactly where the Latin School was located. If King's Chapel was to be enlarged, then the school had to go. The issue was an emotional one. The land and school both belonged to the town, and any change would have to be approved at the annual meeting. Since the chapel was Anglican and the town was Congregational, the petition was bound to be received with some coolness.

At the regular town meeting in March, the request was referred to a committee, one of whose members was Thomas Hancock.[24] Uncle Thomas had been a selectman of the town for nearly a decade, so discussion of local politics at home was nothing new, but with his school and teacher involved, young Johnny now undoubtedly listened with much keen interest.

William Shirley was a member of the chapel's vestry and a close friend of Hancock's; indeed, he was more than a friend, since without his assistance and good will it is unlikely that Thomas would have received so many of his lucrative government contracts. Shirley was very much in favor of a grander chapel and almost certainly made this known to his friends and anyone else in the town with whom he had influence.[25] Lovell was outraged at the suggestion that he move, and tried everything he could to stay where he was. Nevertheless, when the report came in, it supported moving the school to make room for the church.[26]

It was somewhat unusual for the full meeting to resist a committee's recommendation; however, it soon became apparent that the committee's report was not going to have smooth sailing. Lovell had too many friends, and the Anglicans too many enemies, for that to happen. When the vote came, some insisted that it be by written ballot, at which point John Pidgeon, a supporter of the church, tried to stuff the ballot box. That piece of chicanery was unnecessary; when the tally was taken, it was 295 in favor and 197 against. That was not the end, of course. Lovell was as adept in town politics as he was in the classroom, and for weeks he was able to delay construction as he bargained with the vestry. All this prompted a local wag, John Green, to write:

> A fig for your learning! I tell you the Town
> To make the church larger, must pull the school down.
> Unluckily spoken replied Master Birch,
> Then learning I fear, stops the growth of the church.[27]

For the boys at Latin it was intriguing to watch Master Lovell as he did battle with the town and church. After some negotiation the parties reached an acceptable compromise. In exchange for the old school and land, the vestry agreed to purchase a small plot across the street, owned by Richard Saltonstall. On that site, not more than a hundred yards from the old Latin, they would build Mr. Lovell and the town a new brick school. The agreement was more than fair — even Lovell could see that — and construction began immediately. The new brick Latin was finished in short time, and on Monday, May 8, 1749, the old bell rang out from its new location as Hancock and his schoolmates took their seats.[28]

By the spring of 1750 Hancock's time at Latin was drawing to a close. He had finished the school's curriculum and was now ready for college. Naturally, the choice was Harvard; armed with a distinguished lineage, money, and recommendations from Master Lovell, John had no trouble being admitted.

As Aunt Lydia and the servants helped him pack for the trip to Cambridge, Hancock may well have reflected on his first half-decade in Boston and life with Uncle Thomas. He had watched his uncle navigate deftly through the shoal waters of eighteenth-century business and politics. Thomas had matched wits and purses with some stiff competition, and in nearly every case had won. His principles were no better or worse than those of the people he dealt with, so at times this minister's son may have looked to some as if he were in league with the devil himself, as he pushed and pulled on his political levers.[29]

War and politics had made Uncle Thomas rich, and his connections promised to make him richer. Yet wealth, even in the amount possessed by Thomas, had its limitations, and somehow he could never escape that nagging feeling of inferiority at being a colonial. Again and again he told his British correspondents how well he was doing, what a fine house he had, how lovely his gardens were, and anything else that, consciously or unconsciously, he thought would impress them. He ordered all the trappings of wealth he could afford, from silver shoe buckles to fine china and crystal. In all these ways he continually asserted, as best he could, his equality with those in England. Still, no matter how elegant his style of living, the horrid fact remained that he was dependent on the whims of distant bureaucrats he never saw and great merchants who treated him like a junior partner.

Politically, too, he was hemmed in, for no matter what he did or how important he became, there were absolute and arbitrary limits to his rise. The man at the top, the royal governor, was almost always an outsider, yet his word was final. To be sure there were good governors, like William Shirley, but this true friend was treated shamefully by the home authorities, which left the colonials to wonder if the ministry understood the colonies.[30]

Such insensitivity was most often subtle, but at times it grew quite blatant. Regular army officers dismissed the colonial militia as rabble, and even those Americans who made it into regular service were looked down upon. Naval officers had an even livelier contempt for Americans. In Boston they pressed

local seamen without the approval of the governor and contin-
ued to do so even when it was of questionable legality.[31] British
callousness toward Americans reached a peak at the Treaty of
Aix-la-Chapelle, in 1748, when the government blithely returned
Louisbourg, recently bought with American blood, to the
French.[32]

Thomas resented being treated like a country cousin, but his
annoyance was quickly submerged in a sea of contracts that
concealed any ill feelings. Only at a later time, when the euphoria ebbed and conditions changed, would these minor insults become major vexations.

In the fall of 1750, John Hancock, Latin alumnus formerly of
Braintree now of Boston, entered Harvard College. At thirteen
and a half, he was the second-youngest boy in his class of
twenty, and he was ranked number five.

Unlike most of his freshman classmates, Hancock did not live
on campus. His uncle's wealth and an apparent shortage of
rooms allowed him the luxury of boarding in Cambridge at the
home of the Reverend Nathaniel Appleton, where the routine
was easier, the food better, and there were no prying upperclassmen seeking to torment him. Appleton made extra money
by boarding freshmen, and, along with Hancock, he took in
Benjamin Church and Jonathan Webb, a minister's son from
Boston.[33]

He lived here only for the first year, and in the fall of 1751,
when he returned as a sophomore, he moved into Massachusetts
Hall to room with Thomas Malbone of Rhode Island. Malbone
was only the first of five roommates that Hancock had in his
years as an undergraduate. They were, for the most part, an
unimpressive group and included his cousin Jonathan Bowman
of Dorchester, Asaph Rice of Westborough, Elizur Holyoke of
Boxford, and Anthony Wibird of Portsmouth, New Hampshire.
By far the most interesting of the lot was Wibird.[34]

It was a strange twist of fate that threw him and Hancock
together. In 1754, when they both left the college, Wibird went
off to Braintree as minister of the First Church and took up
residence in Hancock's childhood home. What an odd couple
the two of them must have made! Hancock was of medium

height and thin, with carefully groomed brown hair, a hand-some face, and impeccably tailored clothes. Wibird, seven years senior to this young aristocrat, looked quite otherwise. His ap-pearance is best described by John Adams, who arrived at Har-vard one year after Hancock and knew both men well.

> P[arson] W[ibird] is crooked, his head bends forwards, his shoulders are round and his Body is writhed, and bended, his head and half his body, have a list one Way, the other half declines the other Way, and his lower parts from his Middle, incline another Way. His features are as coarse and crooked as his Limbs. His nose is a large roman Nose with a prodigious Bunch Protuberance, upon the Upper Part of it. His mouth is large, and irregular, his Teeth black and foul, and craggy. His Lips [. . .] to command, when he speakes, they dont move easily and limberly pliant. His lips are stiff, rigid, not pliant and supple. His Eyes are a little squinted, his Visage is long, and lank, his Complexion wan, his Cheeks are fallen, his Chin, is long, large, and lean.[35]

Even accounting for Adams' usual dose of acidity, Wibird must have been an awkward, ugly creature beside the graceful and aristocratic Hancock.

John settled easily into college life. As a freshman, he found that one of his first duties was to attend a service in the chapel with all the other freshmen, where a sophomore read to them the college laws they were now bound to obey. Soon after that he went to receive his Hebrew grammar and was then intro-duced to his class tutor, Henry Flynt.[36]

Other than a few ancient elms and oaks in the Yard, "Father" Flynt was probably the oldest living thing at Harvard. He had graduated with the class of 1693 and, aside from a short and unhappy sojourn spent preaching, had never really left the school. The old man was well acquainted with the Hancock family. His sister was married to Edmund Quincy of Braintree, and every holiday Flynt returned to his brother-in-law's home, where a special study was kept for him. He was almost as familiar a figure in Braintree as in Cambridge. On one of his visits, John's father and grandfather tried to interest him in marrying one of the Bishop's daughters, but marriage apparently held no interest for him and he went to his grave a bachelor.[37]

Although Flynt was generally well liked by his students, his advanced age and peculiar habits made him a source of fun that was too good to miss. Benjamin Church, who with his pithy verses was fast becoming an early graffiti poet, directed some of his rhyme toward the old tutor:

> *An ugly Monster, he in Sight appears,*
> *Form'd so by Nature not deform'd by Years:*
> *His matted Wig of piss-burnt horse-hair made,*
> *Scarce covers half his greasy shining Head.*
> *His Face a mixture of Deformities,*
> *Like flaming meteors, shine his Gorgon Eyes,*
> *A very Scare-crow is his awful Nose.*
> *A frightful Grin his hideous Jaws disclose;*
> *You, when he yawns, tremendous teeth may see,*
> *And hence he's call'd his Dental Majesty.*[38]

Each day began the same: prayer at 5:00 A.M. followed by a light repast of bread and home-brewed beer. Then came study hour and the first class at eight. Flynt, despite his age and failing eyesight, ran the class and lectured to his charges in Latin from a prescribed text. After the morning lecture, some time between eleven and twelve, Hancock and his chums sat down to their main meal of the day.

According to college law, everyone, tutor and student alike, was required to take this meal together in the commons. At the front of the hall sat Flynt and the other tutors, with the students, perhaps a hundred or so, sitting in front at their bench and table. Waiters, students working to earn wages, brought the food from the kitchen. Each student had a wooden bowl (which was washed once a week) provided by the college, but his eating utensils had to come from home.

On its face the menu was substantial, albeit boring:

Two sizes of bread in the morning; one pound of meat at dinner, with sufficient sauce (vegetables) and a half pint of beer, and at night that a part pie be of the same quantity as usual, and also half a pint of beer, and that the supper messes be but four parts, though the dinner messes be of six.[39]

Despite appearances, though, there were frequent complaints of scanty servings, along with the more usual comment about the food's being "rotten." Small wonder, then, that students who could afford it, Hancock among them, often cut commons and ate elsewhere. The college authorities, quite wisely, chose not to enforce the rule on compulsory dining, with the result that eating in commons was principally for those who did not have the money to eat outside the college.

After dinner, each student repaired to his tutor's chamber, where he spent the afternoon reciting and disputing the morning lesson. Around five there was more prayer; then supper at seven-thirty. After the last meal, time was available for study or socializing, but given the poor lighting and the early hour the students had to arise, sleep was probably more in order than any other activity.

Hancock's course work was continuation of his studies at Latin, and quite likely he was overprepared, compared with some of his less fortunate classmates whose preparation had been accomplished by men less able than Master Lovell. The emphasis continued on language (Latin, Greek, Hebrew) and the traditional liberal arts, but in Hancock's time some modest changes were under way, so he also got a taste of geography, geometry, arithmetic, and astronomy. There were no courses labeled "history" or "politics," but through a reading of the classics Hancock got a heavy dose, though a romantic and aristocratic one, of both these disciplines. There is no certain way to tell how well he did in his courses, but it did not really matter. For someone of his station, with the future secure, it was enough simply to acquire a socially acceptable patina of intellectualism, nor is there anything to indicate that his learning ever went much beyond this level.

Hancock's modest interest in his studies left time for the lighter side of college life, which he was not wont to neglect. Since he lived off campus as a freshman, he probably missed a good deal of the hazing and funmaking that the first-year men had to endure, cleaning the Yard, running errands for upperclassmen, and the like. Once he moved into Massachusetts Hall, though, he wasted little time getting into mischief.

Like a good many students, Hancock first came a cropper

with the authorities over a drinking incident. Along with four other sophomores, including Jonathan Webb, his roommate at Appleton's, and his old friend from Latin, Sam Quincy, he took to drinking. One day in late August or early September the three of them, accompanied by Samuel Foxcroft and Samuel Marshall, went to a local tavern kept by one Jonathan Sprague. There they began a drinking spree, during which they got a black servant so drunk that they "endangered his Life . . ."[40] The prank did not amuse the college authorities, and the students were haled before the president and tutors for judgment.

Penalties for misbehavior could range all the way from a simple warning, to a fine, to being degraded — that is, having one's place in the class lowered — and finally the ultimate — expulsion. After hearing the allegations, the president and faculty decided that Foxcroft and Marshall were the ringleaders, so they were degraded seven places. Hancock, "for very much promoting the . . . Affair," was pushed down four places. Sam Quincy had to make a public confession in chapel, and Jonathan Webb was simply "admonished."[41]

The family's reaction to all this, especially that of Uncle Thomas and Aunt Lydia, is not recorded, but they could not have been pleased. Both his father and grandfather had gone through the college with nary a blemish, a tradition that the third John Hancock had now broken.

From his sophomore year on, John either mended his ways or became more skillful at avoiding detection, for never again was he severely punished. He did continue imbibing, of course, and even wrote a college drinking song, "A Pot of Good Ale," in which he poked fun for six stanzas at a number of people, including widows (his mother?) and ministers (father? grandfather?):

> Our old Parish Vicar when he's in his liquor
> Will merrily at his Parishioners rail
> Come pay all your Tythes or I'll kiss all your wives
> When once he shakes hands with a Pot of Good Ale . . .
>
> The widow who's buried her Husband of Late
> Has scarcely got time to weep or to wail
> Thinks every day ten, till she's married again
> When once she shakes Hands with a Pot of Good Ale.[42]

Whether Hancock wrote the song with anyone particular in mind is not certain. However, while he was at Harvard his widowed mother did take her third husband, the Reverend Daniel Perkins of Bridgewater.[43]

Perhaps it was while singing these verses that Hancock forgot to go to chapel in his junior year. At any rate, he was fined for his absence; then, a few days later, he was caught in a more pious mood, praying when he should have been studying. He was fined for that, too.[44]

On the first Wednesday of July 1754, Hancock and his class received their bachelor's degrees. As usual, the commencement was conducted with great style and pageantry. All the colony officers were present, including His Excellency the Governor and the sheriff of the county. Along with the official guests were hundreds of others who swarmed in to buy, sell, and make merry, giving the whole affair a carnival spirit. In the audience were Uncle Thomas and Aunt Lydia, and his mother, brother, and sister. Grandfather Hancock was not there. The old Bishop had died in the winter of 1752.

Hancock sat with his class, listening restlessly as the student orators droned on in Latin. At last, he went up to receive his degree from the president. That afternoon he bade farewell to his friends and "Father" Flynt, collected his memories, and set off with his aunt and uncle to his home on Beacon Hill. His mother could not have been insensitive to the fact that the young boy, her son, who had left Lexington some years before would never return. More than ever now he belonged to the world of Beacon Hill, and despite some suggestion that he ought to become the third Reverend Mr. Hancock, that was not his inclination and it most certainly was not what Uncle Thomas had in mind.

Chapter 3

Boston to London
and Home Again

*T*HOMAS WAS GLAD to have his nephew back home. During the years John had been cloistered over at Cambridge, business had been slack, for the halcyon days of Jenkins' Ear and King George's War were over, and, with the outbreak of peace, came readjustment and dislocation. For someone so deeply involved in government work as Uncle Thomas, it was especially difficult to begin his search for new contracts while trying to shore up the old. However, the situation was even more complicated, for not only did the business need attention from him, but so too did his nephew. If John was to learn the ropes, Thomas needed to be there to teach him. Feeling the pressure of these demands, and perhaps just a bit tired, in John's senior year Thomas decided to decline his usual election as a selectman of Boston, and, for the first time in a dozen years, Thomas Hancock did not hold public office in Boston.[1]

John may have been Thomas' nephew, but that seems to have counted for little when he came into the business. There is no mention of his arrival, nor was there any noticeable change in the conduct of Thomas' affairs. Although John had a degree from Harvard, he was very much a novice, and Thomas was not the kind of man to rely on anyone, no matter who he was, until he had proved his ability. Besides, whatever hopes he harbored, Thomas knew that John was free to do what he wished, and it was still not altogether certain that he was destined to follow the mercantile way.

Thomas loved to dress well; he wore silver buckles on his shoes, well tailored and elegant clothes, and carried a gold-tipped cane. He saw to it that John did the same, and the two of them must have cut fine figures in the town. The old man took his nephew in tow to meet other merchants and government officers, usually at a local coffee house or perhaps even a tavern, where young John could watch bills of exchange being discounted and swapped or listen to the latest rumor.[2] One of their favorite stops was the Long Room in the British Coffee House, down by Long Wharf. But they could also be found at the nearby Admiral Vernon, Blue Anchor, or any of several other taverns in the neighborhood. With more than 150 licensed houses in the town, to say nothing of the coffee houses, there was no lack of places to meet.[3]

By his own account, Thomas was often left with hardly a minute to himself; but an objective assessment of the rhythm of the business and its relative prosperity would lead one to believe that Thomas had a good deal of time and money on his hands. He did pay special attention to his overseas correspondence, but that never amounted to more than five or six letters a month.[4]

What did Thomas do with his time and money? To be sure, he was no ascetic — his house and table testified to his fondness for the good life; nevertheless, his Calvinist background, diluted though it may have been, dictated that he spend his time and money responsibly and not in idle frolicking. That was a burden Thomas willingly shouldered, and he hoped that his nephew would do the same; for if it was important to know how to make money, so, too, the young heir should know how to spend it. Aside from his family and business, Thomas had only two other great loves in his life — the town of Boston and Harvard College. The first is easy to understand; the latter more difficult.

Thomas Hancock gave a good deal of himself to Boston. His dozen consecutive years as a selectman stand close to being a record, and when this is coupled with the plethora of committees on which he served, he emerges as one of the town's busiest citizens. It goes without saying that all of this was not done with the cleanest of motives; after all, for a man in his position, it was vital for Hancock to be informed and potent in local affairs. Still, election to office, like the old Calvinist notion of election to heaven, was something to be sought after as a sign of worth and an attribute of fame. To Thomas, service went with his station. He willingly accepted the chore and encouraged John to do the same.

In a very practical way it was this neat grafting of public service with private interest that encouraged Thomas to watch lovingly over Boston Common as if it were his own. He personally saw to the cleaning of the Frog Pond so that he would not have a stinking hole in his front yard. Along the east border of the Common, running down Beacon Hill, he had planted at his own expense a long line of lime trees, a strange and disastrous choice for the New England climate. The experiment was a flop, but Thomas simply replaced the exotic fruits with prosaic but sturdy elms.[5]

Ponds and trees made up only a part of Hancock's vista. On the far southern edge of the Common, along the aptly named Frog Lane, was a burial ground. It was there long before his mansion was built, so there was little he could do about it; but in the spring of 1754, it became a worry when complaints were heard that it was "so crowded with Dead bodies, that it is scarcely possible for the Sexton to dig a Grave as it ought to be dug . . ." Expanding accommodations for the dead by encroaching on the living, especially in the Common, was almost certainly not to Thomas' liking. When the town took up the matter, they naturally turned it over to a committee, and, even though he had declined to serve as a selectman only a short time before, Thomas felt that this matter was too close to home to allow others to control the outcome. He served on the committee and probably chaired it. Not surprisingly, the group recommended against enlarging the present site and suggested that an alternate site be found. The Common was safe.

As the future master of Beacon Hill, John shared the concern for the Common and the hill, as well. Over the years the Hancocks had bought a good deal of Beacon Hill and turned much of it into grassy slopes and manicured orchards. In the days when John was a young boy, and even for a time after he returned from Harvard, the Hancock mansion was the sole occupant of the hill; the remainder belonged to the town and lay empty. Occasionally, some of the town's portion fell into disrepair. Erosion, broken fence rails, and wandering livestock seemed to be the most frequent problems. Thomas was never slow to bring these matters to the attention of the town, even to the point of directing a committee "to repair Beacon Hill . . ."[6]

Thomas' civic example for his nephew did go beyond beautification. He helped oversee the almshouse, visited the schools, surveyed the highways, and gave suggestions on how to repair the granary.

Despite his background, Thomas Hancock was never a very spiritual or philosophical man. He understood the things of this world and, like most people, expected the things of the next to take care of themselves. He was an active member of the liberal Brattle Square Church — Congregational, of course, which was practically the civic religion — presided over by the Reverend Samuel Cooper. The Cooper family had something of a lock on the Brattle pulpit. Samuel's father, William, had ascended it in 1716 and was followed by his son in 1745. Hancock supported both ministers and even left a small legacy to Samuel in his will.[7] But despite this personal relationship, there is little to suggest anything close to religious fervor, and the suspicion is that, for Thomas, Brattle Square was merely another charity to which he gave his support.

As Thomas moved through his daily affairs, John was by his side, watching and assisting. Since his graduation, the pace of business had picked up again, thanks to a new war. The opening gambits in this phase of the imperial conflicts had taken place down in Pennsylvania, with the actions of a brash young Virginia colonel, George Washington, who attacked a party of trespassing French. That incident helped to rekindle the Anglo-French struggle, which finally turned into a full-fledged war under the guise of the French and Indian War.[8]

For Thomas, who remembered fondly the profits from the last

war, it was an opportunity for more of the same. Back then, John had been too young to appreciate the complexity and style of his uncle's operation; now he was part of it.

At first the war did not go well for the empire; but after some initial setbacks, the British forces, at the urging of the extraordinarily able prime minister, William Pitt, went on the offensive. It was Pitt who recognized that, unlike prior struggles, this one would be won or lost in the colonies; so it was to those theaters that he sent the empire's forces. With the arrival of ships and men came contracts, and Thomas was not slow to use his skills in wrangling some of these for his own house. As a mark of his importance, in 1758 he was appointed to the Governor's Council, one of the greatest distinctions any colonial could receive.

Unfortunately for the Hancocks, Pitt's policies were too successful. In 1759 the fortress at Quebec fell, and with it went the backbone of French resistance in North America. Soon all of Canada was British, and though the war would continue elsewhere in the world, for the American colonies and Thomas Hancock it was effectively over. Even before the official peace, in 1763, they were beginning to feel once more the pangs of postwar contraction.[9]

It was during these war years that John began to take a more active part in the business, and by 1759 his signature appears in the official correspondence.[10] He was yet too young, barely twenty-two, and inexperienced to be given much responsibility — and Thomas was too close to allow him much — but John was clearly giving an impression that he was the heir apparent.

As John moved about absorbing his uncle's civic and religious values, along with some business acumen, he even began to act like Thomas. This is especially clear in his relationship with his young brother, Ebenezer, for just as Thomas watched so carefully over John, John watched over Ebenezer.

Ebenezer Hancock was the youngest of the Braintree brood. He had stayed with his mother and sister when they moved to Bridgewater and had grown up in that quiet spot while John was up on Beacon Hill. Perhaps because of his distant relationship with his mother and the death of his father, John felt a special responsibility toward Ebenezer. The Bridgewater house was the third parsonage that Ebenezer had lived in, so it is small wonder that nearly everyone expected that when he went off to Harvard in 1756, it was in preparation for a clerical career. Even John, feeling guilty, perhaps, that he had not done it himself, anticipated that his younger brother would take up the family tradition.

Like John, Ebenezer had a relatively undistinguished career at college, although he did behave better. In four years the only blemishes on the record are two small fines for being absent from class.[11] It is not altogether clear who paid for Ebenezer's years at school. He did receive a small scholarship of twenty-four shillings a year, but that amount of money would hardly have bought his books.[12] Perkins may have given some aid, but it is more likely that Thomas, with his usual largesse, supported Ebenezer, just as he had John.

John played the role of elder brother to the fullest. When Ebenezer wished to buy new clothes, he came to John, who granted him permission and then told him to send the bill to Uncle Thomas. He dispensed brotherly advice on all matters and used his uncle's influence to get Ebenezer excused from classes so that they could set out early for Bridgewater.[13]

Perhaps because he was the youngest and, in many respects, the only son left to her, Mary Hawke Thaxter Hancock Perkins seems to have lavished a good deal of care on her Ebenezer. When he went off to Harvard, she, like everyone else, only more so, hoped that he would follow his grandfather, father, and stepfather into the ministry. Yet her hope for his future must have been tinged with a bit of fear; the last time she had bade goodbye to a son, he never came home.

The summer of 1760 was Ebenezer's commencement time. The festivities were a bit muted this year, for Boston had begun to feel the tightness of a straitened economy that had been dealt a sharp blow by a terrible fire which had swept through the town in March.[14] Nevertheless, the trappings were there and the ceremony went on, with the graduates trooping forward to receive their diplomas. It was a happy day for the family; yet, for all of his care and concern, John was not there. He was in London.

In an age devoid of elaborate credit checks or instant com-

munications, business relationships tended to follow the more
familiar route of friendship and kinship. Trust and reputation
meant a good deal, so it made sense to deal with those whom
you knew or to whom you were related, preferably both. It was
this logic that, more than three decades earlier, had carried
Thomas to England, and now for the same reasons he decided
it was important for John to go. His surrogate son should know
the people with whom he would be dealing, and they should
know him.

While Lydia and the servants packed his trunks, Thomas
coached John on matters of business and protocol. What should
be said, to whom, and when. What bills ought to be presented
and what debts should be paid. Perhaps most important, his
uncle probably counseled him to abjure the affliction of youth
— talk. He ought to bridle his tongue and listen. He was moving
from being a very important man in a very small place to a
very small man in a very important place, and it was vital for
him to understand that. Thomas dealt with men of consequence,
and although John was certainly not to let himself be awed by
them, he should nevertheless not be too cocky, lest he offend.

To ensure that his nephew would have access into proper
London society, Thomas made arrangements for John to travel
with His Excellency Thomas Pownall, the recently relieved
royal governor, who, after a distinguished career, was on his
way home to England.[15] Sailing with the governor meant missing his brother's graduation, but the sacrifice was well worth
it. The governor was an old friend of Thomas' and, indeed, had
left him in charge of several thousands of pounds of investments
in the colonies. Taking John under his wing was a kind deed to
accommodate his friend and business associate.

The sailing date was set for June 3. John hurried to say last-
minute goodbyes. Friends and relatives put in their orders for
an assortment of items they wanted him to bring back. Thomas
gave him a parcel of letters of introduction and bills on which
he could draw, and finally, of course, there was Aunt Lydia, the
person who would miss him the most. She probably gave him
some motherly advice, ending with the admonition "Write."

A large throng of well-wishers snaked their way down to the
wharf to say goodbye, not to Hancock, of course; aside from his

family, few spectators even noticed he was there. The send-off was for Pownall. The party boarded a gaily decorated barge whose oarsman carried them out to Nantasket Roads to the province ship *King George,* where they spent the late afternoon feasting and toasting. Toward dusk, as the tide turned, the entourage transferred to the merchantman *Benjamin and Samuel,* and at 8:00 P.M. she hoisted sail and headed out past the harbor islands, bound east to England.[16]

The first few days out, the ship hit some dirty weather coming in from the northeast, but it passed, and the rest of the voyage was apparently just as a June crossing should be — smooth, uneventful, and boring. Each day's tedium was broken up with reading, games, conversation, and, of course, meals, which were taken at the captain's table, where the food was decent and the company refined. Much of the conversation undoubtedly centered on London and its society. Pownall was eager to know what had happened since his last visit home, and Hancock hungered for any scrap of information about the great metropolis. The young officers on board could tell him all the places to see, where to eat and gamble, and what theaters had the best plays and what taverns the prettiest barmaids.

About a month out of Boston, *Benjamin and Samuel* picked up the southwestern shore of Cornwall and headed up for port, probably either Falmouth or Plymouth. From there, Pownall and Hancock traveled by coach, arriving in London shortly after July 10.[17]

The journey overland was anything but pleasant. The roads were dismal to poor, covered with dust, and at times downright dangerous. As the coach rumbled into the city, dust gave way to pavement, but it was hardly an improvement, since London streets were made of round stones whose special mission seemed to be to discomfort the passengers. Hancock, though, was likely oblivious of the ride, for while his bones were being jounced, his eyes were riveted on a thousand sights in the great city.

The most immediate impressions contradicted one another — the city seemed huge, yet without space. Streets were narrow, windy, filthy, and spotted with strange-looking people. Kennels carrying off the day's effluent ran down the middle of the road, and householders casually dumped their refuse in the most convenient spot in the street. The stench was unmistakable, but the air in the summer was at least spared most of the heavy, acrid coal smoke that fouled everything in the colder months. In the way of cleanliness and neatness, Boston offered a more pleasant prospect.

But the eyes of a young man coming into such a metropolis for the first time were less likely to notice the filth on the street than the excitement and energy in the air. London showed all the signs of being the great mart of the empire. The river was teeming with vessels; docks were piled high with goods arriving and leaving; there were bustling crowds; and, everywhere, there was noise.

Quarters were the first thing on his mind as he stepped down from his coach, and, although it is not certain where he finally decided to put up, there can be no question, that, given his tastes, they were appropriate for a young merchant prince. Once settled, with Pownall's assistance and his uncle's letters, John began his rounds. The first visits were to business associates. At the time, the Hancocks dealt with several firms in London. Among the most important were Trecothick, Apthorp, and Thomlinson; and Kilby and Barnard. To these gentlemen Hancock presented the bills entrusted to him by his uncle so that he could draw on them for his own needs. He also used them as agents for purchasing and selling, as well as guides into the labyrinth of the government bureaucracy.

John's relationship to some of these merchants was sometimes a tender one. Although they consistently told his uncle what a fine nephew he had and how impressed they were by him, the suspicion is that things were not always well. To some extent this was probably the natural reaction on the part of these powerful men to the intrusion of a third party into what had heretofore been a successful duo. On the other hand it is quite likely that John could be a bit arrogant and irritating. Ostensibly, he was in London to listen and learn, but it is hard to imagine this pampered young man remaining silent when he felt he ought to speak. Unfortunately, despite his apprenticeship in Boston, he still had a great deal to learn, especially about the London side of the operation. Inevitably, there were some misunderstandings. On one occasion he went to Thomas' London banker, Trecothick and Company, to draw £1000 to pay a debt owed Pownall. He did this on his own, without a specific authorization from Thomas. The bank, undoubtedly a bit jittery about giving over such a large amount of money without everything being in perfect order, refused to honor his request.[18] His response was one of predictable fury. He refused to have anything more to do with them and immediately went over to Kilby and Barnard, who graciously advanced him £800. When Thomas heard of the insult, he, too, was annoyed and in a forbidding tone of cold wrath he simply wrote to John, "I shall not forget . . ."[19]

Although these London business affairs were highly important, they were hardly time-consuming, and John had plenty of leisure on this junket for less weighty matters — which was exactly as it had been intended, for the trip was to be a small grand tour in the European style. It is unlikely that John wrote home about all his experiences, which is just as well. Thomas would have worried about the cost; Lydia, the rectitude. Nevertheless, John took in the sights by night and day. Perhaps it was here in London that he first developed his high life style, for which he was so famous later in his life. Thomas had given him a good start in Boston, but London was beyond anything he could have ever imagined.

During his year abroad John spent at least £500 sterling in cash, which can be directly accounted for, and probably an additional fair sum, which cannot be traced.[20] This was at a time when a very successful and skilled London artisan could expect to make in the same period £100 sterling. Wherever John traveled and whatever he did was done with an elegance that sometimes reached extravagance. His uncle, who was certainly no ascetic himself, was somewhat taken aback by the stories seeping back to Boston about his nephew's London habits.

In a strange new city, with all of its exotic allurements and beyond the watchful gaze of Puritan Boston, John did live extravagantly. When his uncle gently upbraided him for it, John made no excuses and freely admitted that he was "pretty Expensive" and found "Money some way or other goes very fast . . ."[21] He was moving in high company, and if Thomas wanted him to keep up — and he surely did, for the sake of acquiring contracts and influence — then he would have to foot the bill. What else could he do?

For someone with money and energy, the diversions of London life were almost endless. The more cerebral might take in a gallery, concert, or the meeting of a learned society. Surely Hancock, if for no other reason than to preserve an image, attended his share of these quiet affairs. More mundane pursuits were there as well, and, though he may not have been a regular customer, young Hancock paid his respects to some of the better-known taverns around town, especially those down at Covent Garden, the center of London's night life. It was an area of "fashionable disorderly houses," where anything could be had for a price.

Gambling and sports also drew Londoners. The better sort paraded to cricket and boxing matches and then lurked anonymously to watch the vulgar and brutal cockfighting and bear baiting.

In the daytime, and particularly on Sundays, a visit to pleasure gardens was much in order. Both Vauxhall (Spring Garden) and Ranelagh were only a short distance from Westminster and were undoubtedly visited by Hancock. For a slight admission fee a visitor could have coffee or tea served in an elegant garden. In the evening, dinner might be served in one of the graceful buildings and then the evening topped off with a colorful fireworks display. City life was busy and dear.[22]

One sure way to expand the mind and decrease expenses was to leave the company of London society and head for the country. In September, Hancock took just such an excursion. He went down to Bristol, visited a brief time there, and then headed north to Manchester. Apparently, he did not at this time cross the Channel to tour the continent. He may have made such a journey later — his uncle's agent in Amsterdam, Henry Hope, mentioned expecting him — but if he did go, there is nothing in any of his surviving letters or in his later life to indicate that he ever saw or did anything on the continent that had a significant effect on him or left any kind of lasting impression.[23]

Late in October 1760, London society and Hancock got an unexpected and unwelcome rest from their diversions. His Majesty George II died. Despite the mournful eulogies, the king had never been very popular. He was vulgar, cantankerous, dissolute, and German. His final departure took place, fittingly enough, not in the royal bedchamber, surrounded by his loving relations, but rather in "a water-closet at Kensington."[24]

In life George II had had no effect on John Hancock, but in death it was otherwise, for with the nation in official mourning, all of Hancock's playful pastimes came to a halt. He complained that, with the country so quiet, he was at a loss for something to do; all the theaters were closed "and no Diversions are going forward." There were, of course, numerous memorial services to take in, but it is not probable that the son of a New England minister would find much comfort amidst the incense and candles of an Anglican lamentation, although he did use the occasion to go out and buy even more clothes.[25]

When the official grief subsided, London came alive again, but Hancock was in no condition to enjoy it. Throughout his entire life John Hancock was cursed with a fragile and uncertain constitution. To be sure, he was always ready to play ill health for any conceivable advantage, from encouraging Aunt Lydia's pampering to avoiding a hot political issue; nevertheless, it seems reasonably clear that his health did frequently fail him. The winter of 1760-61 was such an occasion.

Perhaps it was the infamous London air and dampness or bad food, but something brought him low. Fortunately, as soon as he became ill, Jonathan Barnard insisted that he leave his bachelor quarters and come to his home, where he could be properly cared for. At Barnard's there was a young servant girl who took special care of John and for whom he displayed some affection. He told his brother that she was "Remarkably Tender and Kind . . ."[26] So kind, in fact, that she reminded him of his own Aunt Lydia. Later in his life, when Hancock became a public figure, his enemies homed in on this episode, hoping to find some juicy scandal. Their best efforts turned up very little except some allegations that

> he kept sneaking and lurking about the kitchen of his Uncle's correspondent, drank tea every day with the housemaid, and on Sunday escorted her to White Conduit House . . . but his

old schoolfellows and intimates know that, though nature had
bestowed upon him a human figure, she had denied him the
power of manhood. The girl was therefore in perfect safety.[27]

Not even in eighteenth-century Boston would this make a first-
class scandal, and besides, the latter insinuation reduced the
potency of the former. As for the rest of the story — who knows?
Hancock was young, rich, good-looking, and far away from
home. This would not be the last time that his name would be
associated with a minor sex scandal; still, it is hard to imagine
him a Lothario, and he most certainly was not the Ben Franklin
of Boston.

Originally, John had planned to stay abroad for a year and to
sail for home some time in the summer of 1761, but the death
of the king altered his plans somewhat. Hancock became intrigued with the tantalizing possibility of staying in London for
the coronation of George III. If the funeral of the old king was
high pageantry, then the coronation of the new ought to be a
show not to be missed. Reluctantly, Uncle Thomas gave him
permission to stay.

George III and John Hancock never met, yet from the beginning of the young king's reign, their destinies seemed to cross.
John's plan to stay for the coronation began to fall apart because
of the king's romantic problems. He needed a queen. His mother
and the Earl of Bute decided that she would have to be German,
so an agent was dispatched to find an appropriate candidate.
Six princesses appear on the final selection list, each uglier than
the other. The winner was Princess Charlotte of Mecklenburg-
Strelitz, the ugliest of the lot; so ugly, in fact, that even the
taciturn king "winced when he first saw her" — but married
her nevertheless.[28]

The search for a queen delayed the coronation, and Thomas
now began to reconsider. The coronation would not take place
until October, which for John would mean a late and possibly
dangerous crossing. Lydia fretted and with each passing day
seemed to grow more depressed and melancholy at the thought
that John would not soon be home. Her spirits sank even lower
in April, when her father died. Thomas had no choice: he asked

John to forgo the coronation and come home as quickly as possible.[29]

John did not resist his uncle's request. He was growing tired of London and longed to be home in Boston with his family and friends. In the short time he had been gone much had changed, and he wanted to get home, where he really belonged.

Ebenezer, for example, had completely altered his course. After a brief venture into the ministry he had decided that the life of a clergyman was not nearly as exciting or profitable as being a merchant, especially when his uncle was one of the richest. John was a bit surprised at the change, but Thomas took in Ebenezer, and he was off on his mercantile pursuits.[30]

Ebenezer was not the only Hancock whose life was taking new directions. Sister Mary, too, had gone off on a new tack while John was in London. In October she married her step-brother, Richard Perkins.[31] The relations of John and Ebenezer with that side of the family had become somewhat strained. Because of the distance and inconvenience, Ebenezer hardly ever visited Bridgewater, and, conversely, John complained that he hardly ever heard from Bridgewater.[32] Nevertheless, John was pleased at the news and congratulated his sister on the event.

The tugs toward home were irresistible, so in June John began his round of farewells and then headed down for Portsmouth to board a vessel for home. In these last hectic minutes there was just one more item of business to take care of before he left. He met with Matthew Woodford, a government contractor who supplied the troops in Nova Scotia and Newfoundland. Woodford needed an American contact, and Thomas wanted the job. John's diplomacy apparently worked, and on July 11, just before he left, Hancock got Woodford to sign an agreement bringing the House of Hancock into the operation.[33]

Once that piece of business was out of the way, John got his not inconsiderable baggage on board, and, by mid-July, was bound for home.[34] The welcome was joyous. Thomas and Lydia came down in the grand coach to greet him. At the house everyone gathered, including the slaves, Molly, Agniss, Cato, Prince Holmes, and Hannibal, as well as the white servants, Hannah and Betsey. John had brought gifts for everyone, and there was great excitement as he parceled them out.

Over dinner, Thomas quizzed him about politics and business, though Lydia was probably more interested in fashions and gossip. All in all, Thomas was pleased. John had done well. He had done an excellent job representing the firm, expanded its contracts, and enhanced its reputation.

The impressions and news did not flow all one way, and John was as eager to have his questions answered as Thomas was his. One thing that needed no inquiry was Thomas' health. It was obvious from his appearance that Thomas had not been well. Despite the exhilaration of his nephew's return, he was showing his near three score years. He had slowed down considerably and was even talking about retirement from business. Although he had been elected to the Governor's Council in 1758, his duties on that body were relatively light and far less burdensome than the ones in the old days, when he had been a selectman. It was not the assertive and combative Thomas that John came home to, but a plaintive and tired man. Ironically, it may well have been his nephew's return that slowed the old man even more; he now knew that at last he could let go, for there was someone to take hold.

Less than a year and a half after John's return from England, Thomas made the formal announcement of an event long before accomplished. On the first day of 1763 he declared, "I have this day Taken my Nephew Mr. John Hancock into Partnership with me having had long Experience of his Uprightness [and] great abilities for Business."[35]

With his "great abilities" John quickly moved to the fore. He took over an increasing amount of the correspondence, especially with Woodford regarding the contracts in Nova Scotia and Newfoundland. He also encouraged Thomas to take a flyer into an old business, whale oil. Although Thomas himself was practically bedridden with gout, it was an opportunity he did not dare miss, so he gave the go-ahead to John to negotiate with the Nantucket firm of Folger and Gardner, in a bold attempt at nothing less than cornering the market.[36] He left the details to his new junior partner, and in the summer of 1763 John went over to Nantucket and made the final arrangements. Folger and

Gardner would buy the oil on the island; the Hancocks would ship it; Barnard would market it.

Thomas had a new vessel built especially for the trade, *Boston Packet*. The first voyage brought some profit, but not nearly enough for these hungry investors, so they laid plans on a grander scale for the 1764 season. *Boston Packet* was joined that year by a sleek new brigantine, *Lydia*. Like most grand schemes, there were flaws, and despite great promise, things began to go awry. John complained that Captain Folger was not doing his part — a charge that Folger threw back at him — and both thought Barnard a bit lax. The two vessels were packed to the gunwales with barrels of oil and sent off to England in July. When they arrived, the cargoes sold well — or so they thought. However, by the time all the costs were tallied, the partners discovered their great profits had been piddled away. Communication was so bad that even after their mistake was discovered, it was impossible to stop additional shipments, so, having lost money on early shipments, they had to stand idly by while their losses were compounded on later ones.[37] Certainly, John cannot be entirely blamed for these troubles, but there is a lingering impression that youth was prevailing over experience and that the steadying hand of Thomas was growing weaker, to the detriment of the House of Hancock.

The spring and summer of 1764 saw the Hancocks busy with the usual array of business — oil, real estate, government contracts, and general merchandising. In June, Thomas' declining health remitted for a while, and he told Woodford that he was feeling better. His physician, Dr. Thomas Bulfinch, father of the famous architect, came down to treat him with the normal eighteenth-century pharmacopoeia, including emetics, diarrhetics, and, possibly, an occasional bleeding.[38] On August 1, Thomas felt well enough to take himself down the hill to the State House for a meeting of the Council. He arrived and climbed the circular stairs to the second floor, where the Council chamber was located. As he entered, suddenly he crumpled to the floor in a heap. Other Council members rushed to his side, and he was quickly carried back to his home. Two hours later, Thomas Hancock was dead.[39]

Chapter 4

On His Own

*E*VERYONE IN BOSTON knew that Thomas was a wealthy man, but it took his death to show just how profitable his life had really been. For someone who had started out with very little, he had come a long way. To Lydia, he left £10,000 in cash, the mansion, and all its furnishings. He divided an additional £8000 among an assortment of sisters, nieces, nephews, and friends, including several ministers. Harvard College and the town were also beneficiaries. The college got a handsome gift of £1000 to establish a professorship in Oriental languages, and the town received £600 to build a hospital for the insane. Among the others he remembered were the church in Lexington, with £20; the Society for Propagating Christianity (an Indian missionary program), with £700; and his slaves Prince Holmes, £20, and Cato, who got the greatest gift of all — the gift of freedom, when he reached thirty-three years of age.[1]

Aside from cash, there was something else Thomas had an abundance of — land. He owned more than 22,000 acres of undeveloped land in central Massachusetts and Maine, as well as several developed parcels in Boston and other parts of Suffolk County. The undeveloped land, which was apparently being held for speculation, was divided among the relatives; the more valuable items were held intact and given to Thomas' major heir, John. Everything that was not specifically mentioned went to this favored nephew. He got the business, including warehouses, shops, ships, inventory, along with all of the real estate in the town and elsewhere that was not bequeathed to someone else. What did all of this amount to? A good estimate would be that John now had two thirds of an estate valued at £100,000, making him easily, in modern terms, a millionaire.[2] The only significant item John did not get was the mansion, but that was quickly remedied. Thomas was buried on Monday. The following Friday, Lydia signed over the house and its contents to John, asking only that she be allowed to live there for the remainder of her life.[3] With that acquisition, John had both the power and the symbol of the House of Hancock.

At twenty-seven, John Hancock was now one of the richest men in America. He had been training for this moment since the day he first arrived on Uncle Thomas' doorstep. He quickly took charge and announced the melancholy news of Thomas' death to his overseas correspondents, while also reassuring them that nothing had changed and that it would be business as usual. Through the local newspapers he sent the same message to his neighbors, adding that those indebted to his uncle should now promptly pay him to "prevent trouble."[4]

Looking after the business was only one of the cares John inherited from his uncle. Unmentioned in the will, but no less real, was his new responsibility for Aunt Lydia, who, with her own money, was pretty much independent, and Ebenezer, who had neither money nor much ability to make it.

As it happened, however, it was Lydia who looked out for John, rather than vice versa. She continued to watch over him as she had since his schoolboy days. She also kept charge of the domestic side of the household, supervising the staff, arranging menus, and making plans for the numerous social affairs Hancock enjoyed. To please her, Hancock commissioned Boston's best-known portrait painter, John Singleton Copley, to execute a portrait of Thomas, which he presented to Harvard for its library.[5]

Aunt Lydia represented a very happy part of Hancock's world. She brought into his life a certain sense of stability and peace. Ebenezer's role was quite otherwise. Ever since his days at college, he had shown a distressing proclivity toward failure.[6]

Through a combination of misfortune and incompetence, he seemed always to be either on his way to or from disaster. Since his graduation, in 1760, he had been under the wing of Uncle Thomas, who gave him some minor duties in the business, keeping him occupied and out of trouble. But Ebenezer did not relish working for his brother, so he decided, with John's blessing, to fly the nest and try things on his own. John used his influence to establish Ebenezer's credit with the proper houses, and that, coupled with the younger brother's small inheritance from Thomas (£666 and 3000 acres of Maine land), enabled him to go into partnership with Edward Blanchard, a hardware merchant in Boston.[7]

Under the pellucid sky of the crisp New England fall, Hancock took the helm. His warehouses and store down on the waterfront were kept stocked with a variety of English and India goods, which he sold both wholesale and retail. Much of his inventory was delivered in his own bottoms, which on the outward-bound leg carried back to England an assortment of raw materials, especially potash, whale oil, and timber. Trading at various levels was his prime business, but there were other ventures that occupied his time. He carried on Thomas' land speculations and added some of his own. The Point Shirley project started by Thomas was one for which he showed special care. It involved a large parcel of land across the harbor in what is today the town of Winthrop. Originally, Thomas and several other Boston merchants purchased the tract with the intention of developing a large-scale fishing operation. War brought that project to a close, but the merchants continued to develop the land; and in recent years it was beginning to turn into something of a summer retreat for Bostonians.[8]

His fortune and his bachelorhood made Hancock a very eligible young man, a status he thoroughly enjoyed. He was, after all, a handsome man who enjoyed good times. Though not tall, he was slender and well proportioned. He had dark brown hair, which he usually hid under a short white wig, and bushy eyebrows sitting atop dark, almond-shaped eyes. Most Hancockian of all was his nose. It was aquiline, just like the Bishop's, Uncle Thomas', and Ebenezer's. The mouth was undistinguished, ex-

cept that one could hardly miss it on the way to noticing the
large dimple on his wedge-shaped chin.

Under Lydia's direction, the household staff staged some of
Boston's most elegant soirées. The menus included all kinds of
meats and poultry, vegetables, fruits, sweets, and generous servings of wine. Hancock made no secret of his fondness for good
wine. He told one supplier, "I like pale Wine . . . I like rich
Wine," and then, to prove it, he ordered more than 400 gallons
of the best Madeira.[9] When not entertaining at home, he often
joined others either at private parties, of which there was an
abundance, or at public functions in local taverns and, less
frequently, at Faneuil Hall. He associated with all the "best"
people, from the royal governor on down. There can be no
question that Hancock loved entertaining and being entertained. Boston was not Babylon, but, judging by Hancock's
style, it was closer to that than to being "the City Upon a
Hill."[10]

In this very pleasant world there were some inconveniences.
Trade was slumping, and several businesses in Boston had col-
lapsed.[11] As serious as the economic situation was, it certainly
did not forecast doom; after all, similar things had happened
during other postwar periods. However, this time there were
some new ingredients, the implications of which were only
slowly being realized.

It would have taken the combined efforts of Solomon and the
prophets, along with a battery of consultants, to unsnarl the
problems of the British Empire in the mid-sixties. Events would
prove that George III was no Solomon and his ministers no
prophets.

Money was the apparent issue. Britannia had come through
her most recent war with the French wrapped with victories,
possessions, and influence, the like of which the world had not
seen since the days of Rome. But with the glory went the bills,
and the nation was staggering under a national debt of more
than £130 million.[12] That debt, paired with the huge costs of
administering and protecting these new domains, was putting
a wretched strain on an already thin exchequer. New money
had to be found. Over the coming years the search would twist

its way down narrow avenues, up dead-end alleys, always meeting the same responses — protests, boycotts, riots, and eventually revolution itself. The last finally came when the participants understood that the question of money was only a stalking
horse for the real issue — ideology.[13]

Despite the fact that he was to be so much a part of this
impending ideological conflict, it would have required something beyond human knowledge for Hancock to understand his
role at this time. Hancock was not, nor would he ever be, a
philosopher. He knew his history and was well aware of current
issues in British policies.[14] Politically, he was a Whig, not in
any formal sense, but, as with most of his colleagues, in a vague,
almost instinctive, manner. There were numerous influences
that explain his leanings, including history, or at least his view
of it; his Puritan Yankee roots; the Congregational Church;
Harvard College; Uncle Thomas; the town of Boston; and any
number of other sources from which eighteenth-century Bostonians took their beliefs. Although the elements were there,
most of them had yet to come together in any positive form.
There was no need, as long as there were no issues. Still, Hancock did hold certain fundamental tenets. One was that naked
political power went about like a lion, seeking to devour its
natural prey — liberty. Power, therefore, needed to be restrained, and this could best be done through the agency of a
representative government and a vigilant populace.[15] To Hancock, this watchful agency was local government, both town
and colony. Despite the *Sturm und Drang*, for more than a
century and a quarter these institutions had served their people
well. When measured against the sometimes corrupt and venal
antics of British politics, made so much of by the eighteenth-
century Commonwealthmen whose works were devoured on
both sides of the Atlantic, Bostonians felt they could rightfully
take great pride in themselves as exemplars and protectors of
virtue and liberty. It was against this background of ideology
and home rule that the ministry began to play out its hand,
reaching after new revenue for a strapped empire.

In April 1763, George Grenville became the king's first minister. To him fell the unhappy task of divining new sources of

money. After some consideration he hit on a scheme to cut the levy on molasses, a by-product of sugar refining, to one-half the current rate; and, in an unwonted spirit of efficiency, this time it would be collected. Added to this in the bill were new duties on some items and a healthy increase on the old, all intended to raise the modest sum of less than £50,000, barely a fraction of what it cost to administer and defend the empire.[16] The Sugar Act and its promise of rigorous enforcement was bad news for smugglers, of whom there were a number in America, but it boded ill for others, as well. New England floated in a sea of molasses, and anything that disrupted its flow was bound to have a rippling effect throughout the economy. More ominous, though perhaps less recognized, than the economic impact of the measure was the admission by the ministry that the act was specifically designed to raise revenue. This was a new departure. In the past, Parliament's legislation for America had always been regulatory in nature; now it had moved boldly and perhaps foolishly into the taxing business.

For both political and economic reasons, the act caused consternation in Boston. The town meeting denounced it; the House of Representatives called for the creation of a Committee of Correspondence to share its misgivings with other colonies; and James Otis penned his pamphlet, *The Rights of the British Colonies Asserted and Proved*, avowing the principle of no taxation without representation.[17]

All the hubbub in the town, including a movement against importing British luxuries and a return to the more simple life, caught Hancock at a bad moment. His business, like almost everybody else's, was bad and growing worse. Hancock warned Barnard and Harrison, Barnard's new partner, of great "uneasiness" and pointed to the failure of several Boston firms as examples of the town's distress. He did not, however, mention any philosophical or political objections that he had about the recent measures; rather, he confined himself strictly to business issues.[18] At this point in his career he was either not sensitive to the political implications or simply so overwhelmed with reorganizing after Thomas' death that he neglected them. The former seems more probable.

Had wiser heads prevailed, His Majesty's ministers would have waited to see the results of the first act before raising the curtain on the second. That was not the case, of course, and even as the Sugar Act was beginning to be enforced, Grenville was already preparing another new measure to better the health of the exchequer — a Stamp Act.

From his vantage point, Grenville saw nothing radical about a stamp duty. Such duties had been in use in England at least since the reign of Charles II, and on several occasions in the past suggestions had been made to extend them to America. They provided a relatively simple and painless method of raising money. Stamps of differing denominations would have to be affixed to various items, including newspapers, diplomas, licenses, and even playing cards. The stamps would be sold by special stamp masters, appointed by the ministry. It is a measure of Grenville's insensitivity to colonial opinion (a flaw he shared with most of his colleagues) that he could not appreciate how this act would infuriate Americans and raise a storm of protest that would eventually imperil the empire.[19]

Although Hancock may have had only a glimmering of the political implications of the Sugar Act, the Stamp Act moved him to strong action. The reason for the change in attitude has to do with both the substance of the acts and Hancock himself. There can be no question that the Stamp Act was far more threatening to the rights of Bostonians than the Sugar Act. People might quibble about whether the latter was in fact a direct tax, and thereby lessen its import, but such fine distinctions were totally irrelevant in the case of stamp duties. There was no way of escaping the fact that the Stamp Act was a direct tax and that it was intended to raise revenue. Even that fact, though, might not have had the strong impact it did unless, in the months between the two measures, something else had not happened.

Those intervening months saw in Hancock an evolution of thought taking him more in the direction of his later image as the great revolutionary. This change came about principally as the result of his widening circle of political acquaintances. Moving about in his business and social spheres, he was brought into contact with numerous people who influenced his thinking. Since 1762 he had been a member of the Masonic Lodge of Saint Andrew, which, with the other Lodge of Freemasons, Saint John's, counted among its brothers Sam Adams, James Otis, and Joseph Warren. He was also active in the Merchant's Society and probably other social clubs as well. In a town the size of Boston, overlap in membership between the clubs was considerable, and membership in one invited membership in others. Young, ambitious, able, and gregarious, Hancock seemed to relish his roles and even ended up a member of the famous Long Room Club, a collection of staunch Whigs, among them Paul Revere, Samuel Cooper, and Benjamin Church.

All this made it a near certainty that Hancock would venture into politics, and in March 1765 the political bug bit. His first prize was the position of selectman. The election could hardly be called a smashing victory, since the outcome was preordained. Hardly spontaneous, Boston politics were controlled and guided by an influential alliance of merchants, lawyers, and an old political club known as the Caucus. Through their dominance of the town meeting, they were able to direct the affairs of the town.[20]

Hancock's election at a youthful twenty-eight made him the youngest of the five selectmen and marked him as a rising star. He was chosen for two reasons. First, he was "safe"; that is, it was reasonably certain that he was of Whiggish persuasion and would always defend the rights and interests of the town against any encroachment. The second consideration was, of course, his wealth, which gave him the kind of leverage easily translated into political advantage.

Within the New England cosmography, the town, especially the premier one of Boston, exercised considerable independence. As a selectman, Hancock became involved with the budget (approximately £10,000 per year), regulation of markets, law enforcement, schools, streets, morals, and almost anything else the town might wish to consider. Coping with these problems was an ideal way to begin his political career, and through this school he soon learned that philosophy counted for less than compromise, cajolery, and concession.[21]

It has sometimes been suggested that Hancock moved ahead in politics because he was a rich, empty-headed dilettante whose vanity could be played on by clever men for their own advantage. Of his flamboyant vanity there can be no doubt, but in an age hardly known for its self-effacing personalities, that trait was one he shared with many. Was he inattentive and casual about his duties? The record certainly does not show that. In his first year as a selectman, the board met, on an average, twice every week, and Hancock was present more than 80 percent of the time. Considering the demands in his life, especially his business affairs, that can scarcely be considered the record of a dilettante.[22]

Less than two weeks after his election as selectman, in March 1765, Parliament enacted the Stamp Act. Hancock's initial reaction was a very pragmatic one. The act was bad because it would injure trade. At first, he seems to have been almost naïve about the politics of the business, and wrote to his uncle's old friend Thomas Pownall that he "seldom meddle[d] with politics and indeed [had] not time . . . to Say any thing on that head."[23]

Perhaps his insouciance came from a belief that the act would never really go into effect. After all, it was not scheduled to begin until November 1, and with each passing day the tide of opposition was growing higher. Local newspapers everywhere in America were filled with items damning the act and demanding a united front against it. From his point of view as a Boston politician (despite his disclaimer to Pownall) and merchant, Hancock could see nothing but evil consequences from the act. He hoped that Parliament, too, would sense the future and move to avert disaster. His faith was ill founded.

As the countdown toward November 1 ticked off, the Boston press became more strident in the opposition, and Hancock grew less sanguine. Nevertheless, no matter what he thought of the wisdom of the act, he was, after all, a loyal subject of His Majesty, and he confided to Pownall that, although the act might ruin America, "we must submit."[24]

To the south, a fiery redhead took exception to Hancock's submissive attitude. He was Patrick Henry, a rabble-rousing back-country lawyer and orator. In the closing days of the May session of the Virginia House of Burgesses, Henry introduced a series of seven resolves. Not all of them passed, but all did circulate through the colonies to become a rallying point for American opposition to the Stamp Act. At the heart of the resolves was the assertion that the colonists could be taxed only by their own assemblies and that anyone who thought otherwise was an "Enemy."[25] Henry's resolves were the catalyst that plainly brought to the surface one of the fundamental issues troubling the empire — sovereignty.

Hancock believed, as did most eighteenth-century men, that sovereignty was indivisible and had to rest "somewhere in every Commonwealth." In the case of the empire, that place was Parliament, whose only restraints were "judgment, righteousness and truth."[26] But how did this concept square with Patrick Henry's assertion? If Henry was right, then Parliament was not sovereign. What, too, of the Boston town meeting and the colony government? How did they fit into this sovereign scheme? For generations no one had ever bothered to ask these questions, because there had been no need. Now the need was arising, and for Hancock and his peers the answers were uncomfortable.

By the time news of the resolves reached Boston, the Massachusetts General Court had already taken action to call a general meeting of representatives from all the colonies, to take place in New York during the fall. Nine colonies sent delegates to this Stamp Act Congress, which met during October 1765. The gathering adopted resolutions sympathetic to the Virginia resolves, though more moderate in tone. Nevertheless, the delegates did assert the rights of the colonies, making an important distinction between legislation and taxation. Only the former was allowed to Parliament.[27]

The acceleration of events carried forward both Boston and Hancock. With the well-oiled Boston "machine" ready, and the gray eminence, Sam Adams, taking his role, it looked to be a very unpleasant summer ahead for the royal authorities in the town.

Boston could be a violent town. For some time, two local gangs, the North End and the South End, had been in the habit of celebrating Pope's Day by parading through the town with their effigies of His Holiness until they finally stumbled upon one another, signaling a general donnybrook.[28] It took little effort to channel these high spirits into more purposeful political violence.

On the morning of August 14, an effigy of Andrew Oliver, rumored to be the stamp master, was found hanging from a tree down on Newbury Street. That was the sign for a night of tumult. As soon as the sun set, a well-managed mob appeared, carrying Oliver's image. They marched down to the waterfront and surrounded a new brick building of Oliver's that was whispered to be the place from which he intended to distribute the hated stamps. In a few frenzied moments they managed to level the structure, and then, with nothing left to do there, they tramped off in the direction of Oliver's home. Fortunately, Oliver and his family had had the good sense to flee to a neighbor's. When the crowd arrived, they were disappointed to find only an empty house, but they proceeded to ransack it, anyway. Pleased with their night's work, the happy warriors retired. The next day a delegation of local citizens visited Oliver and suggested to him that he had seen only a preview of what was to come unless he resigned his post. Oliver resigned.[29]

For the next ten days the leader of the mob, Ebenezer MacIntosh, a South End shoemaker and consummate rioter, kept the town quiet. It was about this time that those who opposed the Stamp Act began to call themselves "Sons of Liberty," a description given to Americans in Parliament by Colonel Isaac Barre during one of his speeches against the Stamp Act.

Oliver's misfortune was disquieting to Hancock. After all, Andrew Oliver was a respected member of the community, whose roots went deep into Boston's history. He and Hancock had a good deal in common, and to see him so intimidated and shamed was distressing. On the day following the attack, Hancock joined with the rest of the town in decrying the violence. That was the old conservative-merchant side of him. The new political side was not quite so certain. He told Harrison and Barnard that Oliver's misadventure was proof positive of the "General dissatisfaction" and that he personally had come to the conclusion that the only way for America to avoid ruin was for the "whole Continent" to exhibit the "same Spirit." [30] In less than three months, Hancock had moved from submission to resistance.

On August 26, the "spirit" erupted again. This time the mob was after bigger game, Andrew Oliver's brother-in-law, Lieutenant Governor Thomas Hutchinson. To warm up for the assault, half the mob first went to the home of William Story, an official of the Vice-Admiralty Court, where they caused quite a commotion. At the same time, the other half gave a "blessing" to Benjamin Hallowell, the comptroller of the port. Once finished with those side excursions, both groups moved in well-ordered fashion up to North Square and the Hutchinsons' home. Like the Olivers, the Hutchinsons had wisely retired and were at this time staying at their country home, in Milton. The crowd wasted little time getting on with their work. They broke through the doors, smashed windows, threw furniture and papers out onto the street, and made a general shambles of what had been one of Boston's loveliest homes. [31]

To many, it seemed that both Oliver and Hutchinson had gotten no less than they deserved. They were, after all, officials of a government that was imposing unfair and, in the minds of some, unconstitutional measures on the colonies. These mob scenes were an emotional but shrewdly devised addition to the memorials and petitions, which had thus far been ignored.

Hancock had had enough of this lawlessness, so he joined with the other selectmen in summoning a special town meeting to consider the problem. Faneuil Hall was packed to the rafters, and by an overwhelming margin the rest of the townspeople showed that they, too, had had enough, as the town meeting members voted to condemn the violence. To show that they were serious in this matter, the town officers ordered MacIntosh arrested and his accomplices sought. He was quickly released, though, when the word was passed that if he was not, then the Custom House would be leveled stone by stone. As for the others who were arrested, they were set free by a more informal means — a mysterious jailbreak in which no one was ever recaptured.

Violence has a way of becoming more acceptable with use, and though Hancock's class biases might tell him that the riots were the work of Boston's mudsills and that street violence was wrong, he could certainly understand how it had come about, especially in light of his own frustration with the ministry's policies. It cannot be said (as it occasionally has been) that he was falling into the sinister clutches of Sam Adams and the "Sons"; but it is true that in many ways Hancock was what might be described as a ripening radical, who could not have helped being influenced by the patriot arguments in the face of a seemingly intransigent and ignorant ministry.

As the political winds grew more tempestuous, Hancock ran with them. In September he allowed himself to be nominated for the seat in the General Court made vacant by the death of Oxenbridge Thacher. He lost that election to none other than Sam Adams, but the mere fact that he could be considered a candidate stands witness to the town's growing respect for him. The election was also a sign of Adams' rising popularity and the political sentiments of the town, which Hancock observed with great interest.

As November 1, the infamous date on which the Stamp Act would go into effect, drew nearer, Hancock represented continuously to his London correspondents how insane he thought the measure. By September and October, his letters were filled with far more than the old bad-for-business rhetoric. Contrary to what he had told Pownall back in July, he was now "meddling" in politics, and "submission" was no longer his policy. He wrote instead of rights and liberties, and on October 14, in a very long and forceful letter, he announced that if any of his ships arrived after the 1st, he would lay them up, for "I have come to a serious Resolution not to send one Ship more to sea nor to have any kind of Connection in Business under a Stamp"; and to be sure that everyone would know why he was taking these steps, he told them, "This letter I propose to remain in my Letter Book as a Standing monument to posterity, and my Children in particular that I by no means Consented to a Submission to this Cruel Act and that my best Representations were not wanting in this matter."[32] With his concern for fame and history, he wanted to be sure that present and future citizens should know of his patriotism. One week later he wrote, "I have a right to the Libertys and privileges of the English Constitution, and as [an] Englishman will enjoy them."[33]

Hancock's dramatic stand undoubtedly won him many admirers. Fortunately for his business, though, events did not turn out as dreadful as he feared. Some 250 merchants of the town did enter into a nonimportation agreement, pledging not to import a long list of British items until the act was repealed. Contrary to what might be expected, however, this agreement had little effect on Hancock's business; indeed, if it had any effect at all, it was toward improving it.[34] During the period of nonimportation, business was actually better for him. One reason is that he had probably laid in a large inventory, in anticipation of the agreement, and therefore could continue to deal from stocks on hand. It is also true that the effects of nonimportation on American merchants were minimized because the agreement took effect during the winter, which was always the slackest season. As a result of these mitigations, Hancock's business seems to have suffered little direct injury from the boycotts.

Whatever the reality of the situation, it was known only to Hancock and his clerks, and even then unclearly; so it was possible for him to portray the image of a much-aggrieved citizen. He was in the enviable position of being able to enhance his reputation as a great patriot at virtually no cost.

Although the economic costs of the Stamp Act were less than they appeared, there were other difficulties arising from it that were to complicate Hancock's life. Naturally, the flurry of local activity brought on by the reaction to the Stamp Act created a herd of new undertakings, from letter-writing, to enforcing the nonimportation, to delivering memorials to the governor. Add to this the countless difficulties arising from doing business without stamps, and the result was that, for a prominent merchant and town officer like Hancock, there was a deluge of new responsibilities. He found himself so increasingly "engaged in publick matters" that he had to let some of his business accounts slide.[35]

Inconveniencing him even further was Ebenezer's recent departure. He had run the retail store down at Faneuil Market. That post was now vacant, and, much to his annoyance, John was having considerable trouble finding someone to go behind the counter.[36]

Although Harrison and Barnard, who continued to be his principal partners, joined with him in opposing the recent measures, they were not inclined to tolerate late accounts.[37] When they pressed him to bring his affairs up to date, which, translated, meant "Pay your bills," Hancock replied coolly, "Really Gent. it seems to me that you are rather more strenuous with me than with many other of your Correspondents . . ."[38] Increasingly, there was a very noticeable edge to Hancock's letters. He was as much angered by a partner who pressed him as a ministry that taxed him.

Nonimportation was working. Trade was down, British merchants were screaming, and Parliament was listening.[39] Sensing the shift as early as mid-January 1766, Hancock, with cautious optimism, was ordering goods to be shipped to him as soon as repeal took effect so that he might be ready for the spring season.[40]

Naturally, despite the hectic pace they imposed, business and politics did not gobble up all his attention; in the grand tradition of Uncle Thomas, John played the role of the great patron. He went off to Harvard to accept the accolades and thanks of the college at the public installation of the first Hancock Professor. The ceremony was conducted with elegance and style and was second in pomp only to the commencement itself.[41]

Having stood in for Thomas on these occasions, John then turned around and on his own donated a thousand volumes to fill the library shelves and gave "a set of the most elegant carpets to cover the floors of the Library, the Apparatus and Philosophy Chambers."[42] Hancock was rapidly becoming Harvard's chief benefactor.

Neither did Hancock neglect the house on the hill. He ordered trees and vegetables planted, fences erected, roads repaired, and anything else needful to keep it the grandest home in the town. The austerity of the times kept him from importing the kinds of elegant furniture and accessories that Thomas had been so fond of; but still, what there was spoke of high style and grace that even John would have been hard put to improve on.

The rooms were richly carpeted and filled with mahogany and walnut furniture. For the most part, the downstairs area, with its great hall and sitting parlors, was done in conservative style, with the usual assortment of paintings and prints on the walls and silver on the tables. Upstairs, though, in the private chambers, the ambience was a bit freer. Here, the furniture was still walnut and mahogany, but instead of the subdued colors employed downstairs, he used crimson and yellow for the draperies and bed coverings.

His home reflected his style — generous and, at times, histrionic. His largesse extended in all directions. Aside from formal charities, he seems also to have been a kind creditor. Although it cannot be proven, it seems likely that he was most willing to extend credit to the friends of nonimportation; then, if they were squeezed, he never dunned them for repayment. With such favors he contributed to the cause of nonimportation while embellishing his own reputation.

Business favors were only one way Hancock used his wealth to political advantage. He was often accused by his enemies of being Sam Adams' "milch cow" and of funneling great subsidies into the pockets of Boston's Whigs.[43] To what extent this is true can never be known; politicians in any age are not wont to keep incriminating records, and certainly Hancock was no exception. Nevertheless, it can be reasonably assumed that he did support those people and causes with which he agreed. However, given the nature of local politics, which were relatively open, this support most often was given in a public manner — barrels of wine on the Common, sumptuous dinners at a local tavern, fireworks displays, and so forth. The openness was essential, because if one was to achieve political success in Boston, he had to have the support of the common folk. In England, of course, the situation was otherwise. There, power rested with fewer people, who were swayed not by grand displays but by cash and preferment. The difference in style does not mean that Boston was democratic and virtuous — it was neither — but it does suggest that Hancock's money was put to a different kind of use from what it might have been if he had been operating in England. In Whiggish Boston his money was used to buy the town; in Georgian London, the purchase of only a few men would have done.

On April 17, 1766, the *Massachusetts Gazette* carried the long-awaited news — the Stamp Act was repealed. The news was a bit premature; the town was to wait several weeks for official confirmation. The delay gave the Sons and their allies time to savor their victory and plan a gala celebration. As a member of the winning team, Hancock was riding high, and at the elections for the General Court, held on May 6, he was chosen to sit as one of Boston's representatives.[44]

This victory, coming so soon after his defeat in September, would not have happened without the support of Sam Adams and the Sons of Liberty. After the repeal, an act for which they claimed a good deal of credit, their influence was at flood. The spring elections of 1766 saw the popular faction gaining strength as they drove supporters of the ministry to ground. In doing that, they had enjoyed Hancock's support, and, as they glanced ahead to future battles, he seemed to them to be a resourceful ally, one they wished to weld to their cause.

Regarding his election, there are two apocryphal stories that enjoy an undying currency. Both involve that "arch conspirator," Sam Adams. One has Adams and his cohorts, a few days before the election, discussing the candidates. As they went down the list of their choices, they came to the name of John Rowe, a prominent merchant and sympathizer, who was up for re-election. The others were satisfied to keep Rowe, but Adams supposedly turned his eyes toward Beacon Hill and asked cryptically, "Is there not another John that may do better?"[45]

The other story is set on election day and involves Sam and his cousin John. The brace of Adamses were strolling across Beacon Hill, near Hancock's mansion, when Sam remarked, "This town has done a wise thing today . . . They have made that young man's fortune their own."[46]

Like most stories of this sort, these two have both a touch of truth and a good deal of folklore. The old images are there — Hancock, the vain popinjay who is clay in the hands of a cunning and sly Adams. The truth is that the relationship was more symbiotic than parasitical. Hancock was no fool, and the seat in the General Court was as much his right as it was a gift.

Through his extensive business contacts, land holdings, and acts of charity, to say nothing of the name alone, he was one of the best-known people in Boston. Nor was he a political novice. He had acquitted himself well as a selectman. The suggestion, therefore, that Adams was playing Hancock's Pygmalion is simply off the mark. Adams was Hancock's tutor, not his creator.

At last, on May 16, 1766, the official news of repeal arrived. The town went wild with joy: bells were rung, cannon fired, and ships in the harbor saluted. The selectmen declared that Monday next would be a day of general thanksgiving. It was the grandest celebration Boston had ever seen, and Hancock was there to garner his share of the plaudits.

> By the Generosity of some Gentlemen remarkable for their Humanity and Patriotism, our Gaol was freed of Debtors. At one o'clock the Castle and Batteries and Train of Artillery fired a Royal Salute and the Afternoon was spent in Mirth and Jollity. In the Evening the whole Town was beautifully illuminated: — On the Common the Sons of Liberty erected a magnificent Pyramid, illuminated with 280 lamps. The four upper Stories of which were ornamented with the figures of their Majesties and fourteen of the worthy Patriots who have distinguished themselves by their Love of Liberty. On the Top of the Pyramid was fix'd a round Box of Fireworks horizontally. About one hundred Yards from the Pyramid the Sons of Liberty erected a Stage for the Exhibition of their Fireworks, near the Workhouse, in the lower Room of which they entertained the Gentlemen of the Town. John Hancock Esq. who gave a grand and elegant Entertainment to the genteel Part of the Town and treated the populace with a pipe of Madeira Wine, erected at the Front of his House, which was magnificently illuminated, a Stage for the Exhibition of his Fireworks, which was to answer those of the Sons of Liberty.[47]

A week after the Stamp Act festivities, the Great and General Court of the Colony of Massachusetts Bay convened for its spring session. Among the freshmen members was John Hancock of Boston. According to custom, one of the first orders of business was the election of the speaker. The choice was the brilliant, if somewhat erratic, James Otis. Because of his important role in the Sons of Liberty, "Jemmy" Otis had done a good deal to bring misery into the life of Francis Bernard, the royal governor, and for that reason his choice as speaker was nothing less than a calculated insult to His Excellency. Hancock's first committee assignment was to present this name to Bernard for his approval. On May 28, the committee, Hancock included, was ushered into the governor's chamber to tell him something he already knew. His prompt and predictable but no less shocking answer was no — Jemmy Otis would not be speaker. At the same time he announced that four of the councilors elected by the House were also unacceptable and that he was returning their names, as well. The House quickly replied with a new candidate for speaker, Thomas Cushing, but refused to provide more councilors. Bernard accepted Cushing and fumed about the councilors. Hancock had just had his first scuffle with Governor Bernard.[48]

Throughout the month of June, the House met in almost daily session. Hancock quickly became one of the more active members and served on more than thirty committees, which considered everything from potash production to auditing the treasurer's books. He was an active and highly visible legislator, and was particularly active in matters of finance and visitations to the governor. The former was crucial to the power of the House; the latter was often an occasion to present to His Excellency the latest challenge to his authority. It was the nature of the beasts and the temper of the times that the governor and the Court were quite often in adversary positions, so these committee visits were rarely pleasant, and they were giving Hancock an early education in confrontation politics, as well as making him highly noticeable to the governor under not altogether pleasing circumstances.

Political pursuits were swallowing up a good deal of Hancock's time, forcing him to pay less attention to business matters. This shift in attention came at a very bad moment. Trade was stagnant, the whale oil business was foundering, and, in general, the Hancock fortunes were slipping. Only to a small extent were Parliament's recent legislative forays to blame for Hancock's distress. He was a supplier of raw materials, so most of his trade fell neatly into the mercantile mold and was, therefore, not directly affected by the new laws. His problems were rooted in the more general malaise that seemed to infect the empire, as well as in some bad decisions he and his associates had made in the oil business. Hancock, however, was too involved with day-to-day survival to appreciate the more general view. Both he and his associates found it more convenient, and logical, to blame a fumbling ministry.[49]

By no means did all the economic problems rest on Hancock's side of the Atlantic. His agents, Harrison and Barnard, were having their own traumas. Jonathan Barnard, the doyen of the firm, had recently retired. He was succeeded by his son John, but in these troubled times the old man's expertise was sorely missed.[50] The firm was being pressed by creditors, so to raise cash Harrison, in turn, was urgent with Hancock to settle his overdue bills. That was a mistake. Hancock took the dunning as a personal insult and accused Harrison and Barnard of trying to make a fool of him. He could not understand how it was that a man of his eminence in Boston could be treated so shabbily in London.[51] He would have none of it. It was a nasty exchange, and, though he continued at least for a time to do business with them, never again would Harrison and Barnard have his full confidence.

Compounding Hancock's problems was a disaster at home. A fire broke out in a baker's shop down by the Mill Creek, not far from Faneuil Hall. The shop was run by Mr. Bray, but that building and seven others nearby were owned by Hancock. Before the fire could be extinguished, they were all destroyed. The loss was considerable, and gave him more cause for worry. Cleverly, though, he did manage to convert some of the financial loss into political gain by graciously and publicly contributing to a fund for the burned-out families.[52]

As usual, the winter in Boston was slow. The General Court and the selectmen met several times during February and March 1767. In the spring he was re-elected to both posts. This time, he was the number one vote-getter in the General Court race, outpolling both Sam Adams and Otis. Compared with the fury of the Stamp Act days, things were dull in Boston. There were still some back eddies swirling around, but, for the most part, there was little to stir the emotions except the occasional exchanges between the General Court and His Excellency, some of which Hancock was there in person to observe.

Chapter 5

John Hancock —
Hero and Martyr

*I*F FAME was his pole star, then Hancock was steering wisely, for his course through the Stamp Act crisis had brought him a good deal of notice and acclaim. Still, it would be folly to assume that from this success Hancock derived knowledge of the future and was now poised to pursue the career of the great revolutionary. The situation was much otherwise, for at this stage of his involvement he still lacked two characteristics essential to revolutionaries: paranoia and vision. As yet, he had no sense of a ministerial conspiracy afoot to enslave Americans, nor did he look ahead to a great future for young America. Instead, what he saw was a medley of mistakes perpetrated by an uninformed bureaucracy, the principal result of which was to make miserable the lives of loyal subjects. Events would soon upend this happy conception.

Despite all the vexations, life in Boston did once again become reasonably calm. The revocation of the Stamp Act and the subsequent ending of nonimportation greatly relieved tensions, and for a time all that could be heard in the town were the usual rumblings between the governor and the House, where the Adams-Otis faction was jockeying for position and trying its best to embarrass His Excellency. The State House cant, though, was hardly an engine powerful enough to drive the populace, and, despite their best efforts, the Whig faction could barely get a rise out of a somnolent citizenry.[1]

Hancock remained nominally allied with Adams and company, but his real interests seemed to rest far less with political questions than with the more prosaic issues of buying, selling, and surviving. He continued his service in the House and on various committees, most especially those whose function was the delivery of bad news to the governor. But even that duty had become a bit ritualistic and seemed to lack some of the old combative spirit of days past.

The lightness of activity in the House was mirrored in town affairs, as well, and as a result, in early 1767 Hancock turned in one of his worst attendance records ever at selectmen meetings. He made less than one third of the meetings.[2] With little to whet his political appetite, Hancock inevitably turned back toward business. It was, in his judgment, time for expansion, and with his usual enthusiasm he pushed out. On February 19, 1767, he closed one of his biggest real estate deals by buying Clark's Wharf, soon to be known as Hancock's Wharf.[3] Next to Long Wharf, this was the largest docking facility in the town, and the usage fees, along with the rents from the dozen or so stores located along it, gave him a nice profit of £150 a year.[4]

Income alone would have been sufficient reason to buy the property, but for Hancock that was only partly the goal. He had a much larger scheme in mind, a sea venture that might see his new wharf crowded with Hancock ships. Ever since he had taken over the business, shipping had come to play an important part of his operations. His *Lydia* and *Boston Packet* were regular members of the Hancock line on the transatlantic run. *Lydia* was a sleek vessel whose usual commander was Captain James Scott, one of Boston's best seamen and a close friend of Hancock's. Under his command, passengers could expect to make London in a month, with a return trip of about two.[5] In addition to her and *Boston Packet*, he owned shares in several other vessels, and it is not unlikely that, in dickering for the wharf, he envisioned someday playing host to a whole fleet of vessels, all flying the flag of the House of Hancock.

His interest in shipping was by no means at odds with the long but rocky romance he had been having with another siren — oil. The dream of cornering the oil market was a persistent one, and when he could enlarge it with the vision of Hancock

ships, holds crammed with Hancock oil, it was just too much
to resist. He started again to invest heavily in Nantucket whalers, shipping their product to Harrison and Barnard and hoping
for a good market.[6]

Hope was about all there was, for in England the oil business
was again turning out to be a very slippery affair. Quite mis-
takenly, Hancock thought that if he cornered the whale market
in America, he could strangle London. Somehow, he overlooked
the nasty fact that other whalers operated out of England, Hol-
land, and Germany. Instead of dispatching precious cargo into
a starved market, he found himself trying to feed an already
bloated one, with the result that as each of his barrels hit the
dock in England, the price dropped a notch. When the final
tally came in, Hancock and his friends had lost no less than
£3600. It stands as testimony to both his wealth and nerve that
when he read the red ink, he blithely told Harrison and Barnard,
"It cant be helpt."

He knew better, and so did they. His London agents were not
satisfied with either his answer or attitude. They even went so
far as to allege that Hancock had shipped them inferior oil and
suggested that they ought to dispatch their own inspector to
prevent a recurrence. For the man on Beacon Hill, that was a
piece of effrontery he would never tolerate, and he quickly told
them so. These pointed exchanges were slowly poisoning Hancock's relationship with his agents, as the feeling of trust gave
way to suspicion and doubt.[8]

Inevitably, the problems with oil spilled over into other areas.
The news of Hancock's difficulties caused some people to wonder about his ability to make good on his obligations. Thomas
Pownall was just such a person. When he left Boston in 1760, he
had made an understanding with Uncle Thomas that the latter
would oversee the governor's considerable interests in Massachusetts. These included property as well as monies owed to
him. The total value came to almost £5000, a large sum even
for men like Hancock and Pownall.[9] Some time after Thomas'
death, Pownall apparently decided to liquidate his American
holdings, and so instructed his new agent, John Hancock. Probably more out of inattention than anything else — after all,

these were the days when John was learning the business and savoring politics — he neglected to follow Pownall's orders. The governor waited patiently. However, he needed cash, and finally, a bit nervous after hearing of Hancock's recent problems, he wrote and demanded his money. To show what little faith he had, Pownall made the unusual demand that he be paid in specie. He would not accept any of Hancock's bills, for fear that he could not get them honored. Like all American merchants, Hancock was chronically short of cash, even in the best of times. It was clearly impossible for him to comply with Pownall's request, and the matter was to drag on for some time, much to the embarrassment of his honor and credit. It also meant the loss of a good and powerful friend.[10]

While Hancock and his English friends pecked away at one another, at more lofty positions others were making decisions whose import was only dimly perceived. One of these men was "Champagne Charlie" Townshend, chancellor of the exchequer, a consummate politician and a brilliant speaker, who, according to Parliamentary legend, was at his best when dead drunk. In early 1767, Townshend accepted the call from His Majesty, kissed hands, and took the post as chancellor of the exchequer, accepting the unenviable task of replenishing the coffers of His Majesty's treasury. To an expectant Commons, Townshend announced that he had a plan to raise money in America painlessly. Having teased his countrymen with the promise of taxing Americans and thereby untaxing themselves, Townshend left the chamber hanging in suspense, awaiting his miracle. Sensing that it all might well be a clever charade, the opposition engineered a reduction in the land tax, which caused an immediate shortfall in revenue. This, in turn, forced Townshend to unveil his plan for additional revenue.[11]

Townshend's plan was remarkable for its unimaginativeness. What it amounted to was the collection of duties on certain goods being imported into American ports. The articles to be blessed included glass, red and white lead, painters' colors, paper, and tea. To those who argued that the act could be construed as a violation of American rights, Townshend merely answered that his duties were consonant with the long tradition of trade regulation and were, in fact, external duties. The latter point was a fine distinction that Benjamin Franklin had alluded to in testimony before the House during the Stamp Act crisis. Townshend was making the heroic assumption that all Americans could appreciate such subtle points.[12]

Townshend had seen enough of past failures to understand that the levying of duties was one thing but collection could be quite another. The customs apparatus was creaky and sievelike and desperately needed to be repaired if it was to deal with American smugglers, who thus far, through a combination of bribery and subterfuge, had made it into something of a joke. To remedy this, Townshend was determined to close the holes and strengthen the collection process. One section of the act declared that income from the duties would be used, if "it shall be found necessary," to pay the salaries of judges and civil officers, thus freeing them from their hat-in-hand relationship to the colonial legislatures. The act also gave specific authority to Superior Courts to issue writs of assistance, which would give crown officers *carte blanche* to knock down doors and conduct searches and seizures with practically no restrictions. Such power in the hands of angels would have been dangerous; with bureaucrats, it was a catastrophe.

To tighten the collection mechanism even further, a board of five commissioners of the customs was created, to be headquartered in Boston and, from that port, to direct operations along the entire Atlantic coastline. Violators could be haled before nonjury Vice-Admiralty Courts, where, much to the smuggler's distress, justice was usually done. Under the act these courts had their jurisdiction expanded and were increased in number.[13]

Townshend's plan got through Parliament easily and received the king's signature on June 29. It was to go into effect on November 20.

On September 4, 1767, the effects of a dissipated life and a virulent fever caught up with Charles Townshend, and he died, never having had a chance to view the wreckage his handiwork created. Indeed, he probably went to his grave believing that he had succeeded where others failed, for in the weeks before his death there were only mild tremors; on the whole, the American spirit seemed quite subdued.

Everyone, of course, had heard rumors of impending legislation, but as long as the menace remained distant, most Bostonians, Hancock included, were content to limit their discontent to table-pounding in the local taverns, mutterings in the newspapers, and oral assaults in the House and at town meetings. Hancock admitted to having difficulties, but for the most part he attributed them to that perennial problem — "Scarcity of Cash."[14] In a blustery letter written to Harrison and Barnard in midsummer, he told them of his intention "to Suspend the Transportation of goods for a year or two till matters take a Better turn . . ."[15] His motive in offering this threat, which he never did carry out, was economic and personal: he wanted to save money, and was miffed at these gentlemen for annoying him.

In August came the official news. Hancock read the acts with dismay. He felt abused and betrayed. Despite the problems of trade, the repeal of the Stamp Act had given him hope that the ministers did at least have the interests of Americans at heart. They might make mistakes, but they were amenable to reason. Now he was not so sure. In a tone of anger and frustration, he wrote to William Reeve of London:

> It is surprizing to me that so many attempts are made on your side to Cramp our Trade new Duties every day increasing in short we are in a fair way of being Ruin'd we have nothing to do but unite & come under a Solemn agreement to stop importing any goods from England . . .[16]

He went on to say that, as for himself, he would work for nonimportation and sooner shut up his windows than import a single pane of glass.

Now that there was a crisis to chew on, Boston started to come alive again. The Sons of Liberty were back on the scene, and on October 28 the town meeting adopted a limited nonimportation agreement.[17] The mildness of the agreement reflected Hancock's views. The subscription that was circulated through the town bemoaned high taxes, loss of trade, lack of money, and the unfavorable balance of trade with England. To remedy these misfortunes, the signers pledged to support local manufactures, live a frugal life, and after December 31, 1767, not to import a long list of goods, including shoes, gold and silver thread, silks, gloves, and numerous other items, most of which could rightly be termed luxuries. Conspicuously missing from the subscription was any grand statement of constitutional issues, liberties, rights, and the like. All of this was quite acceptable to Hancock, and, though he publicly joined the move toward the simple life, he continued to order large quantities of rich wines, fine food, and — barely two weeks before nonimportation was put into effect — 100 panes of glass.[18]

If Hancock's rhetoric and behavior seem a bit inconsistent, he was in good company. Most of Boston's politicians were still seeing through a glass darkly, and it would take time for events to sort themselves out and opposition to rally. Even the great James Otis kept his opposition within decorous bounds. In his statements against the acts, he conjured up all the hallowed images from the heroic days of the seventeenth century; but then, lest the townsmen think he was advocating violence, he quickly retreated to a more comfortable position of good order and told them that, whatever their grievances, there was nothing yet to warrant "private tumults and disorders."[19]

When one considers the eruption of public sentiment over the Stamp Act, it is sometimes difficult to explain why it took Americans so long to rouse themselves against the Townshend duties. Back in 1765, Bostonians had been ready to meet their enemies on the beach; now they seemed content not only to allow them ashore, but to grant them enough time to dig in. The essential difference, of course, is time. The spirit had not diminished; only the time in which to stir it. For a year before its passage, Grenville had played John the Baptist to the Stamp Act, giving Americans plenty of opportunity to ponder their misery and coordinate their response. On the other hand, the Townshend Acts hit like a meteor, giving little warning. The tide was rising, but it would take time to flood.

On the next-to-last day of the year, Hancock threw on his coat and muffled himself for the familiar walk down his hill to the

State House. It was time for another session of the General Court to meet. After the rituals were over, the members got down to the main business at hand — the state of the province. Hancock came to the session armed with instructions from the town meeting, telling him and the other representatives to work for industry, frugality, and an end to the unfavorable balance of trade. He took his charge seriously and did what he could to move the House in just such a direction. All the same, their motion was glacierlike.

Among the items of business debated by Hancock and his peers was a letter to Dennys De Berdt, the London agent for the colony. In a strange way, this letter summed up both the strengths and weaknesses of the Bostonians. It was written in a conservative tone by James Otis. On behalf of the House, he asserted paradoxically, "We are taxed, and can appeal for relief, from their [Parliament's] final decision, to no power on earth; for there is no power on earth above them."[20] This was precisely what Hancock had said back in the days of the Stamp Act, and he still subscribed to it. He was not yet sufficiently alienated that he could move beyond the point where he was ready to accept anything but submission. His vision went no farther than reason and justice; if those were not sufficient weapons to win the battle, then surrender was the only recourse. There was a way to cut this Gordian knot, the same method Alexander had used — the sword. For the present, it was an alternative Hancock would not consider.

Ministerial policies were a part of his life over which Hancock had no control; he was merely an anonymous pawn being pushed back and forth across the board. Perhaps it was because he felt so helpless in that greater world that he began to take decisive action in his own smaller realm. His relationship with Harrison and Barnard was beyond resuscitation. The oil fiasco, compounded with allegations from both sides of negligence and incompetence, had pushed the partnership to the brink. On October 16, in a letter fairly dripping with acid, Hancock told them, "I look back on myself a Man of Capital & I am not to be put on a footing with every two penny Shopkeeper that addresses you."[21]

That was the beginning of the end; from this point on, Hancock severed all connections with them. It did not happen suddenly; there were too many threads to cut through on one swoop. In December he sent one of his trusted captains, William Cazneau, to wrap up some loose ends. The visit was hardly pleasant. On the first encounter Cazneau met with a clerk, who, when he learned that Cazneau had come from Hancock, began to berate and insult him. The captain left in a huff. A few days later, he returned to see John Barnard himself. He was ushered into Barnard's office and presented him with a personal letter from Hancock. Cazneau was quick to report home what happened then. "Barnard (when I gave him your letter) took it with an air of disdain and gave it a fling upon his desk and began to tell me of your affair." Cazneau, who was accustomed to barking at others on the quarterdeck and not having them bark back, grew red in the face and came perilously close to beating "the little Rascal."[22] Barnard was lucky to escape intact. But his good fortune was short-lived. Within a year after losing Hancock's business, the House of Harrison and Barnard was bankrupt. The fall distressed Hancock not a whit. He shed a few crocodile tears and suggested that he had warned the partners about their loose business practices but they had not listened and were now paying the price.[23]

Dealing with young Barnard was only half of Cazneau's mission, for, while he was closing one door, simultaneously he was opening another. The new connection was with a man named George Hayley. Allying with him was transparently political, for Hayley was not just another merchant. He was a well-known Whig with good political credentials, but, more important, he was married to the shrewish sister of the notorious John Wilkes, scourge of the ministry, whose rapier pen had more than once punctured their grasping pretensions.[24]

Wilkes's lever for raising havoc was *The North Briton*, a scurrilous rag, at least according to his opponents, that he first brought out on June 5, 1762. No one was spared attack in its pages. After forty-four lively issues, the forty-fifth, in which he pilloried Lord Bute, the king, and even the king's mother, struck such a raw nerve that George III made it a personal goal to silence and punish him. Amidst great clamor, Wilkes was tossed into the Tower. His friends secured a writ of habeas corpus and finally got him discharged, on the basis of his immunity as a member of Parliament. By the time he left the Tower, Wilkes had become the idol of London, and everywhere he went crowds mobbed and saluted him, cheering, "Wilkes and Liberty."

George III was nothing if not persistent, and, rather than give up the chase, he found other ways to pursue the infamous Wilkes. By express order of His Majesty, Wilkes's commission as colonel of the Buckinghamshire militia was revoked. That not being enough, through some clever machinations the king's friends then had Wilkes expelled from Commons. Expulsion meant the loss of parliamentary privilege and made poor Wilkes vulnerable to the law, so, in advance of arrest, he fled England and retired for a time to the comforts of Paris.[25]

To American Whigs this peripatetic curmudgeon became a person with whom, in their own struggles against the ministry, they could easily identify. "Wilkes and Liberty" became as much a rallying cry in Boston as in London. By "connecting" with George Hayley, Hancock was drawing as close as he could to this symbol of resistance and liberty.[26]

Although they would never meet, through this business and familial alliance Hancock and Wilkes grew to know one another. They shared a common *bête noire*, the ministry, and to a remarkable degree their careers over the coming critical years paralleled one another. There were many moments when, in his ruminations, John Hancock must have thought of himself as the American Wilkes.

The simmering state of Boston politics gave Hancock time not only for his business but also for the personal chores as Lord of the Beacon Hill Manse. Cato, Aunt Lydia's black slave, and his wife had a baby daughter, Jenny, so for the first time in the history of the house the cries of an infant could be heard. The event pleased the Hancocks, no less than Cato and his wife, and Lydia made arrangements for the child's baptism. Jenny took the waters at the Brattle Square Church by the hand of Reverend Samuel Cooper. Moved by the spirit, or perhaps his wife, three weeks later Cato himself went down to the church, and he, too, was baptized.[27] For Cato this was more than just the beginnings of a Christian life; it represented another step toward the freedom that had been promised him in Thomas' will.

Cato was apparently the last of the two or three household slaves kept by Hancock. When he was freed, there were no others. It is no special condemnation of John Hancock that he owned slaves; it is merely a commentary on the general insensitivity of the eighteenth century to the evils of the people trade. It is to his credit that in all of his vast business dealings there is no evidence to suggest that he himself ever bought or sold this commodity.

Natural increase was one way to add to the household, but another was by bringing in more servants. Under some rather special circumstances, this happened up on Beacon Hill in November of 1767. Elizabeth Momper was a young white girl who had recently emigrated from Newfoundland. Quite likely she had come in on a Yankee fishing boat. Since she was penniless, her indenture was sold to a local man, Mr. Prey. Prey turned out to be a scoundrel, who abused Elizabeth to such an extent that the selectmen were called in her behalf. After a brief investigation, in which they found "that there was too much truth in the information," they ordered Prey to give up the girl. Then the question arose as to what to do with her. Without an indenture there was only one place in the town to send a destitute person, the almshouse. At least Elizabeth would not be abused at the house, but, still, living there did not present a very pleasing prospect. Hancock, who had seen the poor girl's plight firsthand, decided to intercede. He took Elizabeth's indenture, and the lucky girl went from living in the house near the bottom of the hill to the lovely mansion on top.[28]

Elizabeth's problem was easy to solve — all it took was money — but closer to home there were more perplexing puzzles, for which money seemed not to be the answer. Despite his uncle's example and his brother's admonitions, Ebenezer had not been applying the diligent hand, and he was up to his watch fob in debt. It hardly helped that he had recently gotten married; that only increased his obligations and multiplied the distractions.

Of course, even as John would admit, times were not the best — postwar slump, Stamp Act, and now more uncertainty with the new duties. Nevertheless, Ebenezer seemed to have a knack for making bad times worse.

Shortly after Uncle Thomas' death, when he had first ventured out, John had written some of his correspondents, urging them to grant Ebenezer credit. Now that he was on the brink of bankruptcy, John was having second thoughts, and he was most concerned that Ebenezer's sinking situation would reflect on him and might even impair his new arrangement with Hayley. With that in mind, he wrote to Hayley in late February 1768, setting out the general problems of trade and the particular problems of his brother. He backpedaled from his previous recommendations and told Hayley to be "cautious who you Credit, [for] what I mention'd with respect to Messr. Blanchard & [Ebenezer] Hancock I would not have you take as meant by me to extend their Credit with you." In a not altogether admirable way Hancock was putting some distance between himself and his brother. But if not a praiseworthy exercise, it was a wise one, for within a year Ebenezer was bankrupt.[29]

As Hancock fretted over Ebenezer, his friend Sam Adams was working his way with the House of Representatives. He had been trying to educate his peers to the evils of the Townshend Acts. After some disappointments, his efforts finally paid off, and on February 11, 1768, he introduced a Circular Letter, concerning "the great difficultys that must accrue . . . by the operation of several acts of Parliament imposing Duties & Taxes on the American Colonys." The letter then went on in a respectful fashion to assert that the Townshend Acts were "Infringements" on the "natural & constitutional Rights" of Americans, since they were not represented in the body that created the acts. Lest anyone think the mere placing of a few token Americans in Parliament would satisfy the issue, the letter went on to point out that such representation was impractical. The logical conclusion, but one not explicitly stated, was that only local assemblies could tax their constituents. The letter also protested strongly the use of revenue to pay the salaries of the governor and judges.

Hancock much approved of the letter. So, too, did his fellow representatives. It passed overwhelmingly and was sent to other colonial assemblies, as well as to London.[30]

Adams, Hancock, and the others were pleased with their work, but the reaction in the governor's mansion was otherwise. Bernard felt as if he were being pursued by the Furies. Each day brought a new crisis, a new challenge, or just another insult. Early in March, a particularly obnoxious piece of slander appeared in the local press, attacking in vile terms, but never actually naming, His Excellency.[31] The governor laid the piece before the Council, which joined him in condemning it. The reaction of the House was much less pleasing. They noted the possibility of hyperbole in the language, but, since no one was named, it could not affect the king, the government, or the General Court. Besides, whatever damage the piece might have done, it should be suffered so that freedom of the press be maintained. This maddening response was delivered up to the Council and governor in person by Hancock.[32]

Bernard was quick to report all these events to London, embellishing them with tales of "Tumults," "Violent Opposition," and assorted assaults on crown officers, all of which could have added up, in London, only to an image of a man under siege.[33]

March 14, 1768, was a glorious day for John Hancock. Once again the people of Boston honored him. At the town meeting they re-elected him selectman, fire warden, and member of a committee to examine the town accounts. Then, as their highest accolade, they named him to a committee of the town's leading patriots "to prepare and publish a letter of thanks" to John Dickinson, author of *Letters from a Farmer in Pennsylvania to the Inhabitants of the British Colonies*.[34] Dickinson's *Letters* had been written in opposition to the Townshend duties. They appeared in newspapers throughout the colonies and became instantly popular. In them, he reminded Americans of their past successes with economic coercion and suggested that the same weapon could be used again. Hancock was impressed with Dickinson. He had himself come to much the same conclusion long before the *Letters* but had not been able to express his position with the same power and intellect. Apparently, Dickinson's *Letters* were the final element needed to coalesce opinion, for while the town voted thanks to him, the merchants of Boston, led by Hancock and others, were forging a new nonimportation agreement.[35]

All this activity made the commissioners of the customs nervous. Everywhere they went, they saw dark figures lurking after them, hurling insults and even an occasional stone. In one of his typical letters to London, Governor Bernard described the affair of poor Mr. Burch, a commissioner:

> Mr. Burch . . . had a large Number of Men with Clubs assembled before his Door great Part of the Evening, and he was obliged to send away his Wife & Children by a back Door.[36]

Hancock, of course, never took part in such proceedings, but it is an open question as to whether his money bought the rum that was always an ingredient in these affairs, helping the participants find their courage before the fray and celebrate it afterward.

The beset commissioners implored Bernard to send for troops. He wisely refused and offered them only a safe haven in Castle William, out in the harbor, and a proclamation calling on all officers to render assistance to the commissioners.[37] Two days after the governor's proclamation, the people of Boston turned out to celebrate the second anniversary of the Stamp Act repeal. As usual, the taverns were full and the Liberty Tree was festooned with effigies, this time of the hated customs commissioners. That was enough for those gentlemen; if Bernard could not be relied on to protect them, they would appeal directly to London. On March 28, they wrote to the lords of the treasury, citing the recent evidence of violence as a dire portent of things to come. Troops must be sent.[38]

This letter and Bernard's somber reports all came to the desk of the Earl of Hillsborough, a hardliner, who had just recently been appointed secretary of state for the colonies. Hillsborough was both determined and inexperienced, a dangerous combination. He would not tolerate unlawful behavior, and, reacting to the most recent complaints, some from a frustrated governor and the rest from skittish commissioners, he decided to take stern measures. Hancock would soon have reason to know of this stiffening posture.

Despite all the myths, John Hancock was not the king of colonial smugglers.[39] Smugglers are not wont to keep good records, so we can only speculate, but, judging from the general nature of his trade, about which we know a good deal, Hancock's business was not the kind that required a great number of clandestine operations. Nevertheless, whatever smuggling he did engage in was magnified in the minds of British officials because of politics. He was a natural target, made even more tempting by the fact that thus far in their crack-down they had precious little to show for their efforts.

Politics was certainly sufficient reason to pursue Hancock, but even if it was not, the commissioners had a personal account with him that was overdue. Hancock had done everything possible to snub these men. He refused to attend any function where they might be present, thus giving any host the choice of having him or them present, but not both. Social life in Boston was made a bit difficult by this. After all, what hostess was willing to forgo the presence of Boston's richest young bachelor? Others followed the example, and the commissioners were effectively snubbed.

Such a mixture of politics and personal animosity caused the commissioners to keep a most careful watch on Hancock's ships. On April 8, the customs officers boarded and seized *Lydia*. It was a careless venture, and when the case came before Attorney General Jonathan Sewall, he declared that the search was illegal because the officer lacked authority to go below deck.[40] Hancock beat them this time, but the customs people were resolved to get him; this rebuff made them more determined than ever to run him to ground.

Although he could never prove it, Hancock was convinced that there was a conspiracy among the governor, Lieutenant Governor Thomas Hutchinson, Comptroller of the Port Benjamin Hallowell, and David Lisle, the solicitor of the board of customs commissioners, to destroy him. If they could get a large judgment against him, it would ruin him financially, thus depriving the Whigs of their milch cow. The plot against Hancock was not entirely unlike the one against Wilkes in London. It was to end with much the same result.[41]

At the town meeting on May 4, Hancock was again elected one of the town's representatives to the General Court. On May 25, the new House assembled. A quick glance at the membership told Bernard it was not going to be a happy session. The legislators proceeded to the election of a speaker, Thomas Cushing, and then went on to choose councilors. This year one of their selections was John Hancock. It was an honor that Uncle Thomas had enjoyed, and John had every reason to think that he ought to have it, too. The very next day when Hancock's name, along with the others, was presented to the governor for his approval, he made Hancock's honor even greater by rejecting him.[42]

Back in the House, Hancock received the not entirely unexpected news with mixed feelings. He was not insensitive to the position that he had lost, but, on the other hand, martyrdom became him. As these thoughts ran through his mind, he was listening to the clerk read warm letters of support from the assemblies of New Hampshire, Connecticut, and New Jersey, endorsing the Circular Letter of the previous February. There was also some less pleasing news on the floor. H.M.S. *Romney*, fifty guns, had arrived from Halifax and was making herself most unwelcome by molesting boats in the harbor. The House sent a committee, Hancock included, to complain to the governor. He rebuffed them and would accept no complaint unless it was presented in writing.[43]

At every turn, each side was doing its utmost to make life difficult for the other. Indeed, with every new development, whether it was *Romney*'s activities or the refusal of the selectmen to allow Faneuil Hall to be used for a dinner if the commissioners were going to be present, the gap between the two sides grew wider. Thus far, though, the struggle had been carried out, for the most part, in the form of economic boycott and psychological warfare. What violence had taken place was relatively trivial. However, the *Liberty* case was to push events onto a far more ominous course.

Late in the afternoon of May 9, *Liberty*, a small sloop owned by Hancock and named in honor of John Wilkes, nosed her way past Boston Light, eased into the harbor, and came up to Hancock's Wharf. She was inbound from Madeira, under the command of Captain Marshall. Ordinarily the customs officers would have gone on board immediately, but since it was sunset and the light was fast fading, they decided to wait until the morning.

That night, under Marshall's direction, the crew worked overtime. The customs officers might have had trouble working in the dark, but apparently Hancock's men did not. When the customs inspector came back the next morning, he found the captain's body lying on the deck — he had died when he "overheated himself" — and a hold with only twenty-five pipes of wine, a fraction of its capacity.[44] Not surprisingly, witnesses proved impossible to find. Hancock, who in public had said that he intended to "run his Cargo of Wine on Shore," remained on Beacon Hill in dignified silence. Privately, he was chortling at having beaten the harpies once again. Liberty was unloaded and ordered to prepare for another voyage.

Hancock underestimated his enemies, however, for Bernard, Hutchinson, and company were not so easily put off. It took them a month, but finally, through the force of a few pounds in the right hands and the threat of punishment, they found a witness and pried him open. He was Thomas Kirk, one of the tide-waiters from the customs office who had been inspecting Liberty. Under oath, Kirk recited the tale of May 9. Just after dark, he said, Marshall had come on board Liberty and told him and the rest of the crew to open the hatch and unload her. For some reason, Kirk refused to help, at which point he was tossed below and locked up for the next three hours. Below, Kirk could hear footsteps going back and forth across the deck, the creak of block and tackle, and the sound of wooden casks being piled on the dock and then hauled away. When the night's work was finished, Kirk was let go and told that if he ever talked about what he had heard, it might well be his last mortal act.[45]

It was no secret in Boston that, ever since the morning of May 10, the customs officers had been working diligently on the Liberty case. Hallowell's doggedness especially was a worry, and he had been warned by no less a figure than Dr. Joseph Warren, a "High Son Of Liberty," that there might be dire consequences should the government continue to pursue this matter. That type of threat had just the opposite kind of effect from what Warren and his friends wanted. Or did it? Perhaps Warren was playing a crafty game of his own. If that was the case, Hallowell gulled down the bait.

Kirk's statement was enough for Lisle to recommend seizing *Liberty*. Hallowell personally went down to the wharf and did the deed, but not before *Romney* sent over a boat to tow the sloop out into the harbor and snug her under the warship's stern. Hallowell's movements were being watched, and as soon as he left his office, word swept through town that something was up. Hancock was informed but, suspecting what was about to happen, he decided to stay away. Four to five hundred other people in the town did not stay away, and soon a large hostile crowd was gathered down on Hancock's Wharf.

As the lines from *Romney*'s boat to *Liberty* grew taut, the sloop eased away from the wharf — and a hail of rocks came hurtling from the crowd. (The unpaved streets of Boston and even those that were paved provided a nearly inexhaustible source of ammunition for occasions like this.) As the sailors pulled into the channel and out of range, the crowd turned their attention to Hallowell and the collector who had come with him, Joseph Harrison. The two men made the mistake of walking back through the mob. They were lucky to escape alive. They were followed all the way home, and even after they barred their doors they were hardly safe. The crowd smashed windows and took one of the collector's small boats, hoisted it on their shoulders, and carted it up to the Common, where, within sight of Hancock's home, they set it afire. Realizing the precariousness of their position, the commissioners evacuated the town and for a time took up residence on board *Romney*. They then moved into more comfortable quarters at Castle William, putting deep water and stone walls between themselves and the Boston mob. All in all, it was the best example up to that time of organized lawlessness in Boston.

While the less cerebral Bostonians were chasing customs men

and burning boats, up on Beacon Hill the Whig leaders were pondering their position. Initially, Hancock's business instincts told him that his goal ought to be to get *Liberty* back under his control. With that in mind, he dispatched his lawyer to Messrs. Hallowell and Harrison, informing them that if they would return his sloop, he would give his personal bond that she would be available for the court's judgment. Hancock knew full well that litigation of this sort often took months, and to have his vessel idle for that long would mean a great loss. From a legal and business point of view, his offer made great sense. On Saturday afternoon, June 11, the offer was made. Hallowell accepted, and it was agreed that Hancock should have *Liberty* back on Monday morning.

The Sabbath was not a day of rest for Adams, Otis, Warren, and other Whig leaders who had gathered in Hancock's parlor. Over generous amounts of Madeira, some of it recently arrived, they discussed their strategy. It was neither business nor law that these gentlemen debated; it was politics, and their political sense told them that Hancock had made a bad deal. Dealing with the customs men implied concession, and Adams and Otis advised against it. Better that Hancock should stand firmly on his rights and refuse to have anything to do with the rascals. Such a stand, even though it might cost him money, would redound to his credit, and buy the Whig cause, and John Hancock, great repute. The arguments were persuasive, and Hancock, albeit a bit tardy, came around. At midnight on Sunday, Dr. Warren rapped on Hallowell's door to deliver the bad news. There would be no deal.

Although Governor Bernard was not directly involved in this affair, at least not overtly, he was certainly more than a mere spectator. For weeks he had been watching the "radicals" stacking kindling, waiting for the spark; now that they had it, he feared insurrection and told the ministry so. With this kind of information flowing across the Atlantic, it is small wonder that the *Liberty* affair reinforced decisions that Hillsborough had already made. He told Bernard to order the House immediately to rescind the Circular Letter of February 11. To General Thomas Gage, in New York, he sent instructions to send two regiments to Boston for the preservation of the king's peace and authority.[46]

On the business of the Circular Letter, Hancock had the pleasure to deliver the House's response — Never. By a vote of 92 to 17, they refused to comply. After that, the House took up the next piece of business. They drew up a petition demanding the recall of Francis Bernard. The situation left the governor no choice. He dissolved the chamber with the gloomy foreboding that his action could well cause "an . . . insurrection."[47] Not surprisingly, when the order to dissolve was read in the House, practically no one was there to hear it. Adams, Hancock, Otis, and the others had left.

The *Liberty* affair and the events resulting from it catapulted Hancock from being merely a member, though a very rich one, of the radical faction to the loftier level of hero and martyr. His central role in the affair gave him an honored place, and his name was fast becoming indelibly linked with those struggling against the ministry. Bostonians felt a common bond with others, both in America and in England, who were fighting for the same cause. Indeed, if London could find a martyr to liberty in John Wilkes, then Boston need look only to John Hancock for its symbol.

Chapter 6

Francis Bernard versus
John Hancock

THE TEMPO of Hancock's life hastened as a steady stream of people made their way up the hill to meet with and pay homage to the man who had become in his own right a symbol of resistance. Whether he truly merited the encomiums being passed his way, or whether he was merely a tool made use of by politicians more clever than he, is a question that has often been hotly disputed. Was he a victim of circumstances, or was he a shaper of events? To be sure, had it not been for the intercession of Adams, Otis, and Warren, he probably would have kept his deal with the authorities over *Liberty*, which would have defused that issue, much to the detriment of the patriot cause. Nevertheless, when Hancock was given the wise counsel of friends, he had the sense to act accordingly.

Scarcely had the fury of the *Liberty* riot quieted when another incident in the harbor threatened to reignite the town. With its usual callousness, the Royal Navy stopped a coaster and pressed one of its seamen. In more ordinary times this would have been serious enough, but in the charged atmosphere now existing, it threatened to blow the top off the town. Hancock and the other selectmen waited on the governor and Council to seek the man's release. Meanwhile, the townsmen, led by the Sons, moved on their own accord. They held a mass meeting at the Liberty Tree and demanded a town meeting. They marched off to Faneuil

Hall, but there were too many for that building, so they adjourned to larger quarters at the Old South Church, only a short distance away. After some peppery speeches, they elected a committee of twenty-one to ride to Roxbury for the purpose of talking with Bernard.

In the afternoon all twenty-one met at Hancock's home, climbed into their carriages, and set off across the Neck to visit the governor at his country place. Apparently, the meeting was reasonably pleasant. Bernard could take some comfort from the fact that this grievance was not of his making; in fact, he was almost as annoyed as the Bostonians by the impressment. But if he was as annoyed, he was also as helpless, since he had practically no authority over the navy.

The group returned directly to Hancock's. Nothing had been accomplished, but at least a nominal protest had been lodged and, most important, violence had been avoided. This was important to Hancock, who wished to preserve Boston's reputation as a loyal and law-abiding town.[1]

In summer afternoons Hancock often took his visitors out to sit in his gardens. From there they could look across the Common toward the rolling Blue Hills, or past the roofs of the town to the outer harbor, dotted with green islands. Those peaceful vistas were quite unlike the view closer in, along the waterfront. The inner harbor was filled with warships bristling with angry cannon. The most noticeable was H.M.S. *Romney*, floating in the harbor like a giant aquatic bird of prey and dwarfing her prize catch, *Liberty*. Bostonians hated her, and occasionally, in a show of bravado, a Yankee skipper would pass by without giving the customary salute. If *Romney*'s crew were awake, there would be a quick flurry of activity on deck, a cannon fired, and some billingsgate spouted. No one was hurt in these brief encounters, and they amounted to nothing more than a little bluster on both sides. Still, they invariably received attention from the local press and helped to keep the pot boiling.[2]

While *Romney* was taking random shots at scampering Americans, lawyers on both sides were droning on in court over the fate of *Liberty*. The case got under way on July 7.[3] There followed several continuances, so the actual proceedings were delayed

for more than three weeks. It is not fully clear who represented
Hancock, but a reasonable guess would be John Adams. Adams
was in Boston at the time; he and Hancock knew one another;
he was politically reliable; and he was an experienced admiralty
lawyer. For more than two weeks, the court drama went on, as
witnesses were called and testimony taken. Finally, on August
17, to absolutely no one's surprise, the presiding judge, Robert
Auchmuty, found against *Liberty*. She was put up for sale by the
commissioners, but without much luck, since anyone who valued
either his principles or his life was not likely to bid for her.
Then, on September 6, Harrison bought her for use by the
commissioners themselves. Perhaps believing there was nothing
like a smuggler to catch a smuggler, they armed *Liberty* and
sent her off to patrol the coast. Her career was short-lived. In
July 1769, her captain, William Reid, so infuriated the town of
Newport with his searches and seizures that a mob stormed the
vessel while she was in port and burned her to the waterline.[4]
Although he had lost his sloop and a good deal of money, this
news from Rhode Island brought some consolation to Hancock.
If *Liberty* could not be his, neither would it serve the commissioners.

From the beginning, Hancock understood what *Liberty*'s fate
would be. Even if the charges were not true, Vice-Admiralty
Court was hardly a place where he could expect any benefit.
The knowledge that so many of the legal processes were inimical
to him heightened his resolve to greater efforts in those extra-
legal areas where he could be much more effective. The most
promising of these was, of course, a renewal of nonimportation.
On July 18, the Merchants' Standing Committee, a kind of executive committee for the merchants of Boston, met to draw up
just such a plan. Hancock was one of the half-dozen present,
and it is quite likely that the agreement which finally emerged
was partly of his making. On August 1, at a plenary session in
Faneuil Hall, the majority agreed to the plan.[5]

They pledged not to import British goods from January 1,
1769, to January 1, 1770. The agreement covered nearly everything, although exceptions were made for coal, woolcards, duck,
cardwire, shot, and items necessary for the fisheries. The one-

year time limit did not apply to tea, paper, glass, or painters' colors. Those were dutied under the Townshend Acts and would not be imported until the acts were repealed.

The nonimportation agreement did leave one interesting loophole. No. mention was made of banned goods being carried in ships belonging to merchants who had signed the agreement. Thus, it was possible for the ships of a signing merchant to carry prohibited goods as long as they did not belong to him. Whether this happened by design or oversight is not clear; however, some merchants, including Hancock, stood to benefit from this slip, and, given their deep involvement in the carrying trade, it seems unlikely that such a thing could have gotten by without being noticed.

Meetings at an average of nearly one a day, conferences with lawyers, innumerable social obligations, and the general press of business, put a heavy load on Hancock's always delicate psyche. Before long he was complaining, "I am very unwell."[6] The nature of his indisposition was never specified but, under the circumstances, with business bad and the promise of its getting worse, the loss of *Liberty* and the continued threat of litigation, a good guess might be anxiety and depression.

On August 4, 1768, the *Boston Weekly News Letter* published an item from Halifax: troops were being called into the town from the outlying posts. At first, the news brought little reaction from Boston, but when it became apparent that the soldiers being assembled were bound for Boston, the town reacted quickly.

Since the General Court had been sent packing in June, the Boston town meeting took the lead in rallying the opposition.

On September 12, they sent a committee, made up of Hancock and other leading citizens, to the governor. They wished to know about the expected regiments of "His Majesty's Troops . . ." and humbly asked that he explain to them why the troops were being sent.[7] They also requested that he convene the General Court. To the first, Bernard replied that he knew nothing, marking him either a fool or a liar. To the second, his response was that the matter was out of his hands and that the General Court could be reconvened only with the approval of the ministry — hardly a reassuring answer to those who held any notion of home rule.[8]

Frustrated by the governor's answers, the town meeting called a special convention of all the towns in the colony to meet at Faneuil Hall. Nearly 100 communities sent delegates to the meeting, which convened on September 22. Such a respectable turnout indicated clearly that the discontent in Boston had spread across the Neck and into the countryside. After some deliberations, those assembled drew up and presented to the governor an address, which he peremptorily rejected.[9] Five days later, the troop transports lumbered into the outer harbor and signaled for pilots to bring them up so that they could deposit their pernicious cargo.

For a time the ships moored off Nantasket. They swung leisurely at anchor, and their 1200 impatient passengers could do nothing but gaze over the rail at their distant destination, while hungry gulls and long-necked cormorants played about. As the soldiers made do with their boredom, their commander was busy ashore, trying to pave the way for their arrival.[10]

Lieutenant Colonel William Dalrymple was an officer of good record and a gentleman of fine bearing. He was correct, competent, and patient. The last virtue was most important, given the assignment he now had to undertake. He went quickly to make arrangements for a meeting with the selectmen so that he could secure suitable quarters for his men.[11]

Since Hancock and his fellow selectmen had had ample warning of the troops' arrival, they had plenty of time to concoct their strategy. At the least, they wanted to keep the troops as far away as possible. The key to this was in the answer to "Where will they be quartered?" If they were allowed to barrack themselves within the town proper, it would mean trouble for the patriot cause. The surge of a red tide into the town might well flush to the surface dozens of closet Tories. If that happened, nonimportation would be threatened. The fear was quite legitimate.

Under the circumstances, the best the selectmen could hope for was that the troops would be housed out at Castle William, in the harbor. Even that was too close, but it was better than having them live cheek by jowl with the townspeople. Such a solution was not acceptable to the colonel, and he asked to have an interview with the selectmen to discuss the matter. They set the meeting for Saturday afternoon, October 1.[12]

There was certainly no mystery about what Dalrymple was going to say, so the selectmen had sufficient opportunity to rehearse their answer. By now they were a weary bunch. They had had five meetings in four days, and the pressure must have shown on their faces. They were troubled by what they had heard and seen in the harbor. Early Friday morning, small boats were visible moving about the inner harbor, with sailors casting the lead lines over. There could be only one reason for that: they were taking soundings in order to find the best anchorages for their ships. In the afternoon, nearly a dozen warships came up close to the town and dropped anchor, with each broadside facing the shore. Before long, troopships followed in their wake, and by evening the whole fleet was only spitting distance from the docks. Boston was under siege.[13]

By Saturday afternoon, when Dalrymple arrived for his appointment with the selectmen, the whole town was alarmed. Considering the show of force in the harbor, it looked as if the colonel had made his decision about where the troops were going to stay.

Some of the more feisty Bostonians would probably have liked to stand toe to toe with the Regulars and resolutely refuse quarters. There was some legal ground for such action, and, besides, the government's assertion that the troops had to be brought in because the facilities at the Castle were inadequate was open to question. Furthermore, the governor's own Council, which had gone over to the patriot side, refused to support His Excellency's request for quarters in the town. Whatever the emotions, though, good sense dictated moderation, and as Hancock faced the colonel he knew full well that, in any practical sense, their options were quite limited.

Hancock understood that the potential for violence in such a tense situation was extremely high. He continued to believe that this latest piece of stupidity on the part of the ministry was the result not of any malevolent design, but of bad information.

As he told George Hayley, "We have been grossly misrepresented," and if only the authorities in London knew the truth, they would see Bostonians "as Loyal a people as any in the King's Dominion."[14] The misrepresentation, of course, was the governor's; if there was an evil presence at work, it was Francis Bernard.

Hancock and the other selectmen listened stonily as Dalrymple made his request. Avoiding violence was the goal, for if it erupted, it would only give credence to the lies already being spread about the lawless Bostonians. The colonel's ease and composure helped to defuse the situation. In his performance with the selectmen, he gave the impression of being a reasonable man.

He began by stating his request for quarters sufficient for both his regiments. The selectmen, quite predictably and adroitly, skirted the issue with the finesse for which Boston politicians were becoming well known. According to them, they had no power to act, and even if they had, they could move forward only on the express order of Parliament.[15]

Being a soldier and not a politician, Dalrymple probably had little use for the legal nuances of these arguments. What he did care about, though, was finding shelter for 1200 men. Keeping them on board the transports was impossible. Cramped quarters between decks were an invitation to disease and disorder. Ashore, the New England fall had already begun to paint lovely hues of red and yellow, but those colors were the beautiful prelude to a miserable happening — winter. The colonel told the selectmen "that he had not a sufficient number of Tents for his Troops and entreated of them as a favor the use of Faneuil Hall for one Regiment to lodge in till Monday following, promising upon his honor to quit said Hall at that time . . ."[16]

Putting his request on a humanitarian level worked. The selectmen could now concede to Dalrymple's petition without surrendering the principle. That same night, the troops entered Faneuil Hall.

Historians have designated so many incidents as turning points on the road to the Revolution that the path often takes on the image of a corkscrew. Nevertheless, it certainly seems that the arrival of the Regulars at Boston in October 1768 deserves to take its place among the ranking candidates. By bringing troops into Boston the ministry was sowing dragon's teeth in fertile soil. To eighteenth-century Whigs, professional soldiers were nothing more than "gangs of restless mercenaries, responsible only to the whim of the ruler who paid them, capable of destroying all rights, law, and liberty that stood in their way."[17] The roots of antimilitary feeling were deep. Even the groundlings who may never have heard of or read any of the Whig tracts would have agreed with the sentiments expressed in a popular slogan: "A messmate before a shipmate, a shipmate before a stranger, a stranger before a dog, and a dog before a soldier."

Despite the revulsion that many people felt at the sight of the troops, they could not help being impressed by the power they represented. The longboats from the transports made their rhythmic way toward the dock, guarded by warships with open gunports and shotted cannon. Several times they shuttled back and forth, bringing their cargo ashore. Each time, more soldiers scrambled out of the boats and formed ranks, until both regiments and their train of artillery were assembled and ready to march. The bands struck up a martial tune, flags unfurled, and, with a quick step, the troops set off up King Street and toward the Common.

These men were soldiers of the Fourteenth and Twenty-ninth Regiments, infantrymen with a grand tradition. The Fourteenth had fought in Flanders for King William and would, in a few generations, be at Waterloo under Wellington. The Twenty-ninth was equally proud, having fought with Marlborough at Ramillies, and would later distinguish itself in the Peninsular War.[18] Now both had the ignominious duty of cowing an unfriendly town.

Spectators' emotions ran the gamut from anger to relief, depending on their political sympathies. Among the crowd down on the dock were a number of the Sons, including the town's best silversmith and engraver, Paul Revere. He was there on assignment, taking notes and making sketches, which he brought back to his shop in the North End. There, he executed what became one of the best-known engravings in American history. It was a scene depicting the landing of the troops, and it soon appeared throughout the continent so that others could see the evil happening to Boston.

The presence of 1200 troops in a town with barely 15,000 inhabitants had a devastating effect. Everywhere they looked, Bostonians saw red — in Faneuil Hall, around the courthouse, in private homes, on the streets; and, perhaps most distressing, especially for Hancock, they were all over the Common.

His Common, the land Uncle Thomas had fretted over and he had nurtured, now looked like a barbarian encampment.[19] Gone was the grass and in its place were mud and grime, with men slipping and sloshing through the muck. White tents dotted the field, stinking latrines were along the fringes, and the air was filled with the stench of cooking fires, human waste, and animal dung. If the scene offended Hancock's sight and smell, so too it assaulted his hearing, for every day the sounds of officers and noncommissioned officers, barking orders and calling cadence, drifted up the hill to remind him of the demise of the neighborhood. No one in Boston had more reason to hate the British than John Hancock.

The presence of the troops plunged Boston into mourning. Hancock's social life, once filled with dinner parties and gay evenings, ground to a halt. Although many of the pleasantries of life disappeared, there did emerge in the town a new pastime, one that would not have been possible without the troops — enticing men to desert. Considering the harshness of the service, it was an easy thing to do, and many soldiers slipped away and tried to melt into the population.[20] For the unlucky who were caught, the punishment was quick and severe, and it was not unusual to hear the agonizing cries of men being flogged for their indiscretion.

At nearly every turn Hancock felt the bite of the British lion. At home, he found them camped on his doorstep. At selectmen's meetings, he had to sit and listen to Dalrymple repeatedly explain why his soldiers were still in Faneuil Hall despite his promise to leave. Out in the harbor, Captain James Scott, of his brig *Lydia*, was prevented from sailing on schedule because of harassment by naval authorities. To a man with Hancock's pride, all this was absolutely infuriating. He was a man of long memory and some temper who had no intention of meekly accepting abuse.

While Hancock was cataloguing his grievances, others who shared his outrage were taking more decisive action. On October 13, there appeared in a New York newspaper the first installment of a series that would soon become one of the most remarkable propaganda efforts in American history. It was first published under the title "Journal of Transactions in Boston" and eventually under the better-known "Journal of Occurrences." The "Journal" purported to be a chronicle of events in Boston that was "strictly fact." That declaration could be questioned, but not the overall effect of this wondrous piece of propaganda. For nearly a year (October 13, 1768, to August 1, 1769) the installments were printed and reprinted on both sides of the Atlantic. Next to John Dickinson's *Letters*, they were probably the most widely read items in America. It was through this medium that Hancock became well known beyond Boston. He is mentioned more often and in a better light than any other person associated with the patriot cause. In some measure, the account read like an eighteenth-century novel, with Hancock, liberty's protector, beset by evil-doers.

Of course, even the cleverest of propagandists could not have enshrined Hancock without the aid of wicked adversaries, and these the British government seemed eager to supply. Like the Furies, they were determined to pursue and destroy their quarry. The better known he became, the more resolute was their pursuit.

While his enemies sought his ruin, up on the hill Hancock went on with business. As usual, Harrison was dunning him for money, which he refused to pay; the selectmen kept meeting to hear the latest tales of soldiers' atrocities; and he was busy launching and fitting out his newest vessel, christened, appropriately enough, *Last Attempt*.[22]

Down in the town, relations between the local people and the military were growing worse. On October 29, after some tortuous negotiations, the regiments were marched off the Common and put into winter quarters at various locations around the town. Two days later, they trooped back, not to camp, but to witness an execution. Bostonians had seen executions before — pirates, thieves, and murderers had gone to their reward at the end of a rope down on the Neck or out in the harbor — but this one was different. It was gruesome pageantry, the like of which the town had never seen.

As the regimental drummer rolled a slow cadence, the victim, a young deserter from the Fourteenth regiment, was marched solemnly to his place. He was dressed all in white and accompanied by a psalm-reading chaplain. Once the firing squad had done its job, the body was left to lie in a bloody pool while the regiments were marched by so that any with similar ideas might take a lesson. Naturally, this grisly display was made much of by the "Journal." Special note was taken of the fact that this was the poor man's first desertion and that the commander had taken no note of the pleas made in his behalf by the women of the town. None of this would have happened, according to the "Journal," if the troops had been quartered where they belonged, out at the Castle.[23]

Two days after the scene on the Common, the town was animated again. On Wednesday evening, November 2, officers of the regiments were ordered to hold their troops in readiness for the morning, "as a large mob was then expected."[24] No one was certain what "mob" was expected or why. The town's temperature was running a bit above normal, but that was the result of a low-grade infection that had been present since the arrival of the troops. Putting the troops on a special alert obviously meant that something was about to happen.

Arodi Thayer felt quite uneasy as he and his aide trudged up Beacon Hill on Thursday morning. He was the marshal of the Vice-Admiralty Court, a job akin to being the Angel of Death, and he knew that what he was about to do might well earn him a coat of tar and feathers. He was on his way to serve papers on John Hancock.

Since everyone in town knew who he was, the minute Thayer started up the hill the news swept through Boston. Remembering what had happened to Joseph Harrison when he had only seized *Liberty*, Thayer, who was on his way after the great man himself, had good cause to fear for his safety. Fortunately for him, he had something Harrison never enjoyed — the backing of two regiments. They did not have to be in the streets for their presence to be felt. No mob could stand against them, and the patriots wisely refrained from provoking violence.[25] Thayer made his trip in peace.

The marshal was acting on the orders of the judge of Vice-Admiralty for Massachusetts, Robert Auchmuty, the same man who had judged the *Liberty* case. On information filed by Attorney General Jonathan Sewall, Auchmuty had issued warrants for Hancock and four others.[26] The action, of course, was directly linked with the *Liberty* affair and was based on a recent statute of 1764, intended to strengthen the revenue laws. It provided that

> if any Goods or Merchandizes whatsoever, liable to the Payment of Duties in any British Colony or Plantation in America, by this or any other Act of Parliament shall be *loaden on board any Ship or Vessel in ward bound*, before the respective Duties due thereon are paid, agreeable to Law; or if any prohibited Goods whatsoever shall be imported into, or exported out of, any of the said Colonies or Plantations contrary to the true Intent and meaning of this or any other Act of Parliament; *every Person who shall be assisting, or otherwise concerned* Either in the Loading outwards, or in the *Unshipping or landing Inwards*, such Goods, or *to whose Hands the same shall knowingly come* after the Loading or unshipping thereof, shall for *each and every offence* forfeit *treble the Value of such Goods* . . . [Italics added.][27]

For Hancock the possible penalty came to at least £9000 sterling, a sum that would not bankrupt him but would certainly put a crimp in his business and announce to the rest of the merchants that they had best toe the mark. After some quick consultation with his friends and attorneys, Hancock and his fellow defendants, Nathaniel Barnard, Daniel Malcolm, John Matchet, William Bowes, and Lewis Gray, decided to put up bail, which was set at £3000 for Hancock and £2800 for each of the others.

On Monday, November 7, Hancock appeared in court to answer the charge. He had the best lawyer in Boston — John

Adams. After the preliminaries, Auchmuty continued the case until the 28th. That was only the beginning. Once the case was renewed, it dragged on for weeks. The crown's strategy was to prove that Hancock had helped to plan and execute the "frolic" the night *Liberty*'s cargo disappeared, and, to prove it, Sewall called nearly everyone that he thought could give the slightest evidence. Friends, relatives, business associates, and employees were all called. Some, as was permitted in Vice-Admiralty Court, were questioned in private, giving rise to charges of "Star Chamber." Sewall even thought of quizzing Aunt Lydia.

Tedious was the best way to describe it. In later years Adams wrote: "I was thoroughly weary and disgusted with the Court, the officers of the Crown, the Cause, and even with the tyrannical Bell that dangled me out of my House every Morning."[28]

That was defense counsel's point of view; others thought differently. To the authors of the "Journal," the length was a blessing, since the court proceedings churned out a steady supply of grist for the propaganda mill. Each day, Sewall summoned more witnesses, none of whom said what he wanted to hear, all claiming either ignorance or loss of memory. With no evidence being uncovered, the interminable proceedings seemed to be nothing more than harassment. Finally, one witness did come across — Joseph Maysel. He was a frail reed to rest on, but Sewall had little choice. As it turned out, Maysel's checkered past allowed Adams easily to impugn his testimony, and his evidence was declared inadmissible. A short time later the Suffolk Superior Court indicted him for perjury, but before he could be brought forward the commissioners spirited him out of town.[29] Having shot every arrow in his quiver without ever hitting the mark, Sewall had no choice, and on March 25, the charges were dropped.

Was this case an example of Hancock's persecution by harpies intent on stealing his fortune to enhance their own? Certainly that was the view put forth to the people of America, but to believe that is to accept at face value Adams' position that Hancock was innocent of any complicity in the *Liberty* case — a heroic if not a fatuous assumption. What gave credence to the charge of venality was that, under law, one third of the monies realized from such a prosecution would be distributed to the prosecutor (Sewall), one third to the governor (Bernard), and one third to the crown. No doubt all would have been somewhat less than human if the thought of several thousand pounds coming their way did not intrigue them. Nevertheless, it should be remembered that Sewall started the proceedings reluctantly, the trial was not rigged, Auchmuty conducted himself fairly, and, based on the evidence, the result was a just one. Indeed, the entire trial was conducted with great propriety.

If there was a villain in the piece, it was Francis Bernard, for it was he who, for political reasons, pressed Sewall to prosecute. But even this was not so much to line his own pockets as to assert royal authority and strike a blow at Hancock and his fellows, whom he had come to detest.[30]

From the crown's perspective, the governor, the attorney general, and the customs commissioners were doing nothing less than their sworn duty. In fact, the commissioners had been sent to Boston for the purpose of tightening the revenue laws. If they allowed Boston's greatest merchant flagrantly to defy them, then they might as well have declared the town to be a free-trade zone, and watched the whole revenue apparatus come crashing down on their heads. It was unfortunate for them that they did not better prepare their case.

Bernard, having set out to destroy an enemy, found that his plan had completely backfired. Hancock was more popular than ever, and, thanks to the "Journal," he was more widely known. Atop the hill, he bathed in the warm praise that flowed in from the town and beyond. Most gratifying of all came a message from liberty's martyr on the other side of the Atlantic, John Wilkes:

> I beg my best compliments to Mr. Hancock in particular. His late persecutions I consider as a consequence of his known zeal to the cause of his country which our common enemies desire to punish, when they cannot suppress it.[31]

No patriot could have asked for a greater endorsement.

There was an inverse relationship between Hancock's political success and the state of his business. All those things which helped the former — nonimportation, court battle, meetings, office-holding, and so on — were harmful to the latter. The truth was that it was expensive to fight the crown, not only in terms of money but in time, as well. In moments of great difficulty, when he should have been devoting every minute to business operations, Hancock was tied up in lengthy court proceedings and politics.

He did manage to continue exporting oil and potash, and through these sales he was able to pay off some old London debts. But due to nonimportation, his vessels often returned with half-empty holds or even in ballast. He would have liked to rid himself of some of his "navigation," but, with trade so depressed, there were no buyers. For a time he was left with four or five vessels when one or two would have been sufficient.[32]

Closer to home, Hancock kept up his wholesale and retail business, operating out of the store down at Faneuil Hall, which was under the direction of his clerk and friend, William Palfrey. Here, he sold everything from shoe buckles to coal.[33] Most of the sales were on credit, and the list of people indebted to Hancock was a long one. Early in May 1769, Hancock ordered a rendering of his debtors. A portion of that list still remains, carrying the names and the amounts owed. Geographically, the list reached up to Portsmouth, New Hampshire, and down through Connecticut to New York and across to England. In one case the amount owed was £1166, but the average was closer to £100.[34]

For the most part the names are those of unremarkable customers; some were probably retailers buying wholesale, and others were consumers buying for themselves. Occasionally, a name does leap out. General Thomas Gage, the commander in chief of British forces in North America, owed £29. Israel Williams, an important Tory leader from western Massachusetts, was being carried for £168, and Theodore Godet, a prominent New York merchant, owed nearly £1000. Altogether this partial list indicates that Hancock was owed at least £20,000 for goods supplied.

Such magnitude of trade alone placed Hancock in the front ranks of Boston merchants, but even that represented only part of his business. He and Aunt Lydia had lent out £21,000 at interest, which represented more than one fifth of all the money lent in Boston. In truth, the Hancocks were Boston's biggest bankers. It is also a fact that Hancock's merchant fleet was large enough to make him the town's biggest shipowner.[35]

Just how large his fortune was is shown by the fact that the net worth of Boston's next richest Whig, James Bowdoin, was only 25 percent of the Hancocks'. Even John Erving, who was reputed to have Boston's greatest fortune, actually had less than the combined wealth of John and Lydia.[36]

Trade, shipping, and moneylending were by no means Hancock's only business interests. He was also heavily involved in real estate in Boston and the countryside. He was continually buying parcels down by the Faneuil Hall area. Some of them were used for his own purposes, but he rented others. Beyond the town he was smitten with the same passion for land speculation that affected so many of his friends. He and Lydia owned thousands of acres of land in Maine, New Hampshire, central and western Massachusetts, and Connecticut.[37]

Economically, Hancock was the most influential private citizen in Boston. No one could match his wealth. He knew this, and there is no reason to doubt that, whenever he fancied, he could easily translate economic influence into political capital. To those who were his allies he could be generous and forgiving, but to those who opposed him he could be stringent and demanding.

Perhaps in relaxed moments Hancock reflected on the irony of his wealth. He had inherited from Uncle Thomas a business built largely on government contracts. He was now using that fortune to oppose that government. He undoubtedly gleaned pleasure from the knowledge that his opponents had supplied him his arsenal. Fortunately for him, the arsenal was well stocked, for thus far he had done little but expend its contents. That hardly bothered him; he had discovered that attention to business could only gain him money, but in politics he might find fame. Luckily, his wealth was so great that simple momentum would sustain it for a considerable time as he devoted himself to politics.

At the town meeting in March, Hancock topped the list for selectman, and in May he was again returned as one of the town's representatives to the General Court. At the same time, in the other towns of the province the patriots were picking up support. They enhanced their hold over the House when seven of the nefarious seventeen who had voted to rescind the Circular Letter were turned out.[38] For Bernard that news was melancholy enough, but on Monday, April 6, true despair must have set in when he read the *Boston Gazette*.

The *Gazette* was published by two High Sons of Liberty, Benjamin Edes and John Gill, known to the Tories as those "foulmouthed Trumpeters of Sedition." Their shop had long been a meeting place for the patriots, and now it was the drop-off point for some purloined letters. Through the efforts of William Beckford, a member of Parliament sympathetic to America, and William Bollan, the former agent of Massachusetts, Edes and Gill obtained copies of letters sent from Bernard to Lord Hillsborough. As might have been expected, the governor's comments on the people of Massachusetts, particularly Bostonians and their institutions, were hardly complimentary. By publishing them, the *Gazette* destroyed whatever effectiveness Bernard had left. The Council accused him of "unmanly dissimulations" and requested his recall.[39]

Compounding the governor's misery was the convening of the General Court. It had last met eleven months ago when he had prorogued it for refusing to rescind the Circular Letter. As usual the members held their election for councilors. Hancock was again among those elected, and he was chosen to deliver up to His Excellency the names of the councilors. Of the twenty-eight names presented, Bernard vetoed eleven, including, of course, Hancock's.[40]

At the opening session, the governor sent a message, outlining what he thought was a proper agenda for the House to undertake. The House, though, had an agenda of its own and quickly turned to that topic Bernard wished to avoid the most — the troops in Boston. The representatives asked the governor to remove the soldiers from the town. Bernard's response was that he had no power to comply with the request. But if he could not remove the troops, he could remove the Court, and on June 16 he ordered it to convene across the river, in Cambridge. Perhaps he hoped that, free of the baleful influence of the Boston mob and the irksome presence of redcoats, the Court would get down to business in this more serene setting.

Hancock was thoroughly annoyed. Traveling the half-dozen miles to Cambridge was a far cry from a short walk down the hill to the State House. Now he had to leave the comfort of Beacon Hill and Aunt Lydia's company and, for as long as the Court was in session, take up residence in Cambridge. His absence meant that both his business and the affairs of the town would have to wait.

If Bernard thought the bucolic air of Cambridge would cure the patriot fever, he was mistaken, for he soon discovered that he still had a tartar on his hands. On June 21 he told the representatives that in four weeks they had not "done any Thing at ALL." There quickly followed an exchange of the usual veiled insults, a call for the governor's removal, and a testy response from His Excellency: he was going home to "report . . . the State of the Province" to His Majesty. The House bade him good riddance and called him an "enemy of the colony, and to the Nation in general." Infuriated, Bernard struck in the only way he knew how — he prorogued the General Court.[41]

Chapter 7

Protest Turns to Violence —
The Massacre

HAVING LEFT CAMBRIDGE on a discordant note, Hancock was pleased to be back home. On the hill, Aunt Lydia reigned supreme. With Cato, Prince Holmes, Molly, and the rest at her side, she held sway, keeping the mansion in fine order and setting one of the best tables in town. As long as she was in charge, this would always be the one place in the world where Johnny could find peace. Such a refuge was much appreciated, for down in the town and out in the province politics were as noisy and tangled as ever.

"Parties" as a label for the battling factions at work in both the town and province would be a misnomer, for the structure and goals nominally associated with the term in later times simply did not exist. Yet, although they did not fit the modern definition, these groups did behave in some respects like parties.[1]

The pattern of politics in which Hancock operated had begun to emerge in the heyday of Uncle Thomas and his friend Governor William Shirley.[2] Through clever manipulation of patronage and spoils during the wartime boom years, Shirley had managed to create a court faction. The fluidity of these groups, and the lack of any strong ideological bond other than office and spoils, makes profiling them a difficult if not dangerous task. However, there is a hint of commonality among them that, over time and through various crises, grew more pronounced.

The court side was, of course, that group most closely associated with the governor. Their political views were Tory and their social views elitist. Despite this conservative image, it is equally true that in many respects these people were accommodative and adaptable and enjoyed a world view that could well be termed tolerant and cosmopolitan. As a recent historian, Stephen Patterson, has noted:

> The marks of the leading Court party towns were economic diversity, social pluralism, and a considerable openness and toleration in matters of religion. There was, in other words, a developing individualism of the sort one associates with modern, urbanized society.[3]

The country faction represented a different perspective. Its strength rested in towns less wealthy than the court faction's. As a group these people were almost always in opposition to the government. To a significant degree they represented the old ways and were distrustful of commercialism, and they looked back to a pristine and virtuous world that probably never existed. They were still Puritans at heart, who held to Winthrop's dream of a City Upon a Hill.

Ironically, Boston in its role as both spring and sink for the colony signified the best and the worst to each side. Elements of the two sides vied for control in the town. It was through this struggle for control in both the province and the town that the country party was welded into an engine for revolution. Despite setbacks and defections, through each trauma of the sixties the country party seemed to coalesce. In Boston, the special problem was holding the merchants in line. In this cause they were helped by the repeated and inept assertions of royal authority that provided common ground on which both the country element and the Boston merchants could unite. This opportunity for rallying support was quickly recognized and exploited by that shadowy eminence of the Revolution, Sam Adams.

Depending on one's angle of vision, Sam Adams is everything from the savior to the devil incarnate.[4] His father, Deacon Samuel Adams, was an old-stock Puritan who pledged his soul to the Almighty and his vote to Elisha Cooke, the leader of an anticourt faction in Boston, fighting "to preserve the remains of the provincial isolationism of the seventeenth century against the encroachment of time and commerce . . ."[5]

Bred to politics with an antigovernment bias, young Adams followed the traditional route via Master Lovell to Harvard College. After graduating in 1740, he tried his hand in business, failed at that, and finally wound up embraced in his perpetual love affair with Boston politics.

Stocky, balding, not very good-looking, and given to trembling, Adams' leadership could not be called charismatic. His genius lay in a shrewd mind, a skillful pen, and uncanny political savvy. His knack for organization is legendary, a knack that, incidentally, seemed never to intrude into his personal life, which was always in a state of disarray.[6]

In great measure his success was due to his single-mindedness. He always sailed on the opposite tack from the royal government, holding to a course that could be called home rule. Contrary to what some have maintained, Adams did not emerge from the womb crying, "Independence." Though he may have toyed with the idea during the sixties, he did not become a firm advocate until the early seventies, by which time he had lost all faith in the justice of the British government. Nor was Adams the great dictator, driving his people like dumb cattle toward the precipice. That assertion gives too little credit to his peers and too much to him.

With his election to the House in 1765, Adams stood with one foot squarely in the town and the other in the legislature. The following year, in the same political battle that saw Hancock elected and the popular forces gain control of the House, he was elected clerk by a single vote, and James Otis was chosen speaker.[7] Bernard vetoed Otis and probably would have done the same to Adams if he had had the power. For the next decade, Adams held this key post.

Even before they entered the House together, Hancock and Adams knew one another. They were both active in the affairs of the town and had been brought together in common cause against the Stamp Act. For his part, Adams had the good sense to recognize Hancock's potential for influence through both his name and money. Together, the four Boston representatives, Adams, Otis, Hancock, and Thomas Cushing, formed a smooth political team.[8]

That Hancock and Adams were able to work together, even for a short time, stands as testimony to the depth of their opposition to the government, for in nearly every other way these two men could not have been more different. Sam Adams could often be found in a tavern, not quaffing spirits, but shaking hands, patting backs, and making plans. This was his natural habitat, one where, according to his cousin John, "bastards, and legislators, are frequently begotten."[9] From his neat little house down on Purchase Street, he would often walk through the town, down to the docks, saying hello to people by name — mechanics, dock wallopers, clerks, and merchants. He was gregarious and egalitarian, equally at home with Harvard men or day laborers. In philosophy and life styles there was a wide gulf between Hancock and Adams. Sam was a Roundhead in his religion, his politics, and his social behavior. According to one unflattering biographer, he detested riches but was envious of those who had them; he suffered from an acute inferiority complex; he had no close friends; and, in general, he fitted the stereotypical image of a dour Puritan.[10] Only his single-minded political drive could have made him repress all his natural antipathy toward Hancock. It is a measure of how much politics counted with him that he was able to work with this gay Cavalier.

Adams' was not the only voice Hancock heard. There were others with whom he regularly consulted. Among them were two whose influence was considerable, the Reverend Samuel Cooper, "Silver-Tongued Sam," and Jemmy Otis. Cooper presided over the Brattle Square Church, to which the Hancocks and other important families in the town belonged. The ministry, though, was only his profession; his love was politics. In 1753 he was appointed chaplain to the House of Representatives, a perennial post where he was quite able to mingle "religion and politics so skillfully that he became the moral validation of the policies of the Whigs."[11]

With his silky tones and sense of the dramatic, Cooper managed to sway his congregation. He was in the habit of wearing an elaborate cassock — "one sleeve would make a full trimm'd negligee" — which gave him an almost Romish appearance. In fact, one old communicant remarked that he suspected Cooper had a Pope in his belly.[12] In private conversation he was just as awesome, and those who met him came away impressed by the apparent breadth of his learning.

From his pulpit, Cooper railed against religious tyranny (the Anglican Church) and political oppression (the British ministry).[13] His own liberality and that of most of his congregation allowed for the intrusion of a good measure of secularization, and Cooper himself is reported to have remarked once that "an ounce of mother wit is worth a pound of clergy." As a member of the Revolution's black legion he was, in the words of John Adams, an "excellent hand to spread a rumor."[14]

Cooper's influence was made even greater by the fact that his brother William was the town clerk. It was William who counted the votes and kept the records, duties he conducted with a noticeably partisan spirit. Together, Samuel and William carried great weight in Boston politics. Beyond Boston, Cooper was well connected through his friendship with Benjamin Franklin and Thomas Pownall. He kept these gentlemen well informed of happenings in Boston, as interpreted by Samuel Cooper, and they in turn told him of the wider world.[15]

Because of Uncle Thomas' and Aunt Lydia's long and devoted connection to Brattle Square, and John's continued association there, Cooper was more than just a minister to the family; he was a close friend.[16] He was one of a very few men who, in the turbulent years to come, remained both a political ally and confidant of Hancock.

Although the story sounds apocryphal, according to local wags weekends were a favorite time for political scheming in Boston. On Saturdays, Cooper, along with his political chums John and Sam Adams, James Otis, and Dr. Benjamin Church, a local physician and Hancock's old schoolmate at Latin and Harvard, could be found down at the offices of the *Boston Gazette*, concocting the next attack on the government. On Sunday afternoons, a more elite group met, made up of only four: Hancock, Sam Adams, Cooper, and Otis. Gathered over port and tobacco, probably at Hancock's, they hatched the week's political schemes.

Like his friends, Jemmy Otis was a Harvard man; indeed, he was a classmate of Cooper's. After college he returned to his family home in Plymouth, where he spent time preparing for the study of law. Some time in 1745 he came up to Boston to study under Jeremiah Gridley, the best lawyer in the province.[17] For three years Gridley tutored young Otis, until he was ready to set out on his own. He would have preferred to stay and practice in Boston, but his father persuaded him to come home to Plymouth. After two years of bucolic practice, he found the lure of the metropolis too much to withstand, and he came back to the capital.[18]

Otis quickly showed himself to have one of the keenest minds in the town, but he also displayed some distressing signs of erratic and intemperate behavior, which would later totally cripple him. Politically, of course, he was a Whig, which naturally inclined him toward the opposition. This inclination became a raging passion when he saw his father swindled by none other than Thomas Hutchinson and Francis Bernard.

It happened when Chief Justice Samuel Sewall died in 1760. Jemmy's father had apparently been promised the post, but Bernard, for political reasons, decided to award the post to Thomas Hutchinson. That was enough for Otis, and in a heated exchange with Hutchinson he "swore revenge."[19]

Otis' bitter hatred for Hutchinson made him a dangerous foe. His roots in the province ran deep and wide. His father was one of the kingpins of Plymouth and Barnstable counties. Samuel Allyne Otis, his brother, was a prominent merchant of Boston, and Jemmy himself could count among his own clients Boston's most eminent men, including Hancock.

His success at the bar and his own desires brought him into politics, and in 1761 he was elected to the House from Boston. He quickly became a major force in that body and was one of the most outspoken leaders of the opposition.[20]

These four men — Adams, Hancock, Cooper, and Otis — were

at the heart of the opposition in both town and province. Ably assisted by others, including Doctors Benjamin Church, Joseph Warren, and Thomas Young, along with a local hardware dealer, William Molineux, better known as "Paoli," they helped direct politics.

With the end of the summer session of the General Court came the final departure of Governor Francis Bernard. No one was fooled by the lame excuse that he was merely going home to report the state of the province to His Majesty. Anyone with an ounce of sense recognized that Bernard's tenure had been a disaster and that he had about as much chance of coming back to Massachusetts as Sam Adams had of being presented at court. On August 1, the whole town exploded with jubilation. Bells were rung, guns were fired from Hancock's Wharf, the Liberty Tree was covered with flags, and in the evening a great bonfire was made upon Fort Hill.[21] Such unseemly glee over the departure of His Excellency was explained officially as having nothing to do with his sailing; rather, it just so happened that the day he was leaving also marked the anniversary of the Hanoverian succession. The sham excuse did not convince or amuse Francis Bernard, and he left Boston in a black mood, ready to poison any ear that would listen about Massachusetts. Not even the consolation prize of a baronetcy salved his wounds.

While their former governor was midway across the Atlantic, the Sons in Boston gathered for their annual celebration of the Stamp Act repeal. Everyone rendezvoused down at the Liberty Tree and then crossed over the Neck to dine at Robinson's, in Dorchester. There, they drank endless toasts and talked of their recent victories. Bernard, of course, was high on the agenda. The general sentiment was one of good riddance, but some also expressed anger, not so much at Bernard as at the ministry for rewarding him. How could the king, at the ministers' suggestion, elevate to the peerage a man who had trampled on their rights?[22] After dinner the Sons snaked back to Boston in a long procession. There were 139 carriages in the cavalcade. "Mr. Hancock preceded the Company and Mr. Otis Brought up the rear."[23]

With Bernard gone, Thomas Hutchinson was left as acting

governor. For the time being, with the House adjourned and Hutchinson content to keep a low profile, tensions seemed to ease a bit. Politics, though, hardly ever remain inert. Movement, sometimes perceptible and sometimes not, is always taking place, and in this instance, once the opposition ceased their momentum, events began to push them back.

The keystone of opposition politics was nonimportation. In that agreement rested all the Hancock-Adams faction's hopes of coercing the ministry. But that could be accomplished only by rallying support and maintaining a united front, and in this they were facing mounting difficulties.

There is little question that many of the merchants who had signed the agreement had done so under considerable pressure. The simple truth was that in many instances a merchant could trade under the Townshend Acts and still make money. His well-developed mercantile instincts told him to do just that. If at any time nonimportation weakened, the economic impulses were likely to take over and bring the whole apparatus crashing down. It was a neat exercise in countervailing power to see which power, economic or political, would prevail. In the fall of 1769, thanks to some fumbling by Hancock, a waspish Scot, John Mein, came close to single-handedly toppling nonimportation.

Mein was an Edinburgh bookseller who, for adventure, ambition, or romance, decided to give up life in Scotland and venture to America.[24] His willingness to take up a new life is the first indication we have of Mein's spirited temperament, which his adopted town of Boston would soon come to know.

By no means was Mein a destitute immigrant. He had had considerable experience in the bookselling business and apparently had brought some cash with him, as well. Soon after his arrival, the *Boston Gazette* was announcing the opening of a new shop run by Mein and Sandeman on Marlborough Street, "nearly opposite to Bromfield's Lane," where books, pamphlets, and other sundries could be purchased.[25]

Mein did well. Boston was a literate town, and its citizens patronized his shop. In less than a year he had expanded his business by buying out one of his rivals, establishing Boston's first circulating library, and starting his own publishing business. Finally, in October 1767, the enterprising Mein took the next logical step in his march toward an eighteenth-century media empire: he founded a newspaper, the *Boston Chronicle*.[26]

Inevitably, he and the *Chronicle*, like the other publishers and newspapers of the town, became politicized. Unhappily for Mein, his astuteness at business did not carry over into the political realm, and though he could reckon accounts well enough, he was careless in political matters. He soon displayed an inordinate ability to offend people.

The fact that he was an outsider and a Tory made it inevitable that sooner or later John Mein would clash with the Sons and their allies. His first sin was in printing excerpts from London papers that were critical of William Pitt.[27] To the patriots, Pitt was a great hero, and their principal mouthpiece, the *Boston Gazette*, published a letter, almost certainly written by Otis, attacking Mein for his defamation.[28] Mein's response was to troop down to the *Gazette*'s offices, seeking to uncover the identity of his attacker. On his arrival he confronted Benjamin Edes and demanded to know who had written the letter. In an early instance of a newspaperman protecting his sources, Edes refused to answer, whereupon Mein warned that if that was the case, he would consider Edes and his partner, John Gill, responsible for the piece.[29] After delivering these not so veiled threats, he stormed out.

The following evening Mein took his revenge. It was Saturday, and as he was walking along the street he met John Gill. What happened then is best described by the court documents.

> John Mein at said Boston on the twenty-sixth day of January last in the evening of the same with force and arms to wit with a large club made an assault upon the said John Gill and then and there gave the said John Gill two violent blows with the said Club upon the back part of the head of the said John Gill and beat wounded and evil intreated the said John Gill in so grievous a manner that his life was despaired of and other enormities the said John Mein did commit upon the said John Gill against the peace of our Lord the King . . .[30]

Ironically, Gill's attorney was none other than James Otis, the author of the offending letter. As usual, Otis did his job well.

The Inferior Court found against Mein in the amount of £130, a sum that, on appeal, was reduced to £75.[31]

Mein was made wise by his experience, and for a while he was content to remain quiet. His views, though, did not change, and he continued to harbor resentment against those who he felt had treated him so ill. His antagonists, of course, were the same men who had so piously brought forth nonimportation. Naturally, when he was asked to sign the agreement, he flatly refused. Refusal was wicked enough, but then he went even further. Appalled at the treatment afforded others, like himself, who had resisted intimidation by being publicly snubbed, listed in the press as enemies of the people, taunted with insults, and just generally harassed and threatened, he decided to retaliate. With the aid of an informant at the Custom House, he managed to get copies of ships' manifests showing that the same men who were lambasting him were actually violating the agreement themselves. They were taking advantage of that loophole which allowed them to import goods on their ships as long as they belonged to others. They were able to make money and still claim faithfulness to the agreement. Even worse, he found evidence of false entries, whereby prohibited goods were entered as items ordinarily permitted to pass. Obviously, according to Mein, something was terribly wrong.

Well armed, Mein stepped up his attacks, and on June 1, he let loose with a salvo that rocked the town.[32] He began to call to account those merchants who, he claimed, publicly professed allegiance to nonimportation but privately violated the agreement for their own greed. These charges traveled through Boston like fire. Soon he followed the opening blast with more, and during the summer and fall of 1769 the *Chronicle* was the most read and most hated paper in town. Not satisfied with simply publishing the evidence, Mein wrote biting satire that was both insulting and effective. Newspapers outside Boston picked up Mein's charges, and before long the Boston patriots found themselves being portrayed as scoundrels and hypocrites in places as far away as Newport, New York, and Philadelphia. This development was not only embarrassing but dangerous, for it threatened to undermine the whole nonimportation movement.

The Mein offensive hit some vital nerves, and when the mer-

chants realized their vulnerability, they made a quick attempt
to close up the loophole and regain their reputations. They did
this by agreeing not to carry any dutied goods on their vessels
regardless of ownership and by extending their demands to a
repeal of all the revenue measures, not just the Townshend Acts.
Such an advanced position found little support in the other
colonies.[33]

When Hancock informed Hayley and his partner, Hopkins, of
his decision to stand by the new agreement, they came back
with an unsettling response:

> We have ventured to deviate from those instructions for which
> we hope we shall have your excuse when we tell you that our
> reason for so doing was that no such orders have been given
> by any of the Owners of the Vessels in the Trade, except
> yourself, or if any such have been given they have been totally
> disregarded by everyone who has been here this Fall . . .[34]

Perhaps Hancock was too honest and Mein was too right.

Because of his visibility and reputation as a leading patriot,
Hancock was Mein's favorite target. On August 21, Mein asked
pointedly how was it that, at a time when everyone was encouraged to be frugal, Mr. Hancock was importing a fine new
carriage for himself? Or how could he explain the importation
aboard his vessel *Lydia* of a quantity of fine linen fraudulently
listed as canvas. Soon after, the front page of the *Chronicle*
carried the manifest from another of Hancock's ships, *Boston
Packet*, which listed more incriminating cargo.[35]

While Mein was delivering his latest barrage, Hancock was
off on a trip to Philadelphia and New York, trying to shore up
nonimportation and persuade those communities to follow Boston's lead in extending it. He took with him young Tom Brattle,
who had a reputation of being something of a rake. Even if the
mission failed, with Brattle along there was bound to be some
fun.[36]

In Philadelphia the most important visit was with John Dickinson, the "Penman of the Revolution," whose *Letters from a
Farmer in Pennsylvania* had helped to form the philosophical
and legal framework within which the Americans had built

their case against the Townshend Acts.[37] Hancock was a fervent admirer of Dickinson's, and their meeting was a bit of high drama that symbolized the linkage of Boston and Philadelphia.

While Hancock was off on his good-will mission, the very difficult task of mounting a counterattack against Mein fell to his chief clerk, Palfrey. In the face of Mein's broadside, Palfrey's retorts sounded like popguns. The *Newport Mercury* reported:

> The Boston News Writers make JOHN HANCOCK Esq. one of the foremost of the Patriots in Boston and the strictest observer of the agreement for non-importation: he would perhaps shine more conspicuously and be less suspected in this character if he did not keep a number of vessels running to London and back full freighted getting rich by receiving freight and goods made contraband by the Colonies.[38]

In New York the whispers of Hancock's duplicity forced him to publish a defense, asserting:

> This is ONCE FOR ALL to certify to whom it may concern, That I have not in one single instance directly or indirectly deviated from said Agreement; and I now publicly defy all Mankind to prove the CONTRARY.[39]

Toward the end of October, Hancock returned to Boston. His trip had not been altogether successful. He had found little enthusiasm for extending nonimportation, and, indeed, even in its present form disturbing cracks were appearing. That somewhat dreary news saddened Adams and the others, but they were no more distressed than Hancock when he was brought up to date on Mein's latest activities. It took precious little time for Hancock to realize that for both personal and political reasons John Mein had to be silenced. The only question was how.

No doubt some of the radicals suggested the direct approach — smash the presses, and tar and feather the editor. Hancock, who had never advocated violence and who now understood after his trip how the activities of street mobs only hurt the image of Boston, counseled moderation. An attack on Mein would force him to seek help from the government, and, since there were already regiments in the town, help would likely be forthcoming. Furthermore, even if they succeeded in running him out, that would merely enhance Mein's credibility and give more substance to his accusations. As they mulled over their problem, Hancock hit on a solution.

For some time as part of his regular business he had been importing books and magazines from Thomas Longman, a prominent London stationer on Paternoster Row.[40]

Coincidentally, Longman also happened to be Mein's principal supplier and a man to whom he was deeply in debt. Unlike Hancock, who was able to make returns to Longman, Mein was in dire financial straits. Thanks to the Sons, few people wanted to deal with him. As a result, his large inventory (most of it on credit from Longman) sat in his shop, collecting dust and interest.

Longman and another stationer's firm (Wright and Gill) who had also supplied Mein were anxious about their investment. After several months of receiving nothing from Mein other than promises, Longman finally wrote to his friend Hancock, expressing his concern and asking that he recommend someone to whom he could give power of attorney for the purpose of pursuing Mein.[41] As strange as it may seem, politics does not appear to have been a consideration in Longman's actions. Given the time it took for transatlantic communication, it was virtually impossible for Longman to have known what was happening between Mein and Hancock. Nor should the fact that he consulted with Hancock be seen as having been politically motivated. Hancock was a highly respected businessman with whom Longman had dealt for many years and whose judgment he trusted.

For Hancock and his friends the inquiry was heaven sent. After some quick consultation he responded to Longman with a generous offer: he himself would undertake the power of attorney as a favor for his friend.[42] It was a disingenuous offer, for with the power of attorney Hancock could now proceed against Mein under cover of law. It was an opportunity for him to silence a critic and embarrass the government through legal methods that would leave the patriot side with clean hands.

As if Hancock needed to be prodded in this matter, on October 26 Mein launched his most scurrilous assault yet. On the front page of the *Chronicle* appeared a lengthy piece titled "Outlines of the Characters of some who are thought to be 'Well Disposed.'" Heading the list was John Hancock, thinly disguised as

Johnny Dupe, Esq., alias the Milch-Cow of the "Well Disposed" a characteristic plate will be given with this [?] representing a good natured young man with long ears — a silly conceited grin on his countenance — a fool's cap on his head — a bandage tied over his eyes — richly dressed and surrounded with a crowd of people, some of whom are stroaking his ears, others tickling his nose with straws while the rest are employed in riffling his pockets; all of them with labels out of their mouths, bearing these words OUR COMMON FRIEND.[43]

The article went on to give similar Hogarthian descriptions to Tommy Trifle (Thomas Cushing), Muddle head (James Otis), and Lean Apothecary (Dr. Benjamin Church). By publishing this, Mein was practically declaring open season on himself. Two days after its appearance, as he was on his way home, a mob began to move on him, screaming, "Kill him; kill him."[44] He barely managed to escape by taking refuge with the guard. When the mob missed this quarry, they turned their wrath on George Gailer, a suspected customs informer. He "was stripped naked, put in a Cart where he was first tarred, then feathered and in this condition carried through the principal streets of the town followed by a great concourse of People."[45]

Although arrogant, Mein was not foolish. Shortly after this street scene, he decided to leave Boston and take refuge in London until the town quieted. He also hoped to take the opportunity to assuage Longman, but it was too late for that; ironically, while Mein was sailing for London, the power of attorney was arriving in Boston.[46]

Longman was quite unsympathetic. He, along with Wright and Gill, had already given Hancock authority to move ahead, so when Mein appeared at his office, he ordered him thrown into debtor's prison.[47] Mein was clever enough to secure his release through an affidavit in which he accused Hancock of seeking the power of attorney for the sole purpose of destroying him.

Despite his abrupt departure, the *Chronicle,* under the guidance of Mein's partner, John Fleming, continued to publish. Mein's exit pulled most of the paper's sharpest fangs, though it still persisted in tormenting the patriots and remained an annoyance they were anxious to be rid of. As a last bit of insurance, Hancock used his power of attorney to destroy the *Chronicle* completely. With John Adams acting as counsel for Hancock, on March 1, 1770, an attachment was served on the paper, the shop, and all of its contents, to the sum of £2000.[48] Some of Mein's friends stepped forward to offer security, but Hancock flatly refused to hear them, since his goal had less to do with satisfying debts than the silencing of the *Chronicle.* The sheriff, though, was more amenable; he was persuaded to accept the pledges of Mein's friends, and for a time, much to Hancock's displeasure, the *Chronicle* stayed in business.[49]

It was only a temporary reprieve. On behalf of Longman and Wright and Gill, Hancock took his case to court, where it trended inexorably toward a preordained conclusion. Mein knew what was coming. In September he wrote to a friend in Boston that he could not get his "Creditors to agree to come in share & share, so it will be catch that catch can, & the court and lawyers will sweep their part."[50] He was right. In November a jury in the Inferior Court found against him. His lawyer took the case on appeal to the Superior Court, where he fared no better.[51]

Hancock immediately went about making an inventory of the prize. Paper, presses, ink, books, and anything else that could fetch cash was put up for sale. For Longman and Wright and Gill, the final reckoning was disappointing. They received less than one half of what was owed, but to Hancock the victory was sweet.[52] Never again would he have to feel Mein's venom. Through a skillful use of the courts he had managed to destroy an enemy while still claiming to abide by "freedom of the press."

John Mein's rout was a great victory for Hancock and his friends, but unfortunately it came at a time when they also suffered a great loss — James Otis. With the possible exception of John Adams, no one else in town could match his intellect. He wrote and reasoned better than almost any of his colleagues. Despite some of the inflammatory attacks on him, he was, like Hancock, a moderate, who always held himself to be a loyal subject of the king. But if his mind was extraordinary, it was also fragile, and in the fall of 1769 it began to slip badly.[53]

On September 5, Otis stormed into a local tavern to confront John Robinson, a customs officer. Robinson had made some uncomplimentary remarks about Otis, and he was determined to have his revenge. Mad with anger, he came at Robinson with a stick. In the brawl that followed, Otis gave a good account of himself but got worse and emerged dazed and bloodied. By the time the local press got through with the incident, they had turned Otis into the martyr of an attempted assassination. As was to be expected, Sam Adams provided the most biased and emotional account. Signing himself "An Impartialist," he wrote in the *Boston Gazette*: "A number of sticks at once were over Mr. Otis's head — a drawn sword — the cry in the room G-d d——n him, meaning Mr. Otis, knock him down — kill him — kill him . . ."[54]

The beating drove Otis' brittle mind even faster on its flight from reality. He started to flirt with the royal authorities, gave up his practice of law, and began to drink heavily. In March 1770 he smashed the windows at the Town House and then fired off his pistol on a Sunday. Sadly, he was losing his mind.

The tragedy of James Otis was a great loss to Boston, but in the long run it was a gain for John Hancock. With Otis' removal from the inner circle of leadership, Hancock became more important as a link to the merchant community and as a voice of moderation. Soon he would even succeed to the position of moderator at the town meeting, a post that for many years had been held by Otis.[55]

Mein's intemperate attacks, the Otis-Robinson brawl, and promiscuous tarring and feathering were all clear measures of a menacing shift toward violence in Boston. Armed troops and an aroused populace are a bad mixture. Young men who, in civilian cast, act in proper and decent fashion tend to lose restraint when clothed in military uniforms at places far distant from home. This was the situation in Boston. Even after we discount the diatribes of the "Journal" and other propaganda, ample evidence suggests a good deal of misbehavior by the troops. Rowdyism, whoring, and drinking were hardly new in Boston, despite what the town fathers said, but never before had these sins been so politicized and publicized as they were now. Of course, the other side was hardly blameless. The Sons were masters at fomenting trouble. Inflammatory newspaper stories, wild accusations about troop behavior, refusing to socialize with "the enemy" — all these were just part of general policy aimed at making life in Boston as uncomfortable as possible for the regiments.[56] Adding to the discomfort of the soldiers was the mischievous behavior of the children of Boston. A quick snowball, with a razor-sharp clamshell embedded in it, or an anonymous rock often found its redcoated marks.

Hancock, of course, never played a role in these street scenes, nor did any of those with whom he was closely associated. That business was best left to the "lower sort," led by a man like Ebenezer MacIntosh, shoemaker and rabble-rouser, or those in the middling ranks, such as William Molineux and Dr. Thomas Young. But even these men, whether out on the streets, leading the charge, or locked up in some loft whispering conspiracy, did not completely control events. Although they planted the seeds, they had little control over how the crop came in.

On February 22, 1770, it finally happened — a street skirmish cost a life. The victim was a young German boy, Christopher Seider. Seider was part of a gang harassing an alleged violator of nonimportation, Thomas Lille. The gang was laying siege to Lille's shop when his friend Ebenezer Richardson, a well-known customs informer, came along to lend a hand. Richardson's appearance raised the fury of the mob higher, and Richardson had to duck into Lille's home for safety. Having run the two foxes to ground, the mob moved in, pelting the house with stones and pushing in the door. At this point Richardson threw open a window and began to wave a pistol at them. Somehow it went off, and Christopher Seider fell to the street, victim, according to the *Gazette*, of a "barbarous Murder."[57]

The Seider incident set the stage for a drama that was to open a fortnight later, greatly misnamed "the Boston Massacre." In good lawyerlike fashion, the editors of the *Legal Papers of John Adams* set forth the case:

> In the evening of 5 March 1770, the lone sentry before the Custom House on King Street became embroiled with a group of people as he stood his post; he called for help; in response six soldiers, a corporal, and Captain Thomas Preston marched down to the Custom House from the Main Guard; the tumult continued; the soldiers fired the bullets, striking a number of persons of whom three died instantly, one shortly thereafter, and a fifth in a few days.[58]

As usual, the facts tell only part of the story; propagandists, historians, and novelists have told and retold the story until, in some instances, it is barely recognizable as having anything to do with the sparse description above.[59] Were Sam Adams and his malevolent minions the real culprits? Did they carefully orchestrate the mob and lead them to their rendezvous on King Street? Or was it a case of innocent civilians being mowed down by the bloodybacks?

In fact, what seems to be the case is that the "massacre" was neither conspiracy nor murder, but the inevitable result of armed, frightened men confronted with an angry crowd. Leaders in Boston were as much startled by the killings as anyone on the British side.[60] An incident of this kind did their cause no good, for it only painted Boston in bloody hues. But if the Sons had not planned the Massacre, they certainly knew how to take advantage of it, and the very next day the propaganda mills were turning.

The muted sound of the musket volley barely reached the top of the hill, and there was turned away by windows closed tight against the cold March night. The knock on the door, though, wakened the household, and soon Hancock was dressed and down in his parlor, making plans for what must come next. That morning a special committee was elected to go to the acting governor and demand, once and for all, the removal of the troops. With Hancock leading them, the group trudged from the Town House over to the governor's residence. According to Hancock, Hutchinson was a gracious but nervous host. Who could blame him? Hancock, with the others behind him nodding their agreement, told him that there were "ten thousand men armed and ready to come into town upon his refusal."[61]

Hancock was bluffing, and Hutchinson knew it. On the other hand, if the troops did stay, more violence was almost certain. Colonel Dalrymple, who was present with Hutchinson, understood better than the governor the weakness of his position. It was conceivable that more bloodshed would so enrage the populace that his few troops would end up in mortal danger. As a compromise, he offered to remove one regiment; then, after some badgering, he said he would take the other, as well, if the governor desired it. Dalrymple had sprung the trap and Hutchinson was caught. After seeking advice from his councilors and friends, all of whom urged him to concede, Hutchinson finally caved in and agreed to remove the troops.[62]

Hancock carried the news back to the town meeting, which exploded with huzzas and cheers.[63] It was a great victory for the town and for Hancock. They had managed to cow His Excellency and drive the troops from the streets.

A few days later, the people of Boston witnessed a most remarkable sight. Dalrymple had expressed to Hancock and the others his concern over the withdrawal. The Fourteenth was removed with no difficulty, but elements of the Twenty-ninth were over in West Boston. They would have to march straight through the town to get to their boats. The colonel wanted a guarantee of safe-conduct. The committee agreed, and on March 10, with a drummer tapping out a quick step, the Twenty-ninth moved briskly across the town and toward Wheelwrights Dock. The town did provide an escort — one man — Will Molineux. He strode beside them unarmed, providing a curious spectacle: one of His Majesty's regiments, part of an army that had won an empire, being now protected by a single man. It worked. Molineux saw them off at the dock, undoubtedly wishing that they were going all the way to England; but for the time being Castle William would have to do.[64]

Chapter 8

The Unfortunate Thomas Hutchinson

A MERICAN HISTORY has few villains. Our Pantheon of evil-doers is a small one, but securely tucked away in one corner is the lonely and sometimes pathetic figure of Thomas Hutchinson. It was the lieutenant governor's unfortunate fate to be a loser in the Revolution and to have his role chronicled for posterity by the winners. Mercy Otis Warren, sister of James, lambasted Hutchinson in her *History of the Rise, Progress and Termination of the American Revolution*. To her, he was "perni-cious . . . dark, intriguing, insinuating, haughty and ambi-tious."[1] That view by one who knew and hated him was softened by later historians more removed from the fray, but the kernel of it remained alive, presenting Hutchinson in a malevolent role.[2]

To have been the man described by Mercy Warren, Hutch-inson would have had to be totally bereft of morals and prin-ciples. That was not the case; he was at least as decent and honest a person as most of his adversaries. His life ended in disaster because he could no longer understand the world around him and therefore lost his ability to act rationally within it. Bernard Bailyn, Hutchinson's most recent, and a somewhat sympathetic, biographer, portrays his faults as an "insensitivity to the moral ingredients of public life and to the beliefs and passions that grip people's minds; and his incapacity to respond to aspirations that transcend the ordinary boundaries of received knowledge, prudence and common sense . . ."[3] Hutchinson forgot, or perhaps he never knew, that politics is as much a matter of passion as it is of intellect. That was an error Hancock almost never made.

Hancock's encounter with Hutchinson over the Massacre crisis was by no means an introductory meeting, for they knew one another well — indeed, in many ways they were quite alike. They were products of bourgeois society and Harvard College. Hutchinson was a quarter-century older than Hancock and had entered politics about the time when Hancock was born.[4] He served in the House, allied himself with Governor William Shirley (as did Thomas Hancock), was elevated to the Council, and made lieutenant governor in 1758. Obviously, he was a well-born man who was rising even higher. Until the crises of the sixties, the only political scars he bore were those received in the celebrated Land Bank controversy. This involved an attempt by inflationists to issue paper money based on land values. As a staunch hard-money man, Hutchinson vehemently opposed the plan and fought it, as did other conservative merchants. Eventually, they triumphed, causing many of those who supported the scheme to suffer severe financial loss. One of the hard-hit inflationists was Deacon Adams, a fact his son Sam never forgot.[5]

By the time of the Stamp Act, Hutchinson was, without a doubt, one of the most influential politicians in the province. Over the years he had managed to accumulate and hold on to a number of offices. He was simultaneously lieutenant governor, chief justice, justice of the Court of Common Pleas for Suffolk County, judge of probate, and Captain of the Castle. With each addition to his treasury of offices came more power, which he shared with friends and relatives. His brother-in-law Andrew Oliver became secretary of the province, judge of the Inferior Court of Common Pleas for Essex County, and a member of the Council. Even in an age of flagrant pluralism, where politicians often held several posts simultaneously, Hutchinson stands out as one of the worst of the lot. As early as 1765, John Adams took note of it all and remarked, "Is not this amazing ascendancy of one Family, sufficient on which to erect a Tyranny? Is it not enough to excite Jealousies among the People?"[6]

Despite the inordinate leverage Hutchinson and his friends could exercise, their machine had a fatal flaw. In the final reckoning, success, even survival, depended on their ability to shape policy being made by distant authorities — king, ministry, and Parliament. When those agencies acted foolishly, or did not act at all, Hutchinson and his cohorts reaped the whirlwind. To be fair, it must be said that some of the policies shaped in London that led to the Revolution were opposed by Hutchinson.[7] Nevertheless, once they were set in motion, Hutchinson, a firm believer in prerogative and Parliament, could do nothing but dutifully take his place on deck as others conned the ship.

Wealth, lineage, and education — these were traits shared by Hutchinson and Hancock. They had others, too. They were both consummate actors and politicians, but they had learned to play for different audiences. Hutchinson had the misfortune of being part of a minority troupe, whose power and influence were waning fast in the face of repeated assaults by the "mob." Hancock, on the other hand, was a patron of the mob and was aware of their desires and needs. The future belonged to him because he held the key to success in this rapidly changing political situation — flexibility, or, as his enemies were wont to say, less kindly, vacillation. In contrast, Hutchinson was as much a prisoner of ideology as was his opponent Sam Adams. Both in their own ways were resolutely inflexible and, even worse in Hutchinson's case, insensitive. As long as the *Zeitgeist* was consonant with their own beliefs, they were secure, but when the former changed and the latter remained static, they were quickly passed by.

Hancock's fortune was on the rise. The town loved him and regaled him with its honors; Hutchinson got nothing but venomous attacks. It is small wonder, then, that in the month following the Massacre, the governor was filled with foreboding, pessimism, and despair. A spirit of gloom hung over him and the diminishing numbers around him.

For Hancock the reverse was true. He was confident, optimistic, and animated. Business difficulties disturbed him little;

the triumphs in politics more than compensated for those reverses. He was an ambitious man ready to move on and advance farther.

There is little doubt that Hutchinson considered Hancock a vain young man of little principle and few brains. The dislike was reciprocated but with a slight difference. Hancock scorned Hutchinson not only for what he was, a pluralist and cunning politician, but also for what he represented. For a man as ambitious and proud as Hancock, it was irksome to realize that the best offices and highest distinctions in the province were reserved for ministerial sycophants or relatives of Hutchinson. As he had shown again and again in his dealings with British merchants, Hancock would not be treated as an inferior. He became angry and contentious when people did not hold him in the same high esteem that he held himself. Yet this was the situation in Massachusetts, for no matter what his status might be in the province he could never be anything but a provincial, which, in the eyes of the ministry, meant being inferior. True, Hutchinson had succeeded, but at what cost? And now for Hancock to advance he would have to place himself at the disposal of a man for whom he had little regard. He had already been rejected as a councilor. It was clear that the royal government held the plums, and if he was to have one, he would have to accept it on their terms.[8]

The Massacre aftershock continued to be felt through the town. On March 12, Adams, Thomas Cushing, and Josiah Quincy were appointed by the town to be a committee charged with writing to several friends in England, "acquainting them with the circumstances & Facts relative to the late horrid Massacre, and asking the continuance of their good services in behalf of this Town and Province."[9] The result was an emotionally charged and highly inaccurate rendering that presented the soldiers as bloodthirsty miscreants and murderers. In his private correspondence with Thomas Pownall, Samuel Cooper corroborated the story of the "Horrors of the Bloody Massacre . . ."[10] Later that month, a more official account was written by a committee headed by James Bowdoin. This piece of propaganda found its way into pamphlet form and was widely circulated. It, too, depicted Hutchinson and the soldiers as men whose hands were dripping with the blood of innocent victims.[11]

The situation in Boston had grown so bad that even Hutchinson, who had for so long prided himself on his political astuteness and ability to manipulate, felt he was losing control. The town meetings, he grumbled, were being packed with 3000 to 4000 people, when there were only 1500 legitimate voters in the town. The demagogues (Adams and his colleagues) held such complete sway that it was impossible for any dissenting opinion to be heard. Boston, in his judgment, had gone mad.[12]

In the midst of the Massacre turmoil, Hutchinson was confronted with another disagreeable problem, one that had been left to him by Bernard. The issue was the meeting place for the General Court. Believing the baleful influence of the town was in part responsible for the Court's obstreperous behavior, Bernard, as already noted, had moved the meeting place to Cambridge. Now, in March, the Court was once more due to come to session, and Hutchinson had to decide where to convene it. He, too, thought Boston ought to be avoided, so on March 15, on the governor's order, the Court met at Harvard College.[13]

It took a week for the representatives to gather. In the intervening days Hancock was re-elected selectman, but as soon as the Court convened it was obvious that the business in Cambridge would overshadow Boston's; so, although he retained his seat, he spent most of his time during the months of March and April at the Court.[14] Hancock sat in the "new Chapel" along with the other House members, and the Council held its deliberations in the library. The Harvard authorities were less than pleased at this legislative invasion of academia, but the students thought it was fun and enjoyed being spectators at this grand political game.[15]

After some polite formalities, the House got off to its usual bad start. This began when the House committee made the traditional visit to His Excellency, informing him that a quorum was present and ready to do business. Four of the five committee members, Hancock and Adams included, were men who had previously been negatived as Council members. That small affront, which helped indicate the direction the House was taking, was followed by the election of Thomas Cushing of Boston as speaker.[16]

Once organized, the House members rolled out their legal and political artillery and fired a barrage on the governor's decision to convene them away from Boston. They charged that Hutchinson's actions were peremptory and illegal, denying them their rights as "Men and Citizens," and violating the province charter and British constitution. For the next two years, these charges, along with the governor's responses, buttressed by innumerable historical and legal citations, echoed back and forth across the campus and the province. In all, the House and the governor exchanged ten major papers on the issue.[17]

Hutchinson argued that he was bound by the king's instructions to remove the Court. When a House committee led by Hancock asked to see these instructions, he refused to show them. That gave rise to suspicions that he might well be acting not on His Majesty's orders, but on his own authority, in secret concert with the ministers as they sought to weaken the House. That suspicion was not without some basis, for, in fact, Hutchinson had never been explicitly told to move the Court; rather, it was suggested to him by Lord Hillsborough as an option he might consider. It was Hutchinson who made the actual decision, and this now placed him in the position of deceiving the House, intentionally or not. In any case, the issue of who ordered the removal became less important as the nub of the question became clear: Could anyone other than the House appoint its meeting place?[18]

For two weeks the House debated nothing but this matter. Hutchinson waited; he knew that in this case time was his ally. As the days wore on, regular business, most of it petitions from constituents, went unattended. Finally, the pressure to get on to other matters became irresistible, and for a time the members were forced to set aside the issue and get on with ordinary business.

No one could have agreed more about the inconvenience of meeting in Cambridge than Hancock. His business was suffering and town obligations were going unattended while he kept temporary quarters in Cambridge, away from the comforts of the hill. In April his friend Cushing took ill and had to leave. Hancock's popularity made him the natural choice as speaker pro tem. Unfortunately, he was not Hutchinson's choice, and the governor promptly vetoed the selection. Both Bernard and Hutchinson had now denied Hancock advancement.[19]

The House adjourned in April to prepare for the spring elections. Boston quickly showed its defiance by re-electing the rejected Hancock with a near-unanimous vote, 511 out of 513.[20] Anyone else would have been jubilant; Hancock, though, was in anguish. Of the two votes he did not get, one was his own, but the other came from a genuine critic, who apparently had made some public utterances reflecting on Hancock's character. Hancock was so accustomed to adulation from his fellow townsmen that he found even the mildest stricture impossible to tolerate. Childishly, he announced that he was resigning. Sam Adams was stunned. The loss of Hancock would be a devastating blow. Luckily, he knew what lever to press, and in a masterly letter he soothed Hancock's wounded ego.

> Your Resolution yesterday to resign your seat gave me very great Uneasiness. I could not think you had sufficient Ground to deprive the Town of one who I have a Right to say is a most valueable Member, since you had within three of the unanimous Suffrages of your Fellow Citizens & one of the negative Votes was your own. You say you have been spoken ill of? What then? Can you think that while you are a good Man that *all* will speak well of you —— If you knew the person who has defamd you nothing is more likely than that you would justly value your self upon *that mans* Censure as being the highest Applause. Those who were fond of continuing Mr. Otis on the Seat, were I dare say to a Man among your warmest friends: Will you then add to their Disappointment by a Resignation, merely because one contemptible person, who perhaps was hired for the purpose, has blessed you with his *reviling* — Need I add more than to intreat it as a favor that you would alter your Design.[21]

Adams' salve worked. Hancock stayed.

After the election of representatives to the General Court, it was customary in Boston for a committee to draft the town's instructions to these gentlemen. On May 8, a committee of five was appointed for this purpose, and one week later they laid their draft before the town meeting, where it was approved unanimously. Josiah Quincy was the principal author, but not even his eloquence and wealth of legal knowledge could hide the basic stridency of this document.[22] More than half of it was taken up with the question of the removal of the Court, a grievance for which the representatives were told to seek redress with "all proper and spirited methods." Quincy put forth a formidable argument against the Tory view that the king's prerogative allowed him to move the Court at pleasure. Quincy asserted that prerogative was limited by tradition, law, and usage, and that in the case at point the General Court was the best judge of these: ". . . we always expect to defend our own rights & libertys so we are unalterably fixed to Judge *for ourselves* of their real existence, agreeable to law." There was, according to Quincy, no "authority upon earth to determine limit or assertain all or any of our constitutional or charter, natural or civil political or sacred Rights liberties and privileges or immunities." Quincy suggested that anyone who thought otherwise was harkening back to Divine Right, which he dismissed as "mistical Jargon . . ."

Quincy did not go so far as to deny completely royal prerogative. He admitted that it could be valid under certain circumstances. He then laid out those circumstances:

> . . . all prerogatives must be for the advantage and good of the people . . .
> The King . . . hath a prerogative in all things that are not injurious to the subject, *in them all* it must be remembered, that the *Kings prerogative stretcheth* not to the doing of any wrong. And finally the best definition of the *prerogative*, which our law books afford is "that discretionary power of acting for the *public good* where the positive laws are silent and if this discretionary power be abused to the publick detriment, such *prerogative* is exerted in an unconstitutional manner."

Was this the situation in Massachusetts?

> Now the clear law laid down (to the spirit of which we do order you punctually to adhere) proves beyond a cavil, that if the late removal of our General Court was not against plain provincial law, yet that such removal is not only unwarrant-

able by the principles of Crown Law, but is directly repugnant
to the fundimental institutions even of prerogative law — For
will any one be so weak or wicked; nay even a Crown lawyer
for his stipend or pension have the front publicly to maintain,
that the late alteration of the Seat of our General Assembly is
"for the advantage and good of the people," or "for the necessary support of society," or that this assumed "prerogative
stretcheth not to any wrong."

Now if all this and much more, is not maintained, then
waving our provincial law relative to the seat of government,
we with good authority say, that the holding the General
Court, from its antient and proper station, is unwarrantable
unconstitutional illegal and oppressive.

Quincy's instructions were highly dangerous, for what he had
done was to take a specific issue (removal of the Court), on
which nearly everyone agreed, and from that derive a doctrine
(limitation of prerogative) whose implications were yet unex-
plored and on which many people might not agree. Very few
people, Hancock included, grasped the dimensions of the issue.
Even though he dismissed the document as a "piece of rant,"
Hutchinson, who had more reason to worry than anyone else,
probably understood the instructions better than those who
received them.[23]

On May 30 the new House, feisty as ever, convened in Cambridge. The Boston instructions set the tone, and soon the House
and the governor were exchanging position papers. On August 3
Hancock delivered to His Excellency a lengthy rebuttal to
assertions of prerogative power. The paper had the mark of
Sam Adams, and, like the instructions, it laid open to question
some fundamental tenets.

Among other things, Adams stated:

> We utterly deny that the Attourny & Solicitor General have
> any Authority or Jurisdiction over us; any Right to decide
> Questions in Controversy between the several Branches of the
> Legislature here; Nor do we concede that even his Majesty in
> Council has any Constitutional Authority to decide such Ques-
> tions, or any other Controversy whatever that arises in this
> Province, excepting only such matters as are reserved in the
> Charter . . .
>
> This House has the same inherent Rights in this Province as
> the House of Commons has in Great Britain.[24]

At this point, Hutchinson would have done well to soften the rhetoric, but, instead, he made a tactical blunder by answering the House's constitutional arguments with some of his own. Both sides now had abandoned the practical matter of whether the meeting place was convenient; they had taken off into the realm of constitutional philosophy. The new game was being played for much higher stakes than the location of a legislature: it was now a question of sovereignty.[25]

Hutchinson prorogued the Court, leaving the issue unresolved. It met again in September, with the same results, and then again in April 1771. In the spring session, the controversy took a slight twist. As of March, Hutchinson had received his official appointment as governor and, with it, a salary paid directly from London. Such a grant was unprecedented. In the past, the governor had always been dependent on an appropriation from the General Court, which gave the legislature a useful weapon in times of political differences. Under the new arrangement, the governor would enjoy greater independence.[26]

On March 5, 1770, the very day that saw the bloody work on King Street, a less sanguinary event had taken place in Parliament: Frederick Lord North moved for the repeal of the Townshend Acts. On April 12, Parliament agreed. However, lest the Americans interpret the repeal as a retreat on principle, North insisted that the tax on tea remain, arguing that "the properest time to exert the right of taxation is when the right is refused. The properest time for making resistance is when we are attacked."[27]

The news of the repeal spread quickly and shot another hole in the already leaky nonimportation agreement. Outside Boston, divisions emerged between those who wished to hold on to the bitter end and those who were more accommodating and saw no point in "disputing about a shadow which cannot be longer realized." In Boston, very little talk of that sort was heard, at least publicly, but the news that other towns were contemplating giving up sent a shudder through the Whig ranks.

Hancock hoped that the tea-duty repeal was only delayed and not refused. In the interim, though, he was determined to stick to the letter of the agreement. Thus, he was saddened to learn that in July the New York merchants voted to end nonimportation. The wall was breached, and soon Philadelphia, Newport, Albany, and other towns followed. If Hancock still intended to wait for the repeal on tea, his English correspondents told him not to bother. He should, according to them, abandon nonimportation and join with everyone else in going back to business as usual. This, he resolutely refused to do.[28]

At the town meeting of August 24, 1770, Hancock was elected moderator. Of all the offices the town had to offer, this was among the most prestigious. By accepting it he was joining a distinguished line of men, including James Otis and Thomas Cushing, who had held the post. As moderator he would help set the agenda, preside over the meetings, and appoint committees.[29]

In September, at a time when nonimportation appeared to be in a terminal state, Bostonians decided on a last-ditch effort to resuscitate the dying patient. Again they called on Hancock and sent him off on another tour to Philadelphia and New York. For six weeks he was on the road, delivering the Boston plea to hold on. It availed them nothing. He returned home in early October, bearing ill tidings. A few days later the Boston Merchants Association, which had been supporting nonimportation, capitulated and unanimously voted to revoke the agreement on all goods except tea.[30]

The fall of nonimportation came on the heels of a slight rupture in the General Court. When the members had reassembled in April, a disagreement arose over tactics. Otis had temporarily regained control of his senses and was re-elected a Boston representative. Adams, urgent as always, wanted the House to refuse flatly to do business outside Boston. Otis objected. He told the members that the governor had the right to convene the House on the "Houssatonick," if he so desired. He asserted that Hutchinson's calling them into session at Cambridge was inconvenient but not illegal.[31]

Despite the allegations by some that this was a radical shift for Otis and that he was, perhaps, courting the Tories, the truth is that it was quite in keeping with his deep-seated regard for the royal prerogative. In the past he had always backed away from extreme positions. His silence up to now may well have been the result of his ill health, or, like so many others, he may simply have been pressed forward by the sweep of events and was only now pausing to reflect. Added to this mixture of motives for the unpredictable Otis was his strong personal dislike of Adams. He abhorred his tactics and was jealous of his popularity.[32]

Hancock sided with Otis. Some thought he, too, was having an affair with the governor, a belief that was given some credence by Hancock's appointment in April 1772 as Colonel of the Cadets in Boston. Such a view must be tempered by the fact that Hancock had been a Cadet for six years and was unanimously elected colonel, leaving Hutchinson very little choice in the matter. The principal function of the Cadets was to provide an escort for the governor and Court on state occasions, but whatever the truth of the matter, Hancock's acceptance of the post did give some suspicion that he was flirting with Tories.[33] Why did Hancock seem to desert his old friends? There are two possibilities.

First, it is conceivable that he agreed fully with Otis on the legal issues and that once Jemmy took the lead he was willing to follow. This explanation suggests that Hancock was moved by philosophical considerations. After four years at Harvard and nearly a decade in Boston politics, he was unquestionably well acquainted with the issues. Indeed, politics was to Hancock's generation what religion was to the Puritans of John Winthrop's time: it permeated everything. Still, not everyone in Puritan Boston was a theologian, nor was everyone in Revolutionary Boston a political philosopher. Hancock was never an intellectual in the sense that the Adamses and Otis were. His mind lacked their power and depth. He wore his political ideology much as he did his religion, as a cloak; it was at least superficially adequate. He was satisfied to leave the grand political issues to others while he dealt on a lower, and for him more comfortable, level.

The second possibility is a simpler one. Hancock saw Adams' challenge to the royal prerogative as legally shaky but, more important, as inflammatory and potentially destructive. His goal was discrete and immediate: return of the Court to Boston. The only person who could satisfy that need was Hutchinson. Assaulting his authority and that of the king was hardly likely to achieve that end, since, on that basis, any concession would strike to the very heart of the constitutional relationship. A more political, if less philosophical, approach would be to petition on the grounds of "inconvenience" and let the other testy issues lie undisturbed. It seems likely, then, that Hancock's agreement with Otis was based not so much on principle as on expediency.

After some negotiation, Hancock, Adams, Cushing, and Otis managed to smooth over their differences, on the surface at least, so, on June 19, the House sent its petition for removal to Boston. The message was more conciliatory than usual; nevertheless, Hutchinson rejected it and shortly after prorogued the Court until April 8, 1772, thereby giving himself a much needed respite.[34]

Hancock came back to Boston a tired man. He was weary of the wrangling in Cambridge and distressed at the state of his much-neglected business. Palfrey, whom Hancock had sent to England in January, was reporting back low prices for American goods. Potash and naval stores, two items he was heavily committed to, were selling cheap. That news, coupled with the fact that Boston was glutted with goods selling at low market prices, meant Hancock had the worst of both worlds: he had trouble selling his wares in Boston and in London.[35]

That news from Palfrey was regrettable. So, too, was his assessment of the political scene in London. He reported that the ministry was so occupied with a dispute with Spain over the Falkland Islands that "the affairs of America are scarcely mentioned . . ." He saw no hope for removal of the tea duty.[36]

There was bad news in the personal ledger, as well. Ebenezer had gone broke, a victim of nonimportation and his own improvidence. He was hiding in Rhode Island to escape his creditors, and it was from there that he turned to John for help. Out of sentiment for his brother and a need to save the family name, John decided to help Ebenezer out of his muddle. By early 1771 matters were well enough in hand that Ebenezer could come out into the open again, but not before John had delivered some stern advice:

> . . . as you are now coming out afresh into Life my serious advice to you is that you would calmly Reflect on your former Imprudencies & Resolve to suit yourself like a Man determined carefully to avoid the Rocks you have heretofore Split upon; Conduct so as the Consequences may reflect Honour on yourself and your Connections And [?] you must think on what you are to depend for a Subsistence in Life. Devise some way for your future . . . Great you are Sensible is my Burthen & Loss in this matter of yours. I shall never throw it in your teeth and always conduct towards you as a brother.[37]

Hancock needed a rest. In August, he and Aunt Lydia went to Bridgewater to visit his mother and stepfather. This was the first time since he had left the manse in Lexington that he had stayed in a parsonage. The routine of the Perkins household and the presence of his mother must have filled his mind with fond memories of Braintree and Lexington. But Bridgewater was somehow different, and those delightful recollections of childhood failed to soften the stiffness he now felt toward his family. He was not close to his mother or sister, and Reverend Perkins was little more than an acquaintance. Beacon Hill was his real home and Aunt Lydia his mother.[38]

The stay was a short one, and Hancock was soon back in Boston. The vacation did little for his health. In October he told Hayley that he had not been well for months and was now confined completely to his house. A few weeks later he wrote again to say that his health was improving but business was slumping. Nothing seemed to be going right for him.[39] He even went so far as to tell Harrison that if matters did not change, he would probably not trade at all, and then remarked in passing that he planned to come to England in the spring. He never made the trip, but the suggestion was characteristic of his feelings toward Britain. As much as he might dispute with their leaders, he always loved the English and England.[40]

The winter of 1771–72 was a gray time for Hancock. In January and February, he continued to be ill and missed most of the selectmen's meetings. His health was hardly improved by the melancholy news that, on February 3, his brig *Lydia* was driven ashore at Nantasket and declared a total loss.[41]

Despite the somber side of life, he did keep his hand in town activities. His principal activity was serving on a committee to select a Massacre Day orator. The town intended to honor one of its citizens by calling on him to deliver a speech in commemoration of that horrible day. The anniversary had become a town holiday, a chance to rally the populace in an antigovernment demonstration. Hancock's choice for 1772 was Dr. Joseph Warren, who obligingly delivered a stirring memorial.[42]

While keeping a relatively low public profile in private Hancock began actively to explore new political opportunities. He was not altogether happy with Sam Adams' leadership. Adams was contentious, uncompromising, and overbearing, and at times he simply went too far. Hancock shared his misgivings over Adams with his friend Cushing. Cushing apparently agreed, and, although the evidence is not certain, it seems likely that in late winter, as the April session drew near, Hancock and Cushing laid plans to outmaneuver the old master. No one in the town could ever keep a secret, and soon even the governor was clucking over this split in the opposition.[43]

Sensing that there might be a chance here for advantage, Hutchinson signaled to Hancock that "upon a change of sentiments . . . everything past would be entirely forgotten, and it would be a pleasure to the governor to consent to his election to the council . . ." Rather than dismissing this as the bribe that it was, Hancock calmly replied that it was not his intention to remain in politics at all. He intended, he said, to return to business. Understanding Hancock's addiction to politics better than he did himself, Hutchinson accepted the explanation but hardly believed it.[44] What followed was a wistful dalliance between the two, beginning with Hancock's appointment as Colonel of the Cadets in 1772. Later, Hancock's enemies would charge that he had been taken in by Hutchinson's wiles. That explanation gives too much credit to the governor and too little to Hancock. Neither man was a political virgin, and it is hard to make a case that one was being exploited more than the other. Each had his good reasons for playing to the other.

Hutchinson, of course, is the easier to divine. He wanted to do anything possible to widen the gap in the Whig ranks. Hancock, on the other hand, is a bit more complicated. Personality was certainly part of the problem, but a more critical element could well be that, in negotiating with the governor, Hancock saw himself in the role of peacemaker. Indeed, his popularity was so high that he was probably the only Whig who could get close to the governor without running the risk of destroying himself.

On April 8, 1772, the General Court gathered in Cambridge. As soon as the gentlemen were seated, Hancock rose to offer a motion that the House "pray [Hutchinson] that in Consideration of the many Inconveniences that attend the sitting of the Court at Cambridge he would be pleased to remove it [to] . . . Boston." "Inconveniences" was the key word, for by petitioning on those grounds Hancock was leaving the prerogative intact. On this basis the governor would have no grounds for objection and could consent to the petition without compromising principle. Hancock could then claim to have been the architect of conciliation.[45]

It was not to be that easy. Hancock had underestimated Adams. The old master was quick to react; perhaps he knew in advance what was going to happen. At any rate, Adams marshaled his forces and sent the motion down to defeat. Next came the announcement that Thomas Cushing was ill and would be unable to take the chair as speaker. Not even his flirtation with the governor nor the defeat of his motion could erode Hancock's position, and he was elected unanimously speaker pro tem. The governor gave his approbation and the session went forward, ending its business on April 25. Except for the opening moments, it was an extraordinarily dull three weeks.[46]

In May the town elections were held. Boston turned in some interesting results. There was a much larger turnout than usual, and of the four men elected to the General Court — Cushing, Hancock, Adams, and William Phillips — Hancock, the man who had stood for compromise, garnered the second largest number of votes, and Cushing, his friend and ally, came in first. Sam Adams was no longer everyone's idol, and the machine was experiencing some difficulty delivering the votes. Perhaps people were tired of controversy, felt that they had accomplished as much as was possible, and were therefore eager to resolve differences without endless wrangling. If that was the case, then Cushing and Hancock were the men to lead them.[47]

A few days before the new Court convened, Cushing and Hancock paid a visit to the governor. They asked him on what terms he would allow the Court to return to Boston. Hutchinson described his response to his friend Pownall: "I let them know that if there was any thing in their address or message which tended to a denial of the king's authority to give instructions to the governor, I would not consent to it."[48] Not wishing to exclude the possibility of accommodation, though, he added quickly that, understanding the temper of the times, he was willing to overlook any "frivolous assertion" of the House.

The governor was pleased when his visitors indicated that they were willing to go along. Their biggest misgiving was Sam Adams. They told Hutchinson that Adams would do everything he could to sabotage an arrangement that did not provide a clear-cut victory for the opposition. Hutchinson nodded and warned them about the man's "art and insidiousness."[49]

On May 27, the Court convened once more in Cambridge. Cushing, fully recovered from his illness, was returned to the speaker's chair. Next came the choice of councilors. The House again elected Hancock as one. Expecting to draw him closer in, Hutchinson, in a reversal of policy, assented to the choice. True to his word, Hancock declined. He was not withdrawing from politics; rather he realized that it would test even his popularity to accept so obvious a favor from His Excellency. Besides, he enjoyed giving Hutchinson's nose a slight tweak; that was always a sure way to please the Boston Whigs.[50]

On May 29, the House sent its first remonstrance of the session against meeting in Cambridge. It was relatively brief and devoid of some of the rhetoric of past messages. The governor's response also had a tone of moderation about it:

> I agree with you that the Powers vested in me by Charter are to be exercised for the Good of the People, and I have made this the great Object of my Administration. I wish to avoid every Thing which shall appear to you to be grievous; and

although I cannot agree with you that unless there be a Necessity of holding the Court in some other Place than the Town
of Boston it must therefore be a Grievance to remove it from
thence: yet I will take the subject Matter of your message into
consideration.[51]

Things went well. After some brief sparring, on June 13 the
governor sent a message to the House: "It is his Excellency's
Pleasure that the Great and General Court or Assembly be Ad-
jour'd till Tuesday next at Ten the Clock in the Forenoon then
to meet at the Court House in Boston."[52]

Two years of acrimony over this issue were ended. Just how
good an accommodation had been reached is testified to by the
fact that both sides celebrated the return as a victory. Hutchinson believed he had successfully upheld the prerogative and
wooed some Whigs. His opponents rejoiced because they were
back in Boston.

For Hancock the victory was especially sweet. He had been
instrumental in undoing a knot that Adams had helped tie. For
the moment, at least, he saw himself as the great reconciler. He
could speak with both sides. He had not been "bought off" by
Hutchinson; he was moved by a greater prize than mere spoils.

Chapter 9

Tea Party

HANCOCK LOVED being the public man. Despite the demands it made on him, and his oft-repeated threats to withdraw, he was like a moth ever drawn to the flame. As he grew more famous, he was likely to do things with the dramatic flair that became his life style and reputation.

The Reverend Mr. Samuel Cooper had never taken a vow of poverty, nor had any member of his congregation. Indeed, cynics might say there was far more wealth than piety in the church. In February 1772, Hancock made a suggestion that was in keeping with the church's prosperity. He moved that the congregation build a new church, and, to prove his support, he offered a gift of £1000 toward the effort. In addition, he pledged "a mahogany pulpit, with its full furniture, a mahogany deacon's seat and the communion table . . ." It took less than a week for the full parish to agree, leaving for the moment only one question: Where would the new church be located?[1]

James Bowdoin, a fellow Whig and Brattle Square member, came forward and offered a plot of land he owned on Tremont Street. Hancock, apparently a bit put out that someone should compete with his philanthropy, opposed moving the church and thought that the old ought to be torn down and the new erected in its place. For nearly a month the issue went unresolved. Hancock's political clout and munificence (Bowdoin only offered £200) made the outcome inevitable. Although he said very little publicly, his position was well known, and, rather than risk offending his well-known ego and losing the money, the congregation wisely decided to erect the new on the foundation of the old.[2]

They planned to spend between £7000 and £8000 for "as grand a house as our native material will admit of."[3] To design their church they relied on John Singleton Copley.[4] Boston had no professional architects, so it was not uncommon to find any person skilled at drawing involved in designing buildings.

Copley submitted his plans in June. They were elegant and grand but, alas, far beyond the means of the church. It was agreed that, though everyone admired Copley's work, no one could afford it. The congregation set the design aside and, in its place, substituted a simpler and less expensive one. The actual construction took a little over a year, but finally, on July 25, 1773, Aunt Lydia and John, along with the rest of the congregation, took their places in the new meeting house to hear Cooper deliver the inaugural sermon.[5]

The church was grateful to Hancock for his generosity, and so, too, was the town, for a gift of a different sort — a fire engine. In the eighteenth century, Boston had more fires than all the other towns of America combined. Narrow streets, wooden buildings, and the ever-present chimney sparks made the cry "Fire" an all too familiar sound in the town.[6] As one of Boston's largest real estate holders, and one who had suffered his share of fire loss, Hancock had more than a passing interest in fire protection.

To help reduce the danger, alleviate his own distress, and perform a public service, he imported a fire engine for the town. He presented it at the May town meeting. The assembly voted their thanks for this "fresh mark of his Regard for the safety and welfare of the Town . . ." They allowed him the honor of appointing the master of the engine and then voted to keep it "at or near Hancock's Wharf and in case of Fire, the Estate of the Donor shall have the preference of its service." Not long after that, the selectmen ordered that the engine be christened "Hancock" and that name was emblazoned on its side.[7]

As the leading patron of the church and of the town, Hancock was much admired. Neither role, however, provided much in the way of the ceremony and pomp that he seemed to relish. For the church such fuss would have smacked of papist behavior, and for the town it would have been a violation of Whig simplicity. One role, though, for which it was approved, indeed even expected, was Hancock's position as Colonel of the Cadets. Here, pageantry was part of the business. Perhaps it was the memory of those resplendent and glamorous officers who were often engaged with Uncle Thomas that led him down this path. Whether it was that or just fanciful romanticism, he found himself caught between the Scylla of antimilitary Whig ideology and the Charybdis of war's romantic image. He drifted toward the latter.

He relished the title "Colonel," and in much of his correspondence and conversation it soon replaced "Mister." He took his job quite seriously. In the weeks following his election, he held several meetings at the company's favorite rendezvous, the Bunch of Grapes Tavern down on King Street, just below the State House. Despite the ambience of the meeting place, Hancock was determined to make the company into something more than a genteel club dedicated to good times and quaffing spirits.

One of his first tasks was to draw together a manual of arms for his men. It was a simple copy of many that were in existence.[8] Next, he approached Colonel Dalrymple to ask if he would lend one of his sergeants to drill the company. Sergeant Harris, who proved to be a very popular drillmaster, was sent over from one of the regiments.[9] If his men were to march like soldiers, they needed to look like soldiers, so the next item on Hancock's list was proper uniforms. The Cadets adopted a uniform worthy of His Majesty's best: a scarlet coat with buff lapels and undercloth, white gaiters with black bottoms, and a cocked beaver hat with a large cockade secured by a golden tie to a gilt button.[10] As a final touch Hancock advertised for fifers who "are masters of musick, and are inclined to engage with the Company . . ."[11]

In the summer the company drilled at dawn on every Wednesday down on the Common. During the cooler seasons it met twice a month in Faneuil Hall. If anyone missed a drill, he was fined. This routine was quite unlike the more casual approach usually found in militia units. Given the makeup of the company — eighty men, of whom at least half were Sons — there was probably as much politicking as marching; nevertheless, Colonel Hancock drilled and trained his men to the point where most people agreed they made a very military appearance.[12]

Ever since the return of the Court to Boston, political tensions had eased somewhat. There were continuing protests over the governor's salary, and rumors were beginning to spread that a similar arrangement was about to be made for judges, but for the time being passions were restrained.

During late July and August of 1772, Hancock found time to take a pleasure trip. He was fond of traveling, especially when he had such convivial companions. He was off on a voyage to Maine in the *Providence Packet,* which he and his friends had chartered for the sail.[13] Accompanying him were Samuel Cooper and his old friend from the Philadelphia trip, Tom Brattle. Also along were three lesser-known gentlemen, Tart Hubbard, Nicholas Bowes, and Samuel Calef. The seventh and perhaps most glittering member of the expedition was Dr. John Winthrop, Harvard professor and one of America's best scientists. He and Hancock were acquainted from the latter's student days, when the professor was teaching "Mathematicks and natural philosophy." They renewed their friendship during Hancock's long stays with the Court at Cambridge.[14]

A summer sail down east can be a delightful experience, and for nearly a month this "Party of Pleasure" sailed along the coast, from Boston around Cape Ann and up past the Isle of Shoals toward the Kennebec, where they probably landed so that Hancock could visit some of his property. The days and evenings were filled with talk of politics, religion, and science. With Hancock along, there can be little doubt that they traveled in comfort; servants were on board, along with a fine selection of food and spirits.

By the 22nd, the group was back in Boston in time to hear distressing news. For nearly a year and a half, ever since he had been appointed governor, Hutchinson had been drawing a salary directly from London. Although everyone knew of the arrangement, it had never been confirmed officially. In July it was. The news sent the Whigs into action. The House made a stinging attack and then threw a personal jibe at the governor by refusing to make repairs on his official residence, using as the excuse the fact that the house was built as a "Residence of a Governor, whose whole Support was to be provided for by the Grants and Acts of the General Assembly . . ."[15] Since, according to the House, Hutchinson was not that man, the House was content to see his home deteriorate.

Foolishly, the ministry never allowed adequate time for the Whigs to recover from the jolt of the governor's salary before launching another new policy, equally obnoxious. In early fall it was confirmed that judges' salaries, like that of the governor, would henceforth be paid from London.[16]

In the cycle of crisis between 1763 and the Revolution, one thing stands out. After each major event, the enactment of the Stamp Act and Townshend duties, for example, there followed a similar pattern: public uproar, government retreat, and a period of calm. The intermission between events allowed enough time for the consequences to be partially muted and made it more difficult for the Whig propagandists to label the actions a conspiracy.

Now the case was otherwise. Removal of the General Court, Hutchinson's salary, and the judges' salary fell in rapid fire, stirring a debate about the fundamental nature of the empire that raised disturbing questions that were difficult to ignore. Had the events been more isolated, as indeed they were in the sixties, they might have been less vexing, but coming so close together, they amplified and distorted one another. It is at this point that Hancock and others truly began to lose hope, and with each succeeding day the future looked more grim and uncertain.

The first loud reaction to the judges' salary came at the Boston town meeting on October 28. After re-electing Hancock moderator, the meeting moved into a consideration of several petitions "relative to a Report that Stipends are affixed by order of the Crown, to the offices of the Judges of the Superior Court of Judicature." The meeting then dispatched a special committee to inquire of the governor if the rumor was true. Hutchinson, forgetting the biblical injunction about soft answers turning away wrath, refused to answer. That was sufficient in itself, and as soon as the committee reported back, the meeting dispatched a second group to His Excellency, this time asking him to convene the General Court in extraordinary session.[17] The governor viewed the request as more Boston ranting and rejected it, leading Sam Adams to move for the creation of a "Committee of Correspondence . . . to state the Rights of the Colonists and of this Province in particular, as Men as Christians, and as Subjects; to communicate and publish the same to the several Towns in this Province and to the World . . ."[18]

The committee, referred to by Hutchinson as the "foulest, subtlest, and most venomous serpent ever issued from the egg of sedition," was composed of twenty-one members, including Otis and Adams but not Hancock or Cushing.[19] Their absence has been seen by some as a result of the alleged ill feeling between those two and Adams, as well as a general distrust of what the committee was about.[20] Hancock himself said he was declining service because of business, which on closer examination turns out to be a not unreasonable excuse. Less than a week before the committee was established, he had taken out a very large loan, £1500. He obviously had some cash problems and may well have felt that he had to spend more time on his long-neglected business affairs.[21]

Still another reason was suggested by Samuel Cooper. According to him, Hancock agreed with the principle but held back because he feared that if Boston stepped forward, she would find herself alone. His instincts told him the other towns were not yet ready. In that he was wrong.[22]

The committee took nearly three weeks to write its first report. On November 20, the town meeting convened again, with Hancock as moderator. The only item on the warrant was the report.

It was divided into three sections:

> First, a State of the Rights of the Colonists and of this Province in particular
>
> Secondly, A list of the Infringements, and Violations of those Rights
>
> Thirdly, A Letter of Correspondence with the —— other Towns

The entire text ran to nearly 7000 words, making this one of the longest committee reports in the history of the town.[23] It left very little unsaid. Underlying the document was a critical assumption: violations of constitutional rights ought to be resisted. Having stated their rights and enumerated their grievances, the town meeting ended its report with a letter that was intended for circulation among the provinces and towns, as well as abroad. The first sentence set the tone.

> Gentlemen We the Freeholders and other Inhabitants of *Boston* in Town Meeting duly Assembled according to Law, apprehending there is abundant to be alarmed at the plan of *Despotism*, which the enemies of our invaluable rights have concerted, is rapidly hastening to a completion, can no longer conceal our impatience under a constant, unremitted, uniform aim to enslave us, or confide in an Administration which threatens us with certain and inevitable destruction.[24]

The report was approved unanimously and sent off immediately to Edes and Gill, who were told to print up 600 copies. Even though Hancock had not served on the committee, his name, as moderator, appeared in bold type across the first page, larger than anyone else's. He may not have helped write the pamphlet, but outside Boston, anyone who saw it would never have known. He supported it wholeheartedly. Because he was moderator, representative, and selectman, the committee gave him two dozen copies to distribute.[25] Some of them quickly found their way to his London correspondents.

Within Massachusetts the pamphlet had a catalytic effect. On receiving it, towns met and debated their response. As Richard Brown puts it: "Now for the first time, under the impetus of the Boston committee a majority of Massachusetts towns met to consider and formulate their basic political beliefs." Despite numerous variations, in the end, according to Brown, they found a consensus in the belief that "sovereignty lay with the people organized in towns not Parliament or even the General court."[26]

With the Boston committee taking the lead, soon there were committees throughout the province. Intense political discussion on a scale rarely seen in any society began to take place.

By January 1773, when the General Court reconvened, the representatives were primed to do battle.

Up to now Hutchinson had not answered the question as to whether the judges were to receive their salaries directly from the crown. In order to flush him out, the Court voted a salary for justices, hoping to force them to reject it publicly because they were about to receive another.[27] After a few parries and thrusts from both sides, the governor responded, on February 4, that "His Majesty has been pleased to Order that Salaries shall be allowed to the Justices of the Superior Court . . ."[28] Instantly, a committee, chaired by Hancock, was charged to respond. Its report was incorporated in a House resolve, declaring that no "judge who has a due Regard to Justice or even to his own Character" would choose to serve under these circumstances.[29]

The usual acrimonious exchange ensued, with Hancock playing a leading role on the House side. By the time the session was over, Hutchinson was tired and depressed. He had tried to find solutions, but everywhere he turned he was confronted by "perverse men" who sought to destroy him. Little did he know that the worst was yet to come, for in late March Thomas Cushing received a package that would, once and for all, put an end to Hutchinson's career in Massachusetts.

The package had been sent from London by Benjamin Franklin, who was then acting as agent for the province. It contained thirteen purloined letters, all of them written in the late sixties and addressed to Thomas Whately, undersecretary of the treasury. Six of them came from Hutchinson; four from his brother-in-law Andrew Oliver; one from Charles Paxton, a customs officer; and another from Nathaniel Rogers, Hutchinson's nephew. The thirteenth letter was one sent to Hutchinson by Robert Auchmuty.[30]

Because they were intended as private correspondence, they were written in an informal and loose style and were full of frank political observations and recommendations. In Hutchinson's case, most of what he confided to Whately he had said publicly. He warned about the "licentiousness of . . . [the] Sons of Liberty."[31] He spoke of Parliament reacting to affairs in

America with "marks of resentment."[32] In the end, though, his most damaging comments were those having to do with American rights and liberties. He spoke of removing the government from "the hands of the populace . . . by degrees."[33] If the connection to the Mother Country was to continue, and he most certainly hoped that it would, then there must be "an abridgement of what are called English liberties."[34]

In sending the letters to Boston, Franklin asked that they be shown only to a select few and that they not be published. Whether he truly believed that, given so deadly a weapon, the Boston Whigs would refrain from using it is open to question. In Boston there never was any doubt — the letters had to be made public.[35]

Cushing first wrote to Franklin and asked him straight out if he would rescind his request not to publish. He refused.[36] In the interim, the letters were passed around, and their existence and content became the best-known secret in town. In May the General Court convened, with the Boston contingent — Cushing, Hancock, Adams, and Phillips — present as usual. Unlike the previous year, when Adams had apparently suffered some loss in popularity, this time all four were within five votes of one another.[37] In the face of new threats the Whigs were closing ranks.

When the House came to order on May 26, the representatives again elected Cushing speaker and Hancock a councilor. Even if Hutchinson approved the election, Hancock was unlikely to accept. The action was in the House and going up to the Council would have meant stepping off center stage. That was never Hancock's style. He declined the election and stood by for the fray.[38]

He and Adams were now working in close concert. According to a prearranged plan that had been made early in the session, Hancock rose from his seat and announced that, while he was strolling through the Common, "somebody" came up to him and gave him copies of what appeared to be the purloined letters. Not wanting to circulate anything that might be false, he asked for the formation of a committee to compare these errant letters with the originals to determine their authenticity.

He himself chaired the committee, and on the sixteenth they made their report.[39]

The letters were, according to the committee, authentic. The committee members then presented a series of resolves, quickly passed by the House, that, even in the heated spirit of the times, stand out for their anger and sharpness. According to them, Hutchinson and Oliver were working only for their own selfish interests. They were responsible for the introduction of troops and other heinous crimes. They were "justly chargeable with the great Corruption of Morals, and all the Confusion, Misery and Bloodshed which have been the natural Effects of this Introduction of Troops." The House concluded by calling for the removal of both men. At the same time, the letters went to the press.[40]

Following close in the wake of the excitement, a second committee on which Hancock was also serving delivered another blast at the judges. Mercifully for Hutchinson and his allies, the session finally came to an end on June 29, but not before it had made a wreck of the governor's career, sent the judges scampering for cover, and left the Whigs crowing over their triumph.

Although the House was adjourned, its work of keeping people politically aware went on under the aegis of its Committee of Correspondence. Like its counterpart in the town, the committee was fairly large, fifteen, and was charged with communicating with the assemblies of the other colonies.[41]

Not unexpectedly, the size of the committee made it unwieldy, and most of the actual work was done in a much smaller subcommittee, dominated by Cushing, Hancock, and Adams. At the last meeting before the House adjourned, Hancock laid before the full committee a letter he had received from Connecticut. Since all those present were preparing to return home within a day or two, they voted to turn over the continuing work of the committee to the three Boston men and William Heath of Roxbury.[42]

Through the summer and early fall of 1773, this small group met at least eight times. Most of their effort was spent collecting bits and pieces of information from the other colonies and abroad, trying to sense any changes in ministerial policies. None was forthcoming, and in late October the four men decided that it was time to communicate their feelings of anger and frustration to their fellow Americans.

The letter was approved unanimously by the House and bears the unmistakable imprint of Sam Adams. At first glance, it may have appeared to be somewhat less violent than some of the other messages being passed around; however, when it was read carefully, it was seen to contain some fearful portents, for toward the end was a hint of revolution.

> We are far from desiring that the Connection between Britain and America should be broken. *Esto perpetua*, is our ardent wish; but upon Terms only of Equal Liberty. If we cannot establish an Agreement upon these terms, let us leave it to another and wiser Generation. But it may be worth Consideration that the work is more likely to be well done, at a time when the Ideas of Liberty and its Importance are strong in Mens Minds. There is Danger that these Ideas will hereafter grow faint and languid. Our Posterity may be accustomed to bear the Yoke and being inured to Servility they may even bow the Shoulder to the Burden. It can never be expected that a people, however *numerous*, will form and execute a wise plan to perpetuate their Liberty, when they have lost the Spirit and feeling of it.[43]

The committee then closed its letter with "a fresh Instance of the temper and Design of the British Ministry . . ." The East India Company was shipping tea to America.

Hancock was in full agreement with the sentiments of the letter. The events of the past year had done much to drain his faith in the ability of the ministry to provide just government for Massachusetts. The salary issue and the revelation of Hutchinson's letters, followed by the ominous tea business, seemed to give credence to charges of corruption and conspiracy. His reservoir of hope and good will was evaporating, and, although he still had some misgivings about Adams' style, he was solidly in the Whig camp. Lest anyone doubt his devotion to the Whig cause, he even went so far, in his usual dramatic way, as to make a public display of his closeness to Adams by commissioning Copley to paint portraits of himself and Adams, which he then hung side by side in his great front parlor.[44]

In the fall of 1773, heavily engaged in politics though he was,

Hancock undertook another job, which, over time, was to cause him no end of grief. He was elected treasurer of Harvard College. The overseers made the choice out of patriotism and a desire to encourage one of the college's most generous alumni to be even more generous. Hancock could hardly refuse the honor, and in September he took charge of the college books and £15,449, 14s, 2p, the entire college treasury.[45]

On October 18, four bluff-bowed, broad-beamed lubberly merchantmen put the coast of England astern and began beating their way toward Boston. They were *Dartmouth, Eleanor, Beaver,* and *William,* all heavily laden with East India tea.[46]

The decision to send these vessels and their cargo of baneful herb to Boston arose out of an attempt to save the British East India Company from collapse.[47] Next to the Bank of England, the company was the largest and most powerful financial institution in the kingdom. In the early 1770s the company found itself saddled with a huge debt and warehouses bulging with unsold tea. Unless something was done soon, the company might well go bankrupt, an event that no ministry could tolerate and expect to stay in office. In their search for a way out of these straits, Parliament and the company directors hit on tea.

Tea was the sole item on which duties were still being collected after the revocation of the detested Townshend Acts, making it of great symbolic value to both the Whigs and the ministry. During the heyday of nonimportation, legal importation practically ceased, and even after 1770, the trade remained in a pitiful state. Americans, of course, did drink tea. Some of it was imported legally, but huge quantities came in via the illicit Dutch route. The smuggled tea was cheaper and more politically palatable. Under the circumstances it made sense for the company to make every attempt to regain the American market, empty its warehouses, and fill the coffers.

The scheme eventually worked out allowed the company to ship its tea directly to the colonies, where it would be sold by company-appointed consignees. To simplify matters and reduce American opposition, the company directors favored eliminating the Townshend duty. Lord North, though, stubborn as usual, balked at that suggestion and insisted that the duty must be kept. Even with the duty attached, the company, by marketing its tea through its own consignees, could actually sell the product for less than the illegal Dutch variety. Everyone was happy, and the whole matter sailed easily through Parliament, with very little opposition or discussion. North and his cohorts apparently believed that Americans preferred cheap tea to liberty.

The Tea Act alarmed Americans. Not only did it carry the threat of duties that would be earmarked for the salary of royal officers, but it also heralded a new fear, one of monopolies. Ordinarily, tea was imported into England, where it was wholesaled to British merchants. These merchants, in turn, sold the tea to their American correspondents, who then imported and marketed it on this side of the Atlantic. In its attempt to cut costs and undersell the smugglers, the company had eliminated all these middlemen and was being allowed to market directly through its own specially appointed consignees. If the marketing arrangement for tea was carried over to other commodities, as indeed it might be, then the government would have a strangle hold on trade. Monopolies might be arranged for exporters of any number of products, with the politically docile rewarded by being named consignees and the obstreperous put out of business. In Boston, the affair looked even more sinister when the names of the tea consignees were announced. There were five. Two of them were Thomas and Elisha Hutchinson, sons of the governor. A third was Richard Clarke, whose daughter was married to young Thomas. The remaining two were Edward Winslow and Benjamin Faneuil.

To Hancock, the act represented a double threat. Although tea was not one of his major imports, the possibility that the government was using this as the opening wedge to monopolize other trade worried him. His business was already in steady decline, and such a move could well ruin any hope for its recovery. Even more important were the political implications. Americans were being asked to finance the subversion of their own rights.

Shortly before noon on Wednesday, November 3, Hancock made his way down Beacon Hill to the Liberty Tree. By the time he arrived, hundreds of people were milling around, awaiting the arrival of the five consignees, who had been told to come to the elm to make a public resignation. When they failed to show up, the crowd became restless, and Will Molineux was sent to bring the Hutchinsons and the others down to the tree. Instead of waiting, the mob followed Molineux and marched to Clarke's store, where they suspected their quarry was hiding. When one of the consignees called out that they would have nothing to do with such an illegal gathering, the crowd turned mean, broke through the doors, and made a shambles of the store. Meantime, the five fled to an upstairs countingroom, where they barred the door and waited for the mob to tire and leave.[48]

So complete was Whig control in Boston that only one voice was raised in defense of the consignees. An anonymous writer circulated a piece entitled "Tradesmen's Protest," arguing that the only reason the merchants opposed the Tea Act was that they feared losing money. No one paid it much heed.[49]

In the midst of the turmoil, the selectmen received a petition for a town meeting. They happily consented, and on November 5 more than 400 men packed into Faneuil Hall. Hancock was again elected moderator. The meeting was more noisy and unruly than usual. Tempers were short, and when someone discovered several copies of the "Tradesmen's Protest," there was a general uproar and an angry call for the person who brought them in to stand and reveal himself.[50]

The meeting might have taken a nasty turn if Hancock had not wielded a swift and skillful gavel. He demanded order. When the noise died down he took a copy of the "Protest" and began to read it to the meeting. After that, he asked all the tradesmen present to separate themselves from the rest of the meeting and to move over to one side of the room. He then looked directly at them and asked "whether they acknowledge the said paper called, 'The Tradesmen's Protest?'" Only a complete fool would have said yes; to a man they all denounced the "Protest," declaring that it was "false scandalous and base . . ."[51]

Following the tradesmen's ordeal, the meeting returned to the debate over tea. To give at least the appearance of open discussion, Hancock asked if anyone present would like to speak in favor of the act. Silence was his answer.

Toward noon, the meeting decided on a temporary adjournment, but not before the members had passed a series of resolves, declaring, among other things, that anyone who supported the Tea Act was an "Enemy to America." Just before the meeting broke for lunch, a large delegation, headed by Hancock, was sent off to demand again that the consignees resign. They were to report back at three o'clock in the afternoon.[52]

Hancock and his committee made their rounds, but the only ones they found at home were Faneuil and Clarke. Winslow was not available, and the Hutchinson brothers, sensing trouble, had slipped out of town and were at the family estate in Milton. Those they could find had the question laid squarely before them. The committee wanted an immediate answer but, instead, got delay and evasion. Faneuil and Clarke told the committee they could not make a reply until they had consulted with the Hutchinsons. That was far from being satisfactory, and as soon as the afternoon meeting heard that reply, they ordered another committee be sent for an answer. Clarke and Faneuil still dodged the issue and replied that they could not possibly resign until they knew more about their own situation. By unanimous vote the meeting declared this response unsatisfactory. At this point the meeting was adjourned again, but not before Hancock and five other gentlemen were directed to find the Hutchinsons and demand their resignation.

Although it was late in the afternoon, they did go to Elisha Hutchinson's home. There they were told by the servants that he was in Milton. Since it was too late in the day to ride out, they agreed to meet early in the morning and head for Milton. When they arrived there the next morning, they were not pleased to learn that they had just missed the Hutchinsons, father and son, who had left to return to Boston. Somewhat ruffled and suspicious, the committee followed them back and went again to the house. This time they were told that Elisha had been at home but had left early in the morning to return to Milton. Now exasperated, the committee trooped over to the governor's residence and read to Hutchinson the town's request. He told them to wait, that he would have an answer for them in fifteen minutes. He returned and handed them a letter from his son Thomas, which repeated the answer they had gotten from the others.

When this was put before the full meeting, it was unanimously voted that these responses from the consignees were "*Daringly Affrontive* to the Town." The Committee of Correspondence was directed to communicate all these transactions to the towns of the province. In customary fashion the town meeting then voted to give their thanks to Hancock "for the dispatch he has given to the Business thereof." Much to everyone's surprise, Hancock objected to the motion. No man, he said, ought to be thanked for doing his duty. The meeting agreed. Henceforth "a Vote of Thanks should be only given upon very special and signal services performed for the Publick." It was an unusual piece of humility and won him much admiration.

For the next few days the town was quiet. By November 11, the governor had grown a bit nervous, and, as a precautionary move, he asked Hancock to hold his Cadets ready. It is difficult to believe that Hutchinson was serious. He knew as well as everyone else that nearly the entire company, from the colonel down to the lowliest private, was a rabid Whig. Not surprisingly, Hancock simply ignored the order — a neat piece of insubordination that, under the circumstances, the governor was incapable of dealing with.[53] However, by alerting the Cadets and then having them fail to muster, Hutchinson covered himself in case violence did break out. He could always say that he had done his duty but the militia failed in theirs, thereby leaving open the possibility of using Regulars.

Boston was ready for something to happen. On Wednesday, the 17th, Hancock's brig *Hayley* arrived from London. As soon as she was secure at the wharf, Captain Scott hurried ashore and went up the hill to report the latest intelligence. His news was alarming. According to him, at any moment the tea ships were due in Boston. Quickly the news spread through the town, and the next morning the town meeting assembled again at Faneuil Hall. Once more they asked the consignees to resign. The answer was the same.[54]

On Sunday morning, November 28, the crisis became acute when *Dartmouth* made her way past Boston Light and into the harbor. The selectmen met at noon, hoping that the consignees would come before them and resign. Nothing happened. All through the night the Whig presses ran, churning out endless handbills calling on the townspeople to rally at Faneuil Hall. On Monday morning, to the pealing of bells, hundreds of Bostonians piled into the hall. The gathering was not a legally constituted town meeting. When the people asked Hancock to serve as moderator, he declined, explaining that he expected at any moment to be summoned by the governor. In his place they elected a local merchant, Jonathan Williams. Faneuil Hall was too small to accommodate the mass of people, so the meeting moved to the Old South Church, where hundreds still had to stand outside. The meeting demanded that the consignees resign and the tea be returned.[55]

On December 2, *Eleanor* joined *Dartmouth,* and on the 7th *Beaver* arrived. Poor *William* never made her rendezvous. She was washed up on Cape Cod, a total wreck. The three other vessels were eventually brought into the inner harbor and tied up at Griffin's Wharf. Although he never officially mustered his company, Hancock and a good many of his men volunteered for guard duty down at the wharf to ensure that none of the pernicious stuff came ashore. Meanwhile, the town waited.

To Hancock and the Whigs the solution to this impasse was simple — return the tea to England. Unfortunately, the situation was too complex to admit of so easy an answer. The familial ties of the consignees certainly did not help matters. The Hutchinsons knew their father would not desert them. At no other port in America where tea was sent was there such a tight bond between the consignees and the government. Without doubt, this knowledge made them bolder and less likely to give in. At the same time, the governor himself was encouraging them not to surrender to the mob's threats.

On top of this personal and political intrigue there was a legal entanglement. Technically, once a vessel entered a harbor she was obligated to pay all duties on her cargo within twenty days. If she failed to do so, the cargo could be seized by customs officers, landed, and sold to pay the debt. The question of what "entry" meant was never defined satisfactorily. In this instance it was taken to mean the moment a vessel came into the harbor.

According to that definition, *Dartmouth*'s time was up on December 17. If on that day the tea duty remained unpaid, the chests would be landed and sold. A governor less threatened and less personally involved might have looked for a way around the impending confrontation, but Thomas Hutchinson was not that person; and his obstinacy, confronted by Whig passions, guaranteed trouble.[56]

As days ticked off, passions in the town rose. The newspapers were full of articles with the usual cant, warning of tyranny, oppression, villainy, and other dangers. The fear of violence was so real that the consignees themselves left town, and the merchant John Andrew wrote, "Twould puzzle any person to purchase a pair of [p]isto[ls] in town as they are all bought up, with a full determination to repell force by force."[57] The selectmen went so far as to order Hancock, John Scollay, and Thomas Marshall "to inspect the Town Arms and call in those that are lent."[58]

On the 14th and 15th, Francis Rotch, acting for his father, the owner of *Dartmouth* and an old rival of Hancock's in the oil business, scurried about, trying to make some last-minute arrangements to get the ship out of Boston. It was hopeless.

Through it all, Hancock remained resolute. He had been present and active at every meeting, and on one occasion at least was heard to remark that "he was willing to spend his fortune and life itself in so good a cause." He knew that if the tea landed, then all was lost, Hutchinson would have his victory, the Whigs would be broken, and the Tories would be in the ascendency.

Thursday, December 16, was a typical New England early winter day, cold, raw, and rainy. But if the weather was common, the day's events were extraordinary. Thanks to the Committee of Correspondence and the wide circulation of newspapers, people throughout the province knew that *Dartmouth*'s time expired at midnight. At first light, groups of people began to make their way across the Neck in carriages, on horseback, or on foot. They were headed for the Old South, where, according to some estimates, more than 7000 people gathered, filling the church and crowding the street in front.

Since this was hardly an official town meeting, they decided to elect an out-of-towner to preside, symbolizing the fact that the concerns went beyond the confines of Boston. They elected Samuel Phillips Savage of Weston. Soon after Savage took his place at the pulpit, Rotch announced that *Dartmouth* would not leave. He was promptly told to go back to the governor and present his case again. Savage then adjourned the meeting until three.[59]

When Savage called the afternoon session to order, Rotch still had not been heard from. News was received that other towns had voted to ban tea, which prompted the meeting to recommend Committees of Inspection be appointed "to prevent this accursed tea" from being used. Sentiments were running strong when Sam Adams and Thomas Young rose to speak, followed by Josiah Quincy, who told the throng, "Now that the hand is at the plough . . . there must be no looking back."

At four-thirty, the meeting shouted their approval to a resolve that the tea must not land. Immediately, there was a move for adjournment, as some were obviously eager to move down to the wharf; but they were persuaded to remain until Rotch returned with the governor's final answer. At six, he came through the door. The look on his face told the story, and glumly he announced that Hutchinson was adamant.

It was dark now, and in the dim candlelight John Rowe was heard to ask "Who knows . . . how tea will mingle with salt water?" A cry went up: "A mob! A mob!" Order was quickly restored in time for Hancock to say "Let every man do what is right in his own eyes." Shortly afterward, Adams gave the signal for the "Indians" to appear when he announced that "this meeting can do nothing more to save the country."

What happened that night needs no retelling here. The "Mohawks" held a grand party, and the next morning windrows of tea were being swept ashore from Noddles Island to Nantasket. Hancock was not at the party, though he wholly approved of it and encouraged others to attend. Although he rejoiced at this blow for liberty, he was not so foolish as to believe that the government would stand idly by and let this night's work pass without notice. He awaited the new year with some trepidation of things to come.

Chapter 10

Hancock Leads the Rebellion

$\mathcal{B}$Y THE NEW YEAR nearly everyone in America's major towns knew of the happenings in Boston. In the first of his famous rides, Paul Revere, the "Patriot Express," galloped to New York and Philadelphia, and from those centers the news quickly spread.[1]

In Boston the Whigs rejoiced while Hutchinson and other friends of the king, stunned, fell into even greater despair. For his part, Hancock stayed fairly quiet. There was no doubt where he stood; still, he carefully hedged his comments in public and denied any direct involvement in the affair. For both personal and political reasons he had no desire to be portrayed as an instigator or perpetrator of a lawless deed that resulted in the destruction of private property. That was wise, for it was by no means clear what the reaction of the government would be, and a man in Hancock's position was all too vulnerable to attack, as the *Liberty* incident of only a few years before had shown.[2]

Aside from political considerations, which dictated his remaining at arm's length from the party, Hancock had another and equally compelling reason for keeping away — his health. Just a few days after the affair down on Griffith's Wharf, he was struck with what quickly developed into his worst attack of gout yet. For weeks he was so ill that he could barely leave his bed. He was unable to attend selectmen's meetings, rarely ventured outside, and left business matters in Palfrey's hands.[3]

His near-invisibility led some to believe that he was retreating. They even suggested that he had committed the greatest crime of all — importing tea and paying the duty on it. He was quick to refute that allegation, but rumors of his vacillation persisted.[4]

Perhaps it was with the motive of putting these rumors to rest that Hancock eagerly accepted the invitation to be the Massacre Day orator in 1774. At noon on March 5, Old South was packed; every pew was taken and the galleries were overflowing. Hancock, still feeling the effects of poor health and a bad winter, climbed the stairs to take his place at the great lofty pulpit. From there, he delivered one of the most memorable speeches in the history of Boston. For at least an hour he held the crowd with what was one of the most important speeches of his life.[5]

He began on a note of humility, telling his fellow townsmen that the business of the day "fill[s] me with an awe hitherto unknown . . ." He spoke of his love for Boston and its citizens and of his devotion to "righteous government . . . founded upon the principles of reason and justice . . ." Pointedly, he asked, "Is the present system which the British administration have adopted for the government of the colonies a righteous government? Or is it tyranny?" His ready response, of course, was that the latter was true, as he went on to speak of the government's "mad pretension" to power.

Singling out the troops who were stationed in Boston, he described them as "unfeeling ruffians" who were sent over "to enforce obedience to acts of Parliament, which neither God nor man ever empowered them to make." Yet, according to Hancock, the troops did not stop at violating Bostonians' civil rights; they also sought:

> to deprive us of the enjoyment of our religious privileges, to vitiate our morals, and thereby render us deserving of destruction. Hence, the rude din of arms which broke in upon your solemn devotions in your temples, on that day set apart by God himself for his peculiar worship. Hence, impious oaths and blasphemies so often tortur'd your unaccustomed ear. Hence, all the arts which idleness and luxury could invent,

were used, to betray our youth of one sex into extravagance
and effeminacy, and of the other to infamy and ruin; and did
they not succeed but too well? Did not a reverence for religion
sensibly decay? Did not our infants almost learn to lisp out
curses before they knew their horrid import? Did not our
youth forget they were Americans and regardless of the admonition of the wise and aged servilely copy from their tyrants
those vices which finally must overthrow the empire of Great
Britain . . . ?"

Hancock went on to conjure up for his audience sanguinary
visions of that horrid night four years before, "when Satan with
his chosen hand open'd the sluices of New England blood, and
sacrilegiously polluted our land with the dead bodies of her
guiltless sons." At this point, the audience were in his hands.
He carried them along on a crest of emotion until they could
almost hear the shots, whiff the gunpowder, and see the bodies
writhing on the street.

If they had trouble remembering that gruesome night, Hancock directed them to look on one in their own company, Christopher Monk, who had been wounded in the Massacre:

> Observe his tottering knees which scarce sustain his wasted
> body, look on his haggard eyes, mark well the deathlike pale-
> ness of his fallen cheeks and tell me does not the sight plant
> daggers in your souls? Unhappy Monk! Cut off in the gay morn
> of manhood from all the joys which sweeten life, doom'd to
> drag on a pitiful existence without even a hope to taste the
> pleasure of returning health.

Seizing the moment, some ingenious soul thought of taking up
a collection for poor Monk, and, as the basket passed from hand
to hand, there could hardly have been a dry eye in the house.

From a remembrance of the past, Hancock brought his listeners to the present and on to the future. "L[et] our misfortunes," he told them, "teach posterity to guard against such
evils for the future." He congratulated his fellow citizens on
their wariness and opposition to the administration schemes.
The Tea Party was a glorious moment. But "restless malice, and
disappointed ambition will still suggest new measures to our
inveterate *enemies*. Therefore let us also be ready to take the

field whenever danger calls, let us be united and strengthen the hands of each other, by promoting a general union among us." To accomplish this goal Hancock urged continued support of the Committees of Correspondence. He then went a step further and became one of the first to endorse the calling of "a general Congress of Deputies from the several Houses of Assembly on the Continent . . . At such a Congress, a firm foundation may be laid for the security of our Rights and Liberties; a system may be formed for our common safety . . ."

He ended his peroration by reminding his listeners whence they came. They were the descendants of brave and honorable men. He exhorted them "by all that is honourable, by all that is sacred, not only that ye pray, but that you act; that if necessary, ye fight, and even die for the prosperity of our Jerusalem . . . Despise the glare of wealth. That people who pay greater respect to a wealthy villain, than to an honest upright man in poverty, almost desire to be enslaved."

Finally, in a flurry of patriotic and religious fervor, he called on them to honor their fellow patriots, especially his old friend Sam Adams. He was leading them to Armageddon to do battle for the Lord as he committed their "righteous cause to the great Lord of the universe."

Its eloquence almost tells us that Hancock did not write the speech alone. It was probably the product of collaboration among Cooper, Adams, Warren, and, of course, Hancock himself. This was hardly unusual; a good deal of the patriot propaganda came from joint efforts at late-night meetings, heavy with the odor of tobacco and smuggled Madeira. Hancock's oration was more than simply the sentiments of one man; he was making a statement in behalf of the entire community.[6]

The patriots could hardly have found a better spokesman. His spirit and delivery made Hancock the talk of Boston, and, in the public eye at least, signaled him as the leading Whig of Massachusetts. It was strictly an emotional pitch aimed at the groundlings. He spun no fine web of constitutional issues; rather, he appealed to his hearers' feelings, with his horrid visions and physical testimony of that dreadful night. It may well be true that had he tried to sail on a higher intellectual plane, his listeners would have known for certain that the script was prepared by another hand.

The applause had barely died down when Edes and Gill were thumping out copies. They soon discovered that they had something of a best-seller on their hands. Within a short time, it went through four local editions and was being reprinted in several other American towns, making it one of the best-known polemics of the pre-Revolutionary period. Although it was a committee project, other than a few in Boston no one else knew; so to most of the world the piece was entirely the work of John Hancock.[7]

Less than forty-eight hours after descending the stairs at Old South, Hancock was present at another public event of a quite different sort. After a long and painful "bilious disorder," Thomas Hutchinson's brother-in-law, Lieutenant Governor Andrew Oliver, died. He was to be buried on March 7, and for the occasion Hancock unexpectedly offered to turn out the Cadets.[8]

Adams was opposed and thought the late and unlamented Oliver ought to go straight to hell, with as little honor as possible. Hancock, on the other hand, maintained that the office, not the man, deserved the honor, so he agreed to muster his company. With the drummer tapping out a melancholy cadence, the procession made its way toward the burial ground. It was a nightmare. Fearing for his own life, Oliver's brother Peter, chief justice of the province, stayed home and mourned in private. A howling mob followed the casket through the streets, shouting taunts and insults. One of Hancock's own men even broke ranks to join them, an indiscretion for which the colonel later punished him. As Oliver was lowered into his grave, the Cadets fired several volleys, each one accompanied by loud huzzas from the crowd.[9]

In the words of John Adams, the "Republican Spirit" was running strong in Boston.[10] Even reports that Parliament was preparing to close the port of Boston until the tea was paid for failed to restrain the boldness of the townspeople. Although they may have been concerned about the future, they had few doubts about their ability to deal with whatever it might bring.

A week after the Oliver funeral, the town meeting met for the regular March session. Hancock was once again elected moderator, but his health was so bad that he declined to serve.[11] Weighed down by illness, and feeling that trade was going to do nothing but get worse, he decided to cut some of his losses. He ordered Hayley to sell two of his vessels then lying idle in London. The proceeds were much less than he expected, but at least the sale gave him some funds, and he was rid of the expense of maintenance.[12] Still, his debts were mounting. He was forced to take out another mortgage, of nearly £700, on his property, but this seems not to have been enough; on June 1, William Semme, his creditor of two years past, was attaching his goods for nonpayment.[13]

Hancock never wanted for care at home, and, as usual, Aunt Lydia catered to her nephew's every need. One thing was different, though, up on the hill; there was a new visitor to the house who had been spending considerable time with John and Lydia. She was Dorothy Quincy.

Dolly Quincy was the youngest daughter of Edmund Quincy and Elizabeth Wendell. She had a distinguished lineage. Her father, one of Boston's best-known failures, seemed always either on his way to or just returning from one of life's reverses. He had made a handsome fortune when a privateer in which he was a principal investor captured a Spanish treasure ship. But that money had long since vanished, and, though the family was by no means destitute, they did live in a style close to genteel poverty and were frequently dependent on the generosity of their well-connected and well-to-do relatives.

Dolly was born in 1747 at the family home on the south side of Summer Street in Boston. When she was five, the family moved back to the Quincy homestead in Braintree. They lived only a few hundred yards from her Uncle Josiah Quincy, who was now the occupant of the old Hancock parsonage. Just where Dolly and John met one another remains a mystery. The two Quincy homesteads had a reputation for being lively places filled with young people. Indeed, young John Adams spent many pleasant hours there when he should have been reading law. It is not unlikely that Hancock visited the Quincys and there met Dolly. However, his acquaintance with her might never have ripened had it not been for Aunt Lydia's playing Cupid.[14]

Dolly's mother died in 1769, leaving Edmund to care for her.

Although there is nothing to suggest that he was anything but a loving and devoted parent, poor Quincy was a man who found it difficult to manage his own life, let alone that of a twenty-two-year-old daughter. It is equally true that, since both her brother and one of her sisters were already married, Dolly found life in Braintree somewhat confining and was eager to move into the social whirl of Boston.

Her chance came when Aunt Lydia invited her up to Beacon Hill. It was a move reminiscent of Lydia and Thomas' care for young John Bastide, but it was also a great deal more than that, for it was no secret that Lydia Hancock was keen to find a good match for her bachelor nephew. He was over thirty, and she wanted him to connect with a good family. There was none better than the Quincys.[15]

At the age of twenty-seven, Dorothy was eager for marriage. Although she enjoyed the reputation of being a flirt, "Dolly" was by no means a buxom beauty. Her hair was dark brown and straight, drawn up onto the top of her head in the fashion of the time. High cheekbones, a narrow face, and slender body gave the impression of a frail person. She and Lydia could not have been more unlike each other in appearance, but they got along quite well.

It was not as if John had been idle in these matters; in fact, some of his activities spurred Lydia to action. She remembered the rumors about his alleged liaison with a chambermaid when he was in London.[16] If that was true, it was a mere pecadillo, of no importance. Of more interest was his relationship with Sally Jackson, daughter of a good Boston family. They saw one another for a time, but something happened, for Sally married Henderson Inches, an acquaintance of Hancock's and a fellow selectman.[17]

A chambermaid and a Boston belle were not the only girls with whom Hancock had had a romantic link. If Mrs. George Hayley had had her way, Hancock might have become her son-in-law. When he had visited London, Mrs. Hayley's daughter was too young to be seriously noticed, but a few years later, when Palfrey came by to pay his compliments and those of his boss, he described her to Hancock as "a *Strapping* Girl of her

Age." His visit caused the girl some embarrassment, for in the middle of his conversation he mentioned that Hancock might come back for a visit in two or three years, and Mrs. Hayley took it that he intended to court her daughter. She blurted out, "In two or three years . . . why dont you think Miss will do as she is?" The remark turned the girl crimson. Had times been better, a transatlantic alliance between the Houses of Hayley and Hancock might have produced a formidable enterprise. Unfortunately, distance, politics, love, and Aunt Lydia doomed the prospect.[18]

Most of Hancock's love life seems to have been relatively straightforward, or at least discreet enough to avoid notice by prying historians. Like the majority of his peers, Hancock held his passions in check as the price to be paid for respectability. Unlike his political hero John Wilkes, he did not choose a life of public profligacy.[19] After all, Boston was not London, and it would hardly do for an American Whig to revile the decadent habits of England while indulging himself.

There is one possible blemish on this otherwise clean canvas. Her name is Dorcas Griffith. Being a port town, Boston offered a full line of services for seamen, including a more than ample supply of "dockside doxies," of which Dorcas was one. She ran a small grog shop down at the waterfront, just a short distance from Hancock's Wharf. There, she dispensed spirits across the bar and sex upstairs. She ran the operation with the help of her daughter, who was learning her mother's trade. Politics were unimportant to her, and she counted among her customers Whig politicians and British soldiers. According to wagging Tory tongues and her own testimony, among those she serviced was none other than John Hancock. If the story is true, then it helps explain Aunt Lydia's interest in bringing Dolly into the family.

The war ended Lydia's anguish. Dorcas opted for the volume the British army could supply and left Boston when the troops did. Eventually, she ended up in London, where she applied for and got a pension for her services to the king.[20]

Despite Lydia's nudging, Hancock avoided matrimony. It took four years before the couple was even betrothed. He was busy

with other things (politics? Dorcas?), and perhaps felt that matters were too unsettled for such an undertaking.

By eighteenth-century standards of public behavior, the Boston Tea Party was a middling disturbance. Indeed, in many
ways it was rather mild. Aside from the tea, no property had
been damaged, and not a single person had been killed or in-
jured.[21] This did not mean that anyone dismissed it lightly.
Bostonians took it seriously, and, as events were soon to prove,
the ministry took it even more seriously.

The ministers resolved that the town and the individual participants must be punished. One of the strongest supporters of
coercion was the commander in chief of His Majesty's forces in
North America, General Thomas Gage. Gage was home for consultation and was not shy about giving his advice on how to
deal with Boston. He told the king, "They will be Lyons whilst
we are Lambs, but if we take the resolute part they will undoubtedly prove very meek . . ." The general's sentiments found
a receptive audience, and Boston's reputation as a den of radicals called forth Draconian measures.[22]

Retribution came in the form of a quadruped commonly
known as the Coercive or Intolerable Acts. The four legs were
the Boston Port Act, the Massachusetts Bay Government Act,
the Quartering Act, and the Administration of Justice Act.[23]

The first of these, the Port Act, declared that Boston was
closed to commerce. The Custom House, therefore, was to be
moved to Plymouth, and after June 1 no vessels could enter or
leave the harbor. Along with the Custom House, the capital, too,
was to be moved. It was going to Salem. The port would remain
under interdict until such time as His Majesty was satisfied that
the town had made adequate restitution for the Tea Party.

Simple punishment was not enough. Lord North was determined to root out what he saw as the basic evil — the structure
of the province's government. In accordance with the provisions
of the Massachusetts Bay Government Act, henceforth the governor would appoint Council members by a writ of mandamus,
rather than having them elected by the House. County sheriffs
were also to be appointed by the governor without consent of
the Council, and they would summon jurors. Most pernicious

of all, by this act the town meeting, perhaps the most treasured of all institutions in Massachusetts, could convene only once a year, and then its agenda must be confined to election of town officers and enactment of local ordinances. Special meetings could be called if necessary, but only with the express permission of the governor. Had this been in effect a few years earlier, nonimportation might never have happened and Committees of Correspondence would have been denied one of their most effective organizing tools. North's observations were sound, but his decision was too late.

The Administration of Justice Act, or "Murderer's Act," as Sam Adams called it, permitted the governor to send to England for trial any crown official accused of committing a crime in the performance of his duties. This would carry him beyond the reach of local justice and, the British hoped, would permit them to undertake more energetic law enforcement without fear of being harassed by local magistrates and courts. Bostonians saw it differently. To them, it meant that crimes committed here might go unpunished in England.

The final piece of reform legislation was the Quartering Act. For too long Bostonians had been able to keep large numbers of troops at arm's length out at Castle William by pleading insufficient quarters in the town. According to this act, the commander in chief had the authority to seize barns and unoccupied buildings for the convenient location of his troops.

Hancock's oration left no doubt as to how he and his fellow patriots would receive the Coercive Acts.[24] News of the Port Act, first of the acts to be passed, filtered into town in late April, and by May 10, the full text was available. That was the same day on which the town meeting met. The mood of the meeting was quickly apparent. By unanimous vote, they elected Hancock as a representative to the House, followed closely by the old standbys, Adams, who was also elected moderator, Phillips, and Cushing.[25]

The communication apparatus so neatly constructed in the previous crisis soon swung into action. Revere was dispatched southward with letters from the Committee of Correspondence and a resolution of the town meeting calling for a "stop [to] all

Importation from Great Britain & Exportation to Great Britain, & every part of the West Indies, till the Act for Blocking up this Harbor be repealed . . ."[26]

Boston's martyrdom brought her support from all quarters. There was an outpouring of sympathy, and messages of encouragement flowed in. Beyond offering emotional support, though, the messages were less reassuring, for contrary to what had been hoped the tide did not seem to be running in favor of another boycott. Instead, the sentiment seemed more attuned to Hancock's earlier suggestion of a General Congress. Sam Adams, impatient as always, did not oppose a Congress, but saw it as a time-consuming operation when what was called for was immediate action.[27] His answer was a "Solemn League and Covenant," which was a new variation on nonimportation. When the Boston Committee of Correspondence issued just such a call, there was an immediate outcry from local merchants, who charged that Adams and his fellows had exceeded their authority. There quickly followed an unsuccessful effort to abolish the committee. Elsewhere in the province, the Solemn League was well received, no doubt assisted by the fact that Gage proclaimed the agreement a "traitorous combination"; but beyond Massachusetts the plan met with a cool reception.[28]

Both to highlight the sternness of the measures and demonstrate their resolve in enforcing them, the ministers decided that Massachusetts needed a new governor. Their choice was General Gage. The appointment made sense. As commander of the army in America, Gage would have no trouble getting troops into Boston. Furthermore, despite his military position, those who knew him respected him as a reasonable and prudent man who happened to have the good fortune to be married to an American, Margaret Kemble of New Jersey.[29] If all went well, the plan was for Gage to preside while Boston repented, and when the contrition was done, Hutchinson would return to the chair.

After a pleasant spring passage of less than four weeks, Gage arrived in Boston on May 13. He landed first at the Castle, where he found Hutchinson disconsolate and sulking. The governor had taken up residence in the fort to avoid the insults of the Boston mob. For four days the old and new governors were closeted together in somber discussion. Hutchinson was weary and bitter. For years he had borne the brunt of the province's refractory politics, and now he was pleased to unload that burden on Gage, describing to him the politics and personalities of the patriot machine.[30]

On May 17, the governor's barge moved out from the Castle and made her way down the harbor toward Long Wharf. Despite their troubles, the people of Boston gave Gage a grand reception. The wharf was lined with soldiers from the regular regiments as well as Hancock's Cadets. When the barge drew alongside and Gage came up the stairs, the military contingents came smartly to attention, as the council, members of the House, selectmen, and other dignitaries came forward to greet His Excellency and escort him up King Street to the State House.[31]

Gage got his first indication of the town's temperament the next evening at a formal dinner in Faneuil Hall. Hancock boycotted the affair. Those who were there offered numerous toasts, but when someone proposed they raise their glasses to Governor Hutchinson, all he got for a response was a loud hiss.[32]

It did not take long for Gage to realize that he had trouble on his hands. The House met on May 25 and elected eighteen councilors. The next day he vetoed thirteen of them.[33]

The House met in Boston for only three days. By order of the governor, and in conformance with the Port Act, the assembly was moved to Salem, there to meet on June 7. The removal issue was brewing again.[34]

After ten days of relatively normal legislative activities, on the 17th the galleries were cleared for a piece of extraordinary business. Since at least March 5, when Hancock had suggested it, the idea of an intercolonial Congress had been a popular one in Massachusetts. Other colonies had indicated support, so when the House Committee on the State of the Province finished its report, someone moved that "it is highly expedient and necessary that a Meeting of Committees from the several Colonies on this Continent be had on a certain Day, to consult upon the present State of the Colonies and the Miseries to which they are reduced by the Operation of certain Acts of Parliament respecting America."

A committee of five was then elected — James Bowdoin,

Thomas Cushing, Samuel Adams, John Adams, and Robert Treat Paine — to repair to Philadelphia or anywhere else where such a meeting could be held.[35]

News of this infuriated Gage, who immediately dispatched a messenger to dissolve the meeting. He arrived too late. The damage was done.

On that terrible 1st of June, 1774, Boston Harbor closed. Within a few days, John Andrews reported on the desolation: "Our wharfs are entirely deserted; not a topsail vessel to be seen either there or in the harbor, save the ships of war and transports."[36] Not even the ferry to Charlestown was allowed to operate. Anyone coming into town from the north had to go the round-about route through Roxbury and across the Neck.

When Hancock returned to his home from Salem he found Boston in a much saddened state. Unemployment was running high, and those fortunate enough to find jobs were consigned to the lowly chore of "mending the streets and cleaning the docks." Without the port, there was little for Boston to depend upon.[37]

Soldiers were everywhere, and with them came trouble. Gage himself was a fair and just man, but those who served under him, as well as some of those in the patriot camp, were not always so well disposed. Street brawls, name-calling, and intemperate newspaper accounts helped build the pressure toward explosion. Affairs were so tense that on one occasion, when church bells were rung to warn of a fire, soldiers ran for their arms, expecting an attack.[38]

In late July, Hancock left Boston for a brief visit with his family in Bridgewater. His mother and stepfather had planned to come up to town themselves in August, but he persuaded them not to, for fear of more disturbances.[39]

As soon as he knew Hancock was back in town, Gage sent him a stunning message. Suddenly and without warning, the governor dismissed him as Colonel of the Cadets. He never gave a specific reason for the firing, although later some vague reference was made to his not attending the governor; probably a reference to his absence at the Faneuil Hall dinner.[40] For Hancock the firing was a severe personal blow. He was proud of his company and what he had accomplished with them. To be treated so cavalierly was insulting.

When he summoned his men to announce the news, they responded in a way that brought him joy and Gage grief. Palfrey described the scene to Sam Adams:

> The Company highly enrag'd at being thus deprived of their Commanding officer immediately chose a Committee to draw up an address to the Governor [and] to return him the Standard. A spirited address was accordingly drawn, purporting that as his Excellency had tho't fit to remove their first officer from his Command without assigning any reason therefore they had no further use for the Standard his Excellency presented to the Company when he took the Chair of Government, they return'd it to him [and] no longer consider'd themselves as his Company of Cadets — The Governor appeared to be much agitated as the Committee came upon him quite sudden [and] unexpectedly. — He told them Collo. H. had us'd him ill, that he had not treated him with the respect which was due as Commander in chief for which reason he depriv'd him his Commission, that he would not be treated ill by Collo. H. nor any man in the Province and added that had he known our intention he would have prevented it by disbanding us before we would put it in execution — This we foresaw but were determined to be before hand with him and I was highly pleased to find that we had out Generaled the General.[41]

Gage's problems were mounting fast. When the general called the selectmen of the town for the purpose of informing them officially of the provisions of the Massachusetts Bay Government Act he found them ready to defy him. But since open defiance would only have invited repression, the selectmen decided on a dodge. When Gage told them he was ready to allow them to convene the town meeting, they responded that his permission was not necessary — the meeting had not officially adjourned. At that rate, remarked Gage, they could hold the same meeting for the next ten years. The selectmen said nothing.[42]

On Wednesday morning, August 10, there was a slight commotion in front of Thomas Cushing's house. The delegates to the Congress in Philadelphia were preparing to take their leave. Bowdoin was ill and could not make the journey, so the other four were leaving without him.[43] Quite likely Hancock and others were there to bid them farewell and wish them luck in

Philadelphia. It is not altogether clear why Hancock elected to remain behind, for certainly if he had wished, he too could have gone along. Two explanations are possible. One is that his health was bothering him and he did not feel up to the rigors of the journey. The other is that he stayed behind out of a sense of duty. With so many key figures on the road to Philadelphia, someone had to remain at the helm in Boston.

Gage fretted over his position. Beyond Boston Neck, his authority was practically nonexistent, to the point where sending troops into the countryside was considered an act of provocation. In September he ordered his men to erect a large fortification on the Neck. The selectmen, who traditionally would not allow one stone to be turned in the town without their permission, were alarmed and annoyed. When pressed, Gage simply responded that he was doing it to protect the town.[44]

Not only was Gage beset by the patriots, but his own men were restless as well. Since the town refused to supply any quarters, many of the newly arrived troops were forced to bivouac in tents. Gage tried to hire carpenters to build barracks, but any man who worked for the king's shilling was a candidate for a warm coat of tar and feathers. Finally, in a move that must have pained him deeply, the general was forced to seek Hancock's help. Gage asked if he would use his influence to help get the barracks built.

Hancock was more than annoyed. After shutting up the port, ruining his business, and throwing hundreds out of work, the general had the temerity to come to him for help. He was asking assistance of the man whom he had fired and whose militia made sport by calling him names and threatening his life. Hancock refused to help.[45]

Earlier in September, Gage had summoned the General Court to convene in Salem on October 5. As the date for the meeting drew near, he began to have second thoughts. Even though some of his worst opponents were away in Philadelphia, there were enough left at home, especially Hancock, to turn the Salem meeting into another patriot tub-thumping session, something he could easily do without. In the present state of the province, allowing them to meet was an invitation to trouble. He ordered the meeting canceled.[46]

Thomas Hutchinson by John Singleton Copley. (Courtesy Massachusetts Historical Society.)

Reverend Samuel Cooper by John Singleton Copley. (Courtesy Massachusetts Historical Society.)

James Sullivan by Gilbert Stuart. (Courtesy Massachusetts Historical Society.)

Paul Revere by John Singleton Copley. (Courtesy Museum of Fine Arts, Boston.)

Ebenezer Hancock. Artist unknown. (Courtesy Massachusetts Historical Society.)

Paul Revere's engraving of the Boston Massacre. (Courtesy Rare Book Department, Boston Public Library.)

British cartoon showing a meeting between Lord North and Hancock. (Courtesy British Museum.)

"The Flight of the Congress." A British cartoon depicting Congress's evacuation of Philadelphia. Hancock is in the center. (Courtesy British Museum.)

John Trumbull's painting of the Committee of Congress presenting the Declaration of Independence to the President of the Congress. John Hancock seated at right. (Courtesy Boston Public Library.)

The action came too late. The House met and waited for the governor. When he did not show up, the representatives resolved themselves into a convention. They elected Hancock their chairman and proceeded to denounce the governor and establish themselves as the protectors of the province's "peace welfare and prosperity."[47] The convention lasted only one day. On the next morning they resolved themselves into a Provincial Congress and elected Hancock their president.

The establishment of the Provincial Congress heralded the beginning of independent government in Massachusetts.[48] Through October and November and into early December, the Congress met, first in Concord and then in Cambridge. They brazenly ordered taxes to be withheld from the royal collectors and then insisted the monies be paid into their own coffers. A Committee of Safety, with Hancock as one of the key members, was organized. In the absence of any executive, the committee was charged with overseeing the security and defense of the province, a job that soon spilled over into other areas, making the group a powerful directing force in all the province's affairs.[49]

On October 29 the Congress took a fateful step when they ordered that at least one quarter of the militia be "form[ed] . . . into companies of fifty privates . . . who shall equip and hold themselves in readiness to march at the shortest notice . . ." To some, such a move spoke of madness, but all seemed to agree that the Congress was composed of "spirited" men whose patience had run short.[50]

This was the birth of the "Minute Men."[51] The political storm was thickening fast. In October rumors flew about that Gage was only waiting on reinforcements before he arrested Hancock. The charge was going to be destruction of the tea, and to make sure it would stick, witnesses were already being bribed.[52] On the 22nd, nature dealt a heavy blow to the patriots. Will Molineux died. He had been Boston's most ardent rabble-rouser, and his passing left a gap in the patriot ranks. On his funeral day a large crowd attended the procession, while on the sidelines the Tories celebrated the end of this "Pest to Society."[53]

In early November, Adams and his colleagues brought home good news from Philadelphia. To be sure, they had spent more than their share of time "nibbling and quibbling," but in the end the Congress did approve some measures highly pleasing to the Massachusetts delegates.[54]

One of the most important of these was the adoption of the Suffolk Resolves. These resolves had been passed by a special county convention held in Milton and then forwarded to Philadelphia by Revere.[55] They asserted that no obedience was due to the Port Act and that people ought to prepare to defend themselves against Great Britain. Joseph Galloway, a conservative Pennsylvanian, declared that by adopting them, the Suffolk convention had made a "complete declaration of war against Great Britain." Galloway was in the minority. Congress adopted the resolves.[56]

Another victory came with the creation of the Continental Association. According to this agreement, as of December 1774 the colonies would import no goods from Great Britain, and, beginning on September 10, 1775, if their grievances were left unredressed, they would halt all exports to Great Britain. There were numerous loopholes in the agreement, and some, Sam Adams being the most vocal, thought the agreement far too weak. Nevertheless, whatever its faults, now, for the first time, all the colonies had put their signature to a document of union.[57]

Before their final adjournment, the members of the Congress agreed to meet again in Philadelphia in the spring of 1775. The optimists in the group felt that such a meeting would be unnecessary, because they were confident that, faced with a united America, the ministry would come to its senses. Indeed, as he was leaving, John Adams confided to his diary that "it is not very likely that I shall ever see this Part of the World again . . ."[58]

Back home, the Provincial Congress apparently did not share Adams' buoyant view, for on December 1 they elected delegates to the next Continental Congress. Only one change was made. Since Bowdoin was still sick, he was replaced by Hancock, who by now was eager to be part of the important events taking place in Philadelphia.[59]

Once the Provincial Congress adjourned, Hancock returned to Beacon Hill. It is a comment on the uncertainty of the times and Gage's lack of direction that Hancock was even allowed to pass across the Neck. After all, he had just finished presiding over an illegal assembly whose chief business had been the flouting of royal authority. Nevertheless, Hancock rode through town, up the hill, and back home to Lydia and Dolly.

For the time being, Hancock had far less to fear from the British government than from lawless ruffians prowling the streets. As things became more unsettled in the countryside, Boston was filling up with Tories whose safety was proportional to the proximity of the redcoats. The influx of civilians and the restiveness of his own troops created problems for Gage. His chief worry came from his own men. They deserted in sizable numbers, sometimes lured away by patriots. Not even the public execution of one poor soldier caught in the act could stem the flow. In the streets, relations worsened. One afternoon a group of soldiers barged through Hancock's gate and onto his property. On the excuse that they were checking out his barn for use as a possible barracks, they went through his property behaving in a rude and insolent manner.[60] When Gage intervened, as he did in this instance, his men saw his action as catering to the Bostonians. Behind his back they began to call him an old woman. Even his own officers were losing faith in him.

In February 1775, the Provincial Congress met again. The delegates convened in Cambridge and by unanimous vote again elected Hancock their president. Through his multiple roles as president, member of the Committee of Safety, delegate to the Continental Congress, and selectman, Hancock wielded enormous influence. To all intents and purposes he had given up business entirely and had become a full-time politician. Although he was yet to realize it, his political prominence placed him in great danger.

As early as January and February 1774, some in the ministry had talked of cleansing Massachusetts by ridding it of Hancock and Adams. They had discussed arresting the two men and shipping them to England for trial. It was only from a lack of courage and a fear of raising up the populace that the idea was dropped.[61] Since that time, affairs had grown more urgent and Hancock more defiant. He was cocky and confident, standing in his new role as leader of both town and country forces. That,

plus his open and unabashed flouting of royal authority, made
him a prime candidate for arrest. One of the few barriers still
standing between him and the prisoner's dock was Gage's own
indecision and reluctance to do anything that might precipitate
more trouble.[62]

Hancock seems to have been oblivious of the danger. He made
no effort to leave town, and even allowed Lydia and Dolly to
stay by his side. Business was at a complete standstill, although
he did send Palfrey on a mission to South Carolina, supposedly
on commercial matters, but in all probability on business having more to do with politics than trade. By the spring he was
ordering Hayley to sell his remaining vessels.

Despite the tautness of the situation, it was decided to go
ahead with the annual Massacre Day oration. For the speaker
they selected Dr. Joseph Warren to do an encore of his 1772
oration.

Since March 5 fell on a Sunday, the speech was postponed
until Monday. On that day a huge crowd filled Old South. The
pews and galleries were groaning with people, and throngs were
milling about through the aisles. Not all the spectators were
friendly. Mixed in the audience were forty to fifty British officers. They were there, according to an account later given to
Thomas Hutchinson, for an ill purpose. If Warren spoke against
the king, one of them was to heave an egg at him, signaling the
others to draw swords and assassinate Hancock and Adams.
The story has the ring of a very creative imagination. Nevertheless, it is true that a number of soldiers were present; so
many, in fact, that they blocked Warren's path to the pulpit,
forcing him to crawl through an open window at the rear. Once
he had finished the oration, which apparently was not insulting
to the king since no egg was tossed, the selectmen moved the
usual thanks of the town. Immediately, the soldiers shouted
"Fie, fie." Some in the crowd thought they heard "Fire, fire."
There was a general din and a stampede toward the doors. At
the very same time, while chaos was reigning inside, out on the
street drums and fifes were marching by, playing a tune.[63]

A week after Warren's speech Hancock was back out in Concord, presiding over another session of the Provincial Congress.
Witnessing the general impotence of the British beyond the

Neck, and encouraged by the countryside's support, the Congress took on a decidedly military bent. The delegates spent many hours drawing up fifty-three articles comprising the rules and regulations of the Massachusetts army and, then resolved "that the present dangerous and alarming situation of our public affairs renders it necessary for this colony to make preparations for their security and defense by raising and establishing an army."[64]

By now Hancock understood his own personal danger and realized that he could not return to Boston. But being away from Lydia, and especially from Dolly, with whom he had fallen in love, was painful. He missed her deeply and told her, in a playful letter smuggled up to Beacon Hill, that he would be with her soon and would try not to be "saucy." The couple was reunited on April 7, when Dolly and Lydia packed what they could and made a hasty exit out of Boston for Lexington. They headed directly for Grandfather Hancock's manse, now occupied by his granddaughter Lucy Bowes and her husband, Jonas Clarke, successor to the old Bishop. It was only a short ride from the parsonage to the Provincial Congress in Concord, so for the time being the house was home to the Clarkes as well as John, Lydia, Dolly, and Sam Adams.[65] It was a crowded and excited household.

While Congress pushed forward, General Gage continued to fret in Boston. He had tried to make some forays into the countryside to make at least a symbolic show of strength. He had almost nothing to show for his efforts; indeed, as he himself realized, Boston was under siege.

In London the ministers were less than pleased with the general's conduct. From their vantage point he seemed lethargic and timid. On April 14, Gage received a letter from Lord Dartmouth that spurred him to action. After repeated requests, Dartmouth promised him that reinforcements were on their way; in the meantime, though, he suggested that the general undertake the initiative to support royal authority. According to Dartmouth, a "first & essential step . . . towards reestablishing government, would be to arrest the principal actors and abettors in the Provincial Congress."[66]

Thanks to a well-placed spy, none other than Benjamin

Church, Hancock's chum from Latin and Harvard days and now a fellow member of the Committee of Safety, Gage was fully aware that, in addition to housing the Congress, Concord was an important arms depot.[67] With that information, Gage laid plans to strike a double blow. He would dispatch a force to arrest Hancock and Adams and destroy the munitions.[68] Thus was born the march to Lexington and Concord.[69]

If Gage was informed of activities taking place in Concord, the Congress was equally aware of what was going on in Boston. At the heart of its network of spies was a group of thirty "mechanics," who had formed themselves into a committee devoted to watching the British and their Tory sympathizers. Among this group was the North End silversmith and messenger Paul Revere. The committee held secret meetings down at the Green Dragon tavern and made special reports to the Congress, usually via Revere.

On Saturday, April 15, the grenadiers and light infantry companies in Boston were "taken off all duties till further orders." This was a sure sign that something was afoot. The next day, Revere himself observed that "the boats belonging to the transports were all launched and carried under the sterns of the men of war." That bit of news, in conjunction with the activities of the soldiers, presaged some sort of sortie out of Boston. With this intelligence Revere rode out that Sunday to Lexington for a visit with Hancock and Adams.

From Revere's information and their own intuition, Hancock and Adams concluded that Concord was a likely target. Hancock summoned a special meeting of the Committee of Safety for Monday. They met and decided to move as much of the arms cache as possible. What they did not have time to move was to be hidden wherever possible.

Satisfied that they had done as much as they could, Hancock and Adams rode back to the Clarke house. Everyone was nervous. Local militia units, including John Parker's company in Lexington, stood by. If Gage meant to move by force of arms, he would find the Americans ready to stand against him.

Hancock was ready to fight. Over the last decade he had battled for the rights of his town and province. During that struggle, the ministry and its agents had treated him ill. He had been insulted and persecuted and had suffered tremendous financial losses. Now the ministry was on the verge of branding him a traitor. More than most, Hancock felt personally aggrieved. Still, he held on to a thread of hope that somehow the Mother Country would come to her senses; in the meantime, if force was necessary to protect his liberties, then force it would be.

Tuesday, the 18th, was a busy day. The Clarke house was alive with activity. People arrived bearing the latest in reports, gossip, and rumors. As usual in a confused situation, the bits and pieces did not always fit together. It was Hancock's job to try to filter out the truth from a maze of wild tales. In the evening Parker posted a guard at the house. The sentries were hardly in place when word came that a mounted patrol from Boston was approaching the Green. Fortunately, when the horsemen arrived at the Green, they bore off to the left on a road that took them toward Concord and away from the manse.

About midnight, the household was startled by loud noises at the door, the sounds of a horse, and challenges from the guard. The rider was Revere, who had hurried out of Boston less than two hours before with the news that all had been expecting: "The British were coming." A half-hour after his arrival he was joined by a second rider from the town, William Dawes, who had taken an alternate route. After a few moments of rest, Revere and Dawes were on their way to Concord. They had ridden only a short distance when they came on Dr. Samuel Prescott. Prescott was on his way home after a late-night date with a local girl, Lydia Mulliken. He managed to convince Revere and Dawes that he too was a High Son of Liberty, so the three rode on together toward Concord. About midway between Lexington and Concord, the Americans stumbled into a British patrol. Dawes managed to escape but had to turn back. Revere was less fortunate and was taken prisoner, interrogated, and then released. Prescott, the only one who really knew the countryside, spurred his mount over a fence and went cross-country into Concord, alerting the town.

Back in Lexington, the whole town was stirring. Parker summoned his men to the Green, where they took up their positions and waited. After a time the men grew restless, so he dismissed them, warning them to stay close and listen for the sound of a drum.

Hancock wanted to be with Parker and his men. Despite his ignominious dismissal, he still considered himself a colonel of the militia and felt that his place was down on the Green. For political reasons, Adams thought otherwise. The risk was too great; he was certain to be either killed or hauled off as a prisoner. His loss at a time like this might well be a mortal blow to the patriot cause. Lydia and Dolly chimed in to support Adams, adding their own personal concern.

While the arguments went back and forth, the drum was heard. Hancock left the house and made his way to join Parker and his men. What happened then can only be guessed, but it seems likely that when he appeared on the scene, Parker told him the same things he had been hearing from Adams, Lydia, and Dolly. He stayed for a few minutes and then made his way back, in time to throw a few of his belongings in a chaise for a hasty exit, with Adams, toward the north and out of the path of the approaching British. Their departure would have been even speedier had not Adams, for reasons of personal comfort, insisted on riding in a chaise rather than on horseback.

Just as they were ready to set off, Revere reappeared after his release from detention. Along with a Lexington militia sergeant, William Munroe, and Hancock's clerk, Lowell, he went along with the chaise as it headed north toward Woburn. They had gone only a mile or so when Hancock remembered that a trunk full of valuable papers had been left behind. Revere and Lowell rode back to rescue the papers and got to the house just as the troops were coming up on the Green. They quickly took the trunk, and as they were scurrying up the road, they could hear the sound of shots behind them. The Revolution had begun.

In his haste to get away, Hancock had left Lydia and Dolly behind. He knew that even if the troops came to the manse (which they did not), the women would be safe. No civilized nation in the eighteenth century, not even the British, made war on women. In a somewhat hysterical vein, and many years after the event, Elizabeth Clarke, the parson's daughter, described the scene Hancock left behind.

Oh! Lucy, how many descendants can I count from the venerable Hancock down to this day, which is sixty-six years since the war began on the common, which I now can see from this window . . . and . . . in my mind just as plain all the British troops marching off the common to Concord and the whole scene: how Aunt Hancock and Miss Dolly Quincy, with their cloaks and bonnets on; Aunt crying and wringing her hands and helping Mother dress the children; Dolly going round with Father to hide money, watches, and anything down in the potatoes and up garret. And then Grandfather Clarke sent down men with carts, took *your* mother and all the children but Jonas and me and Sally, a babe six months old. Father sent Jonas down to Grandfather Cook's to see who was killed and what their condition was; and in the afternoon Father, Mother, with me and the baby, went to the meeting house. There was the eight men that was killed . . . all in boxes made of four large boards nailed up; and after Pa had prayed, they were put into two horse carts, and took into the graveyard.[70]

What happened that morning on the Green and later at the North Bridge marked the end of discussion and the beginning of war to decide the issues between Great Britain and her colonies. Whether at this point Hancock and his cohorts were actually committed to independence does not matter; what was true was that he was now the leader of a rebellion, and if it failed, he was most certainly a dead man. If he was to survive, the movement of which he was a part must triumph.

Chapter 11

Mr. President

AFTER THE BLOODY WORK on the Green, the British reorganized, unfurled their colors, and, with drums and fifes playing, marched off toward Concord. Back on the Green the people of Lexington rushed to help the wounded and mourn their dead. In the manse Dolly and Lydia were in a state of shock. Dolly's first thoughts were for her father, who was still back in Boston. Instinctively, she made ready to ride back to the town. That was as foolhardy as Hancock's wish to be with the militia. Lydia persuaded her to stay, and together they packed the carriage, making ready to follow after Adams and Hancock. Before lunch they were off, and by noon they were all reunited on the outskirts of Woburn, where they paused to enjoy a fine piece of salmon that Lydia had snatched from the table in Lexington.[1]

The refugees spent two nights in Woburn and then moved only a short distance, over to Billerica, spent one night there at the home of Amos Wyman, and then, on April 22, headed for Worcester, where Hancock and Adams planned to rendezvous with the other delegates to the Continental Congress. On the way they managed a slight detour through Lancaster, where Dolly's sister Sarah had settled with her husband, William Greenleaf, a prominent citizen of the town and captain of the local militia. There they decided that, as soon as practical, Edmund would be brought out of Boston to stay with the Greenleafs until matters were resolved one way or another.[2]

Finding a place of refuge for Dolly and Lydia was a bit more difficult. Taking them to Philadelphia was out of the question. Hancock had no intention of exposing the two most important people in his life to the rigors of a long journey to a city where even he did not know where he was going to stay. Staying in Lancaster was equally unsatisfactory; the quarters were far too cramped to accommodate the Greenleafs, Lydia, Dolly, and Edmund. They finally decided that the safest and most comfortable place for the ladies was in Fairfield, Connecticut, at the home of Thaddeus Burr. Burr was an old family friend and business associate, who, as a representative in the Assembly, could be counted on to provide hospitality and protection for his guests. Nor did it hurt that he was also one of the town's wealthiest men, whose home, though not quite the equal of the one on Beacon Hill, was at least far more comfortable than the rustic surroundings of Lancaster.[3]

After spending the weekend settling the family business, the company left Lancaster and made their way to Worcester, arriving late Wednesday. It was here that Hancock expected to meet the other delegates to Philadelphia and, he hoped, pick up some communications from the Congress. He found neither. His departure from Lexington had been so abrupt that, aside from those actually with him, no one knew his whereabouts, making it absolutely impossible for anyone to maintain contact with the congressional party. Likewise, he himself knew very little, other than rumors, about what had happened after the battle in Lexington.

Distressed at his own ignorance and the feeling of being abandoned, he wrote to the Committee of Safety, "How are we to proceed? Where are our Brethren . . . I beg by the Return of this Express to hear from you and pray furnish us with Depositions of the Conduct of the Troops . . ." He told them brusquely that he felt as if he were traveling as a deserter, and that shame he would not tolerate. "I must," he said, "travel in reputation . . ."[4]

The message had its effect. On the next day, the Congress ordered a military escort for the congressional party. On the same day the other members of the delegation arrived, so on April 26 they all set off for Philadelphia.[5]

The route was south through Brookfield to Springfield, then across into Connecticut, with stops at Hartford, New Haven, and Fairfield. There, the ladies fell out to remain with the Burrs.[6]

On May 6, the Massachusetts delegation, along with the gentlemen from Connecticut who had joined them, made a triumphal entry into New York. The news of Lexington and Concord had electrified the town, and people lined the streets to catch a glimpse of these heroes, most especially Hancock, whose carriage was given the place of honor as first in the parade.

Tired, but buoyant with infectious enthusiasm, he wrote to his "Dear Dolly," recounting the spectacle. According to him, the road was filled with people raising the "greatest Cloud of Dust I ever saw." The crowd pushed to his carriage, unharnessed the horses, and pulled it along on their own backs. He estimated that at least 7000 were there, nearly one third of the entire city. Even after he returned to his quarters following dinner, a steady stream of visitors came by to pay their respects. Not until ten in the evening did he have a chance to relax and enjoy a late snack, fried oysters. All the time, he was carefully guarded by militiamen, for fear that the Tories might try some desperate move. With the excitement, the strain, and the diet, it is small wonder that the always less than robust Hancock began to complain of not feeling well. Nevertheless, he was determined to press forward.[7]

On the 10th the party finally reached Philadelphia. The reception was similar to the one in New York. It was eleven in the morning when they arrived on the outskirts of the city, where they were met by hundreds of people. They formed a long procession led by 200 to 300 mounted militiamen with swords drawn. Once more Hancock took the post of honor, and, with Adams in the seat beside him, made a grand entrance, followed by the rest of the delegates from Massachusetts, New York, and Connecticut.[8]

One observer, Judge Samuel Curwen, watched the proceedings with a close eye. By his account, when the procession crossed over the city limits, "all the bells were set to ringing and chiming, and every mark of respect that could be was expressed . . ." Curwen also noted two troublesome elements. The first was the envy he sensed among delegates from other colonies, who "had to digest the distinction as easily as they could." The other was Hancock's appearance. He looked, reported Curwen, not well, and the judge blamed his pallid complexion on the hard journey and his well-known "high living."[9]

On May 10, the Second Continental Congress opened its first session. For the most part the faces were familiar; the Second Congress was largely made up of those who had been at the First. Among the few changes the most notable was the addition of Benjamin Franklin, Thomas Jefferson, and John Hancock.[10]

At the initial meetings, considerable time was spent on simple matters of organization. Charles Thomson, "the Sam Adams of Philadelphia," was re-elected secretary, and Peyton Randolph of Virginia was again chosen to be president. A good deal of debate centered on letters recently received from colonial agents in London; their observations on ministerial politics were devoured and dissected. The delegates also spent many hours carefully examining the mass of documents describing the events at Lexington and Concord and continuing affairs around Boston.[11]

Boston was much in everyone's mind. After Lexington Green and North Bridge, the British had retreated under heavy fire back to Boston. Since that time they had been surrounded by nearly 20,000 militia. With two large hostile forces facing one another, the situation was critical.[12]

On May 24, Congress interrupted its discussion on the state of the colonies to elect a new president. Randolph had been summoned home to preside at a meeting of the House of Burgesses. In his place the Congress elected another southerner, Henry Middleton of South Carolina. He declined the honor because of poor health.[13]

If on its third try Congress had again favored a southerner, it might have been seen as a slight to the north. After the tumultuous welcome in New York and Philadelphia, could anyone doubt who the most likely candidate would be? Hancock was elected unanimously.[14]

Politically, it was a good choice. He was a Bostonian and therefore, almost by definition, tinged with radicalism. Yet he was also a wealthy merchant of good family whose social and economic position carried the unmistakable air of solid respectability. Completing the triptych was his impressive record in legislative bodies. He could point to more than a decade of service in the Boston town meeting and nearly that long in the Massachusetts House. He had served on scores of committees and chaired dozens. His reputation as an active and competent politician had won him election as moderator, selectman, and, most recently, of course, president of the Provincial Congress. There were few present in Philadelphia who had had as distinguished a career.

If Hancock's reputation and the need for sectional balance dictated his election, it did not necessarily define exactly what he had been elected to do. In these beginning stages, Congress had yet to outline carefully the duties or term of its president. By tradition, most colonial assemblies chose their presiding officers anew after each election. The uncertainty of this Congress's power and future made the situation in Philadelphia quite unclear.[15]

The Congress was made up of delegates from each of the thirteen colonies. Every colony could send as many representatives as it desired, but in voting, it was one colony, one vote. In practice, since each colony footed the bill for its own delegation, representation was usually in the neighborhood of two to five men.

Although there appeared to be a good deal of congeniality among the members, much of it was feigned. They came not as Americans, a concept not yet fully developed, but as Georgians, Virginians, New Yorkers, and so forth. Loyalty rested with each man's colony and section. They were nearly as suspicious of one another as they were of the British ministry. Adding to the centrifugal force of sectionalism were the old political differences between Whigs and Tories. Several members of the Congress had Tory tendencies. They feared that their outspoken Whig brethren might push the body to extreme positions.

Counterbalancing these disintegrative forces was the universal concern and dismay over the British government's ill-conceived policies. Hancock's role was to hold the centrifugal forces in check while, at the same time, moving the body forward to action. It was a Herculean task made even more difficult for him by the uncertainty of his own position.

Most confusing of all, and a point that was soon to nettle Hancock, had to do with a peculiar complexity in his own situation. Had Peyton Randolph resigned his seat permanently, or was he merely on a leave of absence and entitled to resume the presidency on his return? For as long as he remained in Virginia, the question was moot.

Hancock was presiding over a very busy assembly. On June 2 the delegates received an important letter from the new president of the Massachusetts Provincial Congress, Joseph Warren. Warren expressed the concern of all members of the Provincial Congress when he observed that his colony was in the awkward state of having an army "without a civil power to provide for and control them." He asked the Congress in Philadelphia for advice on "the taking up and exercising the poweres of civil government," and concluded by requesting that, since "the Army now collecting from different colonies is for the general defence," the Continental Congress ought to take "the regulation and general direction of it . . ." One week later Congress endorsed the assumption of civil authority by the Provincial Congress, and moved to make the army at Boston its own.[16]

With the adoption of an army came the question of command. On June 15 John Adams rose on the floor of Congress to nominate a commander in chief. He later described the scene in his *Autobiography.*

> When Congress had assembled, I rose in my place, and in as short a speech as the subject would admit, represented the state of the Colonies, the uncertainty in the minds of the people, their great expectation and anxiety, the distresses of the army, the danger of its dissolution, the difficulty of collecting another, and the probability that the British army would take advantage of our delays, march out of Boston, and spread desolation as far as they could go. I concluded with a motion, in form, that Congress would adopt the army at Cambridge, and appoint a General; that though this was not the proper

time to nominate a General, yet, as I had reason to believe this
was a point of the greatest difficulty, I had no hesitation to
declare that I had but one gentleman in my mind for that
important command, and that was a gentleman from Virginia
who was among us and very well known to all of us, a gentleman whose skill and experience as an officer, whose independent fortune, great talents, and excellent universal character, would command the approbation of all America, and
unite the cordial exertions of all the Colonies better than any
other person in the Union. Mr. Washington, who happened to
sit near the door, as soon as he heard me allude to him, from
his usual modesty, darted into the library-room. Mr. Hancock,
who was our President, which gave me an opportunity to
observe his countenance while I was speaking on the state of
the Colonies, the army at Cambridge, and the enemy, heard
me with visible pleasure; but when I came to describe Washington for the commander, I never remarked a more sudden
and striking change of countenance. Mortification and resentment were expressed as forcibly as his face could exhibit them.
Mr. Samuel Adams seconded the motion and that did not
soften the President's physiognomy.[17]

The depth of Hancock's disappointment is hard to fathom,
although it is certainly reasonable to assume that the former
Colonel of the Cadets would have dearly loved to be commander
in chief. In fact, he had some claim to the post. No one had
sacrificed more in the American cause, and, though he lacked
combat experience, he was a highly regarded militia commander. Nevertheless, it is hard to believe that even an ego the
size of Hancock's could have blinded him to the elementary
necessity of someone other than a New Englander in command;
and, much to his credit, there is nothing to suggest that, at this
point or any subsequent time in their long relationship, Hancock ever evinced anything but admiration and support for
Washington.[18]

Hancock was ravenous for news from home. He had not been
in Boston since early April, and for most of that time the town
had been shut up like a fortress. It was anyone's guess as to
what the British were doing to his extensive property in the
town. He was happy to learn that his brother, Ebenezer, had
escaped from the town disguised as a fisherman.[19]

On June 12, General Gage took special notice of the absent Hancock and conferred a signal distinction on him. By proclamàtion, he offered an amnesty to "the infatuated multitude" who had been so misled "by certain well known incendiaries and traitors." Everyone was included in this gesture of reconciliation with two exceptions — Samuel Adams and John Hancock, "whose offences are of too flagitious a nature to admit of any other consideration than that of condign punishment." Such honors were hard to come by. Hancock and Adams were more renowned than ever.[20]

Five days after Gage's proclamation, the British assaulted Bunker Hill. Three times the wavering red lines trudged through bush and grass, over fences, on toward the American redoubt at the top of the hill. Twice they were sent reeling back. Then their commanders ordered them to drop their packs and make one more assault, not just for the hill, but for the honor of the British army, which now hung in the balance. Their ammunition exhausted, the Americans fought bravely but were unable to hold. The British infantry broke through and made quick work with their bayonets. Luckily, in the smoke and confusion most of the defenders were able to make good their escape, but the slopes of the hill were covered with the day's carnage. More than 1000 British lay wounded and dying. It was the worst casualty rate in the history of the British army, and it caused the American general Nathanael Greene to remark wryly that he wished he could sell them other hills at the same price.[21]

The Americans, too, suffered losses, though far fewer than the British, but among those who died was Hancock's friend and successor, Joseph Warren. He had come to the hill to fight, and, although he was president of the Congress and a major general in the militia, he chose to stand as a private in the redoubt. It was there that he died.[22]

News of Bunker Hill arrived in Philadelphia by special messenger late on Saturday evening, June 24. The messenger went immediately to Hancock's lodgings, and within two hours at least a hundred people had gathered to hear more. At one o'clock in the morning Hancock and the two Adamses went to the Philadelphia Committee of Safety to ask that they send powder to Massachusetts.[23]

The brave stand on Bunker Hill, coming so soon after the rout of the British at Lexington and Concord, gave further testimony to the military prowess of the Americans. Belief that untrained militia could stand against Regulars would soon die, but in the meantime exuberance was running high in Philadelphia.

Despite the martial stirrings in the air, Congress had not yet abandoned hope for a peaceful reconciliation, and while arming for war, it also made some pacific gestures. Redress was again sought from the king, this time by the Olive Branch Petition. Written by the moderate Pennsylvanian, John Dickinson, it cited America's grievances but pledged allegiance to the king.[24] To balance this soft approach, Congress took a harder line when it voted approval of the "Declaration of the Causes and Necessity of Taking Up Arms." It was a sword-rattling document written with a rhetorical flair designed to stir the hearts of American troops: "Our cause is just. Our union is perfect. Our internal resources are great, and if necessary, foreign assistance is undoubtedly attainable."[25]

Although the sounds of war were audible and growing louder, some in the Congress still clung to the hope of reconciliation. Hancock was not among them, but as the presiding officer he recognized the need for steering a careful course between declaring independence prematurely and stooping to British pressure. Consensus was the order of the day in Philadelphia. Through the endless debate, the heat, and the swarms of flies that invaded the chamber, Hancock sat and presided with an even hand.

He seems to have done well. Benjamin Harrison of Virginia called him "Noble, Disinterested and Generous."[26] His fellow Massachusetts delegates were silent about his presidency, which, considering such vocal curmudgeons as the Adamses, is high praise in itself. As for the president, his major concern was the frantic pace he was forced to keep. He was, in his own words, "worn out." The long days and nights were taking their toll. His gout was acting up, and his eyes began to bother him, forcing him occasionally to wear glasses.[27]

Life might have been even more trying if he had known what was going on in Fairfield. Thaddeus Burr's young nephew Aaron came by for a Sunday visit. Aaron Burr was a handsome and charming man with a well-earned reputation for success with the ladies. Dolly was intrigued by him, and even Lydia seems to have taken a liking to the rascal. Thaddeus thought that "if Mr. H. was out of the way," Dolly might even court him. Burr, though, had other matters on his mind, and Dolly's wiles were hardly enough to detain him.[28]

Hancock knew nothing of Burr's visit, nor was he aware of anything else that was going on in Fairfield, for Dolly hardly ever wrote, and when she did, her epistles were little more than brief notes. Unlike her contemporaries, Abigail Adams and Mercy Otis Warren, Dolly neither enjoyed writing nor was she very good at it. Indeed, it seems likely that her education was in general very shallow and her intellect not much above average. She played the conventional role of an eighteenth-century woman — household manager and social hostess. Her failure to write caused Hancock much anguish, for he loved her deeply and wanted desperately to hear from her. In lonely moments he often lamented her neglect and would write plaintively seeking more attention.[29]

On August 1, Congress adjourned until September 5. Within hours Hancock was on his way north. On his return trip he found no fanfare; only dusty rutted roads and taverns that specialized in bad food. He traveled unceremoniously through Trenton and New York on a direct line to Fairfield. The stay at Burr's was brief; just long enough to settle an important matter. Long engagements are fine when the partners are close by, but life in Philadelphia without Dolly was more than Hancock wished to endure. He would not go back without her. Dolly agreed, and August 28 was set as the wedding day. Having settled that, Hancock decided to use the intervening days to visit Massachusetts, leaving Dolly and Lydia to make plans for the ceremony.[30]

On August 10 he arrived in Watertown, a few miles to the west of Boston. Everything seemed to be in turmoil. The Provincial Congress was struggling with an avalanche of problems.

Chief among them were those connected with the army invest-
ing Boston — paying them, feeding them, ordering them, housing them. Hancock visited with Washington, who himself had
arrived only one month before. He found the general busy with
the duties of managing an army, but gracious enough always to
find time to entertain so distinguished a guest as the president
of the Continental Congress.

Ceremonies done with, Hancock immediately went to work
sending out his personal and political probes. He had much to
catch up on; a good deal had changed since his April departure.

The most obvious alteration was in the structure of the Massachusetts government. The response of the Continental Congress to Massachusetts' inquiry about setting up a civil government had been vague. Although the men in Philadelphia
approved of the colony's moving forward, they certainly provided no blueprint. Not having the time or inclination to experiment, the Massachusetts Provincial Congress elected to return to the old form of government, as it had been before the
tinkerings of 1774.[31]

Although the form was the same, the substance was a bit
different. Under the old government the House had been pretty
well dominated by eastern interests; in the new House that was
not the case. Through the upheavals of the previous months,
back-country folk had come to discover their power, recognizing
that by shear numbers they could bend events in the House and
impose their more democratic views. The Council, on the other
hand, principally through the political maneuverings of Joseph
Hawley, managed to have several moderate men of eastern
connections in its ranks, including James Bowdoin and two
absentees, Hancock and Thomas Cushing.[32]

In the absence of a governor the Council was playing its own
traditional role as well as that of the executive. A moderate,
Hancock was not eager to alter the old methods any more than
necessary, and for the time being this arrangement pleased him,
though he probably realized that, given the difference in
makeup between the two houses, there was a high probability
of conflict. At any rate, in August political affairs in Massachusetts seemed to be well ordered. Unfortunately, the same could
not be said for Hancock's personal fortunes.

Other than the obvious fact that his property was in enemy hands, Hancock knew virtually nothing about its physical condition. He had heard rumors that Gage's officers were casting lots for his property, but he had no proof. Financially, he was suffering. Two of his largest sources of income, trading and real estate, were at a standstill, and those who owed him money were, under the present uncertain conditions, unable to pay.

His property was in danger, but at least his relatives were safe. Ebenezer, he knew, had escaped, and Edmund Quincy had arrived in Lancaster. In the Boston diaspora, not every one of his relatives had chosen the patriot side. Dolly's brother-in-law Jonathan Sewall, the royal attorney general, had been railing against the patriots for some time. In August he decided to pack up his family and sail for England.[33]

Having hurriedly made his rounds to strengthen the old political and personal ties, Hancock left Watertown on August 24, right after the General Court adjourned. With only four days to spare, he set off for Fairfield by way of Lancaster, where he visited Edmund, whose health would not permit him to make the trip to his daughter's wedding.[34]

On August 28, John Hancock and Dorothy Quincy were married. Although the ceremony took place 150 miles from Boston, it had a distinct flavor of that town. The presiding minister was Andrew Eliot the younger, son of the minister of the New North Church in Boston. The older Eliot had elected to stay in the town with his congregation, suffering under tremendous hardships as he ministered to any who needed him. He did manage to send his young children and wife out to safety, and they were in Fairfield with young Andrew.

According to the dictates of Congregational piety and Revolutionary frugality, the ceremony was a simple affair. The next day, after bidding farewell to friends and most especially Aunt Lydia, the newlyweds set off to Philadelphia on their honeymoon.[35]

The journey was quick and devoid of any special pomp. There were no gawking crowds, no pealing bells or booming cannon. The euphoria of last spring had been tempered by a dose of realism. The carnage at Bunker Hill, the incessant call for troops, supplies, and money, had begun to push romantic no-tions aside as people looked ahead to the grim costs of resistance.

As usual, affairs moved slowly in Philadelphia. Hancock settled into a comfortable home with his "agreeable lady." It was a very pleasant change from his lonesome bachelor days. Indeed, even the irascible John Adams was quick to point out how much Dolly's presence softened the harshness of the hitherto male environment and improved the president's humor.[36]

Unfortunately, though Hancock's social life improved, his health did not fare as well. His increasingly chronic gout laid him low again and made it impossible for him to attend Congress's opening session. Dolly, too, was not well, but her malady probably had more to do with homesickness than any physical affliction.[37]

Whether all in Congress approved or not, clearly it had become a governing body. It had an army and post office, was negotiating treaties with Indians, borrowing money, and in general performing a number of acts normally associated with a sovereign assembly. Staying afloat on this fast-rising sea kept Hancock busier than he had ever been before in his life.[38]

Despite his health problems and duties as president, Hancock undertook another task, that of chairing the newly formed Marine Committee. This body, composed of representatives from each colony — Hancock was the delegate from Massachusetts — had charge of all American naval activities, from the recruitment of crews to the construction and disposition of ships.[39] In his career as an Atlantic merchant, he had accumulated a wealth of experience dealing with ships and the men who sailed them. He relished this post.

As chairman of the Marine Committee, Hancock exercised the executive authority that he lacked as president. Because of the committee's unwieldy size, authority gravitated toward those members in whose colonies important naval activity took place. Thus, Massachusetts, and Boston in particular, after the evacuation, led the way. And Hancock, because of his position on the committee and his power base at home, played a large role in naval affairs.

Initially, Congress only chartered or purchased vessels for its fleet. But finding these provisions inadequate, it laid plans to

build its own warships. In December 1775, it authorized the
construction of thirteen frigates, beginning a program that
would eventually see the launching of more than twenty vessels
for the American service. Of the original thirteen frigates, two
were to be assembled in Massachusetts. Their construction became Hancock's pet project and a matter of great personal
pride. While dealing with the daily issues in Congress, Hancock
also had to cope with personal and political problems. There
was a strongly felt need to hold dissension out of sight. Nevertheless, across this artificial horizon of conformity, occasional
islands of friction loomed. As often as not the issues had as
much to do with style as with substance.

One of the first erupted in September 1775, when Peyton
Randolph reappeared in Philadelphia. Some delegates, John
Adams included, thought Hancock ought to step aside gra-
ciously and let the Virginian take his seat again as president.
Hancock, not inclined to surrender any honor, thought other-
wise and simply ignored the problem. Adams related the inci-
dent to James Warren, the speaker of the Massachusetts House.
Warren joined Adams in snorting at Hancock's graspingness.[40]
The issues might well have continued to fester and perhaps
have even come to a head if providence had not intervened.

> On Sunday eve our late worthy President Mr. Randolph died
> very suddenly. He dined at one Mr. Hollis three miles out of
> town; soon after dinner he was taken with choking and one
> side of his face was distorted and about eight he expired.[41]

Later in the fall another issue came up on which the delegation split. This dispute centered more on politics than personality and involved the appointment of high militia officers in
Massachusetts. It was something in which Hancock had more
than a passing interest.

By a resolution passed on July 18, Congress had recommended
to the colonies "that all officers above the Rank of a Captain,
be appointed by their respective assemblies or conventions, or
in their recess, by the committees of safety appointed by said
assemblies or conventions."[42] The members of the Massachusetts House found this much to their liking, since it extended
their power into an area once the sole preserve of the governor.

The Council balked. It viewed itself as the lineal descendant of the governor and therefore the sole heir to his power. To buttress their case, the councilors pointed to the resolve of the Congress that recommended return to the old charter government, in which this power had clearly sat with the governor. Deadlocked on the question, the two houses adjourned on November 11, parting, in the words of James Warren, "not . . . in the best humor."[43]

Since the Continental Congress had issued these contradictory resolves and since Massachusetts' best political talent was sitting in that body, the delegation in Philadelphia was drawn inexorably into the fray. At its last meeting, the Council dispatched Revere with a letter to the delegates in Philadelphia, outlining its concern over the issue.

As one historian has noted, at first glance the issue may seem trivial. However, that was not the case, for just below the surface lurked some fundamental divisions that had yet to be dealt with. It was the first time that the two houses had been in serious conflict, and the outcome of this imbroglio was bound to influence the entire functioning of the government for some time to come.

By composition, of course, the Council tended to be a moderate, if not conservative, group. Of twenty-eight members, twenty-two came from sections east of Watertown. Only one came from west of Worcester.

In contrast, the House reflected a different makeup. It was under the influence of people who wished "to bring government closer to the people." Electing militia officers would certainly be part of that program.

On the more mundane level was the issue of patronage and spoils. If the Council took the governor's appointing power in toto, it would have available to itself a vast array of political plums to pass out. It naturally preferred to exercise that power alone.

As speaker of the House, Warren understood the implications for his own body. At the same time, he harbored resentment toward Hancock for what he viewed as his influence over the parceling out of jobs. Hancock's sway over appointments in

Massachusetts was considerable, and now added to that was his power as president of the Continental Congress. Bureaucracy is the handmaiden of sovereignty, and, with each passing session, the men in Philadelphia followed the immutable laws of nature and fleshed out their governmental skeleton with a bureaucracy.

By informal agreement any Continental position within a colony was filled by local men whose names were provided by that colony's delegation. Hancock was never shy about pushing his friends and relatives forward, and his success caused resentment in both Philadelphia and Watertown.[44] Warren and his friends wanted to be certain that they got their share. That could best be ensured if the House had an active role to play.

The delegates were divided over the proper response to the Council's letter. Hancock and Cushing, both of whom happened also to be members of the council, decided to respond jointly, and the two Adamses wrote separately. The latter gentlemen saw no impediment to the House electing officers, but they were not eager to lay the matter before the full Congress, since it would only advertise the dissension at home.[45]

Hancock and Cushing felt otherwise. The day after the Adamses' letter, they wrote, indicating their intention to bring the matter before Congress. Neither man was willing to commit himself openly, though it seems likely that each favored the Council's view. When John Adams asked Cushing heatedly if he had an opinion, he waffled and refused to answer. As the presiding officer, Hancock could sail under neutral colors, which spared him the need openly to take a position.[46]

Over the next three or four days, Cushing and Hancock informally surveyed Congress and discovered that sentiment seemed to be running in favor of a role for the House. On November 29 they reversed themselves and, in a second letter, advised the Council that they would not put the issue before Congress and that the Council ought to concede a role to the House. Finding little support for its position, the Council granted the point. The House was given the power to appoint officers, and the Council retained a veto power.[47]

In its aftermath, the militia issue left a residue of ill feeling, with Hancock and Cushing on one side and the Adamses on the other. Cushing was seen as vacillating and a bit Machiavellian, and Hancock, as his friend and ally, was similarly tainted. Such feelings were communicated back home and helped exacerbate a widening rift in the popular party. Ironically, the first victim of the split was Cushing, whose bid for re-election to Congress was successfully blocked in December by his new enemies. His replacement was Elbridge Gerry of Marblehead, a person more attuned to popular interests.[48]

Chapter 12

Back to Boston

*C*USHING RODE HOME carrying his defeat as gracefully as a knife in the ribs. Although beaten once, he was by no means out of politics. He managed to maintain his Council seat and was soon parlaying that into a position of considerable influence. At the same time, his old friend Hancock handed him a post that gave him additional authority. He was named Continental naval agent for Massachusetts. Cushing's job was to oversee all matters relating to the ships. His first task was to find shipwrights. Since Boston was still occupied, that port was out of the question, so Cushing traveled north from his home in Dedham to Newburyport, where, in early 1776, he signed a contract with Stephen Greenleaf and the Cross brothers for the construction of two frigates, one of twenty-four guns and the other of thirty-two.[1]

Hancock doted over his ships, writing more to Cushing during the beginning months of 1776 than to any other person. On one occasion he urged Cushing to "spare no Expence," explaining that the two of them were engaged in a race to launch the first ships and that the honor of both Massachusetts and John Hancock was at stake. Not only should their vessels be the first in the water, but they should be the most beautifully wrought. He directed Cushing to "let the heads and Galleries for the ships be neatly Carv'd and Executed, [and] by all means let ours be as good, handsome, strong, and as early Completed as any that are building here or in any of the other Colonies."[2] Besides his role in the construction of the ships, Hancock involved himself in the selection of captains and officers. Isaac Cazneau, a Boston captain and friend, was named to command the twenty-four-gun frigate, and John Manley, another local captain, was given the thirty-two-gun ship.[3]

Cushing lost the race. The Massachusetts frigates were not the first to sea. Hancock, however, quickly recovered from his embarrassment when he learned that the larger of the two vessels, described by Cushing as a "very fine Ship," would be named *Hancock*.[4] This distinction pleased him, and a few months later he was even more delighted when the Marine Committee ordered that all Continental vessels and their prizes brought to Boston must tie up and transact their business at his wharf. Since Boston was to become the busiest American port for the Continental navy, this directive enhanced the president's prestige as well as his purse.[5]

After being launched, the two frigates idled for months in the harbor, waiting to be outfitted. They lacked everything: guns, sails, rigging, men. For Hancock, these details had become tiresome, and as they and other marine matters pressed upon him, he seemed to grow weary and lose interest. In July 1776, he told Cushing that the burden was too great and that he intended to resign from the committee; but he never did, and for the next year, while he hung on to the chairmanship, the navy suffered because of his desultory attention.

Hancock's decision to remain as chairman caused uneasiness among some members of the committee, and they began privately to question his leadership. Others in Congress shared these misgivings, but in the face of Hancock's immense popularity, they kept their criticisms to themselves or shared them only with friends.

The murmurings, though, could not escape the notice of a politician like Hancock. He possessed an uncanny sense for political trends, and he displayed an extraordinary sensitivity to the smallest slight or criticism. Most painful to him was the reported attempt by some men in Massachusetts to discredit him. The principal source for this piece of intelligence was

Cushing, a man who was hardly unbiased in his perceptions. He continued to resent the suggestion of his enemies that he was timid and cautious and blamed his political misfortunes on a cabal in the Provincial Congress.[6] Hancock perceived this attack on his friend as an indirect attack against himself.[7] His fears were well founded, for unhappiness with the president was on the rise in the Provincial Congress, the Continental Congress, and in the Massachusetts delegation itself.

By early February 1776, the two Adamses and Elbridge Gerry had formed a conscious majority in the Massachusetts delegation, and they were, in John Adams' words, "no longer vexed or enfeebled by . . . indecision, or indolence."[8] They welcomed Cushing's departure, and they probably would have been equally pleased if Hancock had left, too.

The new year saw Hancock and Congress busier than ever. There seemed to be no end to the paper work, committee meetings, and general sessions. Six days was the normal work week. Committees often convened at seven in the morning and met until ten. At ten, Congress met and, after a brief break for lunch, sat until about five. After supper committees regrouped and continued their business until ten in the evening.[9]

As president, Hancock was expected to do nearly everything that a delegate did and more. Naturally, he presided, but beyond that he had also to deal with the mounting correspondence flowing in and out of his office. Thomson helped with some of the burden, but it was more than the two of them could handle alone. Various clerks were employed, sometimes paid out of Hancock's own pocket. Other times he employed, again often at his own expense, private secretaries to assist him. One item that the president had to handle personally was the signing of all official documents, especially commissions. This chore caused him and Dolly some late nights, as he sat up affixing that beautiful signature to papers that had to be in the morning post.

Although politics engulfed his daily activities, Hancock was not unmindful of other orbits in which his life was spinning. One of these was his business. He was desperate for cash, and in January he sent William Bant, Palfrey's successor, off on a round of bill-collecting through New England. Bant found Hancock's debtors as tight for cash as the president himself. He reported that he rode 500 miles and "could not collect £100 . . ."[10] It would have been unseemly to press people who were suffering in the patriot cause, so Hancock had no choice but to suffer these debtors as he expected others to endure him.

March brought some good news. On the 17th, after a siege of nearly one year, the British evacuated Boston. Among the first to go across the Neck was Hancock's aide John Lowell. He was pleased to report that the mansion house had not been seriously damaged and was, in fact, in tolerably good shape, a blessing that can probably be attributed to the house's occupant, General Henry Clinton, whose sense of decency helped restrain the vandal-like instincts of his troops.[11]

Not everything had escaped. Hancock's fine wine cellar, one of the best in Boston, had been ransacked by none other than his own cousin William Bowes. With the connivance of the sheriff, Bowes had taken more than £350 worth of the best spirits, some of it probably good smuggled Madeira. Wisely, Bowes had fled to London, so Hancock could do nothing but fume at the perfidy of his own relatives. Later he was to try a lawsuit, but that had no effect.[12]

Elsewhere in the town he did not escape as lightly. Bant did a thorough inventory of all his property and came up with a total loss of nearly £5000.[13] Two houses were completely destroyed, along with one vessel. The "soldiers and whores" who took over his seven brick tenements down by the Mill Creek left them in shambles. The greatest single piece of damage was done by a fire down at his wharf that burned out several stores and left over £1000 in damages in its wake.

Whatever the cost, it was a great relief to have the British out, and as things brightened in Boston, life took a turn for the better in Philadelphia, as well. The Hancocks moved "into a noble house in an airy open place in Arch Street corner of Fourth."[14] At their new location they did a goodly amount of entertaining. Washington was a guest shortly after he left Boston. So, too, were numerous delegates and people on business to the Congress. The more regular visitors included John Dickinson and Robert Morris of Pennsylvania, and James Duane of New York.

From the guest list it is clear that the president, much to the dismay of some of his New England brethren, seemed to prefer the company of the rich and conservative merchants from New York and Pennsylvania. That, plus the somewhat extravagant style in which he lived in his "noble house" offended the highly developed Puritan sensibilities of Sam Adams. By the middle of March, the estrangement between the two men was growing worse. Their relationship took a hard blow when the Congress resolved itself into a committee of the whole "to take into consideration the state of New York."[15] In the past, Hancock had usually selected the Rhode Island delegate, Samuel Ward, to chair this committee, a choice approved by his Massachusetts colleagues. Ward was an old political wheelhorse with impeccable Whig credentials, and Adams and the others assumed that he would again be asked to take the chair. But this time Hancock revealed other plans.

According to John Adams, Benjamin Harrison, a conservative Virginian and close friend of Hancock's, had been courting the president's favor for some time.[16] Hancock, knowing full well how politically obnoxious Ward was to the conservatives, especially to Duane and Dickinson, encouraged Harrison's friendship. And to please his new friends, he passed over Ward for the chairmanship and announced that Harrison was his choice to take the chair. The New Englanders, especially Sam Adams, were outraged at this betrayal, and, for the rest of his time in Congress, they barely spoke a word to the president.

In May he got the good news that the General Court had elected him first major general of militia. Hancock was delighted with the honor and promised that as soon as he got home he would "put the Militia upon a respectable footing . . ."[17] His victory stood as vivid testimony to his popularity and clout, which he could exercise even when 400 miles away. Those who might challenge him took note.

Early in the spring he had planned to take a short leave from Congress and pay a visit to Fairfield. He had not seen Lydia since the wedding, and when he had left her, she had not been feeling very well. She had since improved, but, still, she was over sixty, and her nephew was concerned. A visit was in order.

By mid-April the press of business, especially talk of independence, made such a visit impossible, so he planned, if her health would permit, to bring her to Philadelphia. She never came. On April 15, she suffered a stroke but seemed to recover. On the 25th, Lydia died.[18]

Hancock and Dolly were grief-stricken. She had been a mother to both of them. For Dolly it was even worse than for her husband. She had just learned that she was pregnant and was looking forward to Lydia's arrival to help with the management of her household. Hancock asked if Catherine, Dolly's older spinster sister, would come in her place. She was living with her father in Lancaster, but he let her go, seeing in the request the "providence of God . . . [calling her] to take so long a Journey, as from hence to Philadelphia in order to accompany a Sister who by the same providence, had been conducted thither." Bant, who was on his way to Philadelphia with some cash, was ordered to stop by Lancaster and escort "Kathy." They arrived in Philadelphia late in the spring.[19]

Lydia had left a very handsome estate. She distributed more than £5000 in cash to a wide assortment of friends and relatives. The Brattle Square Church received a large brick house on Queen Street to be used as a parsonage. She also freed her slaves. The remainder of the estate was left to Hancock. Since there was no inventory it is difficult to assess exactly what this meant, but it seems likely that it included a fair amount of real estate in Boston as well as considerable undeveloped land throughout New England. There was also about £4000 in cash.[20]

Following close on the heels of the news from Fairfield came something nearly as distressing from Boston. For the first time in a decade, Hancock was not elected to the House nor was he re-elected to the Council. Hancock was hurt. He wrote to Cushing: "I find I am left out of both House and Council, I can't help it, they have a Right to do as they please. I think I do not merit such Treatment but my Exertions [and] my life are [and] shall be at their service . . ."[21]

He need not have worried. The election results showed the

eastern moderates in control of both the House and the Council. Most likely Hancock was dropped from the list because of his fellow citizens' concern for what smacked of pluralism.[22] He could not expect to be simultaneously delegate to Congress, president of Congress, major general of the militia, member of the House, and selectman of Boston. Whatever his disappointment, he had little time to lament, for the summer of 1776 was an important period in Philadelphia.

A reading of the *Journals of the Continental Congress* for the summer of 1776 would never lead one to believe that this body had under discussion the most important decision in American history — independence. The idea did not spring forth suddenly like Athena from the head of Zeus. It had been mentioned in letters, whispered in corridors, and alluded to in the press. It was obvious that sentiment for a break with Great Britain was on the rise. The critical item was timing, for "the Torrent of Independence" had to be caught at full flood. If Congress made a move that proved to be premature and failed, that would spell disaster. Unless the decision was unanimous, it should not be made at all.

The first of the colonies to take a clear stand was North Carolina. On April 12, the Provincial Congress of that colony resolved: "that the Delegates for this colony in the Continental Congress be impowered to concur with the delegates of the other Colonies in declaring Independency . . ."[23]

North Carolina's zeal was infectious. Other colonies expressed similar feelings. On May 10, the Continental Congress resolved:

> that it be recommended to the respective assemblies and conventions of the United Colonies, where no government sufficient to the exigencies of their affairs have been hitherto established, to adopt such government as shall, in the opinion of the representatives of the people, best conduce to the happiness and safety of their constituents in particular, and America in General.[24]

The resolution passed easily, but not so the preamble, which John Adams framed. Adams' preamble went far beyond what some in the Congress wished. For five days the debate went on;

at last, in a significant victory for the forces favoring independence, it passed. The heart of it stated:

> And whereas, it appears absolutely irreconcileable to reason
> and good conscience, for the people of these colonies now to
> take the oaths and affirmations necessary for the support of
> any government under the crown of Great Britain, and it is
> necessary that the exercise of every kind of authority under
> the said crown should be totally suppressed, and all the pow-
> ers of government exerted, under the authority of the people
> of the colonies, for the preservation of internal peace, virtue,
> and good order, as well as for the defence of their lives, lib-
> erties, and properties, against the hostile invasions and cruel
> depredations of their enemies; therefore, resolved . . .[25]

The position of the other Massachusetts delegates did not
differ from Adams'. They were among the strongest for independence. Gerry, the newest member of the group, had actually
written to James Warren in March urging that the Provincial
Congress instruct the delegates to favor independence.

Unlike the Adamses and Gerry, who seem to have been constantly writing, Hancock, aside from his official correspondence,
wrote very little. He had no time. Evidence as to what he
thought must be gleaned from sources other than his own testimony. One source, highly inimical, is Stephen Higginson, who
many years later, in a series of stinging essays, attacked almost
every part of Hancock's character. He alleged that Hancock
opposed independence "until it became inevitable . . ."[26]

As a source of information, Higginson is worse than tainted;
he is poison. He hated Hancock, was never present in Philadelphia, and relied for information on biased sources and his own
imagination. To rely on him is to take testimony from a Pharisee
about a Sadducee. Had he wished, in his position as presiding
officer, Hancock could have stalled or diverted the trend toward
independence, but he seems never to have done that, and certainly none of his contemporaries, even those who disliked him,
ever complained of presidential foot-dragging.

Congress's decisions on May 10 and 15, advising the colonies
to suppress royal authority, gave the body a proper head, and
on the 16th they ordered Washington to attend at Philadelphia

"in order to consult with Congress upon such measures as may be necessary for the carrying on the ensuing campaign."[27] Congress was at war; independence was only a matter of time.

On the 18th came disturbing news from Canada. The invasion that had been launched in 1775 was turning into a rout as the American forces crumbled in the face of the advancing British. At the same time came confirmation of the rumor that the king had indeed hired German mercenaries to reduce his American subjects.

The pattern was becoming clear. Britain was placing her faith in the force of arms and leaving America little choice — either submit or resist. Reconciliation was impossible. At this crucial moment Hancock made an eloquent and emotional appeal to Americans, urging them to enlist in the struggle:

> The Militia of the United Colonies are a Body of Troops that may be depended on . . . They are called upon to say, whether they will live Slaves, or die Freemen — they are requested to step forth in Defence of their Wives, their Children, and Liberty, and every Thing they hold dear. The Cause is certainly a most glorious one, and I trust that every man . . . is determined to see it gloriously ended, or perish in the ruins of it.[28]

On Friday, June 7, Richard Henry Lee of Virginia offered three resolutions:

> That these United Colonies are, and of right ought to be, free and independent States, that they are absolved from all allegiance to the British Crown, and that all political connection between them and the State of Great Britain is, and ought to be, totally dissolved.
>
> That it is expedient forthwith to take the most effectual measures for forming Alliances.
>
> That a plan of confederation be prepared and transmitted to the respective Colonies for their consideration and approbation.[29]

Lee's resolutions made for a busy weekend in Philadelphia. Congress sat all day Saturday, until seven at night, in heated discussion. Sunday was a day out of the chamber but not away

from politics, and on Monday morning, when Hancock reconvened the assembly, the opposing forces were ready to do battle.[30]

In the first skirmish, the conservatives won a small victory
when they managed to get a decision on Lee's first resolution
postponed until July 1. The proponents of the resolution scored
a gain, though, when Congress agreed that "in the meantime,
that no time be lost, in case the Congress agree thereto, that a
committee be appointed to prepare a declaration to the effect
of the said first resolution." The committee consisted of a tall
redhead from Virginia, Thomas Jefferson, along with John
Adams, the ageless Benjamin Franklin, Roger Sherman of Connecticut, and Robert R. Livingston from New York.[31]

Debate on the floor made it clear that at least six colonies
were, in the words of Jefferson, "not yet matured for fully falling
from the parent stem, but that they were fast advancing to that
state . . ." Time would bring them around.[32]

On Monday morning, July 1, Congress resolved itself into a
committee of the whole to discuss more freely the "great question of independency." For most of the day they wrangled,
until finally they reported it out favorably. Approval was not
unanimous. Pennsylvania and South Carolina had voted no, and
Delaware, with only two delegates present, was divided. "[At]
the request of a colony" the final vote was delayed until the
following day.[33]

On July 2 (not the 4th) Congress declared independence, with
the *Journals* noting laconically, "The Congress resumed the consideration of the resolution agreed to by and reported from the
committee of the whole; and the same being read was agreed
to as follows . . . [Lee's resolution]. Twelve of the thirteen colonies present voted yea; only New York, whose delegates had
received no instructions, abstained.[34] In a state of near-euphoria
John Adams wrote home to Abigail:

> The second day of July, 1776, will be the most memorable
> epocha in the history of America. I am apt to believe that it
> will be celebrated by succeeding generations as the great an-
> niversary Festival. It ought to be commemorated, as the day
> of deliverance by solemn acts of devotion to God Almighty. It

ought to be solemnized with pomp and parade, with shows, games, sports, guns, bells, bonfires, and illuminations, from one end of this continent to the other, from this time forward, forevermore.[35]

It was one of the greatest good fortunes of Hancock's life that Adams was wrong. Simply declaring independence was not sufficient, for in the best traditions of the eighteenth-century Enlightenment, such a radical move had to be justified and explained to a "candid world." To that end Jefferson's committee had prepared a declaration. The draft had been presented on June 28 and was under discussion when the events of July 2 took place.[36] The document, with its ringing phrases and haunting cadences, was principally the work of Jefferson himself. On the 4th, with some minor alterations, it was approved as "The Unanimous Declaration of the Thirteen United States of America."[37]

Contrary to all the romantic images conjured up by novelists, artists, and playwrights, there was no ceremonial signing of the Declaration of Independence. All the delegates did not troop solemnly by the secretary's desk to affix their signatures to what was, in effect, their own death warrant. Only one man signed on the 4th — John Hancock. The other fifty-three signatures were put to the document between then and November 4th.[38]

The apocryphal story of Hancock's signing has been repeated so many times that by now it deserves to be true even if it is not. As he sprawled that handsome signature, his hallmark since the days at Abiah Holbrook's, he remarked, "There! John Bull can read my name without spectacles and may now double his reward £500 on my head. That is my defiance."[39] Hancock need not have done anything else, either before or after the Fourth of July. By this one brief act, his place in history was secured.

Congress may have declared independence, but the war news made final victory uncertain. From the Northern Department, General Philip Schuyler reported a sizable enemy force preparing to advance south. Washington was in an even worse situation in New York, where the British had landed a huge expeditionary force. As the summer wore on, the news got worse, and the enemy, triumphant in New York, marched across New Jersey toward Philadelphia. By early fall the situation was precarious. General William Howe was in pursuit of Washington. Then, with the momentum still in their favor and New York City securely in their hands, the British settled down into winter quarters to await better campaigning weather in the spring. Amidst the gloom there was one good piece of news. Hancock was the father of a girl, Lydia Henchman Hancock.

As Howe's forces closed in on Philadelphia, Congress grew more nervous. The croakers feared that, before retiring to winter quarters, the British would attack the capital. Rather than risk capture, Congress voted, on December 12, to abandon the city and move to Baltimore.[40]

The distance to the temporary capital was not great, only about a hundred miles, but it included some of the worst travel conditions possible. Winter had turned the roads into a quagmire. The presidential party — Dolly barely out of bed, an infant less than a month old, and a few cumbersome wagons loaded with personal possessions and official papers — moved slowly south. The dismal accommodations along the way did not make the trip any more pleasant. Because of the unusually heavy traffic, inns were full and rooms scarce. As president, Hancock could expect no favors, and he took his turn with the other travelers, in dark, drafty, and cramped quarters.

The trip would have been a mite easier if Hancock had not been so burdened with records. Among the mass of documents he was trundling around were those of the treasurer of Harvard College. Ever since his election to that office he had been charged with keeping the college books, as well as caring for more than £15,000 in cash and securities.[41] In April, shortly before his departure for Philadelphia, the college had asked him to turn over the books and cash before he left. In the confusion of the events following Lexington and Concord, Hancock had never had an opportunity to comply with the request, so in his baggage he still had the Harvard College records.[42]

The inconvenience to the college of having its treasurer and his books so far away was considerable. In December, the overseers appointed one of the college tutors, Stephen Hall, to go to

Philadelphia to retrieve the records. Hall left about the 12th. By the time he got as far as Fairfield, he learned that Congress had taken off for Baltimore. Being a prickly and precise academician, he decided that, since his instructions read Philadelphia, he could not go to Baltimore. He wrote back to Cambridge for new instructions, and in the meantime spent several days at ease in Fairfield. It took the college officers several more days to decided whether Hall should go to Baltimore, but, finally, on January 7, they told him to go.[43]

Compared with Philadelphia, Baltimore was a backwater town, hardly prepared for the honor of hosting the Continental Congress. Available rooms were quickly grabbed up at exorbitant prices. Luckily for the Hancocks, Samuel Purviance, a prominent merchant and Continental agent in Baltimore, invited them to move in with his family. When at last they found their own house, it was a change for the worse. The place was small and costly (£25 per month) and in a dangerous part of town. Within two days of their move, thieves had broken in and taken the president's trunk, loaded with linen, books, paper, and money. Their problems caused him to write to his friend Robert Treat Paine that he dearly wished to go home to Boston.[44]

Amidst the melancholy, Hall arrived. He went to Hancock, showed him his instructions from the college, and asked him for the books and money. Hancock was annoyed. He rightly suspected that, along with the papers and money, the college wanted his resignation but hadn't the courage to come straight out and ask for it. Hall left Baltimore with less than he wished. Hancock sent him off with most of the money, but no accumulated interest, only a few of the books, and no resignation. This "small breeze" between the college and the president had all the promise of turning into a gale.[45]

After Hall left, Hancock wrote to Bant and asked him to lay a letter, explaining his position, before the corporation at its March meeting. He also delivered some veiled threats at "vengeance" if the overseers displaced him as treasurer.[46] The reaction of the corporation came in the form of a letter, more than 7000 words long, in which they demanded a better accounting of the college's funds. Still, though, they held back from replacing him, hoping that he would resign. Finally, in July, with the treasurer and many of his accounts still absent, the corporation, without waiting for the post to be vacant, elected a new treasurer, Ebenezer Storer. In September, Hancock accounted for £16,443 to Storer, but that was hardly the end of the story. Hancock and Harvard were destined to have a bittersweet relationship for many years to come.[47]

Hall's brief visit to Baltimore was just another spot of gray in a very drab landscape. Hancock was not alone in his feelings; nearly all the delegates wished to be rid of the town. It was so remote that William Ellery, a Rhode Island delegate, compared life there to living on the moon, and the eminent Dr. Benjamin Rush felt as if he were shut up in a convent.[48] Expense, too, was a problem. According to some, it cost twice as much to live in Baltimore as in Philadelphia, though the City of Brotherly Love was far from inexpensive. All this to live, in the words of Ellery, in "the dirtiest Place . . . [they] . . . ever saw."[49] For two and a half months, the delegates remained in Baltimore, wondering when it would be safe to return to Philadelphia.

They need not have wondered, for events proved that their departure from Philadelphia had been premature. Instead of marching on the capital, the British stopped at the Delaware River. The main body withdrew to New York, leaving only scattered garrisons to protect their forward areas.

One of these exposed encampments was at Trenton, where Colonel Johann Rall and 1200 Hessians stood guard over the town. On Christmas night, while Rall and his men were busy celebrating, Washington crossed the Delaware. His plan was brilliant and well executed. The Americans took the Hessians by surprise. Rall was killed and two thirds of his men were either casualties or prisoners. Eight days later, Washington paid another unannounced visit, this time to the British garrison at Princeton, with similar results.

Trenton and Princeton saved the Revolution and even infused some spirit into the Congress. When it became obvious that the British were not going to occupy the town, Congress decided to go home. On February 27, 1777, the delegates voted to adjourn from Baltimore and to meet again on March 5 in Philadelphia.[50]

After a farewell dinner given in his honor, Hancock prepared for the trip to Philadelphia. To avoid putting his wife, Kathy, and young Lydia through the ordeal of another winter journey, he decided to leave them in Baltimore until the weather improved. As usual, the president's travel plans went awry. There was a mix-up in the quartermaster's department, and not enough wagons were sent to carry his baggage and official papers. Hancock had never been an especially forgiving person, and the stay in Baltimore had made him a bit petulant; he complained bitterly over the confusion and inconvenience. He could have waited in Baltimore until the wagons arrived, but that would have meant days lost. Instead, he climbed into his phaeton and headed alone, with only a servant or two, toward Philadelphia, leaving behind his family and most of his belongings.[51]

Again, innkeepers showed him no favor. At Stephenson's, on the Susquehanna River, he was asked to give up his private room to a married couple and sleep downstairs in the common room, with the other single men. Such inconveniences were wearing at any time, but this trip, which ordinarily should have taken only two or three days, was particularly difficult. High water on the river prevented the ferry from crossing, and almost a week passed before Hancock rode into Philadelphia, on Friday, March 7.[52] From Friday to the following Wednesday, the other delegates straggled in, so not until the 12th were there enough present to make a quorum.

The prospects for an American victory looked no better now than when Congress had left for Baltimore. The Christmastime victories at Trenton and Princeton had given new life to the army, but it was still small, ill trained, and in almost all ways inferior to the British. Howe stood poised with his army in New York, and his intentions for the spring campaign remained a mystery, although everyone assumed Philadelphia topped his list of targets. To the north, the threat was equally grave, as General John Burgoyne pointed his juggernaut south for the march on Albany.

Despite the uncertain prospects, Congress pushed ahead. It

lacked nearly everything necessary to fight a war, especially that most essential commodity — money. Thus far, the French, in a clandestine arrangement, had sent some supplies and munitions, but they were unwilling to commit themselves openly to a cause which would mean war with Great Britain. The delegates struggled valiantly to increase the army and to launch a powerful navy, ignoring the pitiful inadequacy of the foundation they were building on. From the perspective of 200 years, one wonders not that the Americans won, but that they even survived.

Hancock was tired. By September 1777, he had served in Congress for more than two years and had been its president for nearly as long. His health was not good, and his psychological state was not much better. Dolly had hated Baltimore, and Philadelphia did not stand much higher in her esteem. When she had come back to Philadelphia, Hancock had expected that she would remain with him in town. Dolly, though, had a mind of her own and she wanted to go home. And home she went, taking Lydia with her.

Hancock missed his wife and child. Dolly's writing habits had not improved, and he was forced to spend weeks without any word from her. In the summer of 1777 he did receive some news from home, but it was the kind he could have done without. Lydia, not yet one year old, had taken ill and died.[53] Hancock felt more alone than ever, and Dolly's neglect hardly made it easier for him. In her grief, she wrote to him even less than before. Finally, in a fit of pique, he wrote, "I will only say that I expected oftener to have been the object of your attention."[54]

At least once a week during the summer, Hancock and several other gentlemen gathered for an evening of drinking and eating.[55] He loved a good feast, but his rich diet did his health no good. It also did little for his public image, and some complained about the high costs of the presidential household. Hancock had a quick response to such criticism: "I have Expended my own money [and] in that case had a Right to drink wine if I pleased . . ."[56]

More than ever Hancock longed for home. In the fall, Howe was closer to Philadelphia. Washington positioned himself to defend the capital, a political, not a military, necessity. On September 11, his army was defeated at Brandywine Creek, leaving Philadelphia wide open to attack. With no other choice before it, Congress voted to evacuate, going first to Lancaster, Pennsylvania, and then across the Susquehanna to York. To no one's surprise, on September 26 the British occupied Philadelphia.

It was a depressing time for Americans. To Hancock and the Congress, York was Baltimore all over again, only worse, for it was even more isolated and provincial. Nor did it add to the attractiveness of the place that the local farmers were mostly "Pennsylvania Dutch," whose manners were as different from the English as their language.[57]

Life was hardly any better for Washington and his men. On October 4, he attacked Howe at Germantown. It was a close and well-fought battle, but again the Americans were forced to withdraw. Washington kept his army in the field for two more months, accomplishing very little. Then, on December 11, he marched his men toward Valley Forge, where they were soon to begin their wintry hell.

On October 16, Congress received the glorious news of General Gates's victory over Burgoyne at Saratoga. The details were yet to come, but all the preliminary indications pointed to a great success. In the midst of the jubilation Hancock decided he needed a rest. He told Jefferson, "My constant application to Publick Business both in and out of Congress has so impaired my Health, that some Relaxation has become absolutely necessary and tomorrow morning I set out for Boston with the Leave of Congress to be absent two Months . . ."[58]

In typical Hancockian fashion, the president left Congress in a swirl of controversy. He insisted on making a farewell speech. In the short history of the Congress, no one had ever demanded that, and some delegates viewed it as more posturing by a man who was nearly as good an actor as he was a politician. His critics suffered through the address, hoping that it would end their association with the Bostonian. But at its conclusion a delegate moved that "the thanks of Congress be presented to John Hancock." This maneuver was too much for the New

Englanders, and they immediately objected to the motion, claiming that it was "improper to thank any president for the discharge of the duties of that office." The vote on the objection was divided, so it failed, but every member of the Massachusetts delegation, Hancock excepted, supported the objection. The original motion of thanks passed by a margin of only six states to four. The four states who opposed were Massachusetts, New Hampshire, Rhode Island, and Pennsylvania.[59]

For the journey to Boston, Hancock requested a military escort from Washington. The general could hardly spare the men, but he agreed to send a detachment of fifteen dragoons.[60] On the road north, the entourage met William Ellery, the Rhode Island delegate, who was on his way to York after a leave at home. Ellery, a friend neither to pomp nor to Hancock, compared the president with the recently humiliated Burgoyne, perhaps hoping that his star, too, might fall:

> I verily believe that the President as he passes through the Country thus escorted, feels a more triumphant Satisfaction than the Col. of the Queen's Light Dragoons attended by his whole army and an escort of a thousand militia.[61]

Despite Ellery's caustic observations, it seems likely that Hancock was not traveling in great comfort. His gout was bad again, and he rode with his foot wrapped up in gauze and propped up on a seat. He was still taking all sorts of pills for his ailment, none of which seemed to do much good, including a "turkey rhubarb" concoction that, according to one of his secretaries, was being taken as a "precaution . . . that whatever morbid matter may be made loose in the system may have a certain opportunity of being carried off immediately."[62]

If all went according to plan, Dolly was to meet her husband either at Fairfield or Hartford, with a light carriage, servants, and William Bant. Things did not go according to plan. Because the British sat in New York, the Hancock party was forced to make a long detour to the north, crossing the Hudson far above the city. Added to that was the slowness of the cumbersome wagons, which were laden with all of the president's belongings. By November 8, the convoy was still sixty miles from Hartford.

From there, Hancock wrote to Dolly about his "many Difficulties on the Road" but told her, "I shall not mind. The Remembrance of these Difficulties will vanish when I have the happiness of seeing you." Within a few days he had his wish. Dolly met him at Hartford. By Monday, the 17th, the couple was in Worcester. On November 19, after an absence of more than two years, Hancock made his grand return to Boston.[63] With the escort of Continental dragoons prancing ahead, his carriage came across the Neck and into the town, where it was met by a cheering crowd and the Company of Cadets, specially mustered to meet their former colonel.

Chapter 13

Governor Hancock

*A*s HE RODE through Boston, Hancock looked about and saw how much the town had changed in the two and a half years of his absence. None of it was for the better. He passed empty buildings, knocked-down fences, and streets that seemed to have far fewer people in them than before. Compared with the days before the Tea Party, the harbor looked absolutely empty. He was pleased to see that his own wharf was busy — only a quarter of the stores were vacant — but elsewhere along the waterfront empty warehouses and docks were the rule.[1]

As the carriage made its turn off Marlborough Street and up toward Beacon Hill, he got his first view of home. Of all the things he had thus far seen, this had changed the least. With the help of Bant and two groundkeepers, Saunders and Spriggs, Dolly had mended the house and gardens; even though it was late fall, the grounds were neat and crisp in their nakedness, the barn was in good order, and the house stood just as he remembered it.

At the gate some of the old staff was there to welcome him. It was a moment of joy but also of sadness, for as he walked up the brick path toward the front door he thought of the one person who was not there — Aunt Lydia. It was the first time he had ever been in the house without her.

After a brief rest Hancock set about his affairs. William Bant had been a good steward. He was a former Son of Liberty and a minor merchant in the town. In 1776, when Hancock had arranged for William Palfrey to become paymaster general of the Eastern Department, Bant stepped in as chief clerk.[2] They spent several hours together, taking inventory and trying to piece together the remnants of the House of Hancock.

Bant had been traveling from Portsmouth, New Hampshire, to Cape Cod, trying to collect overdue debts and rents. It was a thankless job that, on one occasion, when he was accused of being a horse thief, nearly cost him time in jail. The people he dunned either did not have any money and promised to pay when they did or else paid in depreciated currency, which Hancock was honor bound to accept, although it cost him dearly. At the end of two trips Bant came back with nearly £1500 in cash and saddlebags full of promises.[3]

Bill-collecting was only one of Bant's responsibilities. He also cared for Hancock's property and, in his boss's absence, made some business decisions. One of these had to do with the remnants of Hancock's fleet. Scott had sold his vessel in England and then remained there himself, but at least two others were laid up, *Whalebone* and *Undutied Tea*, one in Boston and the other in Salem. Under the circumstances, converting them to cash made more sense than keeping them, and Bant was able to get rid of them for £1000. Thus ended the dream of a Hancock fleet.[4]

As they reviewed the books it was obvious that the trend which had been under way before the war was now nearly complete. Aside from a few private dealings, Hancock's mercantile pursuits were over. The bulk of his wealth was concentrated in speculative land holdings and Boston real estate. He did have a potash works in Hopkinton, but it seems never to have been large and could not have provided much income.[5] These activities plus interest income, collection of old debts, and salaries paid to him for public service were his only sources of income.

Although it is impossible to tell for certain, it seems reasonable to assume that the war reduced Hancock's income and put him in a cash bind, as it did everyone else. This is partially borne out by the fact that, despite numerous opportunities, he never invested in privateers or confiscated Loyalist property. Perhaps he simply thought these were bad investments, but, given his free-wheeling business style, that seems unlikely, and a better bet is that he did not have the cash. However, if he was short of funds, it did not demonstrably affect his life style, which was as baronial as ever; nor did it force him, at least in the seventies, to dispose of chunks of real estate.[6]

Having surveyed business matters, Hancock was satisfied to leave them in Bant's hands while he continued to move back and forth on the political stage. He never again echoed his prewar complaints that politics took time from business; he was now content to play the role of statesman and leave trade to Bant.

Hancock had need to spend time politicking. The Warren-Adams sniping had found some marks. They had already managed to deal Cushing a blow and would have dearly loved to administer one to Hancock. Driven on by their own sense of republican virtue, which was informed by the Puritan spirit, they found considerable fault with Hancock's high living and popularity-courting. More and more they resented the adulation heaped on him while they bathed in neglect. It could not have gone over well with the proud Adamses that the same crowds and newspapers that were so fascinated with Hancock almost completely ignored them when they returned home from Congress.

In a letter, ironically carried by Hancock himself from Philadelphia, Sam Adams made some characteristically unkind references to the president:

> I hope the Person to be elected in my Room will have understanding enough to know when the Arts of Flattery are played upon him, and Fortitude of mind sufficient to resist and despise them. This I mention *inter nos* . . . In this evil World there are oftentimes large Doses prepared for those whose stomachs will bear them. And it would be a Disgrace to human nature to affirm there are some who can take the fullest Cup without nauseating.
>
> I suppose you have by this time finished a form of Government. I hope the greatest Care will be taken in the Choice of a Governor. He, whether a wise Man or a Fool, will in a great

Measure form the Morals and Manners of the People. I beg Pardon, for hinting the Possibility of one of the last Character being chosen. But alas! Is there not such a Possibility![7]

Such verbal raids did not pose a serious threat, but they were nettlesome. With better organization and more sensitivity to popular sentiment, the Adams-Warren faction would have been potent enemies. As it was, they were influential men whose opinions could not be lightly dismissed and who, when aroused, could raise considerable noise.

A more serious indicator of problems than sly letters were the returns at the polls. Hancock, who had been elected to the House in 1776, was not chosen a selectman in '77, marking the first time in a dozen years that he had not served on the board. He might take some comfort from his re-election to the House in '77, but it was not the kind of victory he was accustomed to: Boston's top vote-getter came in fifth in a field of six.[8]

Hancock's political problems turned out to be niggling. Once back in Boston he easily regained his standing by using the same tactics that had served him so well in the past. He played on his reputation as a great patriot and dispensed his own money for the public good. When it was pointed out that there was an immediate need for "some effectual Method . . . for providing for the poor of the Town during the Winter more especially for the aged [and] infirm persons in the Almshouse, who are improvided with Wood [and] Clothing . . ." he stepped forward and donated 150 cords of wood.[9]

He was also one of the first persons to whom widows and orphans looked for assistance. He helped support the children of Joseph Warren, the hero of Bunker Hill, and was generous in advancing money to friends, including, ironically enough, Sam Adams. He also looked after the families of men who had been taken away by the war. Among them was James Lovell, delegate to Congress, who relied on Hancock to keep a watchful eye on his wife and children.[10] His philanthropy paid a quick dividend. On December 4, 1777, he was re-elected a delegate to Congress, and four days later the town meeting voted unanimously to make him moderator.[11]

For whatever reason, John Hancock was a generous man and

the people loved him for it. He was their idol. The owners of the Newburyport privateer *Civil Usage* made him a gift of an item of cargo taken from a captured prize. It was an "elegant chariot," in which he rode through the streets of Boston, "attended by four servants dressed in superb livery, mounted on fine horses richly caparisoned; and escorted by fifty horsemen with drawn sabres . . ."[12] Even allowing for exaggeration, which seems always to have been part of his life, such splendor was hardly in keeping with Revolutionary austerity; but the populace adored him, and the affection was returned.

Popularity was exactly what Hancock was relying on to bring him the biggest prize yet — the governorship of Massachusetts. In June 1777, over the objections of several towns, the General Court had organized itself into a constitutional convention to draw up a new frame of government for Massachusetts.[13] It was common knowledge that such an instrument would call for a governor's office, and there was no doubt as to who would claim the post. Hancock wanted the office — indeed, he felt it was his by right — and there was no one foolish enough to dispute him for it.

Although he was ready to grab the prize, Hancock was not necessarily eager to play the game. There was bound to be trouble. Easterners were fearful of westerners' motives in pressing for a constitution. Many objected to the role of the House and thought a specially elected convention ought to draw up the document. Others were simply contented with things as they were. At best, the proposal would have rough sledding; at worst, it would not pass at all. Hancock followed the wisest course by remaining aloof. If it failed, he was untainted; if it passed, he could claim the governorship without being accused of designing the post for his own aggrandizement.

After some delay, the House and Council in joint session elected a committee to work on the constitution. As the committee went about its work, periodically reporting back, the House continued its regular business. Hancock served on several committees; he was especially drawn toward those dealing with the militia, where the "general" felt he had some expertise. Still, unlike his behavior in some previous sessions, he seemed content to play a relatively quiet role. Why the change? It may well have been his health. It was winter and his leg was gouty, as usual, but it may also have been politics. Better to let his two able allies in the House, John Pickering and Thomas Cushing, take the point and leave him to follow in safety.

The most controversial issue in the constitution was the chronic question of representation. According to the extreme western position, every incorporated place ought to have the right to send a representative. The more populous east insisted

The architects of the settlement were Cushing and Pickering. Although they were easterners, they had already made a gesture toward the western reformers when they put forward a proposal to deny the governor a veto, a move in keeping with western fears of a strong executive. With a link established, Cushing and Pickering worked assiduously to find a compromise on representation. The result was an agreement stipulating that all incorporated places had the right to send at least one representative, but each had to pay his way. The latter provision made the compromise acceptable to the easterners, who, from experience, knew that small western communities were unlikely to bear the expense of sending a man all the way to Boston for meetings of the House. Possible and real representation were two entirely different matters. The next day, February 28, the convention passed the constitution and sent it out to the towns for ratification.[14]

Considering the subsequent rejection of the constitution by a majority of voters, including those in Pickering's Salem and Cushing's Boston, it is difficult to understand the part of these two men in the convention. As eastern moderates, their courtship of westerners seems inconsistent, but as one historian has put it, "It was precisely such inconsistency upon which they were to thrive politically."[15] Given Cushing's previous experience with some of his eastern colleagues, and what he felt was their betrayal of him and Hancock, it was quite natural that he seek allies elsewhere. It did not worry him that their political views were not his own. For thus far, despite their strength, his new allies had shown themselves to be clumsy politicians who could be easily manipulated by old hands like himself and Pickering. As for the would-be governor, he did not allow himself to be troubled by ideology, and he continued to chart his course by the office he sought.[16]

Although the immediate goal, that of getting a constitution, failed, in the long run the relationships established in its pursuit had a significant effect on Hancock's career and helped to strengthen the faction around him. It served to raise his popularity in the west, which made him one of the few easterners, perhaps the only one, who could find strong support beyond the western edge of Middlesex County. That would be a valuable asset when it came time to run for statewide office.

The predictable gale raised by the constitution spelled its defeat, and any hopes that it would pass were quickly shattered. It seemed to please no one. Some towns claimed that it was too powerful; others, that it was too weak. Foolishly, the General Court had left no provisions for anyone to suggest amendments, so the voters were left in a position of either accepting it or rejecting it in toto. The leading newspaper critic was the Reverend William Gordon of Roxbury, who hated with equal passion both the constitution and Hancock. His opposition cost him his job as chaplain to the Court, but he thought the price worth paying if it would prevent an "imperfect constitution" from being foisted on the people.[17]

The strongest statement of opposition came from Essex County, where delegates from the towns met in Ipswich to set down in writing their objections. The "Essex Result," as it came to be called, was principally the work of a young lawyer from Newburyport, Theophilus Parsons.[18] The Result was a long and detailed critique, citing, among other things, the lack of a bill of rights and a too-liberal policy on property qualification. By midspring, the signs were unmistakable: the people of Massachusetts were rejecting the constitution by an overwhelming majority. Once that was clear, the Hancockians wanted nothing more to do with it, and they adroitly stepped to the rear.

While the constitution was foundering, Hancock sailed blithely on. In the same season that the voters of Boston rejected the constitution, they re-elected him to the House.[19] His victory seemed all the sweeter when he learned what had happened in Plymouth to James Warren. In a victory for Hancock's faction, Warren had been turned out of office. Warren was stunned and expressed his disbelief to Sam Adams:

> Your Curiosity will lead you to Enquire how my Town came to leave me out, and how the Interest I used to have in the House vanished and sunk on this occasion it may not easely
>
> alone. Envy and the
>
> and the policy or rather what you will Call the Cunning of a party here, who have set up an Idol they are determined to worship . . .[20]

Warren's defeat helped pave the way for another Hancock victory. When the House assembled, Pickering was elected speaker.

Since he could not be governor, Hancock decided to exercise his other option and head for Congress. Dolly objected to his going, and his own heart was not in it, but it seemed politically wise to go. Some were already beginning to refer to him as an absentee delegate, and besides, if nothing else, it got him away from Massachusetts while the constitution went down the drain.

He did delay his departure for several weeks, but he had one of the best reasons possible. Dolly was about to have another child. After the sad experience with Lydia, nothing was to be left to chance, so Hancock stayed with her until the delivery. On May 21, 1778, a son was born. Three days later, at the Brattle Square Church, Samuel Cooper baptized John George Washington Hancock.[21]

With the child safely delivered and the mother doing well, Hancock felt he could leave. With his usual flair he went to the House and walked up to the speaker's dais. He shook Pickering's hand and then bade goodbye to his colleagues, asking their permission to return should his health not be adequate for the job. He was never one to be without options, and his health problems, though real, were also remarkably convenient. The scene was vintage Hancock, done with style, drama, and a heavy dose of sentimental gush.[22]

A week before the actual departure a list was circulated for gentlemen to sign if they wished to be in the entourage escorting the general out of town. On June 3 Hancock left Boston "with the Pomp and retinue of an Eastern Prince." Joining him for the trip was Samuel Holton, who had been elected to replace John Adams, now on his way to The Hague.

The journey was tiresome, full of "bad roads and miserable entertainment." After fifteen days of traveling, Hancock caught up with the Congress just where he had left it eight months before, in York, Pennsylvania.[23]

His reception was hardly what he expected. Henry Laurens of South Carolina, who had been elected president on Hancock's departure, showed no sign of stepping down. Even more embarrassing, no one made the slightest move to suggest that he ought to move aside. Having no choice, Hancock took his seat with the rest of the delegation.

The Massachusetts delegation was not a happy group. The arrival of Hancock and Holton brought the delegation up to six members, the others being Sam Adams, Elbridge Gerry, Francis Dana, and James Lovell. Holton and Lovell were friendly to Hancock, but the other three, especially Adams, had little use for him. Adams was convinced that his beloved Boston was falling into a pit of decadence, with Hancock and his friends doing the digging. Corruption, extravagance, and venality, in his view, were driving out the old republican virtues on which the Revolution had been built. Warren's jeremiads painted a picture of a chosen people falling on their knees to worship the golden idol of Beacon Hill. Adams' response was simple and direct: those who followed the idol were "Asses and Slaves."[24]

On the same day that Hancock rejoined Congress, the British evacuated Philadelphia. A few days later, Congress adjourned from York and was on its way back to the old capital.[25]

It was not long before Hancock became weary of Congress. He was annoyed at having to traipse off to Philadelphia after having barely unpacked in York. Nor was he pleased at being denied the president's chair. All in all, compared with the heady days of '75 and '76, when an army was being formed, generals chosen, and independence debated, this session of the Congress was dull. And he was lonely. As usual, Dolly hardly ever wrote,

party. There were at least eighty people present, all in a festive mood. It was an elegant soirée, complete with food, drink, and an orchestra consisting of "Clarinets, Hautboys, French horns, Violins, and Bass Viols." In the center of the room were four large tables, two of them extending the full length of the room, with the others placed in such a fashion as to make a long rectangle. At the head table was a huge pudding that served as both a refreshment and a patriotic symbol. William Ellery described the concoction:

> It was a large baked Pudding, in the centre of which was planted a Staff on which was displayed a crimson Flag, in the midst of which was this emblematic device: An Eye denoting Providence, a Label in which was inscribed an appeal to heaven; a man with a drawn sword in one hand and in the other the Declaration of Independency, and at his feet a scroll inscribed "The Declaratory acts." [26]

Following the dinner, there was an evening of fireworks and street parades.

One week later there was cause for another celebration in Congress. The French fleet, under the Comte d'Estaing, was sighted off the Delaware capes. Among the passengers on board the flagship was Conrad Alexandre Gérard, the first French minister to the United States. D'Estaing put Gérard ashore and then tacked north toward New York. [27] On Sunday, July 12, Gérard arrived in Philadelphia and was met by a special congressional delegation, with Hancock at its head. According to the

Pennsylvania Packet, it was "impossible to describe the joy that appeared in every good man's countenance upon this auspicious event." On Monday, the Massachusetts delegation was the first to come and pay its respects. The conversation undoubtedly centered on d'Estaing's proposed attack on New York. If the attack was successful, or if no attack was made, the next logical target for an assault was the British post in Rhode Island. The prospect of military operations moving back into the New England area intrigued Hancock, for as senior major general of militia he could rightly claim a large role in any operation. Three days after the interview Hancock was on his way home.

Since December 1776, the British had occupied Newport, Rhode Island. From a strategic point of view the occupation did more for the Americans than for the enemy, since it tied down thousands of British troops in a garrison that served very little use.[28] Although there was considerable political pressure on him, from Rhode Islanders in particular, Washington was content to let the British sit there while a small American force kept watch. He knew full well that any attack on Newport would have to enjoy the kind of heavy naval support that the Americans could never provide. Now, however, with d'Estaing in the area, there was some cause for hope, and that hope turned to jubilation when the French announced that, owing to shallow water at the entrance to New York Harbor, they would not be able to attack the city. Therefore, they would move on the secondary target — Newport.[29]

General John Sullivan, the Continental commander in Rhode Island, was told to call "in the most urgent manner" on the New England states for 5000 militia. At the same time, Washington sent two of his best brigades, John Glover's web-footed soldiers from Marblehead and James Varnum's Rhode Islanders. He was also politic enough to dispatch the young Marquis de Lafayette, who was serving the American cause as a major general and who, it was hoped, would ease communication with his countrymen.[30]

Hancock hurried to Boston, not wanting to miss a moment of the forthcoming battle. His sudden arrival surprised some; but other, more experienced Hancock watchers, understood clearly what was going on. As senior major general he took command of nearly 6000 militia, a task somewhat more difficult than watching the early morning evolutions of 100 Cadets on Boston Common."

Unaccountably, once back in Boston he made no rush for the front. He stayed in Boston for two weeks at a moment when he probably should have been in Rhode Island discussing strategy with Sullivan and his staff. By the time he finally arrived in camp, the battle plans had been drawn. Hancock accepted them

strategic or tactical advice. His chief contribution was the magic of his name and the symbolism of his presence. The actual war-making was better left to the professionals, who knew Hancock for what he really was — a politician lightly disguised as a soldier.

Unhappily for the Americans, the same day Hancock rode into camp, August 9, Admiral Lord Richard Howe, better known as "Black Dick," arrived off Newport with a relief fleet to assist the beleaguered British. The spirits of the besieged men in Newport were "elevated to the highest pitch."

For two days d'Estaing and Howe played cat and mouse with one another as each tried to get the advantage. Before they could close for any decisive action a gale blew up, scattering both fleets for miles. In the melee that followed, some single-ship engagements took place but the damage the ships inflicted on one another was nothing compared to the toll of the storm. Howe headed south, back to New York, for refitting, and d'Estaing, for the time being at least, signaled a return to Narragansett Bay.

On the land side, Hancock and his militia had joined with Sullivan's Continentals. Numbering some 10,000 men, the Americans crossed over into Rhode Island and managed to advance to the outskirts of Newport, where they halted before the British fortifications.

On the 20th, d'Estaing hove into sight with his ravaged fleet. He was there only long enough to announce to a much-startled and annoyed Sullivan that he was leaving for Boston. Hancock wrote d'Estaing, asking him to reconsider. He and Sullivan even went to Lafayette and implored him to speak with the admiral.[33] It was no use, and at midnight on the 21st d'Estaing left for Boston. Once abandoned by the French, the American effort was doomed. Outside the high councils, the first to sense this were the militia, and they began deserting in droves. Within a few days Hancock was a general without an army. The wisest course was withdrawal. Thanks to good discipline among the Continentals and able leadership, the Americans were able to retreat with only moderate losses.

The Newport fiasco was hardly one of the high points of the Revolution. In their first joint operation, the allies had not done well. Sullivan was thoroughly miffed at what he viewed as French bad faith, and d'Estaing resented an upstart American trying to give him orders. As for Hancock, in his first campaign he had contributed next to nothing.

For the sake of amity the American press remained silent about Newport, but the Tory papers had a field day. Rivington's *New York Gazette* published a parody on "Yankee Doodle," which included a stanza devoted to Hancock and his militia:

> *In dread array their tatter'd crew,*
> *Advanc'd with colours spread Sir,*
> *Their fifes play'd Yankee Doodle do,*
> *King Hancock at their Head Sir.*[34]

With the curtain coming down in Rhode Island, Hancock decided to follow the fleet to Boston, where, he said, he could be of more help. Since he had not yet met d'Estaing, before he left camp he approached Lafayette for a letter of introduction. Outwardly, Lafayette was always cordial toward him, but inwardly, he despised Hancock. He thought he was "jesuitical, spiritless, and vain . . ." Indeed, he even thought his departure from Rhode Island smacked of cowardice. Hancock's influence and popularity made it impossible for Lafayette to say any of this publicly, and in his letter to d'Estaing the marquis praised Hancock and called him a "living Brutus."[35] A compliment that might have several interpretations.

On the 26th, Hancock was at home, complaining of headaches

and Dolly's failure to write to him when he was away. One
rumor had it that he had come up to order the French back.
James Warren, who was nearly always incredulous at what the
masses would believe about the "Great Man," remarked that
"if it was reported that he came to arrest the Course of Nature,
or reverse the decrees of Providence there are enough to believe
that practicable." Warren took some comfort from the belief
that the more intelligent would laugh at Hancock's escapades
in Rhode Island. That may have been true, but it was hard to

outnumbered the opposition. He was popular with the common
folk in both the east and west, and his old ties and merchant
politics kept him in touch with moderate elements.

D'Estaing beat Hancock back to Boston. By the time the
general arrived on Beacon Hill, the French fleet was riding
safely at anchor in the harbor. It was the most massive display
of naval might Boston had ever witnessed. By the end of August
there were more than a dozen ships of the line swinging on their
cables. Boston braced for the horde of Frenchmen about to hit
her streets.[37]

It was a tradition in Boston to hate the French. For generations, children had been brought up on tales of black-robed
priests and their Indian allies rampaging through the forests,
murdering, pillaging, and raping. Twice in his own lifetime
Hancock had watched friends and relatives march off to war
against the French, and, indeed, the whole foundation of the
Hancock fortune rested on profits made in supplying British
arms against them.

When in Congress, Hancock had been a supporter of the
French alliance, as were the other members of the Massachusetts delegation. Samuel Cooper, his friend and minister, helped
ease the way by preaching the virtues of the French. He did
such a fine job that within a short time they put him on their
payroll, retaining him as one of America's first public relations
experts.

Boston's elite hardly needed to be persuaded to like the
French. They fawned over them. Within a few days of their

arrival, both the admiral and Lafayette were at the Hancocks' for dinner. The first thing Lafayette noticed in the home was a full-length portrait of Washington that Hancock had ordered painted in Philadelphia and then brought home with him. Lafayette practically worshiped Washington and asked Hancock if he did not have a copy he could take home with him to France. It just so happened that Hancock did have one, but he had planned to give it to d'Estaing. It was awkward, but d'Estaing was Lafayette's senior, so there was little he could say. Hancock did promise to get the young marquis another one. D'Estaing accepted the portrait with such ardor that Lafayette claimed never to have seen "a man so glad to possess a sweetheart's picture as the admiral was to have this one of Washington." The admiral even went so far as to make plans for the firing of a royal salute as the portrait was hoisted aboard his flagship, *Languedoc*. For once, Hancock argued against pomp and ceremony, advising d'Estaing that such a display would cause jealousy among Washington's enemies. D'Estaing agreed, but honored the portrait by placing it in his cabin and covering the frame with laurel.[38]

Almost every day the Hancocks entertained French officers. One morning, 150 of them arrived unannounced for breakfast. Taken aback, but not willing to admit she was not ready for such an invasion, Dolly sent the servants scampering out the back door in quest of milk and cake. They got the former fresh from grazing cows out on the Common, and neighbors were kind enough to help with the latter.[39]

On more formal occasions, when proper notice was given, the Hancocks set an elegant and expensive table. It was, according to some accounts, the best in Boston, as it should have been, for he spent nearly £300 a month setting it.[40]

But while the Hancocks presided with the grace and equanimity befitting their station, the servants were having a terrible time. Out in the barn they had to mind a flock of 150 turkeys being kept for the table. Every day, at least two or three of the birds, and sometimes many more, had to be prepared, which meant killing, plucking, dressing, and cooking. It was too much for the cook, and one day in her haste she made a terrible mistake. She served a turkey that had not been fully plucked.

At the time of the misdeed, Hancock happened to be confined to his bed with one of his periodic attacks of gout. His temper, never the best even in serene moments, took a strange twist when he learned of the feathers being served up downstairs.

From his bed he ordered the cook to kill a bird and put it in the oven, complete with feathers and all. The stench from the smoking turkey feathers nearly emptied the house. It bothered everyone except Hancock, who remained calmly in bed with his feet propped up and the windows open. The odor was but the unusual day at the mansion: smoking turkey and popping feathers. Whatever his point, Hancock felt he had made it. The French were silent.[41]

It was during this same siege of gout and entertainment that Hancock took another eccentric fit. He decided that china plates would no longer be used in his home. Henceforth, all meals would be served on plain pewter. Perhaps pangs from his own conscience or barbs from the opposition about his extravagant style of living led him to this theatrical gesture; at any rate, he was determined to carry through with it.

One evening when he was again confined to bed, a large dinner party was going on below. Since his chamber was located directly over the dining room, he could easily hear what was going on downstairs.[42] Some time toward the end of the meal, his ears perked up when he heard the telltale clink of china. He immediately summoned Cato, who explained that it was only a single china plate that was being used to serve cheese. Even that was too much, and Hancock was not amused. He ordered Cato to bring the offending plate to him. After inspecting it, he told Cato to toss it out the bedroom window. He did. The two of them listened for the crash, but nothing. The plate apparently had landed, intact, on the grass. Now even more annoyed, Hancock ordered Cato out onto the lawn, where he told him to pick up the plate and throw it against the wall. That was the end of the plate. Hancock's china phobia was short-lived, for by the time of his death, in 1793, his estate showed at least twenty place settings.[43]

His testiness surfaced in some public displays as well. On

Friday September 25, a grand reception was held at Faneuil Hall in honor of the admiral and his officers. Over 500 people were present. Hancock presided, and, as was customary, there were several toasts during the course of the meal. With each toast a cannon salute was fired. The United States got thirteen guns, the king of France the same, and then someone lifted his glass to the Congress. The aide de camp glanced at Hancock for the signal. He shook his head from side to side. He was still offended by his recent treatment by that body. There were no guns for Congress.

After the meal James Warren, who, by his own admission, had not spoken to Hancock in months, came up to him and bluntly asked why Congress had not been properly saluted. Hancock thought the question impertinent. He told Warren that Congress had been included in the general salute to the United States. Warren was hardly content with that explanation, and, rather than dismiss the issue, he suggested to some that Hancock had deliberately insulted Congress because he wished to exalt the military over the civilian.[44]

By Monday morning, Hancock had heard of Warren's allegation and was furious. He got a chance to vent some of his anger when the House called on him to attend a meeting. He replied that his ill health kept him at home, but then he went on: "I confess my indispostion has been increased by the Reflection which Malice has circulated against me since the entertainment on Friday last; Hell itself could not have invented greater Lies."[45]

While the French officers and the Boston elite were aping one another, the lesser mortals of the town and fleet were not getting along as well. The impact of the Gallic horde on Boston was tremendous. Rumors were easily born. One story had it that the French sailors were spending their evenings down at the Frog Pond on the Common, catching the amphibious residents for their tables. A variation on the same theme was a story about a group of Bostonians, sitting down to dine at a French table, who were aghast, when they removed the top of a soup tureen, to see several pairs of frog eyes staring vacantly back at them.

Out in Hull, at the entrance to Boston Harbor, Admiral

d'Estaing had landed some of his men to set up batteries for the protection of the fleet. Apparently the French soldiers stationed at the fort were all too free with the property of the local inhabitants, causing them to petition the General Court:

> That the Troops of his most Christian Majesty burn and destroy the Fences of the Inhabitants of the Town of Hull. That they take from them their Wood, their Hay from the Cocks, open their Barns and waste their Grain. That they take up their spread Flax and convert it to beds. That they take their Poultry . . . from . . . them . . . take from them their men servants.

Affairs were not much better in Boston. During September and October, the town experienced at least four riots that pitted the locals against the sailors. The most serious was on September 8. It apparently began when some of the townsmen tried to get bread from a bakery set up by the French for their own use. When the crowd was turned away they turned mean, and a fight broke out. A French officer, the Chevalier de Saint Sauveur, stepped in to break it up. That gesture cost him his life.[47]

Street brawls were hardly new in Boston. The town was, after all, a waterfront community much accustomed to rough-and-tumble visitors. It would be a mistake to believe that these scenes between the French and Bostonians represented anything more than what had been going on for generations. Francophobia was not the cause of the riots. It was quite simply what happens in almost every port when the fleet hits town.

If the presence of so many Frenchmen brought with it great entertainment and deadly brawls, it also brought a measure of prosperity. The French had something Bostonians had seen very little of recently — hard money. They bought foodstuffs, timber for their vessels, and a wide variety of other products, all paid for in silver and gold. It is a sad commentary on the town that, though the French had little difficulty getting the supplies they needed, Continental vessels were always left wanting. In Boston, as elsewhere, French gold spoke louder than American paper and promises.

On November 3, d'Estaing and his fleet left Boston. Just before

their departure, Hancock threw a grand ball in the Concert
Hall. Over 200 people were invited. It was a lavish affair, delighted in by some but scorned by others, who saw in it more
evidence of the decline of republican virtue and a wasteful
extravagance at a time when an impecunious Congress and a
fragile army were barely holding the enemy at bay.[48]

The split between the Warren-Adams faction and the Hancockians was a source of considerable embarrassment to some.
Not only was it personally and politically troublesome; it was
also a flagrant violation of the old Whig principle of unity. One
of the embarrassed was Samuel Phillips Savage, an old friend
of both Hancock's and Adams'. In the fall of 1778, he tried to
play peacemaker by writing to Adams, who was then in Philadelphia.

> I most sincerely value you as my Friend, but as much as I
> value you my Country lies nearer my heart, and I greatly fear
> the differences now subsisting between you and your once
> [strong] friend Mr. H. may greatly hurt her interest: the Effects
> are already visible; the enemies of America triumph in the
> Strife and are taking every measure to encrease the Flame.
> The Friends of their Country cannot stand by idle Spectators;
> they see the encreasing Contest with weeping eyes and aching
> hearts and wish a Reconciliation. Permit me my Friend to
> attempt (however inadequate to the Task) a Restoration of
> Friendship between two who once were dear to each other and
> who now perhaps from mistakes and misapprehensions seem
> so distant.[49]

It is not known whether Savage made a similar overture to
Hancock, but in any case it did not matter, for Adams' frigid
response left no room for accord.

> You call upon me by all that is sacred to forgive him. Do you
> think he has injured me? If he has, should he not ask for
> forgiveness? No man ever found me inexorable. I do not wish
> him to ask me to forgive him; this would be too humiliating.
> If he is conscious of having done or designed me an injury, let
> him do so no more, and I will promise to forgive and forget
> him too; or, I would add, to do him all the service in my
> power. But this is needless; it is not in my power to serve him.
> *He* is above it.[50]

The cold war in Massachusetts continued, with each side giving as much as it took. The Hancock side made an attempt to sully Adams' reputation in order to prevent his re-election to ~~Congress. The vilification failed; Adams was re-elected and for the moment the Hancock faction was set back.~~[51]

~~Through the fall and winter of 1778 and 1779 Hancock seems not to have been very active. His gout gave him a nagging lameness that kept him more confined than usual. He attended sessions of the General Court but played no special role, took~~

A move was afoot in the General Court, supported by eastern moderates, to permit certain proscribed Tories to return to Massachusetts. Warren, of course, was rabidly against it and saw in this move more of what could in a modern sense be called "counter-revolutionary action." As usual, in tender situations like this Hancock was cautious. Still, it was well known that he had entertained Tories. The issue of returning Tories was one that would be around for quite a while. Already, though, by late 1778 it was clear that, despite the public invective directed toward them, the barriers to their return were coming down. The old Revolutionaries railed about it, but it was happening, nonetheless.[52]

An even more important and persistent issue than the Tories was the uncertain status of the state government, namely, the lack of a constitution. Since the rejection of the constitution of 1778, there had been a good bit of agitation, especially in the west, for a new frame of government. In August, a meeting of delegates from the Berkshire towns called on the General Court to summon a convention to write a constitution. The Court sidestepped the call for a while, but by January the pressure had built to the point where the Court could no longer ignore it. On February 20, the Court resolved that the citizens of Massachusetts should make their sentiments known. Two questions were put at each town meeting — whether they chose to have a new state constitution, and whether there should be a special convention called for that purpose. By a better than 2-to-1 margin, the towns voted yes to both questions, and in June the

Court issued a call for the election of delegates. Hancock was one of those elected from Boston.[53]

The convention met for the first time on September 1. They elected a Bostonian, James Bowdoin, president. The work of the meeting was assigned to a committee of thirty members. Such a large committee was too large, of course, so the real work was done by a small subcommittee of three — Bowdoin and Sam and John Adams. The final document was principally the work of John Adams.[54]

Through all the deliberations Hancock stayed in the shadows. He had been elected speaker in the fall, a job that required much attention. He had also been given two far less taxing posts that were, in fact, sinecures. He was re-elected to Congress, although everyone knew he would never go, and he was elected Captain of the Castle, which meant that he commanded the fortifications on Castle Island, formerly Castle William.[55] Obviously, though disinclined to participate in the convention, he was not shying away from public affairs, and he most certainly had an interest in a new constitution, since it was a foregone conclusion that he would be the first governor. By staying away from the document, Hancock avoided any chance that his enemies might charge him with designing an office he planned to fill. It was best not to appear too eager but to wait for the call to office.[56]

His temporary shyness did not extend to more personal matters. Once again in the summer, French ships were visiting the town. This time they brought a new minister, the Chevalier La Luzerne. Again, Hancock had to entertain in a high style. In a bit of mock panic he wrote to his brother-in-law Henry Quincy, who was on his way to Rhode Island:

> The Philistines are coming upon me on Wednesday next. To be serious, the Ambassadors, etc. etc. are to dine with me and I have nothing to give them, or from the present prospect of our market do I see that I shall be able to get anything in Town. I beg you to recommend to my man Harry where he may get chickens, geese, hams, Partridges, mutton, etc. that will save my reputation in a dinner . . . and by all means some butter . . . is there any good Mellons or Peaches or any good

fruit near you? Can I get a good Turkey; I walk in Town today. I dine on board the French Frigate tomorrow; so you see
how I have recovered.[57]

that all parts of the constitution were, in fact, approved by the
voters. Nevertheless, on June 16 it was declared ratified by the
convention and was to go into effect on October 25.

The constitution begins with a "Declaration of the Rights of
the Inhabitants of the Commonwealth of Massachusetts" and
then lays out a structure of government. Considering the fac-
tionalized nature of Massachusetts politics, what is most sur-
prising about this document is that it managed to please so
many people. Of the four major factions identified by one historian, three of them come out winners.

The Adams-Warren element now had a government that
hewed closely, at least on paper, to Whig principles. Hancock,
of course, viewed the business as delightful; he could now be
elected governor, which was a powerful post as described in the
constitution. Finally, the moderates, mostly easterners, had
managed to shape a relatively conservative document that
would, for a time, thrust off western reform. The fourth group,
and the ones that got the least, were the westerners. Their
discontent would erupt violently in the mid-eighties.[58]

Ordinarily, the gubernatorial election would have been held
in the spring of 1780, but, rather than wait a full year, it was
decided to hold the election in the fall. All summer the political
cauldron boiled. At first a few of the more deluded thought that
the Hancock machine might actually be stopped. The habitual
schemer and gossip William Gordon even went so far as to work
out a plan. He knew, as everyone did, that the only man with
even a slim chance of beating Hancock was Bowdoin. In a

moment of weakness Hancock hinted to Gordon that he might be willing to serve under Bowdoin as lieutenant governor. With that, Gordon spread the rumor that Hancock wanted to be lieutenant governor, hoping that people would support him for that post and Bowdoin for governor. It was a silly and hopeless plan, and indicated how badly Gordon and some of the other old republicans misunderstood Massachusetts politics. With the broad franchise provided for in the constitution, the gubernatorial election was clearly a statewide popularity contest, yet Gordon was behaving as if it could be decided by a small coterie of the elite. He was playing the game by rules that no longer applied. In a more sober moment even he had to admit that the "common people," who had had Hancock's name "dinged in their ears, will be likely to pitch upon him."[59]

On this score, at least, Gordon was right. The election was a Hancock landslide. Across the state he polled well over 90 percent of the vote, piling up huge majorities in every county.

The choice for lieutenant governor was less clear. Since no candidate could garner a majority, the election was given over to the House and Senate. On the first ballot Bowdoin was elected. He declined, and the job fell to the next candidate, Warren, who could not stand the thought of serving with Hancock, so he too said no. The third choice was none other than Hancock's good friend Cushing. He eagerly accepted, leaving Hancock's opponents to lick their wounds, some of which were self-inflicted.[60]

$\mathscr{W}$E KNOW at least two things about Hancock's inauguration as first governor of the Commonwealth: what the weather was like, and what he wore. The former was detailed by that compulsive diarist from Salem, William Pynchon. According to him, Wednesday, October 25, was "Remarkably fair and pleasant."[1] We have even better evidence for his dress. Carefully preserved in the old State House at Boston are some of the clothes Hancock wore on that day — a crimson velvet waistcoat, with gold trim and buttons to match, and an embroidered white vest. From these we can even tell his size. As of October 25, 1780, John Hancock was approximately five feet, four inches tall; neck, fourteen and a half inches; sleeve, thirty-three inches; waist, thirty-one and a half inches; and chest, thirty-eight inches. Considering his fondness for rich foods and heavy wines, all contributing to his chronic gout, Hancock looked better than he deserved.[2]

About noon a committee of distinguished gentlemen arrived at the mansion to escort the governor-elect to the swearing-in ceremony. He climbed into his favorite yellow coach, and, with the Company of Cadets leading the way, the entourage set off for the State House. All along the route people gathered to catch a glimpse of him, and by the time he reached the State House, he was forced to make his way through a large crowd of well-wishers who were there to observe the oath-taking.

It was an interesting tableau. The person administering the oath was none other than the president of the Senate and soon-to-be lieutenant governor, Thomas Cushing. He must certainly have been gleeful as he swore in his patron and friend. When Cushing was finished, the secretary of the Commonwealth, John Avery, moved out onto the balcony. On the same spot where the royal governors had once received their accolades, one that overlooked the site of the Massacre, Avery proclaimed the new governor. He did so with more than the usual zest. He was Cushing's son-in-law.[3]

Having taken his oath, Hancock made a few remarks about his unworthiness, but then proceeded to promise to do his best. By three o'clock the business at the State House was over. The new governor, along with Cushing, Avery, and dozens of others, made their way out of the chamber and walked the short distance to the Brattle meeting house, where "Silver-Tongued Sam" delivered the first election sermon under the new government. He was eloquent, as usual. For his text he chose a rather fearsome excerpt from Jeremiah wherein those who offended the Lord were thrown into captivity and destroyed. Once their souls were refreshed, the crowd next headed for Faneuil Hall, where a repast of a different sort was being set out.[4]

A few days after the festivities, the new governor came before the General Court with his first message. It was a decent address and the longest that he ever delivered in person. His first priority was winning the war, and to that end he joined with Washington in calling for a strengthening of the army and an end to short-term enlistments. From there he went on to cite the need for sound public faith, for protecting the seacoast, and for supporting judges and clergy. Despite his continuing fracas with Harvard, he even had a good word for the college and urged the Court to continue its support of that institution.[5]

After delivering his message, Hancock retired into what soon became the characteristic pattern of his administration — *laissez-faire*. From 1780 to 1793, with the exception of only two years (1785–86 to 1786–87), John Hancock was governor of Massachusetts. Yet in all that time he never really led. Although he stood head and shoulders over his opposition and was immensely popular with the masses, he never used his strength to deal with the critical issues confronting the commonwealth — principally those involving taxes and the economy.[6] Instead, he became a master at escaping from tight situations. When a difficult issue arose and there seemed no way around it, his favorite tactic was the use of a diversion. The best example of this ploy was the way he dealt with the question of excise and impost.

Like her sister states and the Confederation Congress, Massachusetts faced the problem of raising revenues heavy direct taxes, indirect means had to be found for raising money. Two methods suggested themselves, excise and impost.

On February 3, 1781, Congress passed a momentous resolve. For the first time, it made a bold move to enlarge the scope of its power by calling for national impost that would provide it with an independent source of income. As adopted, the act empowered Congress to levy a 5 percent duty on all imported goods. Congressional approval was only the first hurdle. In order for the impost to become law, it had to have the approval of all thirteen states.[7]

Early in March 1782, the issue landed squarely on Hancock's doorstep. Few knew the problems of an impecunious Congress better than the governor, but, at the same time, he was much concerned over any drift of power, no matter how slight, toward a central government. The Revolution was a struggle for home rule, and in the mind of John Hancock home was Massachusetts. On March 8, just prior to recess, Hancock told the General Court that he had some misgivings about the impost and wanted more time to study the matter.[8] That killed it for the session and allowed him to delay any decision until the spring. When the Court reassembled, the members did pass the impost and send it to the governor for his approval. According to the constitution, he had five days in which to consider the bill. If he held it longer while the Court was in session, it automatically became law.

Hancock knew the procedure, and he most certainly knew the Court, but for five days he said nothing. The bill passed without his comment either way. To save face, he argued that one of the five days was a Sunday and that the Sabbath ought not to count as a day of business. However, he told the representatives that if they wanted to repass the bill in a proper way, he would be willing to sign it. The Court struck a different pose and, in response to his offer, resolved that the bill had indeed been with the governor five days and therefore had "passed all the forms prescribed by the Constitution to Constitute it a Law of the Commonwealth."[9]

The Court's rebuff was embarrassing, but in the overall scheme of things Hancock considered it a small price to pay. He had managed to avoid taking a stand on a controversial issue and had done it in such a fashion as to alienate the fewest number of people. Those who favored the impost got what they wanted. Those who opposed it lost, but in their defeat they could hardly blame the governor.

Five months later when a similar measure, this time a state excise bill, came before him, Hancock did a repeat performance. The measure was highly controversial. On November 3, without stating whether he favored it, Hancock informed the Court that it ought to delay consideration of an excise. It did not. The bill passed, at which point Hancock announced that he was going to recess the session, thereby allowing the bill to die on his desk. It was a neat evasion, but it did not work. The Senate ordered Secretary Avery to tell them at precisely what moment of the day the bill was given to the governor. According to their calculations, he had had the bill for five days, and therefore it was law. Hancock said no. He tried his Sabbath argument again. The Court was not convinced. The excise was law.[10]

Hancock's shenanigans with the impost and excise were typical of his gubernatorial style. He was in a position of power, yet often avoided using it. In this case he dodged the issue even when he had an economic stake in the outcome. He owned both Continental and state securities. An impost and excise would have made those investments more secure. Why, then, did he not act? To some degree, health is the answer. Hancock was a sick man. In November 1782, some were predicting Hancock's death, and, indeed, for the next few months his health was the worst it had ever been. He complained of poor health frequently, and on several occasions he was unable to address the Court in person because he was confined. On one occasion when he did come, he had to be helped into the chamber and to his seat, where he delivered his speech sitting down. To be sure, at times his illnesses were extremely convenient; nevertheless, they were also quite real.

Aside from his health, there was an even more cogent reason why Hancock shirked leadership. He had no need to lead. His political reservoir was so rich, living that he might sense rivals and Adams might nip at his heels, but he hardly felt it. He was living off a huge reservoir of political capital accumulated in the sixties and seventies. He had sacrificed his health, family, and business in America's cause. All this had brought him the fame that he so coveted. As governor he intended to enjoy that glory with as little tribulation as possible. It was for him a safe haven after a stormy voyage.

In late 1780, the French had been in town again. The Comte de Rochambeau and his staff came up from Newport to visit on December 12. Hancock entertained in his usual lavish manner, which the count undoubtedly enjoyed. He would have stayed longer, but only a day or two after his arrival, Admiral de Ternay, the man who had been commanding in Newport, died, and Rochambeau immediately returned to take charge.[12]

Hancock's affection for the French derived from something more than political and social duty. In May 1780, his brother-in-law Henry Quincy, the man who had helped him stave off the "Philistines," died suddenly. So that she could be closer to her family, Quincy's widow moved into Boston. The family had little money, and when it was suggested that the French consul, Joseph de Valnais, and his secretary ought to take their lodgings with the Quincys, it looked to be an excellent opportunity for the family to earn some much-needed income.[13] The move met with Hancock's approval. He felt a special responsibility toward the family and especially for their unmarried daughter, Eunice. Before Henry's death, he had invited Eunice to come live on the hill so that she could assist Dolly in entertaining the continuous stream of guests. If she came, Hancock told her father, "I intend to get her a good husband." For a family chronically embarrassed, that promise from a rich uncle was an irresistible magnet. Monsieur Valnais was too good a catch to let get away. With Hancock's encouragement, he began to court Eunice in December 1780, and in May 1781 they were married.[14] It was a good match, if a somewhat unusual one, a Yankee Protestant and a French Catholic. Hancock was pleased.

Some thought that Hancock's preoccupation with social affairs distracted him from his public duties.[15] They were probably right, but there was one area that he never neglected. He was always vigorous in urging the Court to fill its quotas of men and supplies for the Continental army. He acted with more energy in this than in anything else he did in public life. Often the Court was not as quick to respond as he would have liked, but whenever it faltered he was there to urge it forward. As a result, according to General Heath, who was commanding in the Northern Department, the commonwealth's militia arrived "more punctually and are nearer complete than from any other State (New York excepted)."[16]

The Court's insouciant attitude toward military affairs is partly explained by the members' remoteness from combat. The last important battle in New England had taken place in the summer of 1779, when the Americans had tried unsuccessfully to dislodge the British from their position in Penobscot. Although they continued to hold New York, the enemy showed no inclination to do much more than simply occupy the city as a coastal enclave. British strategy had changed. Having met defeat and stalemate in the north, they had decided to shift their forces to the south. It was this strategy that had brought Cornwallis to a tiny town in Virginia — Yorktown.

Washington, with the aid of the French army and navy, managed to move his forces into positions around Yorktown. Realizing the hopelessness of his situation, on October 20, 1781, Cornwallis surrendered. When Lord North learned of the Yorktown disaster, he is reported to have exclaimed, "Oh God, it is all over."[17] He was right. Although the final peace treaty would not be completed for two more years, for all intents and purposes the war was over in America.

Boston was jubilant at the news of Yorktown. Ringing bells and bonfires symbolized the joy of the town. Hancock, too, rejoiced, but he also reflected, for the prospect of peace brought to mind the need for reordering his life.

In the past he had always been able to rely first on Palfrey and then, when he went off to war, on his successor, Bant. They had been good and faithful stewards, but unfortunately both were now dead. Bant had died at home in Groton in November 1780. In December of the same year, Palfrey bade goodbye to his friends as he boarded the armed ship *Shillela*, bound for France to take up his new duties as consul. That was the last that was ever heard of him.

Without the help of good managers, Hancock's business affairs took a beating. He paid little attention to his considerable real estate holdings. He was far more interested in politics and society.[20] As a result of his lack of attention he suddenly discovered, late in 1781, that he and his partners had lost nearly 20,000 acres of land in northern New England because they had neglected to pay taxes.[21] Taxes on other lands that he owned were also falling in arrears. It seems safe to assume that Hancock needed cash. All this came at a time when by a conservative estimate he was owed nearly £12,000.[22]

In May 1782, Hancock made a move to alleviate his woes. He hired Mr. William Hoskins, "a gentleman Conversant in Business," to collect monies due him.[23] Hoskins was an able dunner. His first discovery was that Hancock's books were not complete. It was necessary to visit Mrs. Bant and examine the papers her husband had left. With her help and her husband's records he slowly pieced the puzzle together.[24]

Once the books were in order, he was off on his pursuit of debtors. In sometimes harsh and acid terms, the kind of language Hancock would never tolerate if directed at him, Hoskins pursued his quarry. Some of the game was of fair size. To General Joseph Palmer of Braintree he wrote:

> It is his Excellency's desire that as soon as your health and Business will admit coming [sic] to Boston that you will call Upon him at his Boston Seat and inform him what has been done and what further is likely to be done toward accomplishing and compleating the long laboured affair Between him and yourself.[25]

With Hancock's connivance, Hoskins extended his rampage to the politically potent. James Otis, periodically insane but still part of a powerful family, was told to pay £400.[26] The high point of this collecting spree came when Hoskins pressed none other than James Warren for a settlement. After some preliminary sparring Hoskins told Warren:

> I made return to the Governor of having Adjusted Act between him & yourself Agreeable to your own Wishes — (of throwing aside the Interest) which was not altogether pleasing to him — I since informed him you had made a payment towards the Balance; the Governor thinks this Balance [sic] ought to have been Immediately paid him; as it has been done for years back and has not availed himself of any Consideration for your use of it.[27]

There is no evidence in the records to indicate how successful Hoskins was in his efforts. On the other hand, there is nothing to testify to Hancock's promptness in paying his own debts. Town gossip always suggested that he was notoriously slow in paying, but few were brave enough to suggest that to his face. In any case, whether he had the money or not, he continued to buy the best: new pewter plates with his crest engraved, furniture for the parlor, a silver tea urn, Wilton carpets for the entire house, and a new carriage.[28]

Hancock's enterprises had never been confined to New England, nor were his collections. Hoskins was soon corresponding with merchants in Nova Scotia and London who, according to him, owed his master money. Several hundred pounds were due from Nova Scotia and considerably more from London.[29] In one case at least £720 was claimed from an English merchant, Winchworth Tonge.[30] Not enough of the papers have survived, especially correspondence received, to make any firm conclusions, but those which do exist suggest that, contrary to conventional wisdom, in Hancock's case at least, British merchants owed more to him than he did to them.[31]

Once peace was official and transatlantic communication was open again, Hancock dreamed of re-establishing the House of Hancock on its former foundation. To Captain Scott, who had remained in England during the war, he wrote that it was his earnest desire to put aside all ill feeling. He planned, he said, to buy a small vessel, go back into trade, and "resign my com-mand of the commonwealth." Hoskins was told to pack his bags and make ready for a trip to England, where he expected to establish the London branch of the new House of Hancock. Whatever Hancock's dreams, things could never go back as they were. The world had changed too much, and he had not changed

America would be independent but would still enjoy the eco-nomic fruits of the empire. Hancock soon discovered that his nation had been born into a world of hostile empires little inclined to favor the fledgling states.

In the midst of all this activity, Samuel Cooper died. For twenty years Hancock had relied on him as minister, friend, and political confidant. His passing meant that, of the men he had been close to in the days before the war, only Cushing could still be counted a friend. All the others, including Adams, Warren, Otis, and Cooper, were either dead or not speaking to him.[32] Feeling depressed at Cooper's death and his own continuing poor health, Hancock moved to carry through on his plan to retire. He went so far as to summon the Council, but at the last moment his friends persuaded him to stay.[33]

Adding to the somber mood were his frequent separations from wife and son. Aside from the Beacon Hill mansion, Hancock kept two summer homes, one only a short distance away on the shore of Jamaica Pond and the other across the harbor at Point Shirley.[34] It was a pleasant place to spend the summer, away from the heat and noise of Boston. Their home was refreshed with a pleasant sea breeze, and they could go down and walk on the beach, looking out across the bay toward Nahant and Cape Ann beyond. Whenever she went, Dolly took Johnny, her father, and some of the servants, leaving Hancock to rattle around in an empty mansion. As the seagull flew, Point Shirley was only a few miles across the harbor, but by boat and carriage the journey took several hours. Dolly and Johnny might well have been in another state.

Dolly's absence put a crimp in the social life on the hill. Whenever she was gone Hancock did little formal entertaining at home and preferred instead to go out with friends. His favorite companion was Nathaniel Balch, a local hatter.

Since Mrs. Balch often visited out at the Point, the two husbands shared moments of bachelorhood. They were an odd couple. The hatter was lively, witty, and majestic in appearance; the governor was often ill, somewhat stooped, and given to melancholy moodiness. In an age when class lines were carefully drawn, tongues wagged whenever people saw the governor in close company with a man who sold beaver hats. Nevertheless, he was Hancock's favorite companion, and they were often seen drinking, dining, and traveling together. Balch's good humor helped sweep away some of the pall that had fallen over Hancock's life.[35]

If Hancock was in need of cheering up, he was also eager for advice, especially of the political variety. Balch was of little help in this department. Cushing and Avery were close and they were sometimes sought out, but the person with the most influence was a relative newcomer to Massachusetts politics, James Sullivan.

Sullivan was born in Berwick, Maine, then part of Massachusetts.[36] His parents were in very ordinary circumstances, and his childhood hardly portended important things. He was lame and epileptic. His older brother, John, had gone to Harvard, but James was not sent to college and remained at home, studying under his father's care. Later, he studied law with his brother and went into practice for himself when he was twenty-three at Georgetown, Maine. Had it not been for the Revolution, Sullivan would probably have spent his entire life as a backwoods lawyer. The war changed that.

He was elected to the Provincial Congress, became a judge of admiralty, and in March 1776 secured appointment to the Superior Court of Judicature. From this point on, his rise never stopped. Early in 1778, he bought a home in Groton and later that year joined his brother, who was now the major general in command of the Continental forces in Rhode Island. At Rhode Island he undoubtedly had a chance to get reacquainted with

Hancock from their days together in the Provincial Congress. Hancock liked Sullivan. The feeling was mutual.

Despite their different backgrounds, Hancock and Sullivan had a good deal to offer one another. Sullivan was ambitious and on the way up. His ends were well served by his latching on to Hancock. For the governor, too, there were advantages. Sullivan had keen political instincts, and he was well acquainted with the sometimes convoluted nature of Massachusetts politics. He also had a very nimble pen. He loved to write, and was a prodigious contributor to the Boston newspapers. He was happy to defend the Governor against critics who posed a threat to the Hancock faction.[37]

Nothing seemed to bother Hancock's charmed political life. The landslide of 1780 was followed by easy victories in '81, '82, '83, and '84.[38] However wide the margins of victory, though, there was still opposition. Many wished and worked for the downfall of the "Great Man."

One of Hancock's most persistent and articulate critics was the lady from Plymouth, Mercy Otis Warren, wife of Hancock's enemy James. Mrs. Warren rarely missed an opportunity to pass a caustic remark on Hancock's character, viewing him as a vacillating incompetent with feet of clay and a head to match. She and her husband were among the most implacable of Hancock's foes, picturing themselves as "the lovers of the early revolution principle . . . [and] lovers of virtue . . ." They were, in their own minds at least, the last bastion against worldly corruption and degeneracy.[39]

Despite the vehemence of the opposition, they remained only a minority, and Hancock had no trouble walking away with the governor's chair. Divisions within their own ranks (they were just as suspicious of one another as they were of Hancock) and the governor's popularity made him unbeatable until 1785. In that year, rising unrest, the question of public morality, and a miscalculation by the governor brought the Hancock faction its first defeat.

Massachusetts was suffering all the hardships of a postwar economy. The traditional industries of fishing and shipbuilding had been left devastated by the war. Trade was laboring under near-fatal handicaps imposed by the British after the war. The lucrative West Indies trade, which had been the backbone of colonial commerce, was practically dead, and transatlantic trade was almost as moribund. Added to this was an influx of foreign goods, a dearth of capital, and heavy taxes.[40]

In the western part of the state, farmers who felt hardest hit by taxes and the shortage of money were meeting in a series of special conventions, trying to find ways to remedy their woes. They pleaded for relief from heavy debts, high taxes, and scarcity of cash.[41] At the other end of the state, eastern merchants were moaning about the flood of foreign goods that was so damaging to their business.

The situation called for strong action. Since Congress was impotent, the only agency competent to act was the state government, yet Hancock did nothing. Instead, he preferred to remain quiet and depend on his popularity with the masses and the skill of his political managers, especially Sullivan, to keep him in office. Never once did he present to the Court a coherent plan to alleviate economic hardships in the commonwealth. By default, he was siding with the fiscal conservatives, supporting a system that had abolished legal tender, consolidated the state debt at a high value, and paid interest in specie. All this was supported for the most part by direct taxes, which placed the heaviest burden on real estate. Although Hancock was evasive, it seems clear that in financial matters he continued to have the heart of a merchant. He was, after all, a major local creditor, to whom private individuals, the state, and Congress owed large sums of money. His own experience with paper money convinced him of the need for a "sound system." Unfortunately, and perhaps paradoxically, that conviction left him insensitive to the plight of the people who supported him.

In the winter of 1784–85 another issue surfaced and changed the political atmosphere even further.

The cause célèbre concerned a Tea Assembly in Boston. The winter of 1784–85 was especially long and severe, and several prominent citizens of the town had organized themselves into this Tea Assembly, or social club, where they could come periodically during those dreary winter months and enjoy an evening of dancing and card-playing. All this was most horrifying to the "Old Radicals," who saw in this assembly, dubbed by them the "Sans Souci," more evidence of the moral degeneracy

Into A Polite Circle. An Entire New Entertainment in Three Acts."[42] As an introduction he wrote:

> If ever there was a period wherein reason was bewildered, and stupefied by dissipation and extravagance it is surely the present. Did ever effeminacy with her languid train receive a greater welcome in society than at this day . . . We are prostituting all our glory as a people for new modes of pleasure ruinous in their expenses, injurious to virtue, and totally detrimental to the well being of society.[43]

The debate went beyond a simple Tea Assembly. As one historian has noted, "The issue was nothing less than the nature of American society."[44]

Despite verbal threats and an actual physical attack by an irate member of the assembly, Observer began his series of articles, and for the next two months the raging battle over Sans Souci was the talk of the town, with Observer, either Sam Adams or Harrison Gray Otis, relentlessly assailing the vanity, extravagance, and immorality prevailing in Boston, epitomized by Sans Souci.[45] Even Mrs. Warren joined in the fray, and a few days after Observer's inaugural attack, she published *A Farce*, a short play parodying some of the more sybaritic citizens of Boston under such names as Mr. Importance, Madame Brilliant, and Mr. Bon Ton.[46]

The moral rigorism and Spartan virtues being preached by Observer, Mrs. Warren, and others boded ill for the Hancockians. Although Hancock himself was never publicly linked to the assembly, his life style corresponded so closely to that being condemned that few could have missed the point.

As the people began to weary of the exchange of diatribes over Sans Souci, another issue arose to take its place, and it served equally well to keep the question of public virtue and morality clear in the minds of the citizens. The new issue (really an old issue brought to the fore) was the importation and wide-spread use of British luxuries. On this issue, at least, it seemed as if most agreed, and the merchants as well as the Old Radicals lamented the prevalence of these goods and called for action to bring a halt to the influx. To some there seemed to be a sinister plot afoot designed to undermine America's virtue. Observer, having taken leave of Sans Souci, attacked those whom he held responsible for this pernicious influence, the returning Loyal-ists:

> It is a maxim in which truth is blended with consciousness that to remedy an evil the cause must be removed. To apply this maxim the Observer must take notice of a certain set of people now among us to whose doors the charge of introducing many luxuries and extravagancies now fostered in our bosom can with the strictest truth be laid.
>
> . . . we daily see those miscreants the *Refugees*, insolently patrolling those streets they would have deluged in a torrent of blood.
>
> If we consider that the Refugees conceived no enormities too flagitious, nor cruelties too brutal, when their countrymen were the objects: That they exhibited a conduct at which the savages with whom they associated could shudder . . . Can we knowing these things entertain one idea of permitting them to tarry . . .[47]

The point was made, since on this issue as on so many others Hancock had taken no measures to correct the evil.

In the midst of this breast-beating and bemoaning of lost virtue, Hancock dropped a bombshell. He actually resigned. On January 29, he wrote out his resignation, citing poor health as his reason for leaving. Many doubted that and saw in his de-parture just more political posturing.[48] They were partially right. Hancock was astute enough to understand that something was seriously wrong in the countryside. His own lawyers were

in court often enough, suing debtors, so he had personal knowledge of what was happening. Furthermore, in Worcester
County, one of the most troublesome areas, his own brother-in-
law William Greenleaf was sheriff, and from him he must have
been aware of the situation. But even if he saw all these whiffs
of smoke, there is no reason to believe that he was prescient
enough to read the message. The troubles of the commonwealth
may well have provided an incentive for Hancock to withdraw
— the immediate cause for his resigning was in all likelihood
and in need of a rest.

He knew that if he stepped down, Cushing would keep the
chair warm for him and return it to him whenever he wished.
All this was assuming, of course, that Cushing could get elected
governor on his own.

In the spring elections, with their leader temporarily absent
and the issue of public morality reaching a crescendo, the Hancockians were forced to fight from the defensive. The contest
narrowed down to James Bowdoin and Thomas Cushing, Hancock's proxy. Each side took full advantage of the press, and for
the first time in the history of the young state there was a real
contest.

James Bowdoin's chief liability, one fully exploited by his
opponents, was his alleged pro-British sympathies. To support
these charges his enemies cited the fact that he had not attended
the First Continental Congress and, further, that his daughter
Elizabeth was married to John Temple, the former British sur-
veyor general of customs for the colonies.[50] By playing on Bowdoin's British connections, his opponents hoped to excite the
anti-British feeling in the state and direct it toward him. However, an examination of the voting returns indicates that this
never happened. In those areas of the state strongest in their
hostility to the British — namely, Essex and Suffolk counties,
where the merchants were the hardest hit by the influx of British goods — Bowdoin scored the highest, carrying both counties
in a heavy turnout, by a 2-to-1 margin over Cushing.[51] The
people of Massachusetts were not concerned about Bowdoin's
patriotism; their concern grew out of the "Puritan ethic." They

were also deeply worried over the future of the commonwealth and the flood of British luxuries. On all these issues Bowdoin stood high, and, in fact, soon after his inauguration as governor he took direct action in all these areas. In June he issued "A Proclamation For the Encouragement of Piety, Virtue, Education and Manners, and for the Suppression of Vice."[52] Not long after that he presented a measure for fiscal reforms, something the General Court had never received from Hancock, and in the fall the governor publicly called for a national meeting to consider measures to regulate American commerce.[53] The pre-election rhetoric condemning the British did not hurt Bowdoin because his sympathies for the merchants were well known, and it was relatively certain he would move to help them once elected.

What threatened Bowdoin's election more than the accusations of his opponents were the divisions among his own followers. In all the previous elections Hancock's partisans had been able to divide the opposition, and, lacking any "centre of Union," Hancock's opponents had contributed to their own defeat.[54] Many feared that the same thing would happen again, and as late as March, Mrs. Warren was expressing her fear that Hancock's alter ego, Cushing, would be elected as a result of the divisions among the anti-Hancockians.[55] However, with the aid of the Essex Junto and his friends in Suffolk County, Bowdoin get nearly enough votes from those two counties alone to throw the election into the General Court.

When it appeared that Bowdoin might make a strong showing at the polls, the Hancock forces resorted to spreading a rumor that Bowdoin had vowed that, if elected, he would not serve. The rumor circulated in Essex and Suffolk counties, but was quickly rebutted in the *Salem Gazette* and in the Boston papers, as well.

The Bowdoinites were not reluctant to let fly a few shafts of their own, and the election soon turned into a scurrilous contest. Not surprisingly, most of the attacks by-passed Cushing and were aimed at his mentor, Hancock. When a writer did bother to attack Cushing, it was only to expose him as a front man for Hancock. In the *American Herald*, "Cincinnatus" penned a vigorous assault on both Hancock and Cushing:

How . . . deplorable is our situation, when a man who can boast no shadow of real merit, and who would have fallen into the arms of Governor Bernard at the most dangerous crisis of our affairs but for the support of a band of patriots (some of whom are dead and others neglected) I say when such a person appears to decline all public offices still desires to govern by proxy, to elevate his favorites, to depress his opponents, and to preside over the election of his countrymen.

Such attacks also appeared in Essex County, where a writer in

[to] . . . guard . . . above all, against those unprincipled men who go about with a shameless face, seeking for office. The way and the only way, to obtain honours, is to deserve them: the road to glory is merit. We should be ashamed to call a man a conqueror, who had not only never seen a battle, but whom we knew to be a coward, and why then, should we presume any man to be a patriot, who, besides never having shone in the race of merit is, in private life of so suspicious a character that we ourselves hesitate to trust him . . .[57]

Bowdoin's heavy vote from Essex and Suffolk counties, plus scattered support from elsewhere, gave him a plurality but not the required majority, so the election was thrown into the Senate, where he quite easily carried the day.[58] His election gave great pleasure to the Old Radicals. Sam Adams wrote to his cousin John, then in London:

You will have heard of the Change in our chiefe Magistrate, I confess it is what I have long wished for. Our new Governor has issued his Proclamation for the Encouragement of Piety, Virtue Education and Manners and for the Suppression of Vice. This with the good Example of a first Magistrate and others may *perhaps* restore our Virtue.[59]

Bowdoin's victory gave to Hancock the only defeat he ever suffered in Massachusetts politics. His mistake in offering his resignation at such an inopportune moment had cost him dearly.

Chapter 15

A Little Rebellion and a Grand Convention

*H*ANCOCK'S RETIREMENT lasted for two years. In that time his health fluctuated. He became one of the chief investors in the first bridge across the Charles River and continued his correspondence with Scott, attempting to collect old debts and start new business. He had little luck at either.[1]

As far as his real estate holdings were concerned, he made some minor purchases and sales in Boston, but his major activities were in Connecticut, where he was heavily involved in land speculation. He bought nearly 170 acres in Windham County on his own account and considerably more than that in association with other investors. As was so often the case, the speculation turned sour, and Hancock ended up counting disappointments rather than profits.

Freed of the burdens of office, he found time to wade once more into the murky waters of the Harvard College accounts. The overseers had never been satisfied with his reckoning. The last time the issue had been brought up was in the summer of 1783. The result on that occasion was disaster. The architect of the fiasco was William Gordon, a man more interested in embarrassing Hancock than in collecting a debt.

In a moment of weakness the overseers, at Gordon's urging and without Hancock present, agreed that if the accounts were not satisfactorily rendered by the next meeting, in mid-June, they would sue. Hancock came to the next meeting. In front of everyone, Gordon took the opportunity to lecture the governor, accusing him of trifling with the college. He then moved that the college immediately launch legal proceedings to recover the monies. The response was absolute silence. No one dared speak. Whether he was in office or not, Hancock was far too powerful to antagonize. Despite the trouble over the treasurer's records, he had always been generous to the college, both in public and private. Supporting Gordon's ill-tempered motion meant arous-

treated in by the college. He continued to support it, but his enthusiasm waned noticeably. Indeed, he went so far as trying to arrange a transfer of two boys at Harvard, for whom he was paying the bills, to Yale.[3]

Not long after the unpleasantness with Gordon, Hancock did forward an accounting to the college. According to his figures, he owed the college £1054, most of it probably in interest. Although payment usually follows accounting, Hancock never sent the money. It is not clear why. It may have been carelessness, or perhaps he simply did not have the cash, or, if he did, he had more pressing obligations. It may also be that he thought the demand for the money unreasonable. He had, after all, returned all the funds entrusted to him. What was due now was interest on that sum. He had lost a fortune in the American cause. Should Harvard not ought also accept some loss? At any rate, for as long as he lived Hancock never paid the college. Harvard had to wait until after his death to get the money, and then it received far less than it claimed.[4]

When Hancock left the governor's office, he told the people that he was happy the commonwealth was "so little divided" and that the future of Massachusetts looked secure and peaceful. He probably said that with tongue in cheek; he could hardly admit that the state had not done well under his administration and that he was leaving when things looked bad. Little did he realize, though, just how poor a prophet he was, for within eighteen months the state was convulsed by a "Little Rebellion."[5]

There is no mystery as to the cause of the rebellion. The newspapers of the period are filled with a recitation of grievances, principally high taxes, no money, and foreclosures. It was a pitiful situation. The people of Massachusetts had sustained themselves through the hardships of the war with a belief that things would improve in peace. Instead, for many life was worse. They felt themselves deceived and abused, victims of a government and system of justice as oppressive as the one they had just thrown off.

As the political tinder grew warmer, spring elections arrived. Hancock showed little interest in public affairs. He was willing to stay snug at his mooring and once again let Cushing tack out into gubernatorial waters.

Despite the stirrings in the countryside, the election was a ho-hum affair. Bowdoin carried every single county, bearing out James Warren's apt observation that "when a Man is once in, it is for Life."[6] Hancock did allow a couple of political whims to take him afield. He consented to stand as a delegate to Congress. Naturally, he won, and then just as easily he was elected president. He managed that without ever bothering to leave Boston, for he had neither the stamina nor the interest to travel to Philadelphia. His election as absentee president was testimony to the sad state into which the Congress had fallen. Since the end of the war many of the states had ignored Congress. They often failed to send representatives, and when they did they frequently sent obscure and second-rate people. It was hardly like the heady days of '76. Having never presided in the spring, he resigned — by mail.[7] His other office was that of town moderator, a job whose burdens were brief.

The summer session of the General Court offered no balm for grievances. Soon calls for special county conventions were being issued, and between July 1786 and February 1787 at least eight of these petitioned for reform. Some questioned the loyalty of the men at these meetings, and a note of hysteria about them began to creep into conversation. Those who had once led a revolution now lived in fear that they would be the target of one. By fall, armed mobs had appeared in Worcester, Middlesex, Bristol, Hampshire, and Berkshire counties. Their immediate goal was always the same — close down the courts so that legal proceedings against debtors would be halted.[8]

In early December, what had hitherto been sporadic and uncoordinated violence became more organized. At the head of the "regulators" was Captain Daniel Shays, a former officer of the Continental army. Under his leadership the insurgents tried to seize the arsenal at Springfield. They were repulsed by state

youth. In winter, one of the pastimes he enjoyed was skating. On a Sunday afternoon in January 1787 he took his skates and made his way to the pond. While out on the ice he fell and struck his head. He died shortly afterward. It is impossible to imagine the Hancocks' grief. Twice they had lost an only child, first Lydia and now John. In accordance with the straitened times, the funeral was a simple affair. The coffin was carried in Hancock's own coach, with mother and father walking behind. Numbers of people followed, including Sullivan, who had just recently lost his own son. Schoolmates of young John came to pay their respects, and some wrote elegies for him. It was the saddest day of Hancock's life.[9]

To help assuage their grief, the Hancocks decided to take a spring trip. They planned to visit friends in New York and Philadelphia. It had been nearly ten years since either of them had visited those places, and they looked forward to seeing old friends again with whom they could reminisce about the exciting days during the war. They planned to travel in comfort: at least three servants would accompany them, and accommodations were planned well in advance.[10]

They never got to take their trip. When the spring came, instead of going south Hancock stayed home and got elected governor. In the aftermath of the rebellion, the voters had brushed Bowdoin aside and returned to their first love. It was a record turnout, and Hancock won by a better than 3-to-1 margin. Cushing, who had stayed on as lieutenant governor under Bowdoin, was elected, as usual.[11]

After all they had been through, Hancock's election brought

a sense of calm to the people of Massachusetts. Even James Warren commented that "I do not regret the change so much as I once should . . ." a magnificent concession, considering his previous views.[12] Hancock was untainted with the events of the last two years, and he could float more easily through the shoal waters of Massachusetts politics. His moderation ensured that vengeance would not be wreaked on the Shaysites; and, indeed, when the new House took its seats it was apparent that the moderates were in full control. Hancock willingly signed legislation that eased the plight of debtors, and as a gesture of economy he even advocated a £300 reduction of his own salary and made a gift to the treasury in that amount.[13]

Although he had been silent during the rebellion, he did not favor repression and had, in fact, refused to subscribe to the loan used for the support of military action against the Shaysites. He signed pardons for all those involved in the rebellion, including Shays himself. Although several men were sentenced to execution, no one ever actually went to the gallows. Thanks to Hancock, the countryside quickly calmed down to such a point that in the summer he was able to tour the western counties, where he found everything in peace and good order.[14]

The conservatives, of course, railed against such moderation. In the newspapers they screamed that murderers and traitors ought to pay with their lives. Those who supported moderation were typed as the "dregs and scum of mankind." The venom came in great quantities, but its potency was limited. Such men were in the minority, and their feelings of frustration left them susceptible to the schemes of those seeking better order through methods beyond the state, perhaps through a new national government.[15]

While Hancock ministered to the wounds of the rebellion, men elsewhere in America were planning a great nation. Their plan grew out of rising discontent over the feebleness of the Confederation government. According to them, the Confederation was unable to deal effectively with issues of national concern. They were unable to raise sufficient money; foreign nations balked at negotiating with them; and commerce was being hobbled.

In a move to remedy these defects, a meeting was held in

Annapolis, Maryland, in September 1786. Only five states sent delegates, but that was enough for the participants to plan a larger meeting which was called to convene in Philadelphia in May 1787. The purpose, as set forth in an address to the states drafted by Alexander Hamilton, was "to render the constitution of the Federal Government adequate to the exigencies of the Union." In the months between the meetings at Annapolis and Philadelphia, Shays's Rebellion took place. How significant it

open to debate. But there can be no doubt that for many Massachusetts men the experience of the winter months made Philadelphia loom as a possible answer to their prayers. A powerful national government based on conservative principles would put a check on reckless state government.[17]

The convention opened on May 25, and, with only a brief respite to celebrate the Fourth of July and a ten-day recess to allow the Committee on Detail to do its work, it was in continuous session until September 17. When the final document was approved, it was forwarded to Congress for transmission to the states. As soon as nine states ratified it, the Constitution of the United States would become a reality.

When Hancock received the Constitution he summoned a joint session of the Senate and House. He laid the document before them, confining his comments to a few general remarks about the high character of the men who had written it. He said nothing to indicate either favor or disfavor.[18]

What did he think about the document? His personal papers are mute, so conclusions can be drawn only indirectly. It is clear that from the beginning he had misgivings and was by no means a staunch advocate of ratification. Elbridge Gerry, a member of the Massachusetts delegation at Philadelphia, and the one person in the delegation who refused to sign the Constitution, wrote an open letter to the legislature in which he outlined his objections.[19] Hancock shared some of Gerry's apprehensions. Chief among these was the threat of a powerful federal government overshadowing and perhaps destroying state sovereignty. Through victory in the field, Americans had won home rule. Now, in the words of Carl Becker, the question was "Who should rule at home?"[20] A second problem area, and one that Hancock found disconcerting, was that, unlike the Massachusetts constitution, the federal one had no bill of rights. Who would protect the people?

Elections for the ratifying convention were held, and the date for the first meeting was set for January 2, 1788. As might have been expected, the political lines over the Constitution were drawn along boundaries similar to those that already marked the divisions within the state. Conservatives tended to favor ratification; those at the other end of the spectrum stood opposed. As usual, Hancock remained silent, although it was generally assumed that he leaned toward the anti-Federalist camp.[21]

Those who hoped for a speedy and effortless ratification were soon disabused of that notion.[22] Even within Boston there were ominous signs. The town had elected twelve delegates to the convention, including Hancock, Bowdoin, and Sam Adams. A few days before the opening session, Bowdoin invited the eleven others to a dinner, where he planned to thump for ratification. The evening did not go according to plan. Hancock and another delegate, John Winthrop, stayed home. The other ten supped well, but then Adams broke the calm by suggesting that he had strong reservations about supporting ratification. He did, however, add that he was "open to conviction . . ."[23] Ironically, Hancock's oblique tilting against ratification and Adams' expressed reservation now provided a common ground on which the two old antagonists could come together.

The first agenda item at the opening meeting was the election of a president. Although he was ill and not even present, the delegates elected Hancock to the office. Since it was understood by all from past experience and present conduct that his health would likely keep him away a good deal of the time, the convention elected a strong vice-president, William Cushing of Scituate. That was a prudent decision, for Cushing spent far more time in in the president's chair than did the president himself.[24]

From the moment the convention opened, it was clear that the Federalist and anti-Federalist forces were fairly evenly balanced. The Federalists could claim the greater talent and money. Their side was heavily endowed with lawyers, judges, politicians, and others of the "better sort." The resources of the antis were more modest, but their numbers (that is, votes) were nearly equal to the Federalists'.

they were best at — writing and speaking to persuade the fence-sitters to join them. On the 14th, with Hancock still absent, the Federalists won an important victory when the convention agreed to debate the Constitution "by paragraph, until every member shall have had opportunity freely to express his sentiments . . ."[25] This was a guarantee of a long convention.

The debates were reported by the press, and the newspapers were filled with essays and letters for and against.[26] Through the storm Hancock sat quietly at home, waiting and watching. He was not necessarily in the anti camp, but he did have reservations. He had not become governor of a sovereign state to watch that sovereignty diminished by a federal government, nor was he pleased by the lack of a bill of rights. Still, those who were closest to him, especially his confidant, Sullivan, were staunch Federalists, and their influence was considerable. They played on those elements of his character which, they thought, made him most vulnerable, especially his belief in firm government and strong fiscal measures. They may also have alluded to the promise of a great office (President? Vice-President?). Perhaps the most persuasive argument for Hancock, though, was the specter of what might happen should the Constitution fail. Could the union, fragile as it was, stand the shock of rejection? As the leader in the Revolution, Massachusetts, by its actions, would have a profound effect on the other states. The forces in the convention were closely balanced, and it seemed that only by Hancock's direct intervention would the Constitution be ratified. He could convince the moderates and sufficiently soothe the irreconcilables so that they would, in the end, at least accept ratification. Sullivan was right — Hancock was the linchpin on which everything depended.

On Thursday afternoon, January 31, after his long absence, Hancock was presiding again. His presence denoted the importance of the moment. He rose to speak. The audience was silent. He told them that it was his hope that the convention would ratify the Constitution. He realized, he said, that it was not a perfect document and that some were anxious about certain omissions. He proposed, therefore, a series of amendments "in order to remove the doubts, and quiet the apprehensions . . ." He suggested nine changes, the sum total of which had the effect of curbing but not crippling the federal government.[27] As soon as he sat down, Adams asked to be heard. For the first time in years, Adams rose to speak in support of the governor. He too had come over. In less than a week the debates were over and the time for voting arrived. Hancock was the last speaker. His remarks were eloquent and statesmanlike. It was his finest hour.

> Gentlemen — Being now called upon to bring the subject under debate to a decision, by bringing forward the question, I beg your indulgence to close the business with a few words. I am happy that my health has been so far restored, that I am rendered able to meet my fellow-citizens as represented in this Convention. I should have considered it as one of the most distressing misfortunes of my life, to be deprived of giving my aid and support to a system, which, if amended (as I feel assured it will be) according to your proposals, cannot fail to give the people of the United States a greater degree of political freedom, and eventually as much national dignity, as falls to the lot of any nation on the earth. I have not, since I had the honor to be in this place, said much on the important subject before us; all the ideas appertaining to the system, as well those which are against as for it, have been debated upon with so much learning and ability, that the subject is quite exhausted.
>
> But you will permit me, gentlemen, to close the whole with one or two general observations. This I request, not expecting to throw any new light upon the subject, but because it may possibly prevent uneasiness and discordance from taking place amongst us and amongst our constituents.
>
> That a general system of government is indispensably necessary to save our country from ruin, is agreed upon all sides.

That the one now to be decided upon has its defects, all agree; but when we consider the variety of interests, and the different habits of the men it is intended for, it would be very singular

that the amendments proposed will soon become a part of the system. These amendments being in no wise local, but calculated to give security and ease alike to all the States, I think that all will agree to them.

Suffer me to add, that let the question be decided as it may, there can be no triumph on the one side, or chagrin on the other. Should there be a great division, every good man, every one who loves his country, will be so far from exhibiting extraordinary marks of joy, that he will sincerely lament the want of unanimity, and strenuously endeavor to cultivate a spirit of conciliation, both in Convention, and at home. The people of this Commonwealth are a people of great light, of great intelligence in public business. They know that we have none of us an interest separate from theirs; that it must be our happiness to conduce to theirs; and that we must all rise or fall together. They will never, therefore, forsake the first principle of society, that of being governed by the voice of the majority; and should it be that the proposed form of government should be rejected, they will zealously attempt another. Should it, by the vote now to be taken, be ratified, they will quietly acquiesce, and where they see a want of perfection in it, endeavor in a constitutional way to have it amended.

The question now before you is such as no nation on earth, without the limits of America, has ever had the privilege of deciding upon. As the Supreme Ruler of the Universe has seen fit to bestow upon us this glorious opportunity, let us decide upon it, appealing to him for the rectitude of our intentions, and in humble confidence that he will yet continue to bless and save our country.[28]

Even with the support of Hancock and Adams, ratification won by only a narrow margin, 187 to 168. It would not have won at all without Hancock's assistance. After the vote, many of the antis, apparently taking their cue from the governor, rose to say that, although they had not favored the Constitution, they would now do everything in their power to encourage their constituents to live peaceably under it.[29]

As usual, Hancock's enemies laid his actions to the basest of motives. He had, according to them, struck a corrupt bargain and sold out to the Federalists.[30] That judgment is both harsh and simplistic. It is hard to imagine what the Federalist forces in Massachusetts could offer Hancock that he did not already have. They may well have alluded to national office, but that was a prize that at this point did not even exist, and should it come into being, they could hardly guarantee delivery. As for Hancock himself, his later actions indicate no particular favoritism toward the Federalists.

What was it that drove Hancock forward at so crucial a time? It was the same engine that had carried him forward in the sixties, sent him to Philadelphia in '75, and brought him to the governorship in '80 — fame. In his *Discourses*, Niccolò Machiavelli wrote: "Of all men who have been eulogized, those deserve it most who have been the authors and founders of religions; next come such as have established republics or kingdoms."[31] Hancock longed to be in the latter category, and he certainly had some claim to the distinction. He had been one of the midwives for the child independence, and now might claim a similar role in the birth of the republic. In those two moments of high drama, he had publicly pledged himself to the new nation.

Hancock emerged from the convention more popular than ever. Even the balladeers were singing of him.

> *Then Squire Hancock like a man,*
> *Who dearly loves the nation,*
> *By a conciliatory plan,*
> *Prevented much vexation.*
> *Yankee doodle, etc.*
>
> *He made a woundy Fed'ral speech,*
> *With sense and elocution,*
> *And then the 'Vention did beseech*
> *T'adopt the Constitution.*
> *Yankee doodle, etc.*[32]

Backed by the moderates and Federalists, he won re-election as governor by a margin that was close to acclamation. There was one element of sadness in the victory. His good friend and ally Thomas Cushing, the man who for a generation had been unwaveringly loyal, was dead. He had died in February. His departure opened the field for the lieutenant governor's chair. Given Hancock's ill health, the post was worth vying for. The winner was the Federalist candidate, Benjamin Lincoln. He was

From Hancock's perspective Lincoln was a poor substitution for his old friend Cushing. The governor was not in sympathy with the general's avid Federalist policies, nor was he personally fond of the man. Indeed, within a short time Hancock presented Lincoln with an insult that precipitated a series of scurrilous attacks on the governor.

The lieutenant governor received a very small salary. To augment that pittance, for some time it had been the practice, under both Hancock and Bowdoin, for the governor to appoint the lieutenant governor (who had always been Cushing) to the post of Captain of the Castle, which carried with it an income of approximately £450 per year. The sum was not inconsiderable, and Lincoln, being a man of modest means, was counting on it to support him. It was a shock, therefore, when Hancock announced that he did not intend to appoint Lincoln or anyone else to the job.[34]

According to Sullivan, the governor's motives were pure. He had simply decided that the job was a sinecure that, in light of the commonwealth's need for austerity, no longer needed to be filled. Cushing's death provided a convenient point at which to break the tradition. Of course, austerity had never been one of Hancock's more conspicuous trademarks, and it was hard to convince the opposition, let alone a much-disgruntled Lincoln, that the governor was acting out of concern for thrift.[35]

Leading the charge was Stephen Higginson, or Laco, as he signed himself in the papers. He and Hancock were not unaccustomed to quarreling with one another. Two years before, Higginson had pushed hard for severe punishment against the Shaysites and Hancock counseled moderation. Higginson was not only politically hostile to Hancock; he was a personal foe, as well, for he was a close friend of Lincoln's.

Laco let loose with a barrage of vituperation the like of which Hancock had never endured in his long political career. According to Laco, Hancock was everything from a common scoundrel to a crook, incompetent, lazy, and any number of other vile epithets the writer could find. The vehemence and intemperateness of the attack probably weakened it. Laco overplayed his hand. Hancock's friends were not slow in responding, and they gave as good as they received.[36]

The climax to the affair came when Theophilus Parsons introduced into the House a censure motion directed at Hancock for his conduct against Lincoln. The motion failed miserably.[37] Hancock now wanted mightily to drop Lincoln, and in the spring elections of 1789 he got his chance. He himself won re-election handily, but the contest for lieutenant governor was close. It was Sam Adams versus Lincoln. Adams won. After their long estrangement, the two old revolutionaries were once more in tandem.[38]

Although his body grew more frail and he seemed old beyond his years, Hancock still hankered for national office. He knew, as did nearly everyone, that the presidency belonged to Washington. But if he could not be President, perhaps he might be Vice-President. Washington was a southerner, so a northerner would be needed for the second spot, and his was a name to be reckoned with. It is impossible to say with what enthusiasm or seriousness Hancock sought the post. It is likely that he got no support from Dolly, and he was fully aware of his own physical problems. He never made any overt moves himself; however, he did allow certain feelers to be sent out in his behalf.[39]

In August 1788, Hancock made a tour, traveling first to Portsmouth, New Hampshire, and then coming back down the coast to Boston. Everywhere, he was well received. The local newspapers carried the news of his visit and speculated about his possible future as Vice-President.[40] In an effort to thwart his becoming Vice-President, Hancock's foes spread a rumor that the governor would accept nothing but the presidency. Sullivan tried to quash the rumor, but it persisted, nevertheless.[41]

Emboldened by the apparent support within his own state, Hancock resolved to test the waters elsewhere. Late in 1788, Sullivan took a trip south to sound out support. The results were disappointing. Aside from the usual amount of personal and political enmity that he expected to find, Sullivan discovered something else. After a career of popping in and out of a sickbed, Hancock had raised doubts in the voters' minds that he was capable of holding the job. Indeed, even those in his own

were the final results of the election. Washington garnered every vote cast by the electors, 69. For the vice-presidency Hancock ran a poor fifth out of eleven. He received only 4 votes, and not one of them from Massachusetts. Instead of supporting him, the Massachusetts delegation cast their ballots for John Adams, who did indeed win the election as Vice-President.[43]

Hancock was not accustomed to being an also-ran. He was not pleased at having been apparently deserted by the Federalists, but he could take solace from the fact that his loss on the national stage seemed to have no effect in state politics, as was proved when he won the governorship in '89 with Sam Adams running beside him.[44]

Vying for the vice-presidency was the last important act in Hancock's political career. He easily retained the governorship — only death removed him — but for him the post was a sinecure. Politics in the commonwealth took on a more temperate tone. For the rest of his life, at least, the political focus was on national affairs.

Although his quest for national office foundered, Hancock showed no animus toward those who were successful. He supported Washington, Adams, and the Constitution. In fact, even before the election, when the anti-Federalist governor of New York, George Clinton, began fishing in troubled waters by suggesting a new Constitutional Convention, Hancock politely but firmly rejected the notion. He told him that such a meeting would be "dangerous to the Union."[45]

Hancock had an opportunity visibly to display his loyalty to the Union and its new President in the fall, when Washington made his grand tour of the northern states. The President left New York on October 15 and traveled north through New Haven and Hartford, going to Springfield and from there to Cambridge and Boston via Worcester. Everywhere the reception was the same — delirious. Washington loved it.[46]

As he neared Boston, Hancock dispatched a message, inviting the President to stay with him while he was in town. Washington's response was a disappointment. He explained that, as a matter of policy, when he traveled he did not stay in private homes, and that he had already sent an aide ahead to find the necessary accommodations in a public house. Hancock felt a bit slighted.

On the 24th, Washington made his grand entrance into the town that he had not seen since he liberated it more than a dozen years before. At the Roxbury line, he was met by a large delegation, which escorted him along the main thoroughfare recently named in his honor. Leading the procession was the Company of Cadets, followed by a band, the selectmen, the sheriffs of Suffolk and Middlesex counties, the Council, The lieutenant governor, and finally the President himself, mounted on an elegant white charger.

Although it was a raw fall day, thousands of Bostonians lined the way to catch a glimpse of America's greatest hero. As he rode toward the center of town, Washington caught sight of a huge arch erected in front of the State House. It was twenty feet high and on one side was inscribed "To the Man Who Unites All Hearts." On the other was written "To Columbia's Favorite Son." At the very peak was a carved American eagle with a fourteen-foot wing span. Everything was in its finest order. Only one item was missing — the governor.

Hancock's excuse for not being present was his gout and the fear of aggravating it by going out in such dank weather. He did invite Washington to come to his home and dine, but the President, mindful of the dignity of his office, refused to call on the governor first; instead, he took dinner at his lodgings with Vice-President Adams.

When Hancock learned of Washington's annoyance with him, he moved quickly to avoid any further embarrassment. The lieutenant governor and two members of the Council waited on the President to express the governor's "concern" that he had not been well enough to personally welcome him. Washington, who knew Hancock's health and ego all too well, was still somewhat suspicious, and he let it be known that under no circumstances would he lessen the stature of his office by calling on Hancock first. The next day, in one of his most bizarre performances, Hancock called on the President. He was borne into the chamber and set down before Washington by four servants. In one chamber and set down before Washington by four servants. In one event Dolly recalled that, on seeing such a pitiful sight, Washington began to cry. Her story sounds far-fetched. Washington was hardly known as a sentimentalist, and Dolly's recollection could only have been secondhand, since she was not present at the meeting. At any rate, with or without tears, Washington was shocked at what he saw. Hancock had become a near-invalid. He accepted the governor's explanation and, judging by the newspapers, so too did the people of Boston.

The winter of 1789–90 did Hancock little good. Although he was only fifty-three, his hand had grown so feeble that his once-bold signature had become a shaky scrawl.[47] His illness confined him more and more to his home and bed. His friend James Winthrop described his indisposition as "fixed." On occasion he did manage public appearances. He made it a point to be present at the grand reception given in honor of *Columbia*'s return from her around-the-world voyage. He was present when John Carroll, the first American Roman Catholic bishop, celebrated mass in Boston, and he also made it out for the festivities in 1792, celebrating the tercentennial of Columbus' epic voyage.[48]

From his chamber, where he now spent so much of his time, Hancock could look out over a magnificent view. His house was still the greatest in Boston, and he the town's most honored citizen. Others whom he had known and loved were not so lucky. His sister-in-law Esther, one of Dolly's older sisters, had fled at the time of the Revolution to be with her Tory husband, Jonathan Sewall. Their life since had been one misery after another. Hancock may have had little reason to like Sewall, but he was very fond of Esther, and when she wrote to him from

New Brunswick he could do nothing but help. He sent them numerous gifts of food and clothing, hoping to ease their exile. Esther wanted to come to Boston, but she knew her husband was too ill and bitter ever to return. When he died in 1796, she did come home, but by then it was too late to thank the man who had been so kind to her.[49]

In periods of remission, Hancock undertook traveling, something he had always enjoyed. In the spring of 1791, he and Dolly made a trip north to Portsmouth, and the following year they took a turn to the south, visiting Newport, and then over to Fairfield, where they visited with their old friends the Burrs.[50]

Although he enjoyed traveling, Hancock took these trips with an eye toward something more than pleasure. He owned large tracts of land in New Hampshire and Connecticut, and he took time during his journeys to meet with his agents and lawyers to discuss his holdings. The reports were not good. The lands were not selling well, and taxes were continually falling due. In the northern lands, squatters were a vexing problem.[51] He was certainly rich in land. His holdings totaled at least 265 acres in Connecticut, 1325 in Massachusetts, 1680 in Maine lands, and 887 in New Hampshire. And his sizable holdings in Boston were valued at nearly £30,000.[52] But if he was heavily endowed with real estate, he was short on cash, and gossip had it that he managed to underwrite a good deal of his extravagant living by simply not paying his bills.[53]

Hancock's last fling in public controversy came in the fall of 1792, when a troupe of actors arrived in Boston. They rented a stable on Hawley Street, fitted it out as a theater, and raised their curtain on a series of "Moral Lectures." The subterfuge was necessary because theatrical performances were illegal in Massachusetts. Despite the thin disguise, no one seemed inclined to enforce the law, and from August to November the company presented its "Lectures" to delighted audiences.

Hancock was one person who was not pleased by the Hawley Street affair. He did not necessarily share the horror, as expressed by some townsmen, at the immorality and evil of the theater; rather, his principal concern was the impunity with which people were violating the law. He saw the violations and the unwillingness of the local authorities "as an open insult upon the law and the Government of the Commonwealth." Having said that, he was just as unwilling to enforce an unpopular law as were the Boston authorities, and he left the matter to the "vigilance and wisdom" of the General Court.

Nothing further happened until December 5, when the Suffolk County sheriff and his deputies broke into the middle of a performance. They literally brought the house down. In the riot that followed, one of Hancock's proclamations was used to escape on a technicality. Not long after, the General Court and the governor, having witnessed what the public wanted, repealed the law against theatrical performances and allowed stage plays to be performed in Boston.[54]

Broken in health, Hancock continued in office as the great figurehead. With Sullivan, Avery, and Adams to assist him, he continued to reign. On September 18, 1793, he made his last appearance before the General Court. He was so weak that he could neither stand nor speak. On Tuesday morning, October 8, he awoke as usual but soon had trouble breathing. Nat Balch and Dolly were by his side. The doctor was summoned, but it was too late. Within the hour he was dead.

It was a grand funeral. If Hancock had planned it himself, it could not have been more majestic. The procession began promptly at 3:00 P.M. The cortège left the mansion and went straight across the Common to Boylston Street, where it took a left and paused at the site of the Liberty Tree. From there the procession marched up Washington Street to the State House, around the building, and then to Old Granary Burial Ground, where Hancock was laid to rest. Everyone of any importance was in the cortège. Militia, justices of the peace, judges of probate, attorney general, treasurer, Senate, Council, House, Vice-President of the United States, judges and secretaries of the United States, and, of course, the lieutenant governor. Despite his age and weakness, Adams was determined to honor his friend. He made it nearly all the way, but at last age took its toll, and he had to leave the procession at State Street.[55]

Nothing more symbolized the grandeur of Hancock's life than

the manner of his leaving it. For nearly three decades he had dominated the politics of Massachusetts and had moved in the highest circles on the national level. He most certainly deserves to be remembered as one of that sainted group, the Founding Fathers. Yet was he a great man?

He lacked the eloquence of Jefferson, the intellect of John Adams, and the character of Washington. He wrote nothing of an extraordinary nature and seems never to have been much interested in any of the great issues of the time beyond those of mundane politics. What, then, did he contribute to the Revolution and the Republic?

He provided a symbol of moderation and decency at a time when the centrifugal forces of revolution threatened to tear the nation apart. To be sure, he did not always understand his role and often acted from ignorance or on the advice of others. Nevetheless, in the Congress and in the state he was "the centre of union" around which a majority always seemed able to coalesce.[56]

Hancock's role, however, does not end with his ability to please politicians. Perhaps more than any of his contemporaries he deserves to be enshrined as America's first modern politician. He grew up in an age of oligarchy and died with its ruins around him. Many of his contemporaries never understood the change, and that obtuseness cost them their careers. From the beginning, Hancock the aristocrat was always a democrat, at least in public. He could win a following with rum on the Common, jobs at the wharf, or mercy for the Shaysites. Simply because he benefited from these gestures does not mean they were all part of an act, for he seems really to have cared about the people he served. He was never bound by rigid ideology. To some, he was vacillating. Today, we should be more likely to say he was flexible and adaptable. He was a man who could cope with changes in his political environment.

From the grave, Hancock managed to startle the town one more time. He died intestate. One of Boston's wealthiest citizens died without having made out a will. Perhaps it was carelessness or perhaps it was his last grab at popularity. If he directed the division of his estate, some would be pleased, but others would be disappointed. This way, everyone could live with the dream that "if only there had been a will I would have gotten something."

Another, more perverse, explanation is that he was sick of the vultures who hovered over him in his last years and that he hoped their just rewards would come in battling one another for the estate. If this was the case, he got his wish and more. For more than a generation the Hancocks were in and out of court squabbling over Thomas's estate among his mother, wife, brother, and sister. They must have been disappointed, for in the final tally John Hancock proved to be worth far less than anyone thought. Because there had been no inventory of Thomas' possessions, it is impossible to make a precise comparison between what John inherited from his uncle and what he left to his scavenging relatives. However, two things are apparent. John left less than half as much in cash and only a fraction of what Thomas had had in land. Strike it up to bad management, the war, or any other cause, but the plain fact is John Hancock had far less at his death than Uncle Thomas had had at his. Whatever his critics might say, the indisputable truth is that this man sacrificed a fortune to support the people of Boston and the Revolution. At a time when many in similar positions were using their influence to make money in shady schemes, Hancock stood aloof. Aside from Laco's wild accusations and his prewar smuggling, no one ever accused him of turning a dishonest dollar. Even John Adams, who in Hancock's own lifetime was not especially fond of him, had to admit that he was "radically generous and benevolent . . ." A suitable epitaph for any man.

Notes

Bibliography

Index

ABBREVIATIONS

BPL   Boston Public Library
BS-*P*   Bostonian Society *Publications*
BUA   Boston University Archives
CL   Clements Library, University of Michigan
DAB   *Dictionary of American Biography*
HSOP   Historical Society of Pennsylvania
HUA   Harvard University Archives
JCC   *Journals of the Continental Congress*
HL   Houghton Library
MA   Massachusetts Archives
MHS   Massachusetts Historical Society
MHS-*C*   Massachusetts Historical Society *Collections*
MHS-*P*   Massachusetts Historical Society *Proceedings*
NDAR   *Naval Documents of the American Revolution*
NEHGS   New England Historic Genealogical Society
NEHG-*R*   New England Historical and Genealogical *Register*
NYHS   New-York Historical Society
PCC   Papers of the Continental Congress
Sibley   *Sibley's Harvard Graduates*
YUL   Yale University Library

CHAPTER I
The Three John Hancocks
(pages 1–15)

1. Charles Hudson, *History of the Town of Lexington, Middlesex County, Massachusetts* (Boston, 1868), 320–321; *Sibley*, 3:429; Josiah Quincy, *The History of Harvard University* (Boston, 1860) 1:440–441.

2. David S. Lovejoy, *The Glorious Revolution in America* (New York, 1972), 194; Corporation Records Harvard College, II, HUA.

3. *Sibley*, 429; Samuel A. Green, ed., *The Early Records of Groton, Massachusetts, 1662–1707* (Groton, 1880), 104.

4. *Sibley*, 3:431; Hudson, 319.

5. Donald L. Jacobus, *The Bulkeley Genealogy* (Boston, 1933), 111–113, 131–132, 152, 213, 446.

6. Hudson, 437; *Massachusetts Province Laws*, 21:813.

7. Lexington, Massachusetts, *Record of Births, Marriages and Deaths to January 1, 1898* (Boston, 1898), 31; Hudson, 84.

8. Clifford Shipton, "The New England Clergy of the Glacial Age," Colonial Society of Massachusetts *Publications*, 32:47–48.

9. *Sibley*, 6:289.

10. Librarian's Papers, 1714–1728, III: 50, 27, 14, HUA.

11. William Waldron to Richard Waldron, December 25, 1723, Waldron Papers, 30, MHS.

12. William Pattee, *A History of Old Braintree and Quincy With a Sketch of Randolph and Holbrook* (Quincy, 1875), 217; Marion S. Arnold, ed., *A Brief History of the Town of Braintree* (Braintree, 1940), 25–27; *The Chappel of Ease and Church of Statesmen . . . the First Church of Christ in Quincy* (Quincy, 1890), 48.

13. Pattee, 217–218; John Hancock, *A Sermon Preached at the Ordination of Mr. John Hancock* (Boston, 1726).

14. Pattee, 217; *Chappel of Ease*, 48.

15. Suffolk County Court, Book of Deeds, Book 49:135; 51:6; *Sibley*, 6:71; George Lincoln, *History of the Town of Hingham* (Hingham, 1893), passim.

16. Pattee, 219.

17. John Hancock, *A Memorial of God's Goodness* (Boston, 1739).

18. Edwin Gaustad, *The Great Awakening in New England* (Chicago, 1968), 25–41.

19. Gilbert Tennent, *The Danger of an Unconverted Ministry, Considered in a Sermon on Mark VI:34* (Boston, 1742).

20. John Hancock, *The Dangers of An Unqualified Ministry Rep-*

Adams recollections of his childhood during his old age. See Herbert S. Allan, *John Hancock, Patriot in Purple* (New York, 1953), 27, 372n.

22. Indenture Agreement, July 1, 1717-July 1, 1724, BS-*P*, 12:99–100.

23. *Boston News Letter*, March 4, 1725.

24. Accounts August 15, 1727, and January 24, 1728, Hancock Papers, MHS.

25. George E. Littlefield, *Early Boston Booksellers, 1642-1711* (Boston, 1900), 220.

26. NEHG-*R*, 67:106-109; William Lincoln, *History of Worcester, Massachusetts* (Worcester, 1862), 1:4; 2:618; Box 15, Folder 6, Hancock Papers, NEHGS.

27. Sarah H. Swan, "The Story of an Old House and the People Who Lived in It," *New England Magazine*, 17:176.

28. Allen Chamberlain, *Beacon Hill, Its Ancient Pastures and Early Mansions* (Boston, 1925), 20-21; Inventory of All the Estate of His Excellency John Hancock, Mss. Cb. 46, NEHGS. Over the next twenty years Thomas added to his domain atop the hill. See Suffolk County Court, Book of Deeds.

29. Thomas Hancock to James Glin, March 6, 1735; December 20, 1736; June 24, 1737; September 3, 1740, in Thomas Hancock Letter Book, Hancock Papers, NEHGS.

30. *A Report of the Records Commissioners of the City of Boston Containing the Boston Records from 1729 to 1742* (Boston, 1885), 245; Robert Seybolt, *The Town Officials of Colonial Boston, 1634-1775* (Cambridge, 1939), passim.

31. Papers Relating to the Estate of the Reverend Mr. John Hancock, Box 6, Folder 2, Hancock Papers, NEHGS.

CHAPTER 2

The Education of a Boston Gentleman
(pages 16–31)

1. The original town of Boston was confined to the Shawmut Peninsula and comprised approximately 783 acres. The town today, with filled-in land and annexations, is 27,364 acres. See Walter Muir Whitehill, *Boston: A Topographical History* (Cambridge, 1973), 22–46; *Boston's Growth* (Boston, 1910), 44.

2. Thomas Hancock to Simon Gross, December 20, 1743, Box 1, Hancock Papers, NEHGS.

3. Although the cause célèbre over Jenkins' Ear provided a neat excuse for war, the real issues involved colonial expansion, British abuse of the Asiento, and the usual mixture of continental politics. Curiously enough, the ear had actually been sliced off in 1731. Jenkins must have carried it around with him for seven years. See Howard Peckham, *The Colonial Wars: 1689–1762* (Chicago, 1964), 88.

4. William Shirley to the General Court of Massachusetts, January 9, 1744–45, in Charles H. Lincoln, ed., *Correspondence of William Shirley* (New York, 1912), 1:159–160.

5. W. T. Baxter, *The House of Hancock* (Cambridge, 1945), 78; John A. Schutz, *William Shirley: King's Governor of Massachusetts* (Chapel Hill, 1961), 73.

6. G. A. Rawlyk, *Yankees at Louisbourg* (Orono, Maine, 1967), 149.

7. Mark A. DeWolfe Howe, *Boston Common Scenes from Four Centuries* (Cambridge, 1900), 30.

8. Herbert S. Allan, in *John Hancock Patriot in Purple* (New York, 1953), 31–32, asserts, without evidence, that John went to live with Thomas immediately on his father's death, and that, for one year after his uncle kept him at home preparing him for the Latin School. It seems more logical to this author that John would have stayed with his mother. As for taking a year to prepare him for Latin, it is highly unlikely that John, who had attended school in Braintree and was the son and grandson of Harvard ministers, would have needed such tutoring. Certainly others entered who were far less prepared.

    South Grammar, or Latin, School was one of five such schools in the town. They were tax-supported and free to the inhabitants of the town. See Robert F. Seybolt, *The Public Schools of Colonial Boston, 1635–1775* (Cambridge, 1935), 2–3.

Pauline A. Holmes, *A Tercentenary History of the Boston Public Latin School, 1635–1935* (Cambridge, 1935), 78.
14. Brayley, 33.
15. Seybolt, 75.
16. Ibid., 68.
17. William C. Bates, "A Boston Writing School Before the Revolution," *Magazine of American History*, 21:499.
18. In his will Holbrook ordered that this work be sold for £100 and that Hancock was to have first refusal. If no one bought it then the piece was to go to Harvard. Harvard got it. See Holmes, 381.
19. Henry F. Jenks, "Old School Street," *New England Magazine*, 13:265.
20. Baxter, 100–101; Jenks, *Catalogue*, 6.
21. *Sibley*, 13:380–397.
22. Violence was not a rarity in Boston, but in November 1747 a particularly bad riot broke out in the town, precipitated by the activities of a press gang. See Carl Bridenbaugh, *Cities in Revolt* (New York, 1955), 115.
23. King's Chapel was first established in 1686. Henry W. Foote, "The Rise of Dissenting Faiths And the Establishment of the Episcopal Church," in Justin Winsor, ed., *The Memorial History of Boston* (Boston, 1881), 1:201.
24. *Boston Town Records, 1742–1757* (Boston, 1885), 136.
25. Schutz, 74–76.
26. *Boston Town Records, 1742–1757*, 145.
27. Holmes, 244.
28. Ibid., 246.
29. Hancock's correspondence often reflects a certain element of ruthlessness and blatant political conniving. See Thomas

Hancock to John Henry Bastide, June 4, 1745, Thomas Hancock, Letter Book, Hancock Papers, MHS; Thomas Hancock to Christopher Kilby, July 27, 1745, Ibid.; Thomas Hancock to unknown correspondent, April 23, 1747, Hancock Papers, NEHGS.

30. Schutz, 234–247.
31. Herbert L. Osgood, *The American Colonies in the Eighteenth Century* (New York, 1924), 3:560–563; Neil R. Stout, *The Royal Navy in America, 1760–1775* (Annapolis, 1973), 72.
32. Rawlyk, 159; Peckham, 119.
33. *Sibley*, 13:380, 498.
34. UA I:70.27.41, HUA.
35. Lyman H. Butterfield, ed., *Diary and Autobiography of John Adams* (Cambridge, 1961) 1:92–93.
36. *Sibley*, 13:378.
37. Daniel Munro Wilson, *Where American Independence Began* (Boston, 1904), 235–236.
38. *Sibley*, 13:380.
39. Josiah Quincy, *The History of Harvard University* (Boston, 1869) 2:97.
40. Sprague apparently kept a house where students could board. This was not the last time his name appears in a student discipline case. See Faculty·Records, I: 342–343, 325; II: 211–212, HUA.
41. Just before graduation the culprits were restored to their original places in the class. *Ibid.*, I: 342–343, 328.
42. The manuscript copy of this song is signed by Hancock. It is possible that he was not the original author but merely copied it from someone else. In either case he had a fondness for the song. Box 53, Folder 1, Hancock Papers, NEHGS.
43. MHS-C (second series), 7:163.
44. John Hancock to John Hastings, college steward, November 1, 1752-January 31, 1752, Box 22, Folder 1, Hancock Papers, NEHGS.

CHAPTER 3

Boston to London and Home Again
(pages 32–47)

1. Thomas himself felt a bit uneasy at prospects of peace. Thomas Hancock to Christopher Kilby. September 10, 1748; Thomas Hancock Letter Book, Hancock Papers, NEHGS;

W. T. Baxter, *The House of Hancock* (New York, 1965), 111–123; *Boston Town Records, 1742–1757* (Boston, 1885), 236.

2. The Hancock Papers at the NEHGS are replete with receipts

8. Lawrence Henry Gipson, *The Great War* , 6 of *The British Empire Before the American Revolution* (New York, 1946), 31.

9. Baxter, 150.

10. The first business paper bearing John's signature is a receipt dated May 8, 1759. See Hancock Papers, MHS.

11. Faculty Records, III: 80, HUA.

12. Corporation Records, II: 91, 108, 119, 127; HUA.

13. John Hancock to Ebenezer Hancock, November 19, 1756, Ch. M. 1.10 (4), BPL; John Hancock to Ebenezer Hancock, October 26, 1759, Ch. M. 1.10 (77), BPL.

14. Thomas was a member of the committee overseeing the rebuilding. *Boston Town Records . . . Miscellaneous Papers* (Boston, 1900), 103; Arthur W. Brayley, *A Complete History of the Boston Fire Department* (Boston, 1889), 60.

15. John A. Schutz, *Thomas Pownall, Britsh Defender of American Liberty* (Glendale, 1951), 175–76.

16. *Boston News Letter*, June 5, 1760.

17. Trecothick and Apthorp to Thomas Hancock, July 10, 1760, Box 7, Folder 3, Hancock Papers, NEHGS.

18. Trecothick and Company to Thomas Hancock, February 12, 1761, Ibid.

19. Thomas Hancock to John Hancock, March 16, 1761, Thomas Hancock Letter Book, Ibid.

20. This figure is taken from John Hancock's Account Book, 1760–1761, MSQ Am. 2084, BPL.

21. John Hancock to Thomas Hancock, January 14, 1761, MHS-P, 43:196.

22. George Rudé, *Hanoverian London, 1714–1808* (Berkeley, 1971), 64–81.

23. Thomas Griffiths to Thomas Hancock, September 16, 1760,

Box 7, Folder 2, Hancock Papers, NEHGS; Hide and Hambleton to Thomas Hancock, July 5, 1761, Ibid. There seems to be no direct evidence to substantiate the claim that Hancock went to Hamburg and Amsterdam. See BS-*P*, 1:57; Baxter, 148.

24. Alvin Redman, *The House of Hancock* (New York, 1961), 91.
25. John Hancock to Ebenezer Hancock, October 29, 1760, HL.
26. John Hancock to Ebenezer Hancock, December 27, 1760, HL; MHS-*P*, 43:195.
27. John R. Alden, "John Mein: Scourge of Patriots," Colonial Society of Massachusetts *Publications*, 34:596.
28. Redman, 97.
29. Thomas Hancock to John Hancock, July 5, 1760; October 7, 1760; March 16, 1761; March 23, 1761, Thomas Hancock Letter Book, Hancock Papers, NEHGS.
30. W. T. Baxter, "A Colonial Bankrupt: Ebenezer Hancock," Business Historical Society *Bulletin*, 25:115–116.
31. *Vital Records of Bridgewater, Massachusetts, to the Year 1850* (Boston, 1916), 2:292.
32. Richard Perkins to Ebenezer Hancock, August 25, 1761, Box 30, Folder 2, Hancock Papers, NEHGS; John Hancock to Ebenezer Hancock, March 31, 1761, MHS-*P*, 43:198.
33. John Hancock to Thomas Hancock, July 11, 1761, EMS Am. 1300 (3) HL; Charter, July 11, 1761, Ms. G. 41.8, vol. 3, no. 32, BPL.
34. Quite likely, he sailed to New York and took a coastal vessel, *Stamford*, from there to Boston, arriving on September 23. *Boston News Letter*, September 24, 1761.
35. Thomas Hancock to Jonathan Barnard, January 1, 1763, John Hancock Letter Book, Hancock Papers, NEHGS.
36. Thomas Hancock to Maj. Gen. Bastide, August 4, 1763; Thomas Hancock to John Hancock, July 10, 1763, Ibid.
37. This unfortunate enterprise is described by Baxter, 168–176.
38. Dr. Thomas Bulfinch bill to Thomas Hancock, 1765, B., Ms. Misc., Countway Library.
39. John Hancock to Barnard and Harrison, August 17, 1764, John Hancock Letter Book, Hancock Papers, NEHGS.

CHAPTER 4
On His Own
(pages 48–67)

4. *Massachusetts Gazette and Boston News Letter*, August 23, 1764, and January 3, 1765.

5. Aunt Lydia's portrait was done at about the same time. Copley did a number of portraits for Hancock, including the famous sitting pose done in 1770. UA I: 5.120, Corporation Papers, HUA; Frank W. Bayley, *The Life and Works of John Singleton Copley* (Boston, 1915), 137; Augustus T. Perkins, *A Sketch of the Life and a List of Some of the Works of John Singleton Copley* (n.p., 1873); Barbara N. Parker and Anne Bolling Wheeler, *John Singleton Copley: American Portraits in Oil, Pastel, and Miniature With Biographical Sketches* (Boston, 1938), 100.

6. *Sibley*, 14:619–623. W. T. Baxter, "A Colonial Bankrupt: Ebenezer Hancock," Business History Society *Bulletin*, 25:115–116.

7. *Massachusetts Gazette and Boston News Letter*, September 13, 1764; John Hancock to Barnard and Harrison, November 17, 1764, John Hancock Letter Book, Hancock Papers, NEHGS.

8. William H. Clark, *The History of Winthrop* (Winthrop, 1952), 90–93; Anne Rowe Cunningham, ed., *Letters and Diary of John Rowe: Boston Merchant, 1759–1762, 1764–1779* (Boston, 1903), 69.

9. John Hancock to Hill, Lemar, and Bissett, November 12, 1767, John Hancock Letter Book, Hancock Papers, NEHGS.

10. Much of the town's social life, at least on Hancock's level, can be traced through diaries, especially that of John Rowe. The entries for household items in the Hancock Papers indicate a very rich diet.

11. John Hancock to Barnard and Harrison, January 21, 1765, John Hancock Letter Book, Hancock Papers, NEHGS; Charles M. Andrews, "The Boston Merchants and the Non-Importation Movement," Colonial Society of Massachusetts *Publications*, 19:181.

12. The people in Massachusetts were told that the debt was £140 million. Jasper Mauduit to the speaker of the Massachusetts House of Representatives, April 7, 1764, MA, XXII, 361–363; *Journals of the House of Commons*, 27:167; 29:432, 760.

13. Obviously this section owes a good deal to Bernard Bailyn's *Ideological Origins of the American Revolution* (Cambridge, 1967), and Pauline Maier, *From Resistance to Revolution* (New York, 1972).

14. Hancock imported numerous books and magazines. Some he undoubtedly sold; others found their way into his library. There is, of course, no guarantee that he read them, and if he did, that he understood them. Inventory of all the Estate of his late Excellency John Hancock, Mss. Cb. 46, NEHGS.

15. Caroline Robbins, *The Eighteenth-Century Commonwealthman* (Cambridge, 1959), Chap. 9.

16. P. D. G. Thomas, *British Politics and the Stamp Act Crisis* (Oxford, 1975), 54n.

17. James Otis, *The Rights of the British Colonies Asserted and Proved* (Boston, 1764). This pamphlet appeared the same week Thomas Hancock was buried. *Massachusetts Gazette and Boston News Letter*, August 9, 1764.

18. John Hancock to Barnard and Harrison, January 21, 1765. John Hancock Letter Book, Hancock Papers, NEHGS.

19. The best general discussion of the Stamp Act is in Edmund S. Morgan and Helen M. Morgan, *The Stamp Act Crisis* (Chapel Hill, 1953).

20. G. B. Warden, *Boston, 1689–1776* (Boston, 1970), 156–157.

21. The selectmen's activities can be best followed through their *Minutes*. In 1766 the town collected £9582, 2s, 3p in taxes. *Selectmen's Minutes, 1764–1768* (Boston, 1889), 294.

22. Ibid.

23. John Hancock to Thomas Pownall, July 6, 1765, Hancock Papers, MHS.

24. Ibid.

25. The misleading account that suggested all the resolves had passed was first published on June 24, 1765 in the *Newport Mercury*; Robert D. Meade, *Patrick Henry* (Philadelphia,

1936), 3:86–88.
30. John Hancock to Barnard and Harrison, August 22, 1765, John Hancock Letter Book, Hancock Papers, NEHGS.
31. Governor Bernard to Maj. Gen. Gage, August 27, 1765, Edward Channing, ed., *The Barrington-Bernard Correspondence* (Cambridge, 1912), 227–228; Hutchinson, *History*, 90–91; R. S. Congley, "Mob Activities in Revolutionary Massachusetts," *New England Quarterly*, 6:108–109.
32. John Hancock to unknown correspondent, October 14, 1765, John Hancock Letter Book, Hancock Papers, NEHGS.
33. John Hancock to Barnard and Harrison, October 22, 1765, Ibid.
34. This is the somewhat unusual conclusion of W. T. Baxter, the historian who has studied the business empire of the Hancock family. W. T. Baxter, *The House of Hancock* (Cambridge, 1945), 236–239.
35. John Hancock to Harrison and Barnard, December 21, 1765, John Hancock Letter Book, Hancock Papers, NEHGS.
36. January 18, 1766, Ibid.
37. Harrison and Barnard to John Hancock, March 18, 1766, Ch. F. 1.86, BPL; Jonathan Barnard to John Hancock, May 18, 1766, Ch. V. F. 1.85, Ibid.
38. John Hancock to Harrison and Barnard, April 17, 1766, John Hancock Letter Book, Hancock Papers, NEHGS.
39. Thomas, 142–153; Benjamin Gerrish to John Hancock, March 1, 1766, Hancock Papers, CL.
40. John Hancock to Harrison and Barnard, January 18, 1766, John Hancock Letter Book, Hancock Papers, NEHGS.
41. *Massachusetts Gazette Extraordinary*, June 20, 1765.

42. Thomas Longman to John Hancock, March 21, 1766, Ms. I, 1.9, BPL; Josiah Quincy, *The History of Harvard University* (Boston, 1860), 2:494.

43. John Mein was among the first to refer to Hancock as a "milch cow." The term also appears in a document that was apparently intended for publication in London. Document April 18, 1775, MSL, MHS.

44. *Massachusetts Gazette,* May 29, 1766.

45. Apparently this story first appeared in William Gordon, *The History of the Rise, Progress, and Establishment of the Independence of the United States* (London, 1788).

46. This story was first recollected by John Adams, more than a half-century later. John Adams to William Tudor, June 1, 1817, in Charles F. Adams, ed., *Works of John Adams* (Boston, 1850), 10:260.

47. *Massachusetts Gazette Extraordinary,* May 22, 1766.

48. *Journals of the House of Representatives of Massachusetts* (Boston, 1972), 43, Part I:5; John J. Waters, *The Otis Family In Provincial and Revolutionary Massachusetts* (Chapel Hill, 1968), 159–160.

49. Baxter, 243–246.

50. Jonathan Barnard to John Hancock, May 18, 1766, Ch. V. F. 1.85, BPL.

51. John Hancock to Harrison and Barnard, December 17, 1766, John Hancock Letter Book, Hancock Papers, NEHGS.

52. William Tudor, ed., *Deacon Tudor's Diary* (Boston, 1896), 26; *Massachusetts Gazette,* February 12, 1767.

CHAPTER 5
John Hancock — Hero and Martyr
(pages 68–87)

1. G. B. Warden, *Boston, 1689–1776* (Boston, 1970), 175. Even Thomas Hutchinson felt things had quieted a bit. See Thomas Hutchinson, *The History of the Colony and Province of Massachusetts Bay,* ed. by Lawrence Shaw Mayo (Cambridge, 1936), 3:118.

2. *Selectmen's Minutes, 1764–1768* (Boston, 1889), passim.

3. Suffolk County Court, Book of Deeds, 110:17.

4. Account of Wharfage and Dockage, various dates, Box 21,

Folder 2; Box 23, Folder 4; Box 24, Folder 1, Hancock Papers NEHGS.

5. Logbook *Lydia*, Hancock Papers, NEHGS.

    (42) BPL; Lt. Gov. Andrew Oliver to Thomas Pownall, September 19, 1768; Peter O. Hutchinson, ed., *The Diary and Letters of His Excellency Thomas Hutchinson* (London, 1883–86), 1:165n, 166n.

11. Robert J. Chaffin, "The Townshend Acts of 1767," *William and Mary Quarterly* (third series), 17:104–106.

12. John C. Miller, *Origins of the American Revolution* (Boston, 1943), 250–251.

13. Carl Ubbelohde, *The Vice-Admiralty Courts and the American Revolution* (Chapel Hill, 1960), 208–209.

14. John Hancock to Harrison, Barnard, and Spragg, July 29, 1767, John Hancock Letter Book, Hancock Papers, NEHGS.

15. Ibid.

16. John Hancock to William Reeve, September 3, 1767, Ibid.

17. *Massachusetts Gazette*, November 5, 1767.

18. John Hancock to Hill, Lemar, and Bissett, November 12, 1767, John Hancock Letter Book, Hancock Papers, NEHGS; John Hancock to George Hayley, December 15, 1767, Ibid.; John Hancock to John Shirley (no date) Box 20, Folder 3, Hancock Papers, NEHGS.

19. *Boston Evening Post*, November 23, 1767.

20. House of Representatives to Dennys DeBerdt, January 12, 1768, in Alden Bradford, ed., *Speeches of the Governors of Massachusetts from 1765 to 1775* (Boston, 1818), 126.

21. John Hancock to Harrison, Barnard, and Spragg, October 16, 1767, John Hancock Letter Book, Hancock Papers, NEHGS.

22. William Cazneau to John Hancock, December 23, 1767, Autograph File, HL.

23. John Hancock to George Hayley, October 4, 1768, John Hancock Letter Book, Hancock Papers, NEHGS.

24. Alfred Beauen, *The Aldermen of the City of London* (London, 1908–13), 2:135, 200, 211.

25. Horace Bleackley, *Life of John Wilkes* (London, 1917).

26. Pauline Maier, *From Resistance to Revolution* (New York, 1972), 162–166; "John Wilkes and American Disillusionment with Britain," *William and Mary Quarterly* (third series), 20:373–395.

27. *Records of the Church in Brattle Square, Boston* (Boston, 1902), 184, 185.

28. *Selectmen's Minutes*, 273–275.

29. *Sibley*, 14:620.

30. *Journals of the House of Representatives of Massachusetts*, (Boston, 1975), 44:164; The House of Representatives of Massachusetts to the Speakers of Other Houses of Representatives, February 11, 1768, in Harry Alonzo Cushing, ed., *The Writings of Samuel Adams* (New York, 1906), 1:184–188.

31. *Boston Gazette*, February 28, 1768; *Massachusetts Gazette Extraordinary*, March 4, 1768.

32. *Journals of the House*, 44:206–207, 211.

33. Governor Bernard to Lord Barrington, February 20, 1768, March 4, 1768, in Edward Channing and Archibald C. Coolidge, eds., *The Barrington-Bernard Correspondence* (Cambridge, 1912), 145-150.

34. *Boston Town Records, 1758–1769* (Boston, 1886), 238, 241.

35. Paul Leicester Ford, ed., *The Political Writings of John Dickinson* (New York, 1970 repr.), 277–406; Arthur M. Schlesinger, *The Colonial Merchants and the American Revolution* (New York, 1957 repr.), 114–115; *Massachusetts Gazette*, March 17, 1768.

36. Governor Bernard to Lord Barrington, March 4, 1768, Channing and Coolidge, 148.

37. *Massachusetts Gazette*, March 17, 1768.

38. John J. Waters, Jr., *The Otis Family in Provincial and Revolutionary Massachusetts* (Chapel Hill, 1968), 174.

39. In the late nineteenth century, one writer even went so far as to attach a precise figure to Hancock's smuggling — $400,000. *Boston Transcript*, February 11, 1884.

40. Oliver M. Dickerson, "Opinion of Attorney General Jonathan Sewall of Massachusetts in the Case of *Lydia*," *William and Mary Quarterly* (third series), 4:449–504.

41. This is the opinion of Oliver M. Dickerson, "John Hancock: Notorious Smuggler or Near Victim of British Revenue Racketeers," *Mississippi Valley Historical Review*, 32:515–

secondary accounts of the *Liberty* affair. Dickerson's (note 41) is the best.

46. Lord Hillsborough to General Gage, June 8, 1768, Clarence E. Carter, ed., *The Correspondence of General Thomas Gage* (New Haven, 1933), 2:68–69.

47. Governor Bernard to Lord Barrington, June 29, 1768, Channing and Coolidge, 163.

CHAPTER 6
Francis Bernard versus John Hancock
(pages 88–105)

1. Anne Rowe Cunningham, ed., *Letters and Diary of John Rowe* (Boston, 1903), 165; John Hancock to George Hayley, October 4, 1768, John Hancock Letter Book, Hancock Papers, NEHGS.

2. *Massachusetts Gazette*, August 11, 1768.

3. L. Kinvin Wroth and Hiller B. Zobel, eds., *Legal Papers of John Adams* (Cambridge, 1965), 2:174–180; George G. Wolkins, "The Seizure of John Hancock's Sloop *Liberty*," MHS-P 55:239–284.

4. *Boston Gazette*, July 24, 1769.

5. Non-Importation Agreement, August 1, 1768, Hancock Papers, MHS.

6. John Hancock to George Hayley, August 24, 1768, John Hancock Letter Book, Hancock Papers, NEHGS; Peter Shaw, *The Character of John Adams* (Chapel Hill, 1976), 64–66.

7. *Boston Town Records, 1758–1769* (Boston, 1886), 260; Edward Channing and Archibald C. Coolidge, eds., *The Barrington-Bernard Correspondence* (Cambridge, 1912), 281.

8. *Boston Town Records, 1758–1769*, 261; Channing and Coolidge, 281–284.

9. John C. Miller, "The Massachusetts Convention, 1768," *New England Quarterly*, 7:445–474.

10. John Boyle, "Journal of Occurrences in Boston, 1759–78." NEHG-R 84:256; General Thomas Gage to Lord Hillsborough, October 10, 1768, Clarence E. Carter, ed., *The Correspondence of General Thomas Gage* (New Haven, 1933), 2:201.

11. *Selectmen's Minutes, 1764–1768* (Boston, 1889), 311.

12. Ibid.; *New York Journal*, October 13, 1768.

13. *New York Journal*, October 13, 1768.

14. John Hancock to George Hayley, October 4, 1768, John Hancock Letter Book, Hancock Papers, NEHGS. Avoiding violence was a goal shared by others in Boston, as can be seen in Pauline Maier, *From Resistance to Revolution* (New York, 1974), 154–155. The fact that the troops found a relatively peaceful town caused the ministry to reflect on their policy. See John Shy, *Toward Lexington* (Princeton, 1965), 298–301.

15. *Selectmen's Minutes*, 311.

16. Ibid.

17. Bernard Bailyn, *The Ideological Origins of the American Revolution* (Cambridge, 1967), 62; Caroline Robbins, *The Eighteenth-Century Commonwealthman* (Cambridge, 1959), 293–294, 339; J. G. A. Pocock, "Machiavelli Harrington and English Political Ideologies in the Eighteenth Century," *William and Mary Quarterly* (third series), 22:549–583.

18. For the careers of these regiments see J. W. Fortescue, *A History of the British Army*, 13 vols. (London, 1899–1930).

19. Hancock's concern for the Common had been expressed less than six months before, when the selectmen "appointed Mr. Hancock to take care that there shall be no Carriages pass and repass the Common without liberty first obtained and to direct Mr. Lloyd not to suffer the Gate to be opened on any occasion except for the carrying in or bringing out Powder from the Magazine." *Selectmen's Minutes, 1764–1768* (Boston, 1889), 289.

20. Within two weeks of their arrival, thirty soldiers deserted. See Esther Forbes, *Paul Revere and the World He Lived In* (Boston, 1942), 141.

21. The "Journal" has been edited and reprinted in book form. See Oliver M. Dickerson, ed., *Boston Under Military Rule*

1768–1769 As Revealed in a Journal of the Times (Boston, 1936).

22. John Hancock to George Hayley, October 27, 1768, John Hancock Letter Book, Hancock Papers, NEHGS; *Selectmen's Minutes, 1764–1768.* As far as owning vessels Hancock seems to have run hot and cold. At times he threatened to sell them all and then he went and bought more. See John Hancock to Daniel Barker, September–November 1768, Box 27, Folder 4, Hancock Papers, NEHGS.

23. *Ibid.*

26. A biographical of Auchmuty can be found in *Sibley*, 12:12–16. A sketch of Sewall can be found in the same work and volume, 306–324. Strangely enough, Sewall and John Adams were close friends, and in later years Hancock married Sewall's sister-in-law.

27. Wroth and Zobel, 2:195–196.

28. Lyman H. Butterfield, ed., *Diary and Autobiography of John Adams* (Cambridge, 1961), 3:306.

29. Wroth and Zobel, 2:183. According to the "Journal," Maysel was given a job on board *Liberty.* See *Boston Under Military Rule*, 84, 92.

30. Chief among those who see Hancock as a victim of the customs officers is Oliver M. Dickerson, "John Hancock: Notorious Smuggler or Near Victim of British Revenue Racketeers?" *Mississippi Valley Historical Review*, 32:515–540. See also Dickerson, *The Navigation Acts and the American Revolution* (Philadelphia, 1951), passim. A different view is taken by Carl Ubbelohde, *The Vice-Admiralty Courts and the American Revolution* (Chapel Hill, 1960), 127n, and Wroth and Zobel, 179n, 185–189.

31. John Wilkes to William Palfrey, July 24, 1769, Colonial Society of Massachusetts *Publications*, 34:414.

32. W. T. Baxter, *The House of Hancock* (New York, 1965), 269–275.

33. Palfrey had a profit-sharing arrangement with Hancock. As Hancock spent less time with the business, Palfrey's role increased. In addition to being a business associate, Palfrey was also a friend and political lieutenant.

34. List of debtors, Ch. M. 3.5, V. 2 (227), BPL.

35. Boston Assessment, 1771, MA, 132.
36. Ibid. This of course includes only the assessment for Boston. Undoubtedly, Bowdoin and Erving, like Hancock, owned property outside the town.
37. Suffolk County Court, Book of Deeds, 115:252; 111:52; 108:181; 110:17; 108:146; 103:215, 216; 106:227; 109:79; 110:178; Appraisal of estate of John Hancock (various documents), Suffolk County Probate Court 20215; Gordon E. Kershaw, *Kennebeck Proprietors 1749–1775* (Concord, 1975), 301.
38. John J. Waters, Jr. *The Otis Family* (Chapel Hill, 1968), 175.
39. *Journals of the House, 1768–69* (Boston, 1976), 45:197–198.
40. Ibid., 122.
41. Ibid., 139, 148.

CHAPTER 7
Protest Turns to Violence — The Massacre
(pages 106–124)

1. An overview of political party development in the United States can be found in William Nisbet Chambers and Walter Dean Burnham, eds., *The American Party Systems Stages of Political Development* (New York, 1967), and Everett Carll Ladd, Jr., *American Political Parties Social Change and Political Response* (New York, 1970).

   This discussion of political factions in Massachusetts is based heavily on Stephen E. Patterson, *Political Parties in Revolutionary Massachusetts* (Madison, 1973). At times, Patterson's descriptions of the factions are too neat; nevertheless, his general framework is a convenient and useful device for an understanding of Massachusetts politics.
2. John A. Schutz, *William Shirley: King's Governor of Massachusetts* (Chapel Hill, 1961).
3. Patterson, 42.
4. An excellent survey of the literature on Sam Adams can be found in James O'Toole, "The Historical Interpretations of Samuel Adams," *New England Quarterly*, 49: 82–96.
5. *Sibley*, 10:421. The article on Adams is heavily biased toward the Tory side and blatantly anti-Adams.
6. The best of the biographies of Adams is John C. Miller, *Sam Adams: Pioneer in Propaganda* (Stanford, 1936). This should be balanced by Pauline Maier, "Coming to Terms with Samuel Adams," *American Historical Review*, 81:12–37.

7. *Journals of the House, 1766* (Boston, 1973), 43, part 1:5.
8. Cushing was a Boston merchant and graduate of Harvard, class of 1744. He served the town in a number of capacities and was elected to the House in 1761. Sibley, 11:380.
9. Lyman H. Butterfield, ed., *Diary and Autobiography of John Adams* (Cambridge, 1961), 1:130.
10. Sibley, 10:420-465.
11. Ibid., 11:307.
12. Alice Morse Earle, ed., *Diary of Anna Green Winslow, a Boston School Girl of 1771* (Boston, ...

England Quarterly, 50:101–124.
14. Charles F. Adams, ed., *The Works of John Adams* (Boston, 1850), 2:262.
15. The Cooper-Pownall Correspondence has been published in Frederick Griffin, *Junius Discovered* (Boston, 1854) and in Frederick Tuckerman, ed., "Letters of Samuel Cooper to Thomas Pownall, 1769–1777," *American Historical Review*, 8:301–330. The Franklin correspondence can be found in both Albert Henry Smyth, *The Writings of Benjamin Franklin*, 10 vols. (New York, 1907), and Leonard W. Labaree and William B. Willcox, eds., *The Papers of Benjamin Franklin*, 20 vols., in progress (New Haven, 1960–   ).
16. In his will Thomas gave Cooper a suit of clothes and £200. Will of Thomas Hancock, August 10, 1764, Ms. H. 5.11, BPL.
17. An excellent examination of the influential role played by the Otis family can be found in John J. Waters, Jr., *The Otis Family in Provincial and Revolutionary Massachusetts* (Chapel Hill, 1968). There are several nineteenth-century biographies of James Otis, Jr., all of them with a pronounced Whig bias. As usual, Shipton provides a more Tory perspective. See *Sibley*, 11:247–287. A biographical sketch of Gridley can be found in the same work, 7:518–530.
18. Waters, 115.
19. The Hutchinson-Otis feud is one of the best known in the history of Massachusetts Bay. Hutchinson put forth his side of the feud in the *Boston News Letter*, April 7, 1763. Bernard Bailyn, *The Ordeal of Thomas Hutchinson* (Cambridge, 1974) 48–50, gives a good account of this incident.
20. John R. Galvin, *Three Men of Boston* (New York, 1976), 35–44; Patterson, 55; Waters, 140–143.

21. Thomas Hutchinson, *The History of the Colony and Province of Massachusetts Bay*, ed. by Lawrence Shaw Mayo (Cambridge, 1936), 3:182.

22. This sentiment was felt throughout the colonies. See Maier, 174.

23. Anne Rowe Cunningham, ed., *Letters and Diary of John Rowe, Boston Merchant, 1759–1762, 1764–1779* (Boston, 1903), 191; "An Alphabetical List of the Sons of Liberty Who Dined at Liberty Tree, Dorchester August 14, 1769," MHS-*P*, 11:140–142.

24. Isaiah Thomas, *The History of Printing in America* (Albany, 1874), 152–154.

25. Samuel Adams Drake, *Old Landmarks and Historic Personages of Boston* (Boston, 1900), 107.

26. John R. Alden, "John Mein: Scourge of Patriots," Colonial Society of Massachusetts *Publications*, 34:581.

27. *Boston Chronicle*, December 21, 1767.

28. *Boston Gazette*, January 18, 1768.

29. Ibid., January 25, 1768.

30. Supreme Judicial Court of Massachusetts, Suffolk Files, 101491, Attachment for John Mein, March 21, 1768.

31. Ibid.

32. *Boston Chronicle*, June 1, 1769.

33. John Hancock to Hayley and Hopkins, September 6, 1769, John Hancock Letter Book, Hancock Papers, NEHGS; Arthur M. Schlesinger, *The Colonial Merchants and the American Revolution, 1763–1776* (New York, 1957), 131–132.

34. Hayley and Hopkins to John Hancock, November 16, 1769, Ch. F. 1.92, BPL.

35. *Boston Chronicle*, August 21, August 28, and September 18, 1769.

36. William Palfrey to John Wilkes, October 21, 1769, MHS-*P*, 47:212; Schlesinger 132; *Boston News Letter*, October 26, 1769; *Sibley*, 14:568–569.

37. Paul Leicester Ford, ed., *The Political Writings of John Dickinson, 1764–1774* (New York, 1970 repr.), 9–22, 277–406.

38. *Newport Mercury*, September 4, 1769. The charges were echoed to the north as well. See *New Hampshire Gazette*, July 6 and 13, 1770.

39. *New York Journal*, January 18, 1770.

40. These activities can be followed in the Hancock Letter Books at the NEHGS.

41. Thomas Longman to John Hancock, July 22, 1769, Hancock Papers, MHS.
42. Thomas Longman to John Hancock, December 4, 1769, Ibid.
43. Boston Chronicle, October 26, 1769.
44. Alden, 587.
45. Boston Chronicle, October 30, 1769.
46. Thomas Longman to John Hancock, December 4, 1769, Hancock Papers, MHS.
47. John Hancock's Power of Attorney Case, Suffolk Files, 101964; Alden, 591.
48. L. Kinvin Wroth and Hiller B. Zobel, eds., Legal Papers of John Adams (Cambridge, 1965), 1:199–230; Suffolk Files, 101964.
49. Nina Moore Tiffany, ed., The Letters of James Murray, Loyalist (Boston, 1972), 169–170.
50. James Murray to Charles Stewart, September 3, 1770, Ibid., 172.
51. Suffolk Files, 101964.
52. John Hancock to Thomas Longman, January 31, 1772, John Hancock Letter Book, Hancock Papers, NEHGS.
53. Waters, 177.
54. Boston Gazette, September 25, 1769; Harry Alonzo Cushing, ed., The Writings of Samuel Adams (New York, 1968), 1:381.
55. Boston Town Records, 1770–1777 (Boston, 1887), 35.
56. The role of the Boston press is examined in Arthur M. Schlesinger, "Propaganda and the Boston Newspaper Press, 1767–1770," Colonial Society of Massachusetts Publications, 32:396–416.
57. Boston Gazette, February 26, 1770. Richardson was tried and convicted but then pardoned, causing a great stir and forcing him to leave Boston. He received an appointment in the customs service at Philadelphia. However, he never took the post, since the mob there would have tarred and feathered him. See Wroth and Zobel, 2:410–411; Maier, 194.
58. Wroth and Zobel, 3:1.
59. The best secondary account is Hiller B. Zobel, The Boston Massacre (New York, 1970).
60. Pauline Maier, "Revolutionary Violence and the Relevance of History," Journal of Interdisciplinary History, 2:123–125. There was general concern at the time of the incident that it would trigger an even more bloody scene. To avoid that, the leaders in Boston worked to calm passions. Samuel

Cooper to Thomas Pownall, March 26, 1770, *American Historical Review*, 8:317.

61. This anecdote was related by Hancock, MHS-*P*, 3:308–309.
62. Accounts of this meeting differ. See Zobel, 206–210; Hutchinson, 3:197–199; Thomas Hutchinson to Francis Bernard, October 30, 1770, MA, 27:48.
63. William Tudor, *Deacon Tudor's Diary* (Boston, 1896), 33.
64. Charles F. Adams, *Works*, John Adams to William Tudor, April 15, 1817, 10:252.

CHAPTER 8

The Unfortunate Thomas Hutchinson

(pages 125–142)

1. Mercy Otis Warren, *History of the Rise, Progress and Termination of the American Revolution* (New York, 1970 repr.), 1:79.
2. In addition to his political duties Hutchinson was also an accomplished historian who wrote in three volumes *The History of the Colony and Province of Massachusetts-Bay*. Not surprisingly, his volumes should be used with care for those years in which he himself was actively involved.
3. Bernard Bailyn, *The Ordeal of Thomas Hutchinson* (Cambridge, 1974), vii.
4. Aside from Bailyn's work, other biographies of Hutchinson include "Thomas Hutchinson" in *Sibley*, 8:149–217; Malcolm Freiberg, "Thomas Hutchinson: First Fifty Years," *William and Mary Quarterly* (third series), 15:35; and James K. Hosmer, *The Life of Thomas Hutchinson* (Boston, 1896).
5. George Athan Billias, *The Massachusetts Land Bankers of 1740*, University of Maine Studies, No. 74 (Orono, 1959), 19.
6. David Edward Maas, "The Return of the Massachusetts Loyalists," (Ph.D. dissertation, University of Wisconsin, 1972), 14. The issue of plural office-holding is examined in Ellen E. Brennan, *Plural Office-Holding in Massachusetts 1760–1780* (Chapel Hill, 1945). To be found in Harry Alonzo Cushing, ed., *The Writings of Samuel Adams* (New York, 1906), 2:265–266, is the following letter, written in 1771 by Samuel Adams to his friend Arthur Lee, regarding Hutchinson's fondness for office:

You will not then be surprised if I tell you that among
the five Judges of our Superior Court of Justice, there
are the following near Connections with the first and
second in Station in the province. Mr. Lynde is Chiefe
Justice; his Daughter is married to the Son of Mr. Oliver,
the Lt. Gov., Mr. Oliver another of the Judges is his
Brother; his Son married Gov. Hutchinson's Daughter;
& Judge Hutchinson lately appointed, who is also Judge
of the probate of Wills for the first County, an important
department, is the Govrs. brother. Besides which the
young Mr. Oliver is a Justice of the Common pleas for

man of the Govr. was sent for out of another province to
fill up the place of Clerk to the Common pleas in this
County; & the eldest Son of the Govr. will probably soon
be appointed a Justice of the same Court in the room of
his Uncle advanced to the superior bench. I should have
first mentioned that the Gov. & the Lt. Govr. are Brothers
by Marriage.

7. Hutchinson had opposed the Stamp Act and was critical of
   other measures as well. See Bailyn, 36; Thomas Hutchinson
   to Robert Wilson, May 11, 1770, MA, 26:480.
8. The question of artificial restraints being placed on the
   upward mobility of Americans is developed by James Kirby
   Martin, *Men in Rebellion* (New Brunswick, 1973).
9. *Boston Town Records, 1770–1777* (Boston, 1887), 10.
10. Samuel Cooper to Thomas Pownall, March 26, 1770, *American Historical Review,* 8:316.
11. James Bowdoin and others, *A Short Narrative of the Horrid
    Massacre in Boston* (Boston, 1770); Arthur M. Schlesinger,
    in *Prelude to Independence: The Newspaper War on Britain,
    1764–1776* (New York, 1965), 21, maintained that the Whig
    propagandists managed to create "folk heroes out of street
    loafers and hoodlums."
12. Thomas Hutchinson to Francis Bernard [?] March 1770, MA,
    26:464.
13. *Journals of the House, 1770* (Boston, 1977), 46:89; Donald C.
    Lord and Robert M. Calhoon, "The Removal of the Massa-
    chusetts General Court From Boston, 1769–1772," *Journal of
    American History,* 55:739; Hutchinson defends his action in
    his *History,* 3:215–220.

14. *Journals of the House*, 46: passim; *Selectmen's Minutes, 1769–1775* (Boston, 1893), 58–59.

15. Lord and Calhoon, 739n; Samuel Eliot Morison, *Three Centuries of Harvard, 1636–1936* (Cambridge, 1946), 136–137.

16. *Journals of the House*, 46:89–90.

17. Hutchinson, *History of Massachusetts-Bay*, 3:470–474. The intensity of feeling on this issue is testified to by the fact that it was included as a grievance in the Declaration of Independence:

> He [the king] has called together legislative bodies at places unusual, uncomfortable, and distant from the depository of their Public Records, for the sole Purpose of fatiguing them into compliance with his measures.

18. Bailyn, 172; Lord and Calhoon, 740.

19. *Journals of the House*, 46:166–167.

20. *Boston Town Records, 1770–1777*, 21.

21. Samuel Adams to John Hancock, May 11, 1770, Cushing, 2:9.

22. The instructions can be found in *Boston Town Records, 1770–1771*, 26–32; John Cary, *Joseph Warren* (Urbana, 1961), 101.

23. Thomas Hutchinson to Francis Bernard [?], May 1770, MA, 26:489.

24. The House of Representatives of Massachusetts to the Lieutenant-Governor, August 3, 1770, Cushing, 2:21, 31.

25. Hutchinson was generally pleased with himself and felt he had answered the House's attack with compelling logic. Hillsborough was not so certain and was a bit uneasy that the two sides should be engaging in such a philosophical debate, which called into question the theoretical foundation of the empire. See Bailyn, 171–172.

26. The salary was made even more onerous by the fact that it was being paid out of the tea duties. See Bailyn, 169; John C. Miller, *Sam Adams: Pioneer in Propaganda* (Stanford, 1964), 258–259; Lord and Calhoon, 749; Samuel Adams to Stephen Sayre, January 12, 1771, in Cushing, 2:250–256; Hutchinson, *History*, 3:258–259.

27. Benjamin Woods Labaree, *The Boston Tea Party* (New York, 1966), 43.

28. *New York Gazette and Post-Boy*, October 8, 1770; Arthur M. Schlesinger, *The Colonial Merchants and the American Rev-*

olution (New York, 1957 repr.), 214–239; John Hancock to Harrison and Ansley, May 10, 1770, John Hancock Letter Book, Hancock Papers, NEHGS.

Boston (New York, 1970), 219.

32. Lyman H. Butterfield, ed., *Diary and Autobiography of John Adams* (Cambridge, 1961), 2:20; John J. Waters, Jr., *The Otis Family* (Chapel Hill, 1968), 178–179; Thomas Hutchinson to [?], June 5, 1771, MA, 27:180–181.
33. Samuel Adams to Arthur Lee, April 22, 1773, Cushing, 3:36.
34. Hutchinson, *History*, 400–404; Butterfield, 2:21n.
35. John Hancock to George Hayley, December 27, 1770, John Hancock Letter Book, Hancock Papers, NEHGS; John Hancock to William Palfrey, January 1, 1771, bMS, AM 1704.3 (82), HL; William Palfrey to John Hancock, February 15, 1771, Ibid.
36. William Palfrey to John Hancock, February 15, 1771, bMS, AM 1704.3 (82), HL.
37. John Hancock to Ebenezer Hancock, January 11, 1771, Ms. 254, BPL; *Sibley*, 14:620.
38. Richard Perkins to Ebenezer Hancock, August 31, 1771, Box 30, Folder 2, Hancock Papers, NEHGS.
39. John Hancock to Hayley and Hopkins, October 6, 1771; Hancock to William Jones, November 14, 1771, John Hancock Letter Book, Hancock Papers, NEHGS.
40. John Hancock to Harrison and Ansley, November 14, 1771, Ibid.
41. John Hancock to Hayley and Hopkins, May 9, 1772, Ibid.
42. The importance of these orations is discussed in Philip Davidson, *Propaganda and the American Revolution, 1763–1783* (New York, 1973), 196–198.
43. Hutchinson, *History*, 3:249; Thomas Hutchinson to Francis Bernard, January 29, 1772, MA, 27:286–287; Miller, 248–249; Bailyn, 178.

44. Hutchinson, *History*, 3:249.
45. *Journals of the House, 1772* (Boston, 1772), 120; Samuel Adams to James Warren, April 13, 1772, W. C. Ford, ed., *Warren-Adams Letters . . . 1743–1814* (Boston, 1917–25), 1:10; Hutchinson, *History*, 3:250–251.
46. *Journals of the House, 1772*, 120–121.
47. *Boston Town Records, 1770–1777*, 78; Robert E. Brown, *Middle-Class Democracy and the Revolution in Massachusetts, 1691–1780* (New York, 1969), 289–290, suggests that the high turnout was "in all probability" the work of the governor in persuading "gentlemen" and "better sort" to vote.
48. Thomas Hutchinson to John Pownall, June 15, 1772, MHS-P, 19:138.
49. Ibid.
50. Anne Rowe Cunningham, ed., *Letters and Diary of John Rowe* (Boston, 1903), 228; *Journals of the House, 1772*, 5–8; Thomas Hutchinson to John Pownall, June 15, 1772, MA, 27:342.
51. *Journals of the House, 1772*, 15.
52. Ibid.

CHAPTER 9
Tea Party
(pages 143–161)

1. Samuel Kirkland Lothrop, *A History of the Church in Brattle Street, Boston* (Boston, 1851), 95; MHS-P, 19:75.
2. Lothrop, 96–97; John Andrews to William Barrell, February 24, 1772, MHS-P, 8:322.
3. Ibid.
4. Barbara N. Parker and Anne Bolling, *John Singleton Copley American Portraits in Oil, Pastel and Miniature, With Biographical Sketches* (Boston, 1938), 7. A previous generation of Bostonians had also relied on a portrait painter to be their architect when they asked John Smibert to design Faneuil Hall. See Henry W. Foote, *John Smibert, Painter* (Cambridge, 1950), 81.
5. MHS-C, 71:186; Lothrop 102; Boyle's "Journal of Occurrences in Boston," NEHG-R, 84:359, 364.
6. Arthur W. Brayley, *A Complete History of the Boston Fire Department* (Boston, 1889), 79; Carl Bridenbaugh, *Cities in*

Revolt (New York, 1964), 100; *Boston Town Records, 1770–1777* (Boston, 1887), 88.

7. *Selectmen's Minutes, 1769–April 1775* (Boston, 1893), 162.

A25, BUA; Anne Rowe Cunningham, ed., *Letters and Diary of John Rowe* (Boston, 1903), 230; John Andrew to William Barrell, June 4, 1773, MHS-*P*, 8:323; *Boston Weekly Newsletter*, May 27, 1773.

13. Cunningham, 232.

14. *Sibley*, 9:240–264.

15. *Journals of the House, 1772* (Boston, 1772), 117, 122; Thomas Hutchinson, *The History of the Colony and Province of Massachusetts-Bay*, ed. by Lawrence Shaw Mayo (Cambridge, 1936), 3:257; Bernard Bailyn, *The Ordeal of Thomas Hutchinson* (Cambridge, 1974), 202–203.

16. Even Hutchinson realized that, by putting the two announcements so close together, the government was courting trouble. Hutchinson, *History*, 3:259.

17. *Boston Town Records, 1770–1777*, 89–93; Richard D. Brown, *Revolutionary Politics in Massachusetts: The Boston Committee of Correspondence and the Towns, 1772–1774* (Cambridge, 1970), 55–57.

18. *Boston Town Records*, 93.

19. MA, 27:461; *Boston Town Records*, 93.

20. *Boston Weekly Newsletter*, November 12, 1772; John C. Miller, *Sam Adams* (Stanford, 1936), 264–265.

21. Attachment of Goods of John Hancock, File 297, Social Law Library, Suffolk County Court.

22. Samuel Cooper to Benjamin Franklin, March 15, 1773, William B. Willcox, *The Papers of Benjamin Franklin* (New Haven, 1976), 20:110–115.

23. *Boston Town Records*, 95–108.

24. Ibid., 106.

25. Brown, 66–67.

26. Ibid., 94.

27. *Journals of the House, 1773* (Boston, 1773), January 21, 1773, 168.

28. Ibid., 208.

29. Ibid., 224.

30. Bernard Bailyn, 224–259; Hutchinson, *History*, 283–296; Willcox, 19:xx, xxxi–xxxiii, 399–409. The letters are reprinted in 20:539–580.

31. Thomas Hutchinson to Thomas Whately, January 20, 1769, Willcox, 540.

32. Ibid.

33. Thomas Hutchinson to Thomas Whately, October 4, 1768, Ibid., 547.

34. Thomas Hutchinson to Thomas Whately, January 20, 1769, Ibid., 550.

35. Benjamin Franklin to Thomas Cushing, December 2, 1772, Ibid., 19:409–413.

36. Thomas Cushing to Benjamin Franklin, March 24, 1773, Ibid., 19:123–125; Cushing to Franklin, April 20, 1773, Ibid., 172–175; Franklin to Cushing, June 4, 1773, Ibid., 228–229.

37. *Boston Town Records*, 129.

38. Hutchinson did not veto Hancock's election. His reluctance did not grow out of any hope of courting Hancock; rather, it would have meant denying the council a quorum, "and it was not a time for such an experiment." Hutchinson, *History*, 3:285.

39. Thomas Cushing to Benjamin Franklin, June 14, 1773, Willcox, 20:235–238; *Journals of the House, 1773* (Boston, 1773), 58–61.

40. *Journals of the House, 1773*, 58–61.

41. The committee was created in response to a series of resolves passed by the Virginia House of Burgesses. Brown, 140–143, 150, 155, 165–166; Edward D. Collins, "Committees of Correspondence of the American Revolution," American Historical Association, *Annual Report . . . For 1901* (Washington, 1902), 1:245–271; Thomas Cushing to Benjamin Franklin, April 20, 1773, Willcox, 20:172–175.

42. "A Journal of the Proceedings of the Committee of Correspondence Chosen by the Honorable House of Representatives," MHS-*P* (second series), 4:85–90.

43. "The Committee of Correspondence of Massachusetts to Other Committees of Correspondence," Harry Alonzo Cushing, ed., *The Writings of Samuel Adams* (New York, 1906),

47. The background to the Tea Act is covered best in Benjamin Woods Labaree, *The Boston Tea Party* (New York, 1966), 3–125.
48. Drake, xxvi-xxvii; Messrs. Clarke and Sons to Mr. Abraham Dupuis, November 17, 1773, Ibid., 283–286.
49. *The Tradesmen's Protest Against the Proceedings of the Merchants Relative to the New Importations of Tea* (Boston, 1773); Labaree, 110.
50. *Boston Town Records*, 141–142.
51. Ibid.
52. Ibid., 144. For the events surrounding this meeting, see Drake, 295–303. Labaree, 111–112; *Boston Gazette*, November 8, 1773; *Boston News Letter*, November 11, 1773; Hutchinson, *History*, 3:304.
53. Thomas Hutchinson to John Hancock, November 11, 1773; First Corps of Cadets Papers, A150, BUA.
54. *Boston News Letter*, November 18, 1773; *Boston Post-Boy*, November 22, 1773; *Boston Town Records*, 146–148.
55. Drake, 320–331.
56. Labaree, 119.
57. John Andrews to William Barrell, December 1, 1773, MHS-P, 8:325.
58. *Selectmen's Minutes*, 202.
59. For descriptions of the Tea Party, see the collection of letters in Drake, lxv-lxxvii, 334–336; Labaree, 126–145.

CHAPTER 10
Hancock Leads the Rebellion
(pages 162–185)

1. Esther Forbes, *Paul Revere and the World He Lived In* (Boston, 1942), 200–201; Arthur M. Schlesinger, *Prelude to Independence: The Newspaper War on Britain, 1764–1776* (New York, 1965 repr.), 181–182; Benjamin Woods Labaree, *The Boston Tea Party* (New York, 1966), 146–169.

2. Hancock had good reason to remain quiet. It was rumored about the town that the patriot leaders were to be seized and sent to England for trial. See Labaree, 151. He told Hayley he was "not acquainted" with the details of the incident. John Hancock to Hayley and Hopkins, December 21, 1773, John Hancock Letter Book, Hancock Papers, NEHGS.

3. William Palfrey to Hayley and Hopkins, January 10, 1774, John Hancock Letter Book, Hancock Papers, NEHGS. *Selectmen's Minutes, 1769–April 1775* (Boston, 1893), 206–227, show that Hancock's attendance did not improve until the fall of 1774. *Boston Town Records, 1770–1777* (Boston, 1887), 162; Elbridge Gerry to Jeremiah Lee and Tristam Dalton, April 23, 1774, Gerry Papers, MHS.

4. John Hancock to John Gray, February 1, 1774, bMS, AM 1704.6, (12), HL.

5. John Hancock, *An Oration: Delivered March 5, 1774* (Boston, 1774).

6. Mary C. Crawford, *Old Boston Days and Ways* (Boston, 1909), 74, and William V. Wells, *Life and Public Services of Samuel Adams* (Boston, 1865), 2:138–140, credit Sam Adams with authorship. John Adams, in his *Diary and Autobiography*, 2: 89–90, 3:384, assigns authorship to Benjamin Church and Joseph Warren. Philip Davidson, *Propaganda and the American Revolution 1763–1783* (New York, 1973 repr.), 197, agrees that Samuel Cooper wrote it. According to still another source, Noah Webster to Ebenezer S. Thomas, July 29, 1840, Norcross Collection, MHS, the speech was a group effort. Whoever wrote the speech, contemporaries felt it was well delivered. See John Andrews to William Barrell, April 14, 1774, MHS-P, 8:327. The collection taken up for Monk yielded over £42. See *Selectmen's Minutes, 1769–1775*, 212.

7. Thomas Randolph Adams, "American Independence, The

Growth of an Idea: A Bibliographical Study of the American
Political Pamphlets Published Between 1764 and 1776 Dealing With the Dispute Between Great Britain and Her Col-

1774 FCC227, Papers of the First Corps Cadets, BUA; George
P. Anderson, "A Note on Ebenezer MacIntosh," Colonial
Society of Massachusetts *Publications*, 26:349–350.

10. Lyman H. Butterfield, ed., *Diary and Autobiography of John Adams* (Cambridge, 1961), 2:93.

11. Robert F. Seybolt, *The Town Officials of Colonial Boston, 1634–1775* (Cambridge, 1939), 354, 358.

12. James Scott to John Hancock, April 19, 1774, Hancock Papers, NEHGS.

13. Attachment of Goods of John Hancock, File 297, Social Law Library, Suffolk County Court.

14. Crawford, 220; Sarah H. Swan, "The Story of an Old House," *New England Magazine*, 17:170, 178–179; Daniel Munro Wilson, *Three Hundred Years of Quincy, 1625–1925* (Quincy, 1926), 171, 210–211; *Sibley*, 7:106–116; Butterfield, 1:66–68.

15. Ibid., 2:87, 87n.

16. Ibid., 65–66.

17. "Boyle's Journal of Occurrences in Boston," NEHG-*R*, 84:262. Sally Jackson died on March 4, 1771, Ibid., 268.

18. William Palfrey to John Hancock, February 15, 1771, bMS, AM. 1704.4 (34), HL.

19. William Purdie Treloar, *Wilkes and the City* (London, 1917), 3.

20. F. W. C. Hersey, "The Misfortunes of Dorcas Griffiths," Colonial Society of Massachusetts *Publications*, 34:15–22.

21. For a general overview comparing American and British mob activity, see Pauline Maier, *From Resistance to Revolution* (New York, 1974), 3–26.

22. George III to Lord North, February 4, 1774, John Fortescue ed., *Correspondence of George III* (London, 1928), 3:59.
23. The full text of these acts and the discussion surrounding their passage can be found most conveniently in Peter Force, ed., *American Archives*, fourth series (Washington, D.C., 1837–1853), 1:35–132, 165–170. Commonly a fifth act, the Quebec Act, is lumped together as one of the Coercive Acts. This was not the intention of the ministry. Ibid., 169–224. The acts and their effect have been the subject of numerous historical inquiries. In addition to works already cited, see Roger Champagne, "New York and the Intolerable Acts, 1774," *New-York Historical Society Quarterly*, 45:195–207; Reginald Coupland, *The Quebec Act: A Study in Statesmanship* (Oxford, 1925); Bernhard Donoughue, *British Politics and the American Revolution: The Path to War, 1773–75* (New York, 1964); Don R. Gerlach, "A Note on the Quartering Act of 1774," *New England Quarterly*, 39:80–88.
24. The general reaction in Boston can be followed in the local press and in Harry Alonzo Cushing, ed., *The Writings of Samuel Adams* (New York, 1906), 3:107 (reaction to intolerables); Cushing included not only Adams' own writings but some of the letters from the Boston Committee of Correspondence, as well. See also Arthur M. Schlesinger, *Prelude To Independence: The Newspaper War on Britain, 1764–1776* (New York, 1965), 195–196. For reaction in the countryside, see Lee N. Newcomer, *The Embattled Farmers* (New York, 1953), 38–57.
25. *Boston Town Records, 1770–1777*, 166.
26. Ibid., 174; Richard D. Brown, *Revolutionary Politics in Massachusetts: The Boston Committee of Correspondence and the Towns, 1772–1774* (Cambridge, 1970), 185–188.
27. Richard Frothingham, ed., "Correspondence in 1774 and 1775 Between a Committee of the Town of Boston and Contributors of Donations" MHS-C (fourth series), 4:1–278. Samuel Adams to Silas Deane, May 18, 1774, Cushing, 3:114–116; Samuel Adams to Charles Thomson, May 30, 1774, Ibid., 122–125; Arthur M. Schlesinger, *The Colonial Merchants and the American Revolution: 1763–1776* (New York, 1957 repr.), 393–396.
28. Schlesinger, *Colonial Merchants*, 319–325; John C. Miller, *Sam Adams* (Stanford, 1964), 301–307; G. B. Warden, *Boston, 1689–1776* (Boston, 1970), 294–295.

29. John R. Alden, *General Gage in America* (New York, 1969, repr.), 44.
30. *Boston Evening Post*, May 16, 1774; Thomas Gage to Lord

ʊ.ɔ̣ʑʊ.

33. *Journals of the House, 1774* (Boston, 1774), 7; Thomas Gage to Lord Dartmouth, May 30, 1774, Carter, 1:355–356.
34. *Journals of the House, 1774*, passim.
35. *Journals of the House, 1774*, 44. To whom credit should be given for the first call is a disputed point. Providence, Rhode Island, seems to have the best claim. See Schlesinger, *Colonial Merchants*, 327. For newspaper support, see Richard Frothingham, *The Rise of the Republic of the United States* (Boston, 1881), 314, 329, 331–333n.
36. John Andrews to William Barrell, June 12, 1774, in MHS-*P*, 8:328.
37. John Andrews to William Barrell, August 2, 1774, Ibid., 337.
38. John Andrews to William Barrell, August 11, 1774, Ibid., 340.
39. William Palfrey to Samuel Adams, September 1774, First Corps Cadets Papers, A158, BUA; Daniel Perkins to Ebenezer Hancock, September 7, 1774, Ch. F. 2.7 (a-b), BPL.
40. Thomas Flucker to John Hancock, August 1, 1774, First Corps Cadets Papers, A142, BUA.
41. William Palfrey to Samuel Adams, September 1774, Ibid., A158.
42. *Selectmen's Minutes, 1769–1775*, 224–225; General Thomas Gage to Lord Dartmouth, August 27, 1774, Carter, 1:366.
43. Bowdoin's nonappearance may also have been political. See William Fowler, "The Massachusetts Election of 1785: A Triumph of Virtue," Essex Institute Historical *Collections*, 111:291.
44. *Selectmen's Minutes, 1769–1775*, 227. By early September Gage had resigned himself to the prospect of bloodshed. He told Dartmouth, "I mean my Lord to recurr all I can by Degrees, to avoid any bloody Crisis as long as possible,

unless forced into it by themselves, which may happen."
See General Thomas Gage to Lord Dartmouth, September
2, 1774, Carter, 1:371.

45. John Andrews to William Barrell, September 26, 1774, MHS-
P, 8:368.

46. General Thomas Gage to Lord Dartmouth, September 25,
1774, Carter, 1:376.

47. William Lincoln, ed., *The Journals of Each Provincial Congress of Massachusetts in 1774 and 1775 and of the Committee
of Safety* (Boston, 1838), 6; General Thomas Gage to Lord
Dartmouth, October 17, 1774, Carter, 1:378; Gage's reaction
was to declare the assembly illegal, *Proclamation* (Boston,
1774).

48. For a Tory perspective of these events, see Douglas Adair
and John A. Schutz, eds., *Peter Oliver's Origin and Progress
of the American Revolution* (Stanford, 1961), 113–118.

49. Lincoln, passim.

50. John Andrews to William Barrell, October 29, 1774, MHS-*P*,
8:380.

51. Ibid., 47; John R. Galvin, *The Minute Men* (New York, 1967),
64–71.

52. John Andrews to William Barrell, October 17, 1774, Ibid.,
377; Joseph Warren to E. Storer, October 18, 1774, Hancock
Papers, MHS.

53. Cunningham, 286; Adair and Schutz, 117.

54. Butterfield, 2:156.

55. Albert Bushnell Hart, *Commonwealth History of Massachusetts* (New York, 1928), 2:548–550; *At a Meeting of the Delegates of Every Town and District in the County of Suffolk*
(Boston, 1774).

56. *JCC*, 1:39.

57. *JCC*, 1:75–81; Miller, *Sam Adams*, 325.

58. Butterfield, 2:157.

59. Lincoln, 55.

60. John Andrews to William Barrell, March 19, 1775, MHS-*P*,
8:401.

61. Alden, *General Gage*, 201.

62. Ibid., 218–232, is very sympathetic to the general. John Shy,
*Toward Lexington: The Role of the British Army in the Coming
of the American Revolution* (Princeton, 1965), 375–418, should
also be consulted.

63. Peter O. Hutchinson, 1:528–529; Allen French, ed., *A British*

Fusilier in Revolutionary Boston (Cambridge, 1926), 36–39; Swan, 179–180; Richard Frothingham, *Life and Times of Joseph Warren* (Boston, 1865), 428–440.

147–201; *Sibley*, 13:390–397.
68. John R. Alden disagrees that Gage intended the arrest of Hancock and Adams. See "Why the March to Concord?" *American Historical Review*, 49:446–454.
69. The events surrounding the affair at Lexington and Concord are well chronicled and often romanticized. Among the primary sources are *Paul Revere's Three Accounts of His Famous Ride* (Boston, 1961); General Thomas Gage to Lord Dartmouth, April 22, 1775, Carter, 1:396–397; eleven accounts published in Henry S. Commager and Richard B. Morris, eds., *The Spirit of Seventy-Six: The Story of the American Revolution As Told by Participants* (New York, 1960), 69–89; Christopher Ward, *The War of the Revolution*, ed. by John R. Alden (New York, 1952), 1:32–51; Harold Murdock, *The Nineteenth of April, 1775* (Boston, 1923); Allen French, *Day of Lexington and Concord* (Boston, 1925); Don Higginbotham, *The War of American Independence* (New York, 1971), 57–77; Arthur B. Tourtellot, *Lexington and Concord* (New York, 1963).
70. Elizabeth Clarke to Lucy W. Allen, April 19, 1841, Lexington Historical Society *Proceedings*, 4:91–92.

CHAPTER 11

Mr. President

(pages 186–202)

1. William H. Sumner, "Reminiscences," NEHG-R, 8:187–188.
2. Herbert S. Allan, *John Hancock, Patriot in Purple* (New York, 1953), 183, suggests that Dolly and Lydia did not remain with Hancock but for a few days "traipsed about the

province in a seemingly aimless manner." I find this unlikely. See Abijah P. Marvin, *History of the Town of Lancaster* (Lancaster, 1879), 329; Henry S. Nourse, *The Military Annals of Lancaster . . . 1740–1865* (Lancaster, 1889), 135. Edmund arrived about May 6. See Ellen C. D. Woodbury, *Dorothy Quincy, Wife of John Hancock* (Washington, 1905), 74. Within a week of Hancock's departure from Lancaster, the Greenleafs baptized their infant son John Hancock Greenleaf.

3. C. B. A. Todd, *A General History of the Burr Family in America* (New York, 1878), 54–55.

4. John Hancock to the Massachusetts Committee of Safety, April 24, 1775, MA, 193, 107–109.

5. Order of the Massachusetts Provincial Congress, Ch. M. 1.12, 239, BPL; Franklin P. Rice, *The Worcester Book: A Diary of Noteworthy Events in Worcester Massachusetts from 1657 to 1883* (Worcester, 1884), 48.

6. Lester J. Cappon, ed., *Atlas of Early American History* (Princeton, 1976), 2; "Extract of a letter From A Gentleman in Pittsfield to an officer at Cambridge, Dated May 4, 1775," *NDAR*, 1:278.

7. John Hancock to Dorothy Quincy, May 7, 1775, Hancock Papers, MHS.

8. William Duane, ed., *Extracts From The Diary of Christopher Marshall Kept in Philadelphia and Lancaster During the American Revolution, 1774–1781* (Albany, 1877), 24–25; J. Thomas Scharf and Thompson Westcott, *History of Philadelphia, 1609–1884* (Philadelphia, 1884), 2:295n.

9. George A. Ward, ed., *Journal and Letters of Samuel Curwen* (Boston, 1864), 28.

10. *JCC*, 2:11; Edmund C. Burnett, *The Continental Congress* (New York, 1964), 64–65.

11. *JCC*, 2:24–44; Burnett, *Continental Congress*, 65–79; Marshall Smelser, *The Winning of Independence* (Chicago, 1972), 43–52; John J. Zimmerman, "Charles Thomson, The Sam Adams of Philadelphia," *Mississippi Valley Historical Review*, 45:464–480.

12. Richard Frothingham, *History of Siege of Boston, and of Lexington, Concord and Bunker Hill* (Boston, 1873); Richard Frothingham, *Life and Times of Joseph Warren* (Boston, 1865), 464–526; G. B. Warden, *Boston, 1689–1776* (Boston, 1970), 318–332; John Cary, *Joseph Warren* (Urbana, 1961), 205–225; Justin Winsor, ed., *The Memorial History of Boston*

(Boston, 1881), 3:67–118; Allen French, *The First Year of the American Revolution* (Cambridge, 1934).

13. *JCC*, 2:58–59; Silas Deane to Mrs. Deane, May 21, 1775, Edmund C. Burnett, ed., *Letters of Members of the Continental Congress* (Washington, 1921), 1:94; Diary of Samuel Ward, Ibid., 98.

14. One apocryphal story has Benjamin Harrison walking up to Hancock after the election, seizing him by the arms, and, as he placed him in the presidential chair, exclaiming, "We will show... Britain how little we care for... See Ch. M. 1.10 (49), BPL. The British reaction to his election is best typified by General Frederick Haldimand's comment, "The insolence of Congress in naming Hancock president!" in Allen French, "General Haldimand in Boston, 1774–1775," MHS-*P*, 66:92.

15. Jennings B. Sanders, *The Presidency of the Continental Congress, 1774–89: A Study in American Institutional History* (Gloucester, 1971 repr.). Many of Hancock's activities as president can be traced in his letter books, PCC, 12A (roll 23). In customary fashion Hancock considered his presidential letter books as his private property, and, on leaving Congress, he carried them with him. Later, an argument arose over their ownership, and this first instance of a dispute over presidential papers was resolved in 1925, when the six volumes were restored to the Papers of the Continental Congress by the MHS. See "Report of the Council, April 9, 1925," MHS-*P*, 58:250.

16. *JCC*, 2:77–78, 84–85.

17. Charles F. Adams, ed., *The Works of John Adams* (Boston, 1850), 2:416–417.

18. William Williams to the Connecticut Delegates in the Continental Congress, *NDAR* 1:728; John Hancock to George Washington, July 10, 1775; Paul H. Smith, ed., *Letters of Delegates to Congress* (Washington, 1976), 1:620–621.

19. John Lowell to Dorothy Quincy, June 5, 1775, Hancock Papers, MHS.

20. Proclamation by Governor Thomas Gage, June 12, 1775, Peter Force, ed., *American Archives*, fourth series (Washington, D.C., 1837–46), 2:967–970; Samuel Adams to Elizabeth Adams, June 28, 1775; Smith, 1:552; Adams to James War-

ren, July 2, 1775, Ibid., 572.

21. Don Higginbotham, *The War of American Independence* (New York, 1971), 70–77; Christopher Ward, *The War of the Revolution* (New York, 1952), 1:73–98. The battle of Bunker Hill was actually fought on Breed's Hill.

22. Cary, 221; Frothingham, *Joseph Warren*, 517–518.

23. John Adams to James Warren, June 27, 1775, Burnett, *Letters*, 1:145.

24. *JCC*, 2:158–162; Burnett, *Continental Congress*, 85.

25. *JCC*, 2:128–157. The authorship of this Declaration has been disputed between Jefferson and Dickinson. Julian P. Boyd, "The Disputed Authorship of the Declaration on the Causes and Necessity for Taking Up Arms, 1775," *Pennsylvania Magazine of History and Biography*, 74:51–73; Julian Boyd, ed., *Papers of Thomas Jefferson* (Princeton, 1950), 1:187–219.

26. Benjamin Harrison to George Washington, July 21, 1775, Burnett, *Letters*, 1:170.

27. John Hancock to Joseph Warren, June 18, 1775, Ibid., 134; Hancock to Elbridge Gerry, June 18, 1775, Ibid., 135; Hancock to Dorothy Quincy, June 21, 1775, Hancock Papers, MHS: Edmund Quincy to Dorothy Quincy, July 22, 1775, NEHG-R, 11:165. On an average Hancock was dispatching at least two official letters per day. See PCC, 12A (roll 23).

28. Sumner, 188; Thaddeus Burr to Tapping Reeve, May 15, 1775, Annie Burr Jennings Memorial Collection, YUL.

29. John Hancock to Dorothy Quincy, June 10 and 11, and July 2, 1775; Henry C. Walsh, "Three Letters from Hancock to Dorothy Q.," *New England Magazine*, 12:532–533; Woodbury, 83–84; John Hancock to Dorothy Quincy, June 21, 1775, Facsimile, MHS.

30. *JCC*, 2:239; John Hancock to Jonathan Trumbull, August 8, 1775; Smith, 699; John Hancock to Dorothy Quincy, August 14, 1775, Photostats, MHS.

31. Charles F. Adams, 3:12–23; Robert J. Taylor, ed., *Massachusetts Colony to Commonwealth* (New York, 1961) 13; William Lincoln, ed., *The Journals of Each Provincial Congress of Massachusetts* (Boston, 1838), 359–360; Stephen E. Patterson, *Political Parties in Revolutionary Massachusetts* (Madison, 1973), 123–124.

32. Patterson, 125–127.

33. *Sibley*, 12:317.

34. Edmund Quincy to John Hancock, September 9, 1775, Quincy Papers, QP 9A, MHS.

35. Allan, 203; *Sibley* 10:151–158; 15:226–227. A photographic

39. in Item 37, Reports of the Marine Committee and the Board of Admiralty, 1776–1781, PCC (roll 44), and Charles Oscar Paullin, ed., *Out-Letters of the Continental Marine Committee and Board of Admiralty* (New York, 1914), vols. 1 and 2, passim.

40. John Adams to James Warren, September 19, 1775, Ford, 1:112; James Warren to John Adams, October 1, 1775, Ibid., 123.

41. Samuel Ward to Henry Ward, October 24, 1775, Burnett, *Letters*, 1:240; John Adams to James Warren, October 24, 1775, Smith, 2:232–233; *JCC*, 3:302–303.

42. *JCC*, 2:188.

43. James Warren to Samuel Adams, November 12, 1775, Ford, 2:426–427; Patterson's account of this altercation is excellent, 129–132.

44. For examples of Hancock's lobbying on behalf of friends and relatives, see John Hancock to William Palfrey, September 25, 1775, bMS, AM 1704.3 (82) HL; James Warren to John Adams, October 20, 1775, Ford, 1:151–152; Hancock to Cushing, February 16, 1776, Misc. Bound Papers, MHS.

45. Samuel Adams to James Otis, November 23, 1775, Burnett, *Letters*, 1:256–257; John Adams to James Otis, November 23, 1775, Ibid., 258.

46. Massachusetts Delegates to the Massachusetts Council, November 24, 1775, Smith, 2:383–384.

47. James Warren to Samuel Adams, December 19, 1775, Ford, 2:429.

48. George Athan Billias, *Elbridge Gerry: Founding Father and Republican Statesman* (New York, 1976), 65–66.

CHAPTER 12
Back to Boston
(pages 203–221)

1. Articles of Agreement . . . Between Hon. Thomas Cushing, Esq. . . . and Jonathan Greenleaf, Stephen Cross, and Ralph Cross of Newburyport . . . March 1, 1776, United States Naval Academy Museum, Annapolis, Maryland.
2. John Hancock to Thomas Cushing, March 6, 1776, *NDAR*, 4:196–198; John Hancock to Thomas Cushing, March 7, 1776, Misc. Bound Papers, MHS.
3. John Hancock to George Hayley, January 9, 1768, John Hancock Letter Book, Hancock Papers, NEHGS; Capt. Isaac Cazneau to John Hancock, April 4, 1776, Box 17, Folder 4, Hancock Papers, NEHGS. Cazneau had not even been mentioned on an earlier list that John Adams had prepared. John Manley was already well known for his exploits as one of Washington's schooner captains. Informed that Cazneau wanted a berth, Hancock used his influence to get it for him. Ironically, Cazneau changed his mind and declined the post. See John Lowell to John Hancock, March 17, 1776, MS 269a, BPL.
4. Thomas Cushing to John Hancock, July 18, 1776, *NDAR*, 5:1123.
5. Marine Committee, August 6, 1776, to John Hancock, C. E. French Papers, MHS.
6. Thomas Cushing to John Hancock, January 30, 1776, Gratz Collection, HSOP; Thomas Cushing to Robert Treat Paine, February 29, 1776, Robert Treat Paine Papers, II, MHS.
7. John Hancock to Thomas Cushing, January 17, 1776, Hancock Papers, MHS.
8. Charles F. Adams, ed., *The Works of John Adams* (Boston, 1850), 3:25.
9. John Adams to Abigail Adams, December 3, 1775; Paul Smith, ed., *Letters of Delegates to Congress* (Washington, 1976), 2:430.
10. William Bant to John Hancock, January 6, 1776, Hancock Papers, MHS.
11. John Lowell to John Hancock, March 17, 1776, MS 269a, BPL; Col. Jedediah Huntington to Andrew Huntington, March 17, 1776, *NDAR*, 4:379.
12. Suffolk County Court, Suffolk Files, 96737.

13. "An Account of damage . . ." Ch. M. 1.10 (147), BPL.
14. John Hancock to Thomas Cushing, May 17, 1776, Safe, MHS.
15. JCC, 4:206–207.

Papers, 10A, MHS, John Lowell to John Hancock, May 20,
    1776, Ms. 269, BPL; Woodbury, 111.
20. Will of Lydia Henchman Hancock, Probate Court, 16409,
    Suffolk County.
21. John Hancock to Thomas Cushing, June 12, 1776, Misc.
    Bound Papers, MHS.
22. Ellen Brennan, *Plural Office-Holding in Massachusetts*
    (Chapel Hill, 1945), 116.
23. *Journal of the Proceedings of the Provincial Congress of North
    Carolina* (New Bern, North Carolina, 1776), 9.
24. JCC, 4:342.
25. Ibid., 357–358.
26. Stephen Higginson, *Ten Chapters in the Life of John Hancock*
    (New York, 1857), 10–11; Originally published as *The Writ-
    ings of Laco as published in the Massachusetts Centinel in the
    months of February and March 1789, with the addition of No.
    VII, which was omitted* (Boston, 1789).
27. JCC, 4:359.
28. PCC, 12A, 148–149 (reel 23).
29. JCC, 5:425–426.
30. For the events surrounding the Declaration, see Burnett,
    Continental Congress, 146–198; Edmund C. Burnett, ed., *Let-
    ters of the Members of the Continental Congress* (Washington,
    1921), 2:529–532; Marshall Smelser, *The Winning of Inde-
    pendence* (Chicago, 1972), 118–161; Carl Becker, *The Decla-
    ration of Independence* (New York, 1922), passim; JCC, 4 and
    5, passim; Thomas Jefferson, "Notes of Proceedings," Julian
    P. Boyd, ed., *The Papers of Thomas Jefferson* (Princeton,
    1950), 1:309–329; JCC, 5:428–429.
31. Boyd, 313.
32. JCC, 5:505.

33. Ibid., 507.
34. Ibid., 509.
35. John Adams to Abigail Adams, July 3, 1776, Lyman H. Butterfield, ed., *The Book of Abigail and John* (Cambridge, 1975), 139.
36. *JCC*, 5:491.
37. Ibid., 510–516.
38. The evidence for this statement is summarized by Boyd, 1:305–308.
39. Boston *Globe*, January 21, 1962.
40. *JCC*, 6:1027. Robert Morris remained in Philadelphia, and on December 21, 1776, he, George Clymer, and George Walton were appointed "a committee of Congress, with powers to execute such continental business as may be proper and necessary to be done at Philadelphia." See *JCC*, 6:1032. Morris actually conducted most of the work, especially the marine affairs. See Charles Oscar Paullin, ed., *Out-Letters of the Marine Committee*, 1:158–82; PCC 137 (roll 150); Edward M. Coleman, "The History of the Third Session of the Second Continental Congress" (Ph.D. dissertation, University of Southern California, 1941).
41. Corporation Records, II, 389, HUA.
42. Ibid., 423.
43. Ibid., 451; James Bowdoin to Commissary Richard Devens, December 16, 1776, Ch. A. 4.23, BPL; Josiah Quincy, *The History of Harvard University* (Cambridge, 1840), 2:189–193.
44. John Hancock to Robert Treat Paine, January 13, 1777, Paine Papers, II, MHS.
45. James Warren to John Adams, April 3, 1777, W. C. Ford, ed., *Warren-Adams Letters*, 1:310; Quincy, 194.
46. William Bant to John Hancock, March 20, 1777, Ch. F. 2.26, BPL.
47. Corporation Records, II, September 8, 1777, HUA.
48. William Ellery to Governor Nicholas Cooke, December 25, 1776, William R. Staples, ed., *Rhode Island in the Continental Congress* (Providence, 1870), 110–113; Benjamin Rush to Robert Morris, February 8, 1777, Burnett, *Letters*, 2:240.
49. William Ellery to Governor Nicholas Cooke, January 4, 1777.
50. *JCC*, 7:164.
51. John Hancock to Robert Morris, February 27, 1777, Burnett, *Letters*, 2:286.
52. John Hancock to Dorothy Quincy Hancock, March 5, 1777,

Photostats, MHS.

53. John Hancock to David Evans, August 11, 1777, Box 22, Folder 1, Hancock Papers, NEHGS.

(Richard Caswell), October 10, 1777, Burnett, *Letters*, 2:514; John Thaxter to John Adams, January 10, 1778, Lyman H. Butterfield, ed., *Adams Family Correspondence* (Cambridge, 1963), 2:383.

58. John Hancock to Thomas Jefferson, October 25, 1777, Burnett, *Letters*, 2:534.

59. *JCC*, 9:852–854; Samuel Adams to James Warren, November 4, 1777, Burnett *Letters*, 2:541.

60. General George Washington to the President of Congress, October 22, 1777, John C. Fitzpatrick, ed., *The Writings of George Washington* (Washington, 1933), 9:513–514.

61. "Diary of . . . William Ellery," *Pennsylvania Magazine of History and Biography*, 11:323.

62. Jacob Rush to Edmund Quincy, January 22, 1777, Quincy Papers, 10A, MHS.

63. John Hancock to Dorothy Quincy Hancock, November 8, 1777, Mary C. Crawford, *Old Boston Days and Ways* (Boston, 1909), 248–249; Edmund Quincy to John Hancock, November 25, 1777, Quincy Papers, 9, MHS; "An Estimate of the Services and Expenses of . . . John Hancock," Box 29, Folder 1, Hancock Papers, NEHGS; "Boyle's Journal of Occurrences in Boston," NEHG-*R*, 85:132.

CHAPTER 13
Governor Hancock
(pages 222–244)

1. In 1770, Boston's population was approximately 15,000. At the time of Hancock's return it was considerably less than 10,000. See *Historical Statistics of the United States, Colonial*

table, taken from page 32 of the best work on the subject, E. James Ferguson, *The Power of the Purse* (Chapel Hill, 1961), gives the figures for Continental depreciation.

Currency Required to Purchase $1.00 Specie

	1777	1778	1779	1780	1781
January	1.25	4.00	8.00	42.50	100.00
April	2.00	6.00	16.00	60.00	167.50
July	3.00	4.00	19.00	62.50	
October	3.00	5.00	30.00	77.50	

4. William Bant to John Hancock, December 2, 1776, Hancock Papers, MHS.

5. Jonathan Hall to William Bant, February 6, 1777, Box 16, Folder 2, Hancock Papers, NEHGS.

6. These statements are based on an examination of the appropriate court records of Suffolk County. See also John T. Hassam, *The Confiscated Estates of Boston Loyalists* (Cambridge, 1895); Gardner Weld Allen, *Massachusetts Privateers of the Revolution* (Boston, 1927).

7. Samuel Adams to James Warren, October 29, 1777, W. C. Ford, ed., *Warren-Adams Letters* (Boston, 1917–1925), I:376.

8. *Boston Town Records, 1770–1777* (Boston, 1887), 282.

9. Ibid., 294.

10. John Hancock to John Hanson, May 6, 1782, Ch. M. 1.10 (67), BPL; James Lovell to John Hancock, November 28, 1779, CL.

11. *Journals of the House of Representatives; Boston Town Records*, 293. Hancock did plan to return to Congress. See John

Hancock to Robert Morris, February 7, 1778, Etting Papers, HSOP.

12. *Pennsylvania Ledger*, March 11, 1778.

16. On May 25, 1778, William Pynchon of Salem noted in his diary:

> Mr. Hancock calls on his debtors, and desires payment in paper currency, preferring that to silver money — the difference in the exchange being at 3½, and from that to 5 paper dollars for one of silver. Does Mr. H., in fact, mean to give his debtors the difference; or to induce his own creditors to take of him their dues at that rate be-because he takes his dues at that rate; or to become popular, and obtain votes at the choice of governor next May?

See Fitch Edward Oliver, ed., *The Diary of William Pynchon of Salem* (Boston, 1890), 54.

17. The returns of the towns are in MA, 156. Examples are in Taylor, 59–73. *Independent Chronicle*, April 2, 9, 16, and 30, 1778; William Gordon to Horatio Gates, April 28, 1778, MHS-P, 63:401.

18. Theophilus Parsons, *Memoir of Theophilus Parsons* (Boston, 1859), 47–53; 359–402; Cushing, 221–226.

19. *Boston Town Records, 1778–1783* (Boston, 1895), 18.

20. James Warren to Samuel Adams, May 31, 1778, Ford, 2:13–14.

21. *Records of the Church in Brattle Square* (Boston, 1902), 190.

22. James Warren to Samuel Adams, May 31, 1778, Ford, 2:14.

23. James Warren to John Adams, June 7, 1778, Ibid., 20; John Hancock to Dorothy Quincy Hancock, June 20, 1778, MHS-P, 48:506.

24. Samuel Adams to James Warren, July 14, 1778, Ford, 2:33.

25. *JCC*, 11:641.

26. The description of the anniversary party is from "Diary of the Honorable William Ellery of Rhode Island June 28-July 23, 1778," *Pennsylvania Magazine of History and Biography*, 11:477–478.

27. William C. Stinchcombe, *The American Revolution and the French Alliance* (Syracuse, 1969), 32; Samuel Adams to James Warren, July 15, 1778, Ford, 2:33.

28. For the British rationale, see J. W. Fortescue, *A History of the British Army* (London, 1911), 3:197. Washington's attitude is reflected in George Washington to Nicholas Cooke, December 21, 1776, John C. Fitzpatrick, ed., *The Writings of George Washington* (Washington, 1932), 6:412. The political situation is described in William M. Fowler, Jr., *William Ellery: A Rhode Island Politico and Lord of Admiralty* (Metuchen, 1973), 85–86.

29. Stinchcombe, 48–49; Charles P. Whittemore, *A General of the Revolution: John Sullivan of New Hampshire* (New York, 1961), 83; Christopher Ward, *The War of the Revolution* (New York, 1952), 2:588.

30. George Washington to John Sullivan, July 17, 1778, Fitzpatrick, 12:184; Washington to James Mitchell Varnum, July 21, 1778, Ibid., 195–196; Washington to Sullivan, July 22, 1778, Ibid., 202; Washington to Marquis de Lafayette, July 22, 1778, Ibid., 202–203.

31. As was so often the case, Hancock gave poor health as his reason for leaving Philadelphia. Abigail Adams to John Thaxter, July 23, 1778, Ms. Am. 229.5, BPL; Samuel Adams to Samuel Phillips Savage, August 11, 1778, Harry Alonzo Cushing, ed., *The Writings of Samuel Adams* (New York, 1908), 4:49.

32. "Diary of Ezekiel Price," NEHG-R, 19:334; Franklin B. Dexter, ed., *The Literary Diary of Ezra Stiles* (New York, 1901), 2:294.

33. Louis Gottschalk, *Lafayette Joins the American Army* (Chicago, 1937), 254.

34. Vera B. Lawrence, *Music For Patriots, Politicians and Presidents* (New York, 1975), 79.

35. Gottschalk, 256–257.

36. James Warren to Samuel Adams, August 25, 1778, Ford, 2:44.

37. A list of the vessels is in Fitz-Henry Smith, "The French at Boston During the Revolution," BS-P, 10:18. There were

probably 7000 to 8000 sailors in the fleet, along with 4000 soldiers.
38. Gottschalk, 264–265; Fitzpatrick, 12:501n. The portrait was

41. Sumner, 189.
42. Plan of the Hancock House, John Hancock Mutual Life Insurance Company Archives, Boston.
43. Sumner, 189; Inventory of all the Estate of his late Excellency John Hancock, MS, Cb 46, NEGHS.
44. James Warren to Samuel Adams, September 30, 1778, Ford, 2:48–49.
45. John Hancock to House, September 28, 1778, Hancock Papers, MHS; James Warren to Samuel Adams, September 30, 1778, Ford, 2:48–49.
46. Smith, 37.
47. Smith, 41; Stinchcombe, 59. The chevalier was buried in the crypt of King's Chapel. As a gesture of friendship, the General Court voted to build a monument, which, because of numerous delays, was not erected until the twentieth century. It stands today in the King's Chapel burial ground.
48. Letter fragment, October 28, 1778, Hancock Papers, MHS. On October 25, 1778, Warren lamented to Samuel Adams, ". . . indeed, all manner of Extravagance prevails here in dress, furniture, Equipage and Living amidst the distress of the public and Multitudes of Individuals. how long the Manners of this People will be Uncorrupted and fit to Enjoy that Liberty you have so long Contended for I know not. I fear you have lost your Labour. they will be soon fit to receive some Ambitious Master." See Ford, 2:59–60. For a different opinion, see Anne Rowe Cunningham, ed., *Letters and Diary of John Rowe* (Boston, 1903), 323.
49. Samuel Phillips Savage to Samuel Adams, October 1778, MHS-P, 43:335.
50. Samuel Adams to Savage, November 1, 1778, Cushing, 4:87–88.

51. James Warren to Samuel Adams, August 18, 1778, Ford, 2:42; Warren to John Adams, October 7, 1778, Ibid., 53. Hancock did manage to outpoll Adams, 431 to 383, but Adams had enough votes to be elected. See *Boston Town Records, 1778–1783*, 62.

52. A full examination of this issue is David E. Maas, "The Return of the Massachusetts Loyalists" (Ph.D. dissertation, University of Wisconsin, 1972). Warren's letters to Adams are replete with comments on this situation.

53. "Proceedings of the Convention for Forming a Constitution of Government for the State of Massachusetts Bay," MA, 160. Events leading up to the adoption of the constitution can be best followed in Samuel Eliot Morison, "The Struggle Over the Adoption of the Constitution of Massachusetts, 1780," MHS-*P*, 50:353–412; Patterson, 218–247; Taylor, passim.

54. Lyman H. Butterfield, ed., *Diary and Autobiography of John Adams* (Cambridge, 1961), 2:401n.

55. According to the papers his election was unanimous, but by Gordon's account there were 53 votes against him. The truth is uncertain. William Gordon to Horatio Gates, June 3, 1779, MHS-*P*, 63:412; *Journals of the House*, October 5, 1779; Hancock's failure to go to Philadelphia brought him considerable criticism. William Gordon to Horatio Gates, June 8, 1779, MHS-*P*, 63:413; James Warren to John Adams, June 13, 1779, Ford, 2:106.

56. John Adams to Benjamin Rush, April 12, 1809, MHS-*P*, 5:90.

57. John Hancock to Henry Quincy, August 30, 1779, Mary C. Crawford, *Old Boston Days and Ways* (Boston, 1909), 337.

58. Patterson, 247.

59. William Gordon to John Adams, July 22, 1780, MHS-*P*, 63:436–437.

60. Book of Votes for the Election of Governor and Lieutenant Governor, 1780, MA; E. M. Bacon, ed., *Supplement to the Acts and Laws of the Commonwealth of Massachusetts* (Boston, 1896), October 27 and 31, 1780, November 2, 7, 11, 13, and 14, December 1, 1780; 53–58; Van Beck Hall, *Politics Without Parties* (Pittsburgh, 1972), 135–136; *Massachusetts Spy*, November 6 and 23, 1780; *Boston Gazette*, November 6, 1780. Chapter II, section 1, article III of the constitution sets forth the procedures for electing the governor and lieutenant governor:

Those persons who shall be qualified to vote for senators and representatives within the several towns of this Commonwealth shall, at a meeting to be called for that purpose on the [first Monday of April annually], give

same to the sheriff of the county, thirty days at least before the [last Wednesday in May]; and the sheriff shall transmit the same to the secretary's office, seventeen days at least before the said [last Wednesday in May]; or the selectmen may cause returns of the same to be made to the office of the secretary of the Commonwealth, seventeen days at least before the said day; and the secretary shall lay the same before the senate and the house of representatives, on the [last Wednesday in May], to be by them examined: and in case of an election by a majority of all the votes returned, the choice shall be by them declared and published. But if no person shall have a [majority] of votes, the house of representatives shall by ballot, elect two out of four persons who had the highest number of votes, if so many shall have been voted for; but, if otherwise, out of the number voted for; and make return to the senate of the two persons so elected; on which the senate shall proceed, by ballot, to elect one, who shall be declared governor.

CHAPTER 14
Resignation and Defeat
(pages 245–261)

1. Fitch, Edward Oliver, ed., *The Diary of William Pynchon of Salem* (Boston, 1890), 77; William Tudor, ed., *Deacon Tudor's Diary* (Boston, 1896), 85.
2. I am particularly grateful to the Bostonian Society and its director, Mr. Thomas Parker, for allowing me to examine Hancock's clothes. The measurements were taken by Mr. William Belezos.
3. *Sibley*, 11:382.
4. Tudor, 85; *Boston Gazette*, October 30, 1780.

5. E. M. Bacon, ed., *Supplement to the Acts and Laws of the Commonwealth of Massachusetts* (Boston, 1896), 23–26.

6. For economic conditions in Massachusetts, see Oscar Handlin and Mary Flug Handlin, "Revolutionary Economic Policy in Massachusetts," *William and Mary Quarterly* (third series), 4:3–26; Handlin and Handlin, *Commonwealth: A Study of the Role of Government in the American Economy: Massachusetts, 1774–1861* (New York, 1947), 33–52; Van Beck Hall, *Politics Without Parties: Massachusetts, 1780–1791* (Pittsburgh, 1972), passim.

7. *JCC*, 19:111–112.

8. John Hancock to Senate and House, March 8, 1782, in Bacon, 96.

9. Massachusetts Constitution, Chapter I, Article II; John Hancock to Senate and House, June 3, 1782, and June 4, 1782; Resolve, June 5, 1782; Samuel Adams to John Lowell, May 15, 1782; Harry Alonzo Cushing, ed., *The Writings of Samuel Adams* (New York, 1968), 4:273.

10. John Hancock to Senate and House, November 3, 1782, and November 14, 1782, in Bacon, 145–147; James Sullivan to Benjamin Lincoln, November 18, 1782, Sullivan Papers, MHS.

11. James Sullivan to Elbridge Gerry, August 13, 1789, Sullivan Papers, MHS.

12. The British had evacuated Rhode Island in October 1779. See William B. Willcox, *Portrait of a General; Sir Henry Clinton in the War of Independence* (New York, 1964), 220–229; Evelyn Acomb, ed., *The Revolutionary Journal of Baron Ludwig Von Closen, 1780–1783* (Chapel Hill, 1958), 47n.

13. Sarah H. Swan, "The Story of an Old House," *New England Magazine*, 17:181.

14. *Sibley*, 14:668; John Hancock to Benjamin Franklin, June 30, 1783, HSOP; *Boston Marriages, 1752–1809* (Boston, 1903), 448.

15. Charles Martyn, *The Life of Artemas Ward* (New York, 1921), 258.

16. Hancock repeatedly referred to this matter in his messages to the General Court during the fall of 1781. For examples, see John Hancock to House and Senate, September 13, 1781, in Bacon, 85; Vote Accepting the Report, October 23, 1781, Ibid., 73; General William Heath to John Hancock, September 22, 1781, MHS-C (seventh series), 5:262.

17. Alan Valentine, *Lord North* (Norman, Oklahoma, 1967), 2:274.

18. *Vital Records of Groton, Mass.* (Salem, 1927), 2:198. Bant had

21. John Wendell to John Hancock, October 29, 1781, Box 26, Folder 4, Hancock Papers, NEHGS. See also John Wendell to Hancock, November 17, 1781, Ibid.; James McFarland to Hancock, March 1781, Ibid.; Levi Lincoln to John Hancock, January 3, 1783, Ibid.

22. Trial Balance Money Due, June 26, 1783, Ch. M. 3.5, v. 2, p. 279, BPL.

23. John Hancock to Capt. James Scott, November 14, 1783, John Hancock Letter Book, Hancock Papers, NEHGS.

24. William Hoskins to Mary Ann Bant, January 25, 1783, Ibid.

25. William Hoskins to Joseph Palmer, January 17, 1783, Ibid.

26. Account between James Otis and John Hancock, January 24, 1783, Ch. M. 1.10 (102), BPL.

27. William Hoskins to James Warren, February 1, 1783, John Hancock Letter Book, Hancock Papers, NEHGS.

28. John Hancock to Capt. James Scott, n.d., Ibid.; William Phillips to John Hancock, January 7, 1783, Archives of the John Hancock Mutual Life Insurance Company.

29. William Hoskins to Thomas Brown, August 15, 1783; to Messrs. Avery and Déschamp, August 15, 1783; to William Allen, August 15, 1783; to John Chipman, August 15, 1783; to Joseph Gray, August 15, 1783. All in John Hancock Letter Book, Hancock Papers, NEHGS.

30. William Hoskins to Winchworth Tonge, August 14, 1783, Ibid.

31. Hancock himself believed that a final settling of his foreign accounts would put him in the black. See John Hancock to Capt. James Scott, November 14, 1783, Ibid. Hancock still had a decent reputation in England, as some merchants made overtures to him for re-establishing trade. See Har-

rison and Ansley to John Hancock, April 26, 1784, Hancock Papers, MHS; Richard and David Owen to John Hancock, November 17, 1783, Ibid.; Cruger, Ledyard, and Mulett to John Hancock, March 5, 1783, Box 27, Folder 2, Hancock Papers, NEHGS. His friend John Wilkes also continued to speak highly of him. See John Wilkes to John Hancock, May 15, 1783, MHS-*P*, 8:459–460.

32. On September 2, 1783, Ezra Stiles noted in his diary, "The difference between Mr. Samuel Adams and Gov. Hancock is incurable." See Franklin B. Dexter, ed., *The Literary Diary of Ezra Stiles* (New York, 1901), 3:90.

33. William Gordon to Elbridge Gerry, December 24, 1783, MHS-*P*, 63:500, 500.

34. The Point Shirley property had been left to him by Uncle Thomas. See Harriet M. Whitcomb, *Annals and Reminiscences of Jamaica Plain* (Cambridge, 1897), 36, 39.

35. Samuel Adams Drake, *Old Landmarks and Historic Personages of Boston* (Boston, 1873), 341. Balch was a former Son of Liberty and a member of the Brattle Square Church. See *Records of the Church in Brattle Square* (Boston, 1902), 51; Henry S. Nourse, *The Military Annals of Lancaster* (Lancaster, 1889), 229–230.

36. Biographical information on Sullivan is drawn from Thomas C. Amory, *Life of James Sullivan, with Selections from His Writings* (Boston, 1859), 2 vols.

37. Sullivan seems to have written reams of items for the local press. Copies of many of his pieces are in the Sullivan Papers, MHS.

38. Book of Votes for Governor and Lieutenant Governor and Journals of the House of Representatives, MA.

39. Mercy Otis Warren to Winslow Warren, March 24, 1785, Mercy Otis Warren Papers, MHS; William M. Fowler, Jr., "The Massachusetts Election of 1785: A Triumph of Virtue," Essex Institute *Historical Collections*, 111:296.

40. Hall, passim; Merrill Jensen points out that British policy was especially hurtful to New England, but the rest of America "was little harmed . . ." *The New Nation* (New York, 1950), 164; Samuel Eliot Morison, *The Maritime History of Massachusetts, 1783–1860* (Boston, 1961), 30–35; Robert J. Taylor, *Western Massachusetts in the Revolution* (Providence, 1954), 103–127.

41. Taylor, 103–127.

42. *Massachusetts Centinel*, February 19, 1785.
43. Ibid.
44. Gordon Wood, *The Creation of the American Republic*

ruary 1785, bMS, Am. 1649.5 (75) HL. In his letter, Dana took particular pains to indicate that Hancock had "at last" resigned.
49. MHS-*P*, 4:33.
50. *Sibley*, 11:522; *Massachusetts Centinel*, April 2 and 4, 1785; *Independent Chronicle*, April 21, 1785.
51. The statewide tabulation showed 9018 people voting in 1785. That was an 18 percent increase over 1784. Unfortunately, a county-by-county comparison for these years cannot be made since the town returns for 1783 and 1784 are missing from the State Archives. The table below gives the county vote in 1785. In addition to Bowdoin and Cushing, there were fifty-two other gubernatorial candidates. That was a record number and another indication of the interest this election generated.

County	Cushing	Bowdoin
Suffolk	525	1002
Essex	235	480
Middlesex	416	277
Hampshire	293	302
Plymouth	276	182
Barnstable	104	85
Bristol	148	260
York	134	20
Worcester	476	509
Cumberland	94	46
Lincoln	33	47
Berkshire	265	238
Dukes	6	71
Total	3005	3519

52. *A Proclamation For the Encouragement of Piety, Virtue, Education and Manners, and for the Suppression of Vice . . .* June 8, 1785 (Boston, 1785).

53. Allan Nevins, *The American States During and After the Revolution, 1775–1789* (New York repr. 1969), 564.

54. Mercy Otis Warren to John Adams, 1783, Mercy Otis Warren Papers, MHS.

55. Mercy Otis Warren to George Warren, March 24, 1785, Ibid.

56. *American Herald*, April 4, 1785.

57. *Salem Gazette*, March 29, 1785.

58. Nevins, 217; Book of Votes, MA.

59. Samuel Adams to John Adams, July 2, 1785, Cushing, 4:316.

CHAPTER 15
A Little Rebellion and a Grand Convention
(pages 262–281)

1. "Historic Processions in Boston From 1689 to 1824," BS-*P*, 5:68; Examples of Hancock's dunning for overdue debts can be found in the Suffolk Files; John Hancock to Capt. James Scott, June 3, 1785, John Hancock Letter Book, Hancock Papers, NEHGS; James Sullivan to Rufus King, October 25, 1785; Thomas C. Amory, *Life of James Sullivan* (Boston, 1859), 2:390; John Hancock to Rufus King, November 30, 1785, Rufus King Papers, NYHS; Deeds Box 25, Folder 6, Hancock Papers, NEHGS.

2. At a Meeting of the Overseers of Harvard College, May 6, 1783, Box 26, Folder 8, Hancock Papers; William Gordon to John Adams, June 28, 1783, MHS-*P*, 63:494–495; Josiah Quincy, *The History of Harvard University* (Cambridge, 1840), 2:189–205.

3. Franklin B. Dexter, ed., *The Literary Diary of Ezra Stiles* (New York, 1901), 2:151–152.

4. Final Settlement signed by Mr. Hoskins, Attorney for John Hancock, Overseers' Records 3, HUA; Quincy, 203–205.

5. Despite the importance generally ascribed to Shays's Rebellion, it does not have an extensive literature. By far the best work on the subject is Robert Feer, "Shays's Rebellion" (Ph.D. dissertation Harvard, 1958); see also George Richards Minot, *The History of the Insurrections in Massachusetts* (Boston, 1810); Marion Starkey, *A Little Rebellion* (New York,

1955); Robert J. Taylor, *Western Massachusetts in the Revolution* (Providence, 1954), 103–177.

6. Even though Hancock was not an active candidate he still managed to garner nearly 1100 votes, four times as many as Cushing. Book of Votes, 1786, MA.; James Warren to John Adams, April 30, 1786, W. C. Ford, ed., *Warren-Adams Letters* (Boston, 1925), 2:271.

7. JCC, 30:282, 338. Hancock gave bad health as the reason for resigning. He was also aware that the President's personal accommodations were not the best. Rufus King to John

8. Van Beck Hall, *Politics without Parties* (Pittsburgh, 1972), 190–226; Taylor, 103–127.

9. *Independent Chronicle and Universal Advertiser*, February 1, 1787; An Elegy Upon the Death of John George Washington Hancock, MSS Co. 4, NEHGS; Amory, 23.

10. John Hancock to Henry Knox, March 14, 1787, Hancock Papers, MHS.

11. *Book of Votes*, 1787, MA. In Newburyport someone wrote Hancock's name on the ballot in gold letters. See *Independent Chronicle*, April 12, 1787.

12. James Warren to John Adams, May 18, 1787, W. C. Ford, 2:292.

13. Taylor, 166; Hall, 251; *Massachusetts Centinel*, June 30, 1787.

14. *Worcester Magazine*, August 1787.

15. Among those who thought sterner measures were needed was young John Quincy Adams. In his diary he made sardonic reference to pardoning the Shaysites: "It is much to the credit of our government that a man who has stole £30 worth of plate should die for the offence, while others commit treason and murder with impunity." See *Life in a New England Town: 1787, 1788 Diary of John Quincy Adams* (Boston, 1903), 33. The impact of the rebellion is also examined in Joseph P. Warren, "The Confederation and Shays's Rebellion," *American Historical Review*, 11:42–67 and Robert A. East, "The Massachusetts Conservatives in the Critical Period," in Richard B. Morris, ed., *The Era of the American Revolution* (New York, 1939), 380–391.

16. Robert A. Feer, "Shays's Rebellion and the Constitution: A Study in Causation," *New England Quarterly*, 42:388–410.

17. The events surrounding the Philadelphia Convention are

well known. In 1913, Charles Beard started a small industry with his book *An Economic Interpretation of the Constitution* (New York, 1913). Since Beard's book, there have been a host of books and articles supporting, refuting or altering Beard's thesis.

18. Message of Governor Hancock to . . . Senate and . . . House, October 25, 1787, *Debates and Proceedings in the Convention of the Commonwealth of Massachusetts* (Boston, 1856), 18.

19. Elbridge Gerry to Senate and House, October 18, 1787, Ibid., 24–26.

20. Carl L. Becker, *The History of Political Parties in the Province of New York, 1760–1776* (Madison, 1909), 22.

21. Hall, 256.

22. James Sullivan was among those who expected easy ratification. See James Sullivan to Rufus King, September 23, 1787, Sullivan Papers, MHS. There are several works on the ratification in Massachusetts: A. W. Clason, "The Convention of Massachusetts," *Magazine of American History*, 14 (1885), 529–545; Samuel Banister Harding, *The Contest Over the Ratification of the Federal Constitution in the State of Massachusetts* (New York, 1896); Forrest McDonald, *We The People: The Economic Origins of the Constitution* (Chicago, 1958), 182–202; J. T. Main, *The Anti-Federalists* (Chapel Hill, 1961), 201–210; George Athan Billias, *Elbridge Gerry* (New York, 1976), 206–217.

23. *Debates and Proceedings*, 31; "Belknap's Notes," MHS-*P*, 3:304.

24. *Debates and Proceedings*, 44. Cushing went on to a distinguished career as an associate justice of the U.S. Supreme Court. See "William Cushing," *DAB*, 2:633–635.

25. *Debates and Proceedings*, 55.

26. Under the pen name "Cassius," Sullivan wrote a series in support that appeared in the *Massachusetts Gazette*. James Winthrop took the opposite position, writing under the pen name "Agrippa." These and additional articles may be found in Paul Leicester Ford, *Essays on the Constitution of the United States* (Brooklyn, 1892), 1–123. See also *Debates and Proceedings*, 335–398.

27. The amendments were as follows:

> *First*. That it be explicitly declared that all powers not expressly delegated to Congress, are reserved to the States, to be by them exercised.

Secondly. That there shall be one representative to every thirty thousand persons, until the whole number of representatives amount to ——.

Thirdly. That Congress do not exercise the powers vested in them by the fourth section of the first article, but in cases where a State shall neglect or refuse to make adequate provision for an equal representation of the people, agreeably to this Constitution.

Fourthly. That Congress do not lay direct taxes, but when the moneys arising from the impost and excise are insufficient for the public exigencies.

Sixthly. That no person shall be tried for any crime, by which he may incur an infamous punishment, or loss of life, until he be first indicted by a grand jury, except in such cases as may arise in the government and regulation of the land and naval forces.

Seventhly. The Supreme Judicial Federal Court shall have no jurisdiction of causes between citizens of different States, unless the matter in dispute be of the value of —— dollars, at the least.

Eighthly. In Civil actions between citizens of different States, every issue of fact arising in actions at common law, shall be tried by a jury, if the parties, or either of them, request it.

Ninthly. That the words, "without the consent of the Congress," in the last paragraph of the ninth section of the first article, be stricken out.

And the Convention do, in the name and in behalf of the people of this Commonwealth, enjoin it upon their Representatives in Congress, at all times, until the alterations and provisions aforesaid have been considered, agreeably to the fifth article of the said Constitution, to exert all their influence, and use all reasonable and legal methods to obtain a ratification of the said alterations and provisions, in such manner as is provided in the said article.

Debates and Proceedings, 79–80.

28. Ibid., 279–280.
29. Ibid., 280–281.
30. Among those who made the charge was Jeremy Belknap. See Jeremy Belknap to Ebenezer Hazard, February 3, 1788, MHS-C (fifth series), 3:15–16.
31. Niccolò Machiavelli, *The Prince and the Discourses* (New York, 1950), 141.
32. *Debates and Proceedings,* 332.
33. Book of Votes, 1788, MA. A brief biography of Lincoln ap-

pears in MHS-*C* (second series) 3:233–253. A longer one is by Francis Bowen in Jared Sparks ed., *Library of American Biography* (Boston, 1847), second series, 13:207–434.

34. Amory, 243; Hall, 317; *Independent Chronicle*, August 7 and 14, 1788.

35. *Independent Chronicle*, January 15, 1789.

36. Laco's letters first appeared in the *Massachusetts Centinel* during February and March 1789. Later they were published in collected form with an addition, *The Writings of Laco* (Boston, 1789). For examples of the responses, see *Boston Gazette*, January 19, February 2, 1789, also *Independent Chronicle*, January 15, February 19 and 26, 1789. Some were written by Sullivan. See "Junius" in *Independent Chronicle*, March 5, 1789, Sullivan Papers, MHS.

37. *Boston Gazette*, February 16, 1789; *Independent Chronicle*, February 12, 1789.

38. Samuel Adams to the Legislature of Massachusetts, May 27, 1789; Harry Alonzo Cushing, ed., *The Writings of Samuel Adams* (New York, 1968), 4:327–329; Book of Votes, 1789, MA; *The Diary of William Bentley* (Salem, 1905), 1:121.

39. As might be expected, William Gordon was not pleased at the prospect. See William Gordon to George Washington, April 3, 1788, MHS-*P*, 63:547.

40. *Diary of John Quincy Adams*, 164; *Massachusetts Centinel*, August 2, 1788.

41. James Sullivan to George Thacher, October 8, 1788, Thacher II, MHS.

42. Benjamin Rush to Jeremy Belknap, October 7, 1788, MHS, 4:319; Henry Jackson to Henry Knox, February 11, 1789, Knox Papers, MHS. Even Washington knew of Hancock's ill health. See George Washington to John Hancock, May 9, 1789, 9317-a, Alderman Library, University of Virginia.

43. Merrill Jensen and Robert A. Becker, eds., *The Documentary History of the First Federal Elections, 1788–1790* (Madison, 1976), 1:xxvii–xxix.

44. Book of Votes, 1789, MA.

45. John Hancock to George Clinton, February 21, 1789, Huntington Library.

46. Washington's visit and the circumstances surrounding it are described in contemporary newspapers, as well as in "Historic Processions in Boston From 1689 to 1824," BS-*P*,

5:74–80; Mary C. Crawford, *Old Boston Days and Ways* (Boston, 1909), 277–281; NEHGR, 8:190; James Sullivan to Tobias Lear, October 18, 1789, MHS-*P*, 8:173–174; Christopher Gore

49. Esther Sewall to John Hancock, November 13, 1790, Ch. F. 2.83, BPL; *Sibley*, 12:324.
50. Eunice Burr to John Hancock, May 1, 1792, Box 17, Folder 2, Hancock Papers, NEHGS; Thaddeus Burr to John Hancock, March 4, 1793, Hancock Papers, MHS.
51. The Hancock Papers, especially Box 17, at the NEHGS are replete with these problems.
52. These figures were compiled from the inventory of Hancock's estate taken after his death. See Suffolk County Court, Suffolk Probate 20215.
53. John Quincy Adams to John Adams, June 30, 1787, *Diary of John Quincy Adams*, 119–120n.
54. John Hancock to Senate and House, November 1792, Hancock Papers, MHS; MHS-*P*, 62:55–58; William T. W. Ball, "The Old Federal Street Theatre," BS-*P*, 8:46–49; Crawford, 428.
55. Crawford, 295; "Funeral Processions in Boston from 1770 to 1800," BS-*P*, 4:131–134.
56. James Sullivan to Elbridge Gerry, August 13, 1789, Sullivan Papers, MHS.

It is not my intention here to provide a definitive list of sources used in my work. That information is well conveyed in the footnote citations. Rather, my purpose in this bibliography is simply to comment on the major sources.

The vast bulk of John Hancock's Papers are located at three institutions, all within walking distance of each other: The New England Historic Genealogical Society, the Boston Public Library, and the Massachusetts Historical Society. Other minor collections, sometimes just one or two items, can be found at widely scattered places, including the John Jay Papers at Columbia University; the Huntington Library, San Marino, California; the Alderman Library, University of Virginia; the Rufus King Papers, the New-York Historical Society, the Houghton Library, Harvard University; the Archives of the John Hancock Mutual Life Insurance Company, Boston; the Historical Society of Pennsylvania; the Clements Library, University of Michigan; and Yale University Library.

Unquestionably, there is a large quantity of Hancock material available; unfortunately, its size belies its quality, since most of what he wrote related to either routine business matters or politics. There is little of the personal or private Hancock in any of his correspondence. His wife is even worse. I was unable to locate a single manuscript letter written by Dorothy Quincy Hancock.

To fill in some of the more private details, I placed a heavy reliance on the comments of others. In this regard some of the more valuable collections were the Palfrey Papers, Houghton Library; Thacher II, the Mercy Otis Warren Papers, the James Sullivan Papers, the C. E. French Papers, the Robert Treat Paine Papers, and the Quincy Papers, all located at the Massachusetts Historical Society. Another source that is of considerable value are the records of Harvard College, located at the University Archives.

Public manuscript sources are also important. The Suffolk County Probate Records contain a wealth of information, including an inventory of Hancock's estate. The Suffolk Files, in possession of the Supreme Judicial Court of Massachusetts, were also useful, as were some items in the custody of the Social Law Library. Deeds recorded in the Suffolk County Court were also consulted.

The Massachusetts State Archives have a series of volumes known conventionally as "The Massachusetts Archives." These are a massive collection of 328 volumes containing the colony records from 1629 to nearly 1800. Several of these volumes were used, especially volumes 25, 26, and 27, containing the Hutchinson correspondence.

No history touching on the era of the American Revolution could be written without consulting the Papers of the Continental Congress. They have been made fairly accessible through microfilm. For Hancock, the most important items are the Letter Books of the Presidents of Congress, and the Reports of the Marine Committee and the Board of Admiralty.

One last manuscript source needs to be mentioned. It is the Phillips Collection at the American Antiquarian Society in Worcester. Henry A. Phillips collected a large amount of material on the Hancock family, apparently planning to write a history of the entire family. Unfortunately for a biographer of John Hancock, Phillips never got much beyond Uncle Thomas.

Contemporary newspapers were often helpful. The best guide to them remains Clarence S. Brigham, *History and Bibliography of American Newspapers, 1690–1820* (Worcester, 1947), two volumes. Among the relevant newspapers are the *New Hampshire Gazette* (Portsmouth), *Massachusetts Gazette and Boston News Letter, Herald of Freedom, Boston Evening Post, Massachusetts Centinel, Massachusetts Spy, Independent Chronicle, Salem Gazette, Newport Mercury, New York Gazette, New York Journal,* and *Pennsylvania Ledger.*

Several newspapers carried the famous "Journal of the Times." This important piece of information and propaganda is most easily available in Oliver M. Dickerson, ed., *Boston Under Military Rule, 1768–1769, As Revealed in A Journal of the Times* (Boston, 1936).

Almost as valuable as newspapers were several contemporary pamphlets: James Bowdoin, *A Short Narrative of the Horrid Massacre in Boston* (Boston, 1770); John Hancock, *Massacre Day*; Stephen Higginson, *The Writings of Laco* (Boston, 1789); and

Published manuscript sources are abundant and essential. On the local level the *Boston Town Records* were often consulted. These were published in twenty-nine volumes during the late nineteenth century. Many of the towns of Massachusetts, especially those in the eastern portion of the state, have had their vital records published, and these, too, were used. Also of local relevance are the *Records of the Church in Brattle Square, Boston, with Lists of Communicants, Baptisms, Marriages and Funerals* (Boston, 1902).

On the colony and state level, the *Journals of the House of Representatives of Massachusetts* (Boston, 1919–1978) are useful although sketchy. Forty-seven volumes are currently in print, covering the years 1715 to 1771. The *Journals of Each Provincial Congress of Massachusetts in 1774 and 1775 and of the Committee of Safety* (Boston, 1830) provide considerable information regarding those turbulent years in Massachusetts.

For the decade of the 1780s the *Acts and Laws of the Commonwealth* should be consulted, as well as E. M. Bacon, ed., *Supplement to the Acts and Laws of the Commonwealth of Massachusetts*. The debates over the federal Constitution are detailed in *Debates and Proceedings in the Convention of the Commonwealth of Massachusetts* (Boston, 1856).

On the national level, the *Journals of the Continental Congress*, thirty-four volumes (Washington, 1904–36), are informative, although, like most legislative journals, rather sketchy. Despite their title, *Naval Documents of the American Revolution*, seven volumes in progress (Washington, 1964–1976), cover a variety of topics and should also be used by anyone dealing with the Revolution.

With the exception of Hancock, nearly all of the great figures of the Revolution have had a good portion of their papers published. The Adams family of Braintree alone can claim several series, including Charles F. Adams, ed., *The Works of John Adams* (Boston, 1850–56), ten volumes; Lyman H. Butterfield, ed., *Diary and Autobiography of John Adams* (Cambridge, 1961), four volumes; Lyman H. Butterfield, ed., *Adams Family Correspondence* (Cambridge, 1963–1973), four volumes; Lyman H. Butterfield, ed., *The Book of Abigail and John* (Cambridge, 1975); L. Kinvin Wroth and Hiller B. Zobel, eds., *Legal Papers of John Adams* (Cambridge, 1965), three volumes; and W. C. Ford, ed., *Warren-Adams Letters* (Boston, 1917–25), two volumes. The writings of Samuel Adams have also been published; see Harry Alonzo Cushing, ed., *The Writings of Samuel Adams* (New York, 1904–08), four volumes.

Other published sources include Edward Channing and Archibald C. Coolidge, eds., *The Barrington-Bernard Correspondence* (Cambridge, 1912); William Bentley, *The Diary of William Bentley* (Salem, 1905–14), four volumes; Leonard W. Labaree and William B. Willcox, eds., *The Papers of Benjamin Franklin* (New Haven, 1960–   ), twenty volumes, in progress; Clarence E. Carter, ed., *The Correspondence of General Thomas Gage* (New Haven, 1931–33), two volumes; Peter O. Hutchinson, ed., *The Diary and Letters of His Excellency Thomas Hutchinson* (London, 1883–86), two volumes; Julian Boyd, ed., *The Papers of Thomas Jefferson* (Princeton, 1950–   ) twenty volumes, in progress; Allen French, ed., *A British Fusilier in Revolutionary Boston* (Cambridge, 1926); Nina Moore Tiffany, ed., *The Letters of James Murray, Loyalist* (Boston, 1901); Fitch Edward Oliver, ed., *The Diary of William Pynchon of Salem* (Boston, 1890); Anne Rowe Cunningham, ed., *Letters and Diary of John Rowe* (Boston, 1903); John C. Fitzpatrick, ed., *The Writings of George Washington* (Washington, D.C., 1931–44), thirty-nine volumes; Edmund C. Burnett, ed., *Letters of Members of the Continental Congress* (Washington, D.C., 1921–36), eight volumes; and Paul H. Smith, ed., *Letters of Delegates to Congress* (Washington, D.C., 1976–   ), two volumes, in progress. In addition to collections, various individual items and series of items have appeared in the published works of various societies. In this area the richest sources are the New England Historic and Genealogical Society, *New England Historical and Genealogical Register* (Boston, 1847–   ); the Colonial Society of Massachusetts *Publications* (Boston,

1895–   ); the Essex Institute *Historical Collections* (Salem, 1859–   ); the Massachusetts Historical Society *Collections* (Boston, 1792–   ) and *Proceedings* (Boston, 1859–   ).

American Portraits in Oil, Pastel, and Miniature (Boston, 1959) and Jules D. Prown, *John Singleton Copley* (Cambridge, 1966), two volumes. John R. Alden, *General Gage in America* (Baton Rouge, 1948) is a sympathetic account. George Athan Billias, *Elbridge Gerry: Founding Father and Republican Statesman* (New York, 1976) is a good account of that irascible Marbleheader.

Hancock himself has had several biographers. W. T. Baxter, *The House of Hancock* (Cambridge, 1945) is a business history that ends at the beginning of the Revolution. Other biographies include Herbert S. Allan, *John Hancock, Patriot in Purple* (New York, 1953); Mabel M. Carlton, *John Hancock: Great American Patriot* (Boston, 1922); John R. Musick, *John Hancock: A Character Sketch* (Dansville, 1898); and Lorenzo Sears, *John Hancock, the Picturesque Patriot* (Boston, 1912). Dorothy Quincy Hancock, too, has a biographer: E. C. D. Woodbury, *Dorothy Quincy, Wife of John Hancock* (Washington, 1905).

Thomas Hutchinson's best biographer is Bernard Bailyn, *The Ordeal of Thomas Hutchinson* (Cambridge, 1974). The other royal governors involved in Hancock's life share one biographer: John A. Schutz, *William Shirley: King's Governor of Massachusetts* (Chapel Hill, 1961) and *Thomas Pownall British Defender of American Liberty* (Glendale, 1951).

On the Whig side there are several relevant biographical works. Among the more important are John J. Waters, Jr., *The Otis Family in Provincial and Revolutionary Massachusetts* (Chapel Hill, 1968); Thomas C. Amory, *Life of James Sullivan, With Selections from His Writings* (Boston, 1859), two volumes; and John Cary, *Joseph Warren* (Urbana, 1961).

No list of biographies for the seventeenth and eighteenth centuries would be complete without mention of *Biographical*

Sketches of Those Who Attended Harvard College (Boston 1873-), sixteen volumes, in progress. This series, begun by John Langdon Sibley and continued for many years by Clifford Shipton, is a priceless source of information, although at times Shipton did display a strong Tory bias.

Frank Freidel, ed., *Harvard Guide to American History* (Cambridge, 1974), two volumes, is the best source for general works on the era of the Revolution. This should be supplemented with John Shy, *The American Revolution* (Northbrook, Illinois, 1973) and E. James Ferguson, *Confederation, Constitution and Early National Period, 1781–1814* (Northbrook, 1975).

Among other works I found most useful are Bernard Bailyn, *Ideological Origins of the American Revolution* (Cambridge, 1967); Edmund C. Burnett, *The Continental Congress* (New York, 1941); Don Higginbotham, *The War of American Independence* (New York, 1971); Pauline Maier, *From Resistance to Revolution* (New York, 1972); James Kirby Martin, *Men in Rebellion* (New Brunswick, 1973); John C. Miller, *Origins of the American Revolution* (Boston, 1943); Edmund S. and Helen Morgan, *The Stamp Act Crisis* (Chapel Hill, 1953); Jennings B. Sanders, *The Presidency of the Continental Congress, 1774–1789* (Gloucester, repr. 1971); Arthur M. Schlesinger, *The Colonial Merchants and the American Revolution* (New York, 1957 repr.); Arthur M. Schlesinger, *Prelude to Independence: The Newspaper War on Britain, 1764–1776* (New York, 1965); Marshall Smelser, *The Winning of Independence* (Chicago, 1972); William C. Stinchcombe, *The American Revolution and the French Alliance* (Syracuse, 1969); Christopher Ward, *The War of the Revolution*, ed. by John R. Alden (New York, 1952), two volumes; Gordon Wood, *The Creation of the American Republic* (Chapel Hill, 1969).

Local history was an indispensable source of information. Any search of this area must begin with John D. Haskell, Jr., ed., *Massachusetts: A Bibliography of Its History* (Boston, 1976). This led to literally hundreds of sources. For Massachusetts, the most useful were Ellen E. Brennan, *Plural Office-Holding in Massachusetts, 1760–1780* (Chapel Hill, 1945); Robert E. Brown, *Middle-Class Democracy and the Revolution in Massachusetts, 1691–1780* (Ithaca, 1955); Harry Alonzo Cushing, *History of the Transition from Provincial to Commonwealth Government in Massachusetts* (New York, 1896); Van Beck Hall, *Politics Without Parties* (Pittsburgh, 1972); Oscar Handlin and Mary Flug Handlin,

Commonwealth: A Study of the Role of Government in the American Economy: Massachusetts, 1774–1861 (New York, 1947); Samuel B. Harding, *The Contest Over the Ratification of the*

Federal Constitution in the State of Massachusetts (New York, 1896); Albert Bushnell Hart, *Commonwealth History of Massachusetts* (Boston, 1927–30), five volumes; Thomas Hutchinson, *The History of the Province of Massachusetts-Bay* (Cambridge, 1936), three volumes; Stephen E. Patterson, *Political Parties in Revolutionary Massachusetts* (Madison, 1973); and Robert J. Taylor, *Western Massachusetts in the Revolution* (Providence, 1954).

own history. Boston leads the way with some of the best, including G. B. Warden, *Boston, 1689–1776* (Boston, 1970); Walter M. Whitehill, *Boston: A Topographical History* (Cambridge, 1959); and Justin Winsor, ed., *The Memorial History of Boston* (Boston, 1880–81), four volumes. For additional histories of Boston and the other towns, see Haskell.

The literature in journals was helpful. In addition to the major journals of the field, state historical journals were also consulted, as well as the publications of the historical societies already mentioned.

One final source needs to be mentioned — dissertations. By far the most useful dissertation, and indeed one of the most valuable works of any kind on the period, is Robert Feer, "Shays's Rebellion" (Ph.D. dissertation, Harvard, 1958). Also used were Edward M. Coleman, "The History of the Third Session of the Second Continental Congress" (Ph.D. dissertation, University of Southern California, 1941), and David E. Maas, "The Return of the Massachusetts Loyalists" (Ph.D. dissertation, University of Wisconsin, 1972).

Adams, Abigail, 195
Adams, John, 8, 9–10, 27, 110, 167, 199, 281; in *Liberty* trial, 90; Hancock's lawyer and ally, 99–100, 110, 120; on Hutchinson, 126–127; delegate to Congress, 174, 178, 205; speech on army, 191–192; on militia, 201; on independence, 209, 212–213; to The Hague, 230; on Mass. constitution, 242; Vice-President, 275
Adams, Samuel, 55, 121, 126; on Stamp Act, 57; in General Court, 60; relations with Hancock, 63–65, 110–111, 131, 139, 148, 165; on meeting place for Court, 133–134, 137; on judges' salaries, 148; on Whately letters, 151–153; on tea ships, 161; and Coercive Acts, 171; delegate to Congress, 174, 188, 205, 230; in Concord, 181–184; estranged from Hancock, 207, 224, 240, 249, 253; on Mass. constitution, 242; "Sans Souci," 257; on ratification of Constitution, 268, 270; lieutenant governor, 274, 275, 279

Adams, Samuel (father), 107–108
Administration of Justice Act, 170, 171
Aesop's *Fables*, 20
Aix-la-Chapelle, Treaty of, 26
Albany, N.Y., 135
Amsterdam, Netherlands, 42
Andrews, John, 160, 174
Andros, Sir Edmund, 1–2
Annapolis, Md., 267
Appleton, Nathaniel, 26
Auchmuty, Robert, 90; warrants issued by, 99; trial presided over by, 100, 101; letter to Hutchinson, 150
Avery, John, 246, 248, 254, 279

Bailyn, Bernard, 125–126
Balch, Nathaniel, 254, 279
Baltimore, Md.: Congress moved to, 214; discomforts of, 215–216; departure from, 216–217
Bant, William: stewardship of, 205–206, 208, 215, 222–224; death of, 251
Barnard, John, 67
Barnard, Jonathan, 43, 47, 67
Barnard, Nathaniel, 99

Barnard & Harrison, 53, 58, 62; difficulties of, 67; and the oil business, 70; Hancock's relations with, 73, 75–76

Barre, Colonel Isaac, 58

Bastide, John Henry, Jr., 22, 168

Beacon Hill: Thomas Hancock's house on, 13–14; Hancock concern for, 34–35

Beaver, tea ship, 154; arrival of, 159

Becker, Carl, 267–268

Beckford, William, 104

Belcher, Mrs., schoolmistress, 9

Bernard, Francis, 65–66, 129; and Townshend Acts, 80–81; refusal of Hancock as Councilor, 83, 104; and the *Liberty*, 86; and impressed seaman, 89; and Halifax troops, 91; trial of Hancock, 101; recall requested, 104; and Otis, 111; departure of, 112

Bible and Three Crowns, the, Hancock shop, 12

Bill of rights, omitted in proposed constitution, 268, 269

Billerica, Mass., 186

Blanchard, Edward, 50, 79

Bollan, William, 104

Boston, Mass., 16; Thomas Hancock's feeling for, 33–35; and Townshend Acts, 73–74, 80–81; and the *Liberty*, 83–85; growing violence in, 121–122, 179; Boston Massacre, 123, 126–129; and the judges' salaries, 147; and tea, 154–161; punishment for, 170–172; harbor closed, 174; besieged, 189, 192–193, 195–197; evacuation by British, 206; Hancock's return to, 221, 232, 234; French in, 235–240, 249; constitutional convention at, 242; post-war issues in, 255–256; Washington in, 276–277; Hancock land in, 278

Boston Chronicle, 114, 120; attacks on nonimportation in, 115, 116

Boston Common: Thomas Hancock's concern for, 34; British troops on, 96, 97; execution on, 98

Boston Gazette, 104, 114

Boston Latin School, 11; Hancock at, 19–24; headmaster of, 19–20; education at, 20–21; in dispute with King's Chapel, 23–24

Boston Massacre, 123; aftermath of, 126–129

Boston Packet, 47, 69, 116

Boston Port Act, 170; reaction to, 171–174; harbor closed, 174

Boston Tea Party, 161; consequences of, 170

Boston town meeting: Hancock as selectman, 55, 59, 67, 80, 104; protest against troops bound for Boston, 91–94; Hancock as moderator, 135, 138, 147, 166–167, 225, 264; committee on judges' salaries, 148–149; on the Tea Act, 156–157, 160–161; session of 1774, 166–167; on Coercive Acts, 171–172, 175

Boston Weekly News Letter, 91

Bowdoin, Elizabeth, 259

Bowdoin, James, 103, 244; on Boston Massacre, 128–129; views on site for church, 143; delegate to Congress, 174, 175, 178; member of Council, 196; president of committee on state constitution, 242; candidate for governor, 259–261; governor, 264; defeat of, 265; in ratification convention, 268

Bowes, Lucy, 181
Bowes, Nicholas, 5, 146
Bowes, William, 99; flight to
England, 206

Lydia's bequests to, 208; in-
augural sermon at, 246
Bridgewater, Mass., 138, 174
British East India Co., 154
Brown, Richard, 149
Bulfinch, Dr. Thomas, 47
Bunker Hill, battle of, 193
Burgoyne, General John, 217, 219
Burr, Aaron, 195
Burr, Thaddeus, 187, 278

Cadets, Boston: Hancock as colo-
nel of, 136, 145–146; alerted,
158; honor guard for body
of Oliver, 166; Hancock dis-
missed, 174–175
Caesar, Commentaries, 20
Calef, Samuel, 146
Cambridge: General Court con-
vened in, 105, 140, 141; Gen-
eral Court at Harvard, 129–131,
133; Provincial Congress in,
177
Cambridge, North Precinct
Church, 2–3
Canada: defeat of French in, 17;
British in, 36; Hancock trade
in, 45, 46, 252
Captain of the Castle, 273
Carroll, John, 277
Castle Island (formerly Castle
William), 242; refuge for cus-

toms commissioners, 85; British troops withdrawn to, 124
Cazneau, William, 76

ald, 260–261
Clarke, Elizabeth, 184–185
Clarke, Jonas, 181
Clarke, Mary, 3
Clarke, Richard, 155, 157
Clark's Wharf (Hancock's Wharf),
69
Cleverly, Joseph, 9
Clinton, George, 275
Clinton, General Henry, 206
Coercive or Intolerable Acts,
170–171; reaction to, 171–174
Colonies, sectionalism of, 190.
See also Continental Con-
gresses; individual states
Committee of Safety, 177; on
British threat to Concord, 182
Committees of Correspondence,
165, 171
Concord, Mass.: Provincial Con-
gress in, 177, 180–181; Hancock
in, 181; as arms depot, 182;
British in, 183–185
Congress, idea of, proposed by
Hancock, 165; sentiment for,
172; General Court's motion
for, 173–174. See also Continen-
tal Congresses
Connecticut: support for Mass.,
83; Hancock land in, 103, 262,
278; Whig contacts in, 152
Constitution of the U.S.: drafting

Constitution of the U.S. (*cont.*)
of, 267; ratifying convention,
268–272; Hancock's speech on,
270–271
Continental Association, 178
Continental Congresses: First,
177–178; Second, 189–195; subsequent, 198; on appointments
and bureaucracy, 199–200; on
independence, 209–211; Lee's
resolutions, 211–212; Declaration of Independence, 213;
moved to Baltimore, 214–217;
in Philadelphia, 217–219; on
taxation, 247; Hancock absentee president of, 264
Convention for ratification of
Constitution, 268–272
Cooke, Elisha, 108
Cooper, Samuel, 35, 55, 77, 143,
148; politics of, 109–110; and
Boston Massacre, 128; on
Maine trip, 146; collaboration
of, 165; and the French, 235;
death of, 253
Cooper, William, 110
Copley, John Singleton: portrait
of Thomas Hancock, 49; de-
signer of new church, 144;
other portraits by, 153
Cornwallis, General Charles, 250
Council, 80; Hancock's election
to, vetoed by governor, 83, 104;
Hancock declines membership
to, 141, 151; under Provincial
Congress, 196; on appointment
of military officers, 199–202;
Hancock not elected to, 208–
209
Covent Garden, 42
Cross brothers, shipbuilders, 203
Curwen, Judge Samuel, 188–189
Cushing, Thomas, 66, 83, 135,
224; relations with Hancock,
109, 204–205, 227, 253, 254; de-

scribed by Mein, 119; and Boston Massacre, 128; Speaker of
House, 130, 131, 140, 141; on
meeting place for Court, 137;
on Adams, 139; in Boston elections, 140–141; letters sent by
Franklin to, 150, 152–153; and
the Port Act, 171; delegate to
Congress, 174, 175; member of
Council, 196; on militia appointments, 200–202; defeated
for Congress, 202; new positions, 203; lieutenant governor, 246, 259, 265; in campaign
for governor, 259–261, 264;
death of, 273
Cushing, William, 268
Customs, Boston, commissioners of, 81–82; enmity for Hancock, 82; and sloop *Liberty*,
83–85, 101; retreat of, 85

Dalrymple, Lieutenant Colonel
William, 92–96, 124, 145
Dana, Francis, 230
"Danger of an Unqualified Min-
istry,"9
Dartmouth, Lord, 181
Dartmouth, tea ship, 154; arrival
of, 158–159; duty due on, 160;
departure refused, 161
Dawes, William, 183
De Berdt, Dennys, 75
Declaration of Independence: ap-
proved, 213; anniversary of,
231
"Declaration of the Causes and
Necessity of Taking Up Arms,"
194
Delaware, 212
Delaware River, 216
d'Estaing, Comte, 231; at New-
port, 232–234; in Boston, 236
Dickinson, John, 80, 97, 116–117,
194, 206–207

Divine Right, Josiah Quincy on, 132
Duane, James, 207

Edes, Benjamin, 104, 114
Edes & Gill, 149, 166
Education: at Boston Latin, 10–11; at Harvard, 29
Eleanor, tea ship, 112; arrival of, 159

England. Thomas Hancock in, 12; wars with France and Spain, 17; attitude toward colonials, 25; after French War, 51–52. See also London; Royal governors
Erving, John, 103
"Essex Result," critique of proposed constitution, 228
Eutropius, 20
Excise tax, Massachusetts, 247–248

Fairfield, Conn., 187; Hancock ladies visit, 188; wedding in, 197
Faneuil, Benjamin, 12; consignee of tea, 155, 157
Faneuil Hall, 83, 246; meeting on Halifax troops, 92; British troops quartered in, 94, 96; Hancock store at, 102
"Farce, A," 257
Federalists, on ratification of Constitution, 268–270
First Continental Congress, 177–178
Fleming, John, 120
Flynt, Henry, 27–28
Folger & Gardener, Nantucket, 46–47
Foxcroft, Samuel, 30

France: with Spain against England, 17; New England expedition against Louisbourg, 17–18; defeat in Canada, 36; aid to colonies by, 218; first Minister to U.S., 231–232; American attitude toward, 233
Franklin, Benjamin, 72, 110; Whately letters sent by, 160–161; at Second Continental Congress, 212
French and Indian War, 35

Gage, General Thomas, 102, 172; troops sent to Boston by, 86–87; on punishment for Boston, 170; appointed governor, 172–173; Hancock dismissed from Cadets by, 174–175; difficulties of, 176–179; military situation of, 181, 193; amnesty proclaimed by, 193
Gailer, George, 119
Galloway, Joseph, 178
Gates, General, 219
George II, death of, 43
George III: coronation of, 44; and John Wilkes, 76–77
Gérard, Conrad Alexandre, French minister, 231–232
German mercenaries, 211; at Trenton, 216
Germantown, Pa., 219
Gerrish, Samuel, bookseller, 11–12
Gerry, Elbridge, 202; in Mass. delegation, 205, 210, 230; opposed to Constitution, 267
Gill, John, 104, 114
Glass, tax on, 71, 73
Glover, John, 232
Godet, Theodore, 102

Gordon, Reverend William, 228,
243–244, 249; on Hancock as
Harvard treasurer, 262–263
Gray, Lewis, 99
Great Awakening, the, 8–9
Greene, Nathanael, 193
Greenleaf, Stephen, 203
Greenleaf, William, 186, 259
Grenville, Lord, 52–53, 54, 74
Gridley, Jeremiah, 111
Griffin's Wharf, tea ships at, 159
Griffith, Dorcas, 169
Groton, Mass., 2

Halifax, N.S., British troops assembled at, 91
Hall, Stephen, 214–215
Hallowell, Benjamin, 59; enmity
for Hancock, 82; and the Liberty, 84–86
Hamilton, Alexander, 267
Hancock, the, 204
Hancock, Dorothy Quincy (Mrs.
John), 197, 274, 277; daughter
of, 214; in Baltimore, 215, 217;
return to Boston, 218; son born
to, 229; at summer home, 253;
at death of husband, 279
Hancock, Ebenezer, 3; death of,
10
Hancock, Ebenezer (nephew of
above), 8; and his brother
John, 36–37; as a merchant, 45;
failures of, 49–50, 61, 78–79,
137; escape from Boston, 192,
197
Hancock, Elizabeth, 3; marries
Jonathan Bowman, 5
Hancock, Reverend John (1671–
1752): education, 1–2; career,
2–5; genealogy, 4; host to son's
family, 10
Hancock, John (1702–1744): genealogy, 4; at Harvard, 5–6; in
Braintree, 6–10; death of, 10

Hancock, John (1737–1793): birth,
8; schools, 9–10; moves to
Lexington, 10; moves to Boston to live with uncle, 11,
15, 18; at Boston Latin, 19–21;
youthful activities, 21–24; at
Harvard, 24, 26–31; apprenticeship with uncle, 32–36; relations with brother, 36–37,
138; to London, 37–45; return,
45–46; partner in business, 46–
47; inheritance from uncle,
48–49, 281; way of life, 50–52,
62–63; politics of, 52; selectman, 55, 59, 67, 80, 104; and the
Stamp Act, 56–61; member of
General Court, 64–66, 67, 69,
75, 80, 83, 104, 131, 140, 171;
business difficulties, 66–71,
102–103, 223–224; ventures in
shipping, 69–70; and Townshend duties, 73; and sloop
Liberty, 83–87, 89–91; and impressed seaman, 88–89; on
nonimportation, 90–91, 102,
116–117, 135; and troops in
Boston, 93–97; trial of, 98–101;
wealth of, 103; political allies
of, 107–112; and John Mein,
118–121; and Boston Massacre
123–124; and T. Hutchinson,
127–128, 139; House session
(1770), 129–134; moderator of
town meeting, 135, 138, 147,
166–167, 225, 264; Colonel of
Cadets, 136–137, 145–146; illness of, 137–139, 162–163;
House session (1772), 140–142;
charities of, 143–145, 225; trip
to Maine, 146; on payment of
judges, 147–150, 152; and
Whately letters, 150–153;
treasurer of Harvard, 153–154,
214–216, 246, 262–263; and the
Tea Act, 154–161; Massacre

Day oration, 163–166; betrothal, 167–170; and Coercive Acts, 171–174; dismissed from ~~Cadets, 174–176; president of Provincial Congress, 177, 179, 180; delegate to Philadelphia, 178, 206, 207, 214–217; dangerous position of, 179–181; in Concord, 182–184; departure north 184, 185; at Second Continental Congress~~

204; losses in Boston, 205–206, 223–224; on independence, 209–213; in Baltimore, 214–217; farewell speech, 219–221; and governorship, 226–228; Congress (1778), 229–231; at Newport, 232–234; host to French, 236, 242–243; as governor, 243–244, 245–250, 255, 256–258; business affairs, 251–253; retirement, 253, 258–259, 262; reelected governor, 265–266, 273, 274, 275; on Constitution, 267–272; and national office, 274–275; death of, 279; funeral, 279–280; role of, 280–281

Hancock, John George Washington, 229, 253; death of, 265

Hancock, Lucy, 3; marries Nicholas Bowes, 5

Hancock, Lydia (Mrs. Thomas): devotion to John, 18, 25, 38, 44–45, 49, 138, 167; inheritance of, 48, 49; as hostess for John, 51, 106; and the slaves, 77; as moneylender 103; hostess to Dolly Quincy, 168; in Concord, 181–185; to Woburn, 186; refuge for, 187, 188; death of, 208

Hancock, Lydia Henchman, 214; death of, 218

Hancock, Mary, 8, 45

Hancock, Nathaniel, 3

Hancock, Thomas, 3, 5, 10; host ~~to nephew, 11, 16; career of, 11–15; house of, 14; war plans, 17–18; as a colonial, 25–26; John in business of, 32–36; and Boston, 33–35; John sent to London by, 37–41; and return of John, 35–36; health of, 36; death of, 37; legacies of; John's~~

Harris, Sergeant, 145

Harrison, Benjamin, 194, 207

Harrison, Joseph, 85, 86, 97, 138

Hartford, Conn., 220–221

Harvard College, 108; 1st John Hancock at, 1–2; 2d John Hancock at, 5–6; 3d John Hancock at, 24, 26–31; Ebenezer at, 37; legacies to, 48; Hancock Professor at, 62; meeting of General Court at, 129–131, 133; John Hancock treasurer of, 154, 214–216, 246, 262–263

Hawley, Joseph, 196

Hawley Street Theatre, 278–279

Hayley, George, 76–77, 79, 94, 138, 167, 180; and nonimportation, 116; daughter of, 168–169

Hayley & Hopkins, 116

Hayley, the, brig, 158

Heath, General, 250

Heath, William, 152

Henchman, Daniel, 12

Henchman, Lydia, 13

Henry, Patrick, 56–57

Higginson, Stephen (Laco), 210, 273–274

Hillsborough, Earl of, 81–82, 130; troops sent to Boston by, 86–87; letter from Francis Bernard to, 104

Holbrook, Abiah, 21, 213
Holton, Samuel, 230
Holyoke, Elizur, 26
Homer, 20
Hope, Henry, 42
Hoskins, William, 251–253
Howe, Admiral Lord Richard, 233
Howe, General William, 214, 217; Philadelphia occupied by, 218–219
Hubbard, Tart, 146
Hutchinson, Elisha, 155, 157, 159
Hutchinson, Lieutenant Governor Thomas, 59, 111; relations with John Hancock, 82, 136–137, 139–140; successor to Francis Bernard, 112–113; and the Boston Massacre, 124; role in American Revolution, 125; career of, 126–128; relations with House, 129–134; on site of Court meeting, 134, 141–142; salary paid from London, 146–147; and judges' salaries, 147–150; letters to London, 150–152; recall requested, 152; and tea, 158–161; replaced, 172
Hutchinson, Thomas, 155, 157, 158, 159

Impost, Hancock's evasion of issue of, 248
Independence: growing sentiment for, 209; approval by Congress, 212–213

Jackson, Sally, 168
Jefferson, Thomas, 189, 212; author of Declaration of Independence, 213
Jenkins, Robert, 17
"Journal of Occurrences" ("Journal of Transactions in Boston"), 97; on Hancock trial, 100, 101
Judges, salary of paid from London, 147; report of committee on, 148–149

Kemble, Margaret, 172
Kilby & Barnard, 40
King, the: powers of, debated by Quincy, 132–133
King's Chapel, 23–24
Kirk, Thomas, 84–85

Lafayette, Marquis de, 232; and Hancock, 234
La Luzerne, Chevalier, 242
Lancaster, Mass., 186
Lancaster, Pa., Congress at, 219
Land Bank controversy, 126
Last Attempt, sailing vessel, 97
Laurens, Henry, 230
Lee, Richard Henry, resolutions on independence, 211–212
Letters from a Farmer in Pennsylvania to the Inhabitants of the British Colonies, 80
Lexington, Mass.: 1st John Hancock, minister in, 3–5; preparations for British, 182, 183; arrival of British troops, 184–185
Liberty, sloop, 83–87; trial relating to, 89–90; burned, 90
Lille, Thomas, 122
Lincoln, General Benjamin, 265; lieutenant governor, 273–274
Lisle, David, 82; and the Liberty, 85
Livingston, Robert R., 212
Lodge of Freemasons, Saint John's, 55
London: Hancock trip to, 37–45; extravagances of, 41–43; Hancock's illness in, 43–44

Longman, Thomas, and John Mein, 118–120

Long Room Club, 55

Louisbourg, French fortress [Cape Breton Island: capture of, 17–18; returned by England, 26]

[Lovell, James, 22, 215, 230]

[Lovell, John, headmaster of Boston Latin 19–20; in dispute with King's Chapel]

zure of, 82; wreck of, 139

Machiavelli, Niccolò, 272

MacIntosh, Ebenezer, 58, 59, 122

Maine: T. Hancock's land in, 48; J. Hancock's land in, 103, 251; J. Hancock's trip to, 146

Malbone, Thomas, 26

Malcolm, Daniel, 99

Marine Committee, 198–199; construction by, 199

Marsh, Joseph, 6

Marshall, Captain, 84

Marshall, Samuel, 30

Marshall, Thomas, 160

Masonic Lodge of Saint Andrew, 55

Massachusetts: Hancock land in, 103; meeting of towns on committee report, 149; independent government begun, 197; western interests represented in Provincial Congress, 196; reorganization of government of, 226–229; west vs. east, 227–228; rejection of constitution, 228; issue raised again, 241–243; state constitution approved, 243; John Hancock governor of, 245–250, 255; excise and impost in, 247–248; postwar economy of, 255–258;

James Bowdoin governor of, 259–261; Shays's Rebellion in, 263–265; role in ratification of Constitution 269, 271. *See also* [Massachusetts General Court]

[Massachusetts Bay Government Act, 170–171]

[Massachusetts constitutional convention, 242–243]

[Massachusetts General Court and Stamp Act 71; John Han-] 171; letter on Townshend Acts passed by, 79–80, 87; recall of Francis Bernard demanded, 87; moved to Cambridge, 105; prorogued by Bernard, 105, 134; S. Adams clerk of, 108; convened at Harvard, 129–137; Hancock rejected as speaker, 131; attempts to return to Boston, 135–137, 141–142; session of 1773, 151–152; session of 1774, 173; moved to Salem, 173, 176–177; changed to Provincial Congress, 177. *See also* Massachusetts Provincial Congress

Massachusetts Hall, Harvard, 26

Massachusetts Provincial Congress, 177, 179, 180–181; request to Continental Congress on army, 191; assumption of civil authority by, 191, 196; on appointment of military officers, 199; J. Hancock reelection to, 225, 229; J. Hancock speaker of, 242

Massachusetts Sentinel, 257; "Observer" articles on "Sans Souci," 257; on British luxuries, 258

Massacre Day Orations: by Warren (1772), 139; by Hancock

Massacre Day Orations (*cont.*)
(1774), 163–166; by Warren
(1775), 180
Matchet, John, 99
Mather, Increase, 2
Maysel, Joseph, 100
Mein, John, 113–120; attack on
Gill, 114–115; on nonimportation, 115; attacks on Hancock
circle, 119; departure of, 119
Merchant's Society, 55
Merchants' Standing Committee
on nonimportation, 90
Middleton, Henry, 189
Military campaigns, 213–219;
winter of 1776, 213–214; British
withdrawal to N.Y., 216; Tren-
ton and Princeton, 216; spring
of 1777, 217; Germantown and
Valley Forge, 219; Saratoga,
219; Yorktown, 250
Militia: Hancock 1st major gen-
eral of, 207; quotas for, 250
Milton, Mass.: Hutchinson es-
tate in, 157; county convention
in, 178
Milton Lower Falls, Mass., 12
"Minute Men," formation of, 177
Molasses, tax on, 53
Molineux, William ("Paoli"),
112, 122, 124, 156; death of, 177
Momper, Elizabeth, 78
Monk, Christopher, 164
Monopolies, threat of, 155
Morris, Robert, 207
Mulliken, Lydia, 183

Navy: Marine Committee, 198–
199, 204; Thomas Cushing as
naval agent, 203–204
Newburyport, Mass., construction of ships in, 203
Newfoundland, Hancock contacts in, 45, 46
New Hampshire: support for

Mass. from, 83; Hancock land
in, 103, 278
New Jersey, support for Mass.
from, 83
New North Church, Boston, 197
Newport, R.I., 278; *Liberty*
burned at, 90; nonimportation
ended in, 135; British occupation of, 232; French fleet at, 249
New York, N.Y.: John Hancock
in, 116–117, 135; nonimportation ended in, 135; Revere's
ride to, 162; Hancock's welcome in, 188; British withdrawal to, 216, 250; French attack on, 232
New York Gazette, 234
Nonimportation: reaction to
Stamp Act, 61, 63; revived, 73,
90–91; effect on Hancock, 102;
imperiled, 113–116; Hancock
in support of, 116–117; and repeal of Townshend Acts, 134–
135
North, Frederick Lord, 134, 154;
and Coercive Acts, 170; on
Yorktown surrender, 250
North Briton, The, 76
North Carolina, 209
Nova Scotia, Hancock contacts
in, 45, 46, 252

Old Granary Burial Ground,
Hancock's grave in, 279
Old South Church: protest meet-
ings in, 159, 160–161; Massacre
Day oration in, 180
Olive Branch Petition, 194
Oliver, Andrew, 58, 126, 150; re-
moval from office requested,
152; death of, 166
Otis, Harrison Gray, 257
Otis, James, 53, 55, 75; speaker of
General Court, 65, 108; letter
on Townshend duties, 75; and

Liberty case, 86; ally of Hancock, 109, 110, 111; attorney for Gill, 114–115; and John Mein, 116; growing insanity of, 121; on site of Court meeting, 135–136, 137; on judges' salaries, 138; dunned by Hancock, 253

Otis, Samuel Allyne, 111

Point Shirley, Mass., 50; Hancock summer place at, 253
Political "parties," Boston variety, 106; court (Tory), 107; country faction, 107; influence of Sam Adams, 107–109; allies of Hancock, 109–113
Portsmouth, N.H., 274, 278
Pownall, Thomas, 18–19, 56, 60, 110, 138; relations with Hancock, 207; on site of meeting place for Court, 133–134; James Otis on, 135–136; question renewed, 147

South Carolina, 180; death of, 251
Palmer, General Joseph, 251
Parker, John, 182; on Lexington Green, 183–184
Parsons, Theophilus, 228
Patterson, Stephen, 107
Paxton, Charles, 150
Pennsylvania, 212
Penobscot, Me., 250
Perkins, Daniel, 31, 138
Perkins, Richard, 45
Philadelphia: Hancock in, 116–117, 135; nonimportation ended in, 135; Revere's ride to, 162; site for Continental Congress, 174, 178; welcome of Mass. delegation in, 188–189; Hancocks in residence in, 197; Congress moved from, 214; Congress returned to, 217; occupied by British, 219, 230; Constitutional Convention in, 267
Philips, Henry, 12
Phillips, William, 140, 171
Pickering, John, 227; Speaker of House, 229
Pidgeon, John, 24
Pitt, William, 36, 114
Plymouth, Mass., 229; James Otis in, 111; customhouse moved to, 170

Prescott, Dr. Samuel, 183
Preston, Captain Thomas, 123
Princeton, N.J., taken by Washington, 216
Purviance, Samuel, 215
Pynchon, William, 245

Quartering Act, 170, 171
Quebec, fall of, 36
Quincy, Catherine, 208
Quincy, Dorothy (Mrs. John Hancock), 167–170; to Concord, 181–185; flight with Lydia, 186–187; in Fairfield, Conn., 188, 195; wedding of, 197
Quincy, Edmund, 27, 167, 186, 197
Quincy, Esther, 277–278
Quincy, Eunice, 249; marriage of, 250
Quincy, Henry, 242–243, 249
Quincy, Josiah, 128, 167; paper on meeting place for Court, 132–133; on ban of tea, 161
Quincy, Samuel, 22, 30

Rall, Colonel Johann, 216
Randolph, Peyton: resignation of, 189, 191; death of, 199

Ranelagh, London (pleasure garden), 42

Reeve, William, 73

Reid, William, 90

Revere, Paul, 55; sketches of landing of British, 95–96; first ride, 162; other rides, 171–172, 178; member of committee of spies on British, 182; ride of April 18, 1775, 183–184

Rice, Asaph, 26

Richardson, Ebenezer, 122

Rights of the British Colonies Asserted and Proved, 53

Robertson, John, 121

Rochambeau, Comte de, 249

Rogers, Nathaniel, 150

Romney, H.M.S., 83; and the sloop *Liberty*, 85; in inner Boston harbor, 89

Rotch, Francis, 160, 161

Rowe, John, 64, 161

Royal governors. *See* Bernard, Francis; Gage, General Thomas; Hutchinson, Thomas; Shirley, William

Royal Navy, seamen impressed for, 88–89

Rush, Dr. Benjamin, 216

Salem, Mass.: customhouse moved to, 170; General Court moved to, 173

Saltonstall, Richard, 24

"Sans Souci," 257

Saratoga, battle of, 219

Savage, Samuel Phillips, 161, 240

Schuyler, General Philip, 213

Scollay, John, 160

Scott, Captain James, 69, 96, 158, 223; postwar activities of, 252–253, 262

Second Continental Congress, 189–195; Hancock president of, 189; organization of, 190–191;

adoption of army at Cambridge, 191–192; reconciliatory moves by, 194

Sectionalism, of colonies, 190–191

Seider, Christopher, 122

Semme, William, 167

Sewall, Attorney General Jonathan, 82, 99; and the *Liberty* case, 100–101; departure for England, 197; postwar in Canada, 277–278

Sewall, Chief Justice Samuel, 111

Shays, Captain Daniel, 265, 266

Shays's Rebellion ("Little Rebellion"), 263–265, 266, 267, 273

Sherman, Roger, 212

Shirley, William, 17, 126; and the King's Chapel dispute, 23–24; and Thomas Hancock, 106, 126

Slaves: of Thomas Hancock, 45, 48; of John Hancock, 77–78

Smuggling: Hancock's part in, 82; and the case of the *Liberty*, 83–85

Soldiers, British: arrival in Boston, 94–96; misbehavior of, 122, 174; demand for removal of, 123–124; and the Quartering Act, 171; difficulties in housing, 176

Solemn League and Covenant, for boycott of Britain, 172

Sons of Liberty, 58, 64; and Townshend Acts, 73; and impressed seaman, 88–89; in the Cadets, 146

South Carolina, 180, 212

Sovereignty: fundamental issue of, 57; an issue in debate on meeting place of Court, 134; debated in Mass. towns, 149

Spain, England at war with, 17, 137

Sprague, Jonathan, 30
Stamp Act: significance of for Boston, 54; opposition to, 56; and Hancock, 56–61; nonim-portation agreement, 61, 63; repeal of, 64–65
Stamp Act Congress (1765), 59
State sovereignty, issue in ratification of Constitution, 262
Storer, Ebenezer, 216
Story, William, 91

Sullivan, James: Hancock's friendship with, 254–255, 256, 265, 279; on the Constitution, 269, 270; on national office for Hancock, 274–275
Sullivan, General John, 232, 233–234, 254

Taxation: Sugar Act, 53; Stamp Act, 54, 56–57; vs. legislation, 57; Townshend's plans for, 71–72; Townshend's Acts repealed, 134; tea tax retained, 134, 137
Tea: tax on, 71, 134, 137, 154; shipments to colonies, 154–155; arrival of tea ships, 158–159; legal complications, 159–160; meetings on, 161; Tea Party, 161
Tea Act, 154–155
Tea Assembly, 256–257
Temple, John, 259
Tennent, Gilbert, 9
Ternay, Admiral de, 249
Thaxter, James, 8
Thaxter, Mary Hawke (Mrs. John Hancock), 8, 31, 37
Thayer, Arodi, 98–99
Thomson, Charles, 189
Tonge, Winchworth, 252

Tories, question of permitting return of, 241
Townshend, Charles, 71–72
Townshend Acts, 71–72; repeal of, 134
"Tradesmen's Protest," 136
Trecothick, Apthorp, & Thomlinson, 40
Trenton, battle of, 210
"Unanimous Declaration of the Thirteen United States of America"

Valley Forge, Pa., 219
Valnais, Joseph de, 249; marriage to Hancock's niece, 250
Varnum, James, 232
Vauxhall (Spring Garden), London, 42
Vice-Admiralty Court: trial of Hancock in, 98–99, 100–101
Virgil, *Aeneid*, 20
Virginia, 57

Waldron, William, 6
Ward, Samuel, 207
Ward, *Lily's Grammar*, 20
Warren, James, 210, 264; on militia appointments, 200–201; sniping against Hancock, 224, 230, 233, 238, 240, 249, 253, 255; defeated for House, 229; dunned by Hancock, 252; on Hancock as governor, 266
Warren, Joseph, 55, 85; and the *Liberty* case, 86; political ally of Hancock, 112; orator on Massacre Day, 139, 180; letter to Continental Congress, 191; death at Bunker Hill, 193; Hancock support for family of, 225

Warren, Mercy Otis, 125, 195, 255, 257, 260
Washington, General George, 35, 220; commander of army, 191–192; in Boston, 196; in Philadelphia, 211; in New York campaign, 213; at Delaware River, 216; at Brandywine, 219; at Valley Forge, 219; and Newport, 232; portrait of, 236; at Yorktown, 250; as President, 274, 275; tour of northern states, 276
Watertown, Mass., 195
Webb, Jonathan, 26, 30
Wendell, Elizabeth, 167
Wendell, John, 12
Whalebone (sailing vessel), 223
Whale oil, investment in, 46–47, 66–67, 69–70
Whately, Thomas: Hutchinson's letters to, 150–151; publication of letters, 152
Whigism, as Hancock politics, 52
Whigs, and the Liberty case, 86

Wibird, Anthony, 26–27
Wilkes, John, 76–77; message to Hancock from, 101
William, the (ship), 154; wrecked, 159
Williams, Israel, 102
Williams, Jonathan, 159
Winslow, Edward, 155
Winthrop, Mass., Hancock land in, 50
Winthrop, James, 277
Winthrop, John, 146, 268
Woburn, Mass., 184; reunion of Hancock family in, 186
Woodford, Matthew, 45, 46, 47
Worcester, Mass., rendezvous of delegates at, 186–187
Wright & Gill, 118
Wyman, Amos, 186

Xenophon, 20

York, Pa., Congress at, 219
Yorktown, Va., surrender at, 250
Young, Thomas, 112, 122, 161